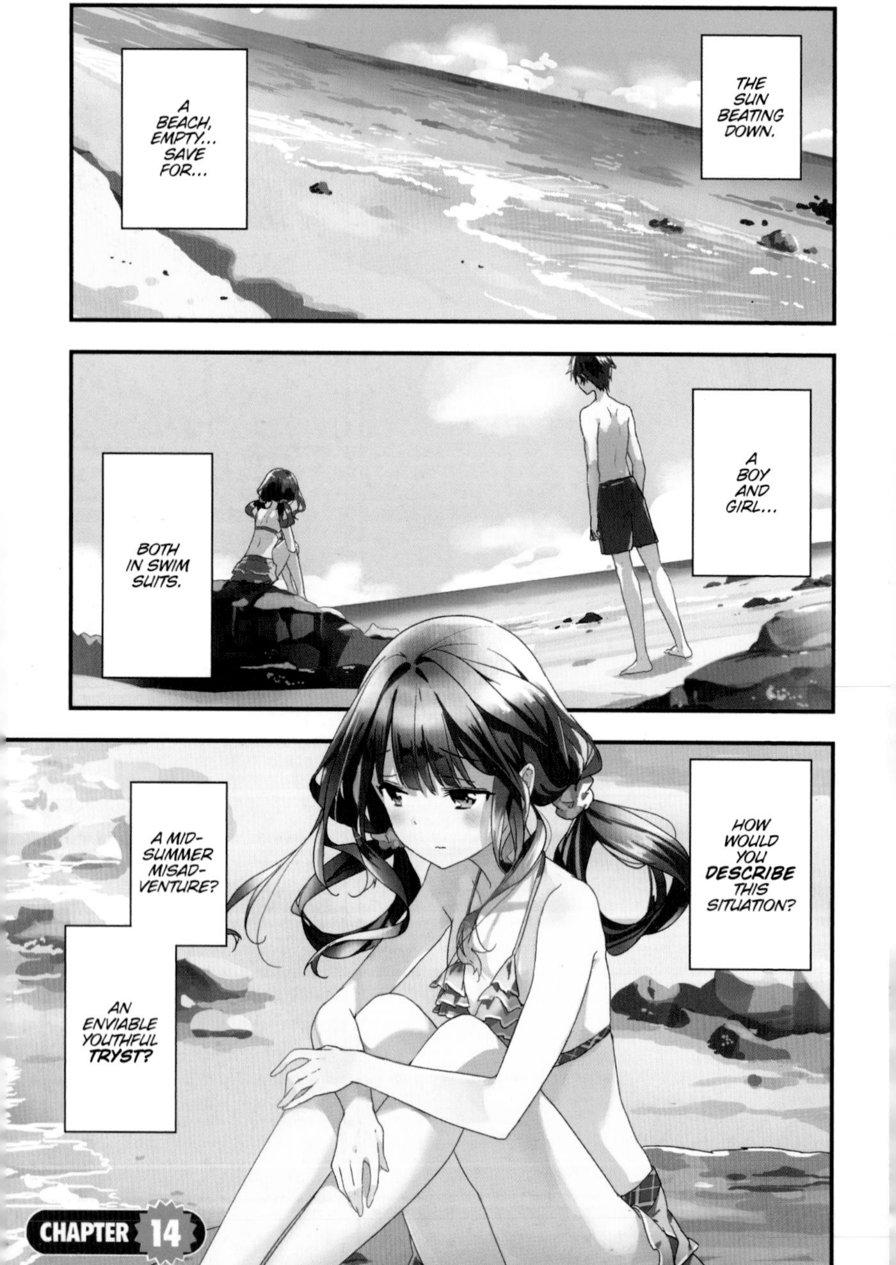
THE SUN BEATING DOWN.
A BEACH, EMPTY... SAVE FOR...
A BOY AND GIRL...
BOTH IN SWIM SUITS.
HOW WOULD YOU DESCRIBE THIS SITUATION?
A MID-SUMMER MISADVENTURE?
AN ENVIABLE YOUTHFUL TRYST?
CHAPTER 14

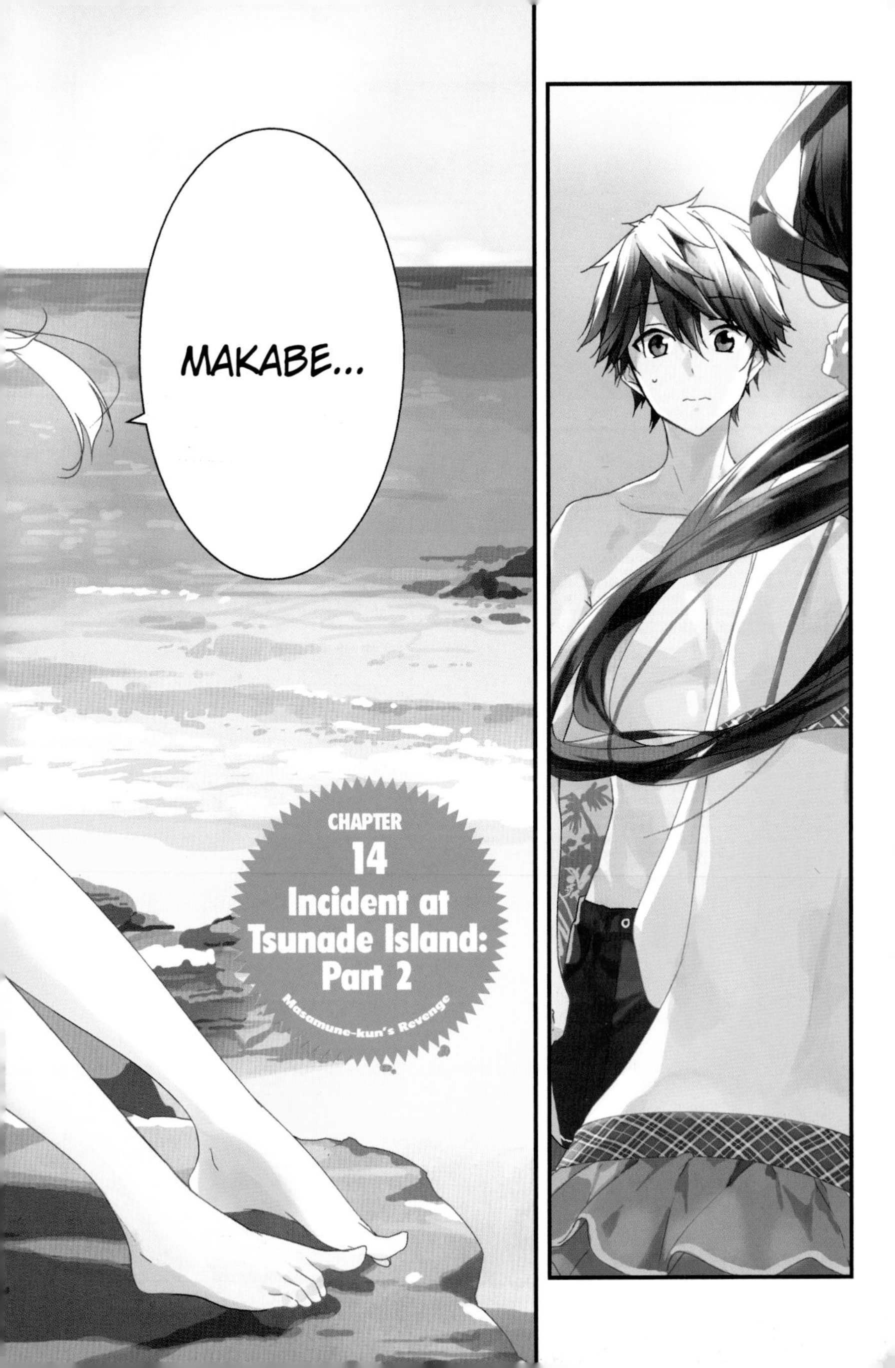
MAKABE...
CHAPTER
14
Incident at Tsunade Island: Part 2
Masamune-kun's Revenge

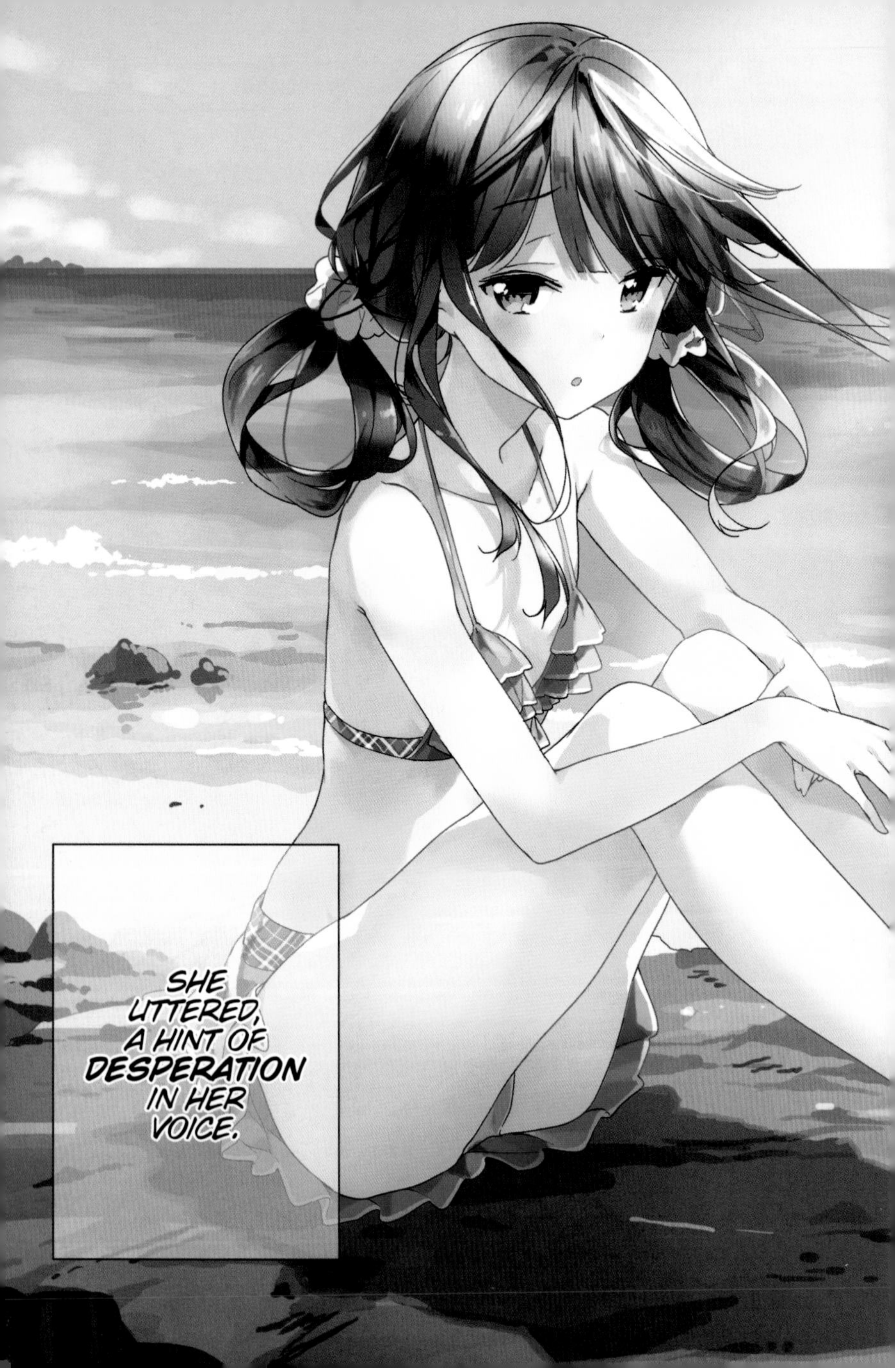
SHE UTTERED, A HINT OF DESPERATION IN HER VOICE.

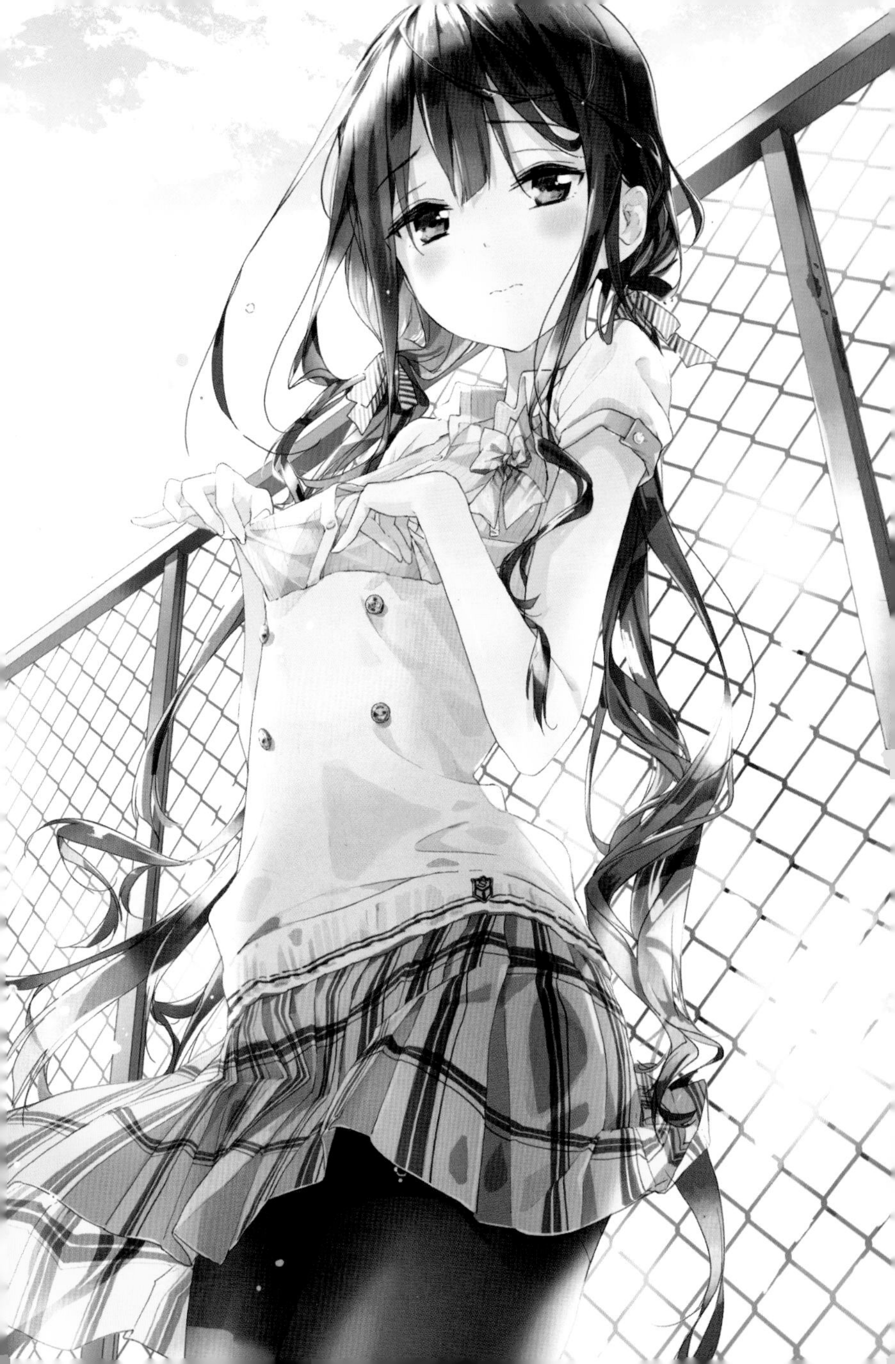

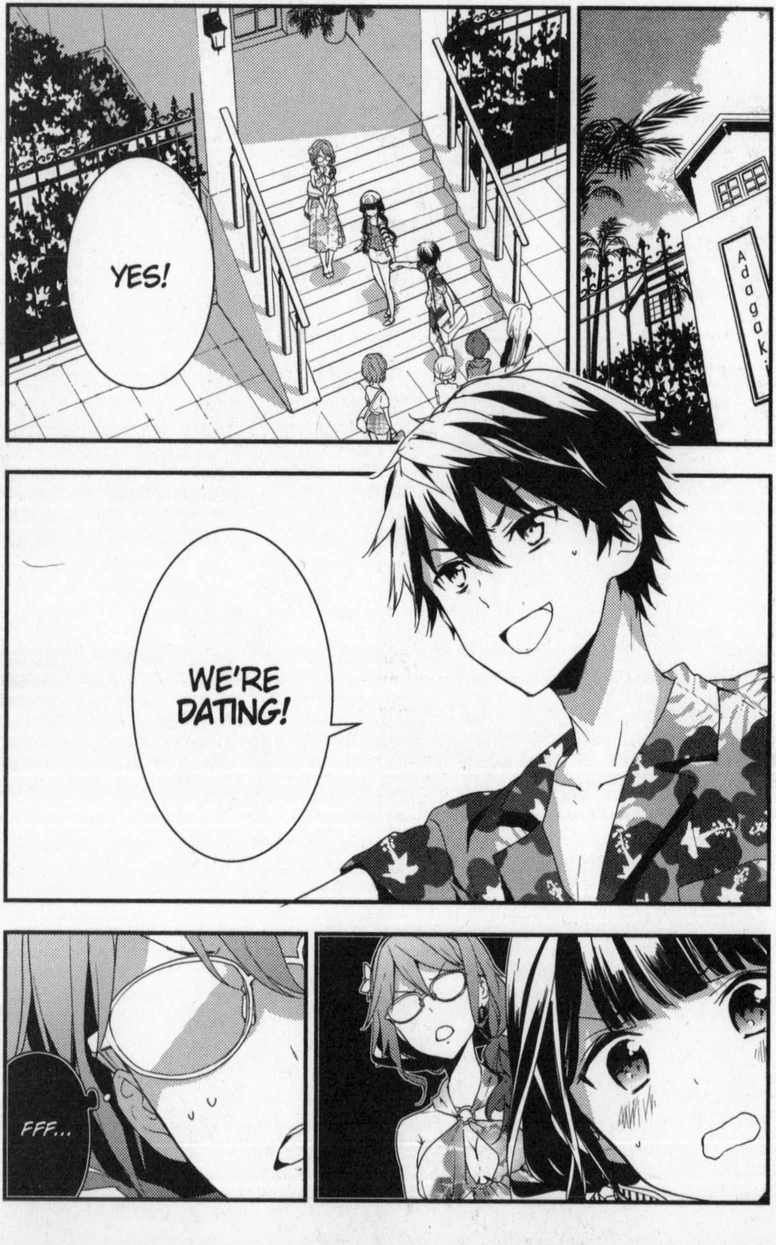
YES!
WE'RE DATING!
FFF...

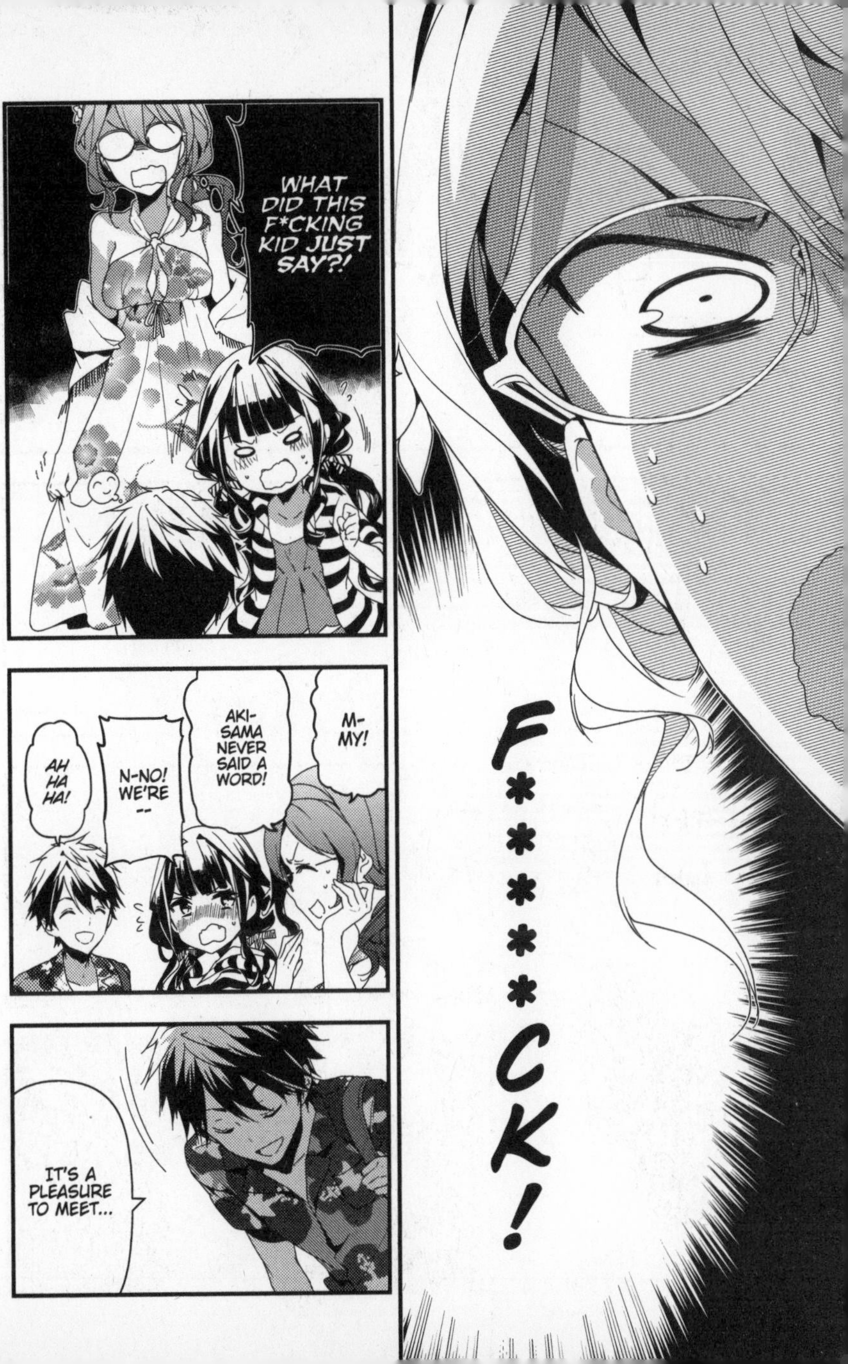
F****CK!
WHAT DID THIS F*CKING KID JUST SAY?!
M-MY!
AKI-SAMA NEVER SAID A WORD!
N-NO! WE'RE --
AH HA HA!
IT'S A PLEASURE TO MEET...

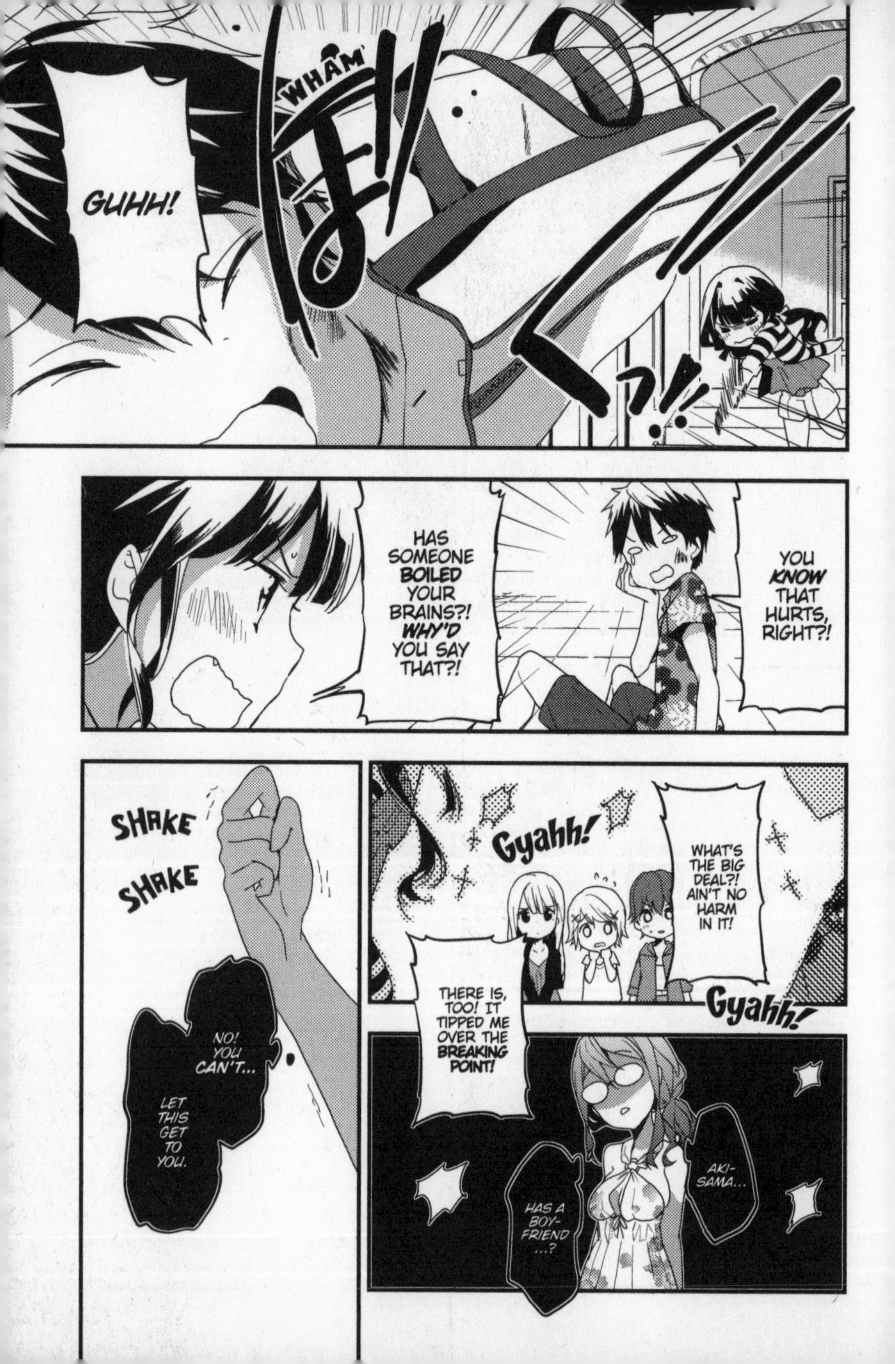
WHAM
GUHH!
YOU KNOW THAT HURTS, RIGHT?!
HAS SOMEONE BOILED YOUR BRAINS?! WHY'D YOU SAY THAT?!
WHAT'S THE BIG DEAL?! AIN'T NO HARM IN IT!
Gyahh!
Gyahh!
THERE IS, TOO! IT TIPPED ME OVER THE BREAKING POINT!
AKI-SAMA...
HAS A BOY-FRIEND ...?
SHAKE
SHAKE
NO! YOU CAN'T...
LET THIS GET TO YOU.

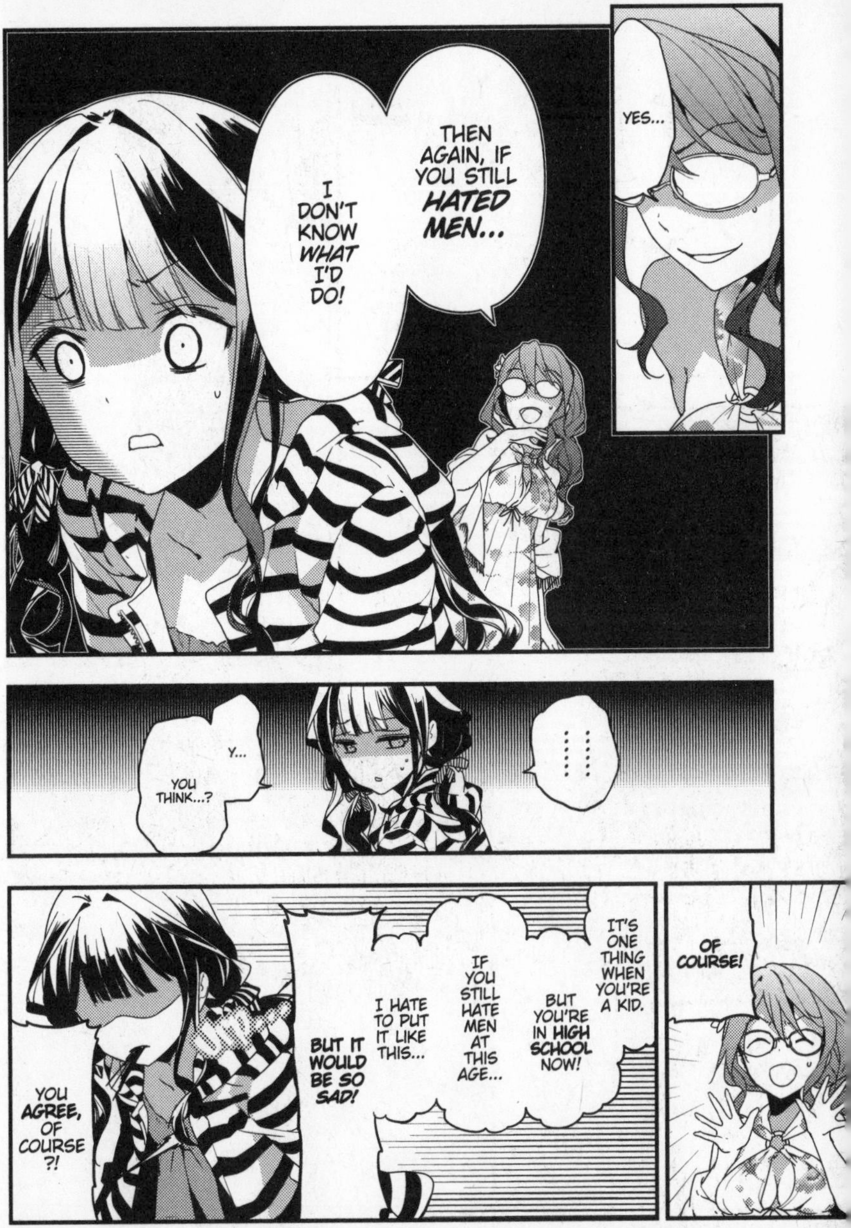
YES...
THEN AGAIN, IF YOU STILL HATED MEN...
I DON'T KNOW WHAT I'D DO!
......
Y... YOU THINK...?
OF COURSE!
IT'S ONE THING WHEN YOU'RE A KID.
BUT YOU'RE IN HIGH SCHOOL NOW!
IF YOU STILL HATE MEN AT THIS AGE...
I HATE TO PUT IT LIKE THIS...
BUT IT WOULD BE SO SAD!
YOU AGREE, OF COURSE?!

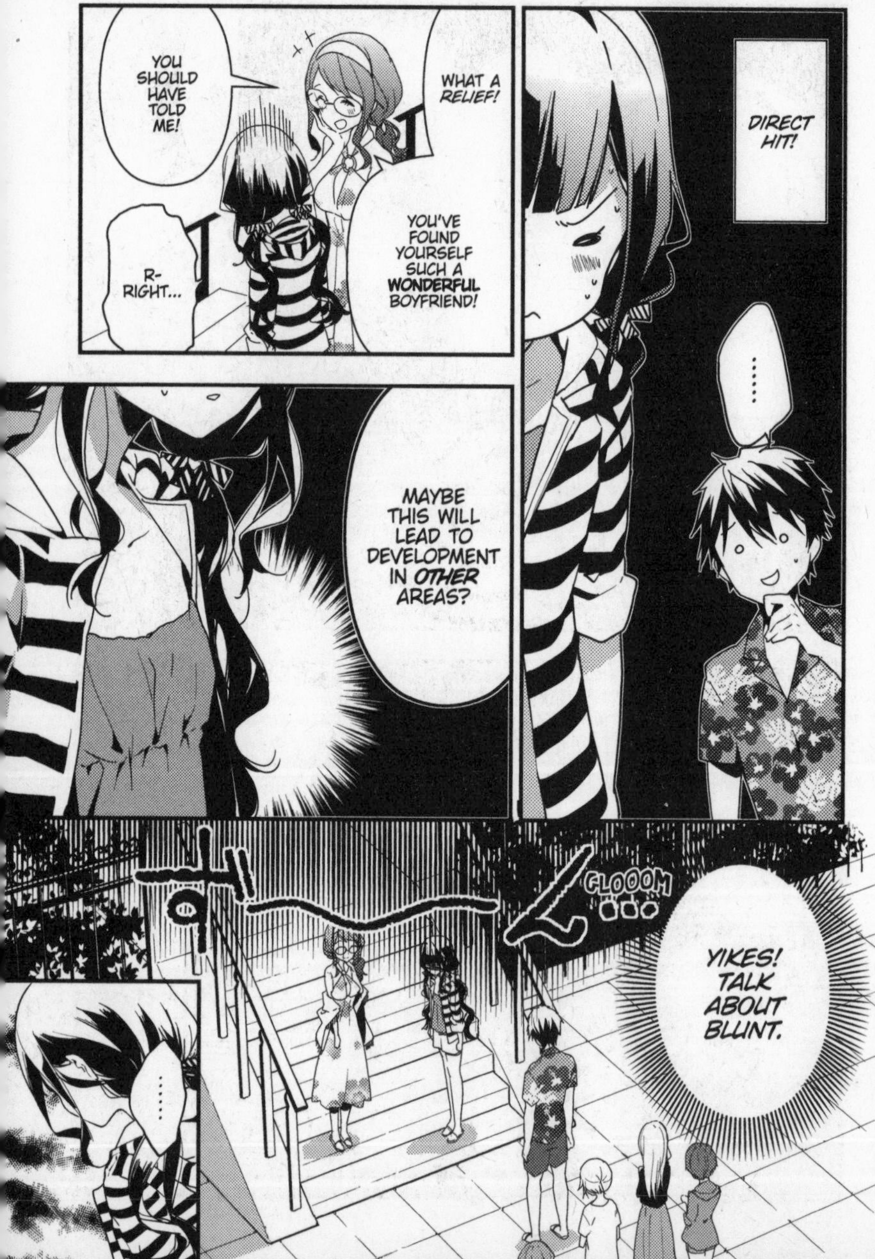
DIRECT HIT!
......
WHAT A RELIEF!
YOU SHOULD HAVE TOLD ME!
YOU'VE FOUND YOURSELF SUCH A WONDERFUL BOYFRIEND!
R-RIGHT...
MAYBE THIS WILL LEAD TO DEVELOPMENT IN OTHER AREAS?
YIKES! TALK ABOUT BLUNT.
GLOOOM...
......

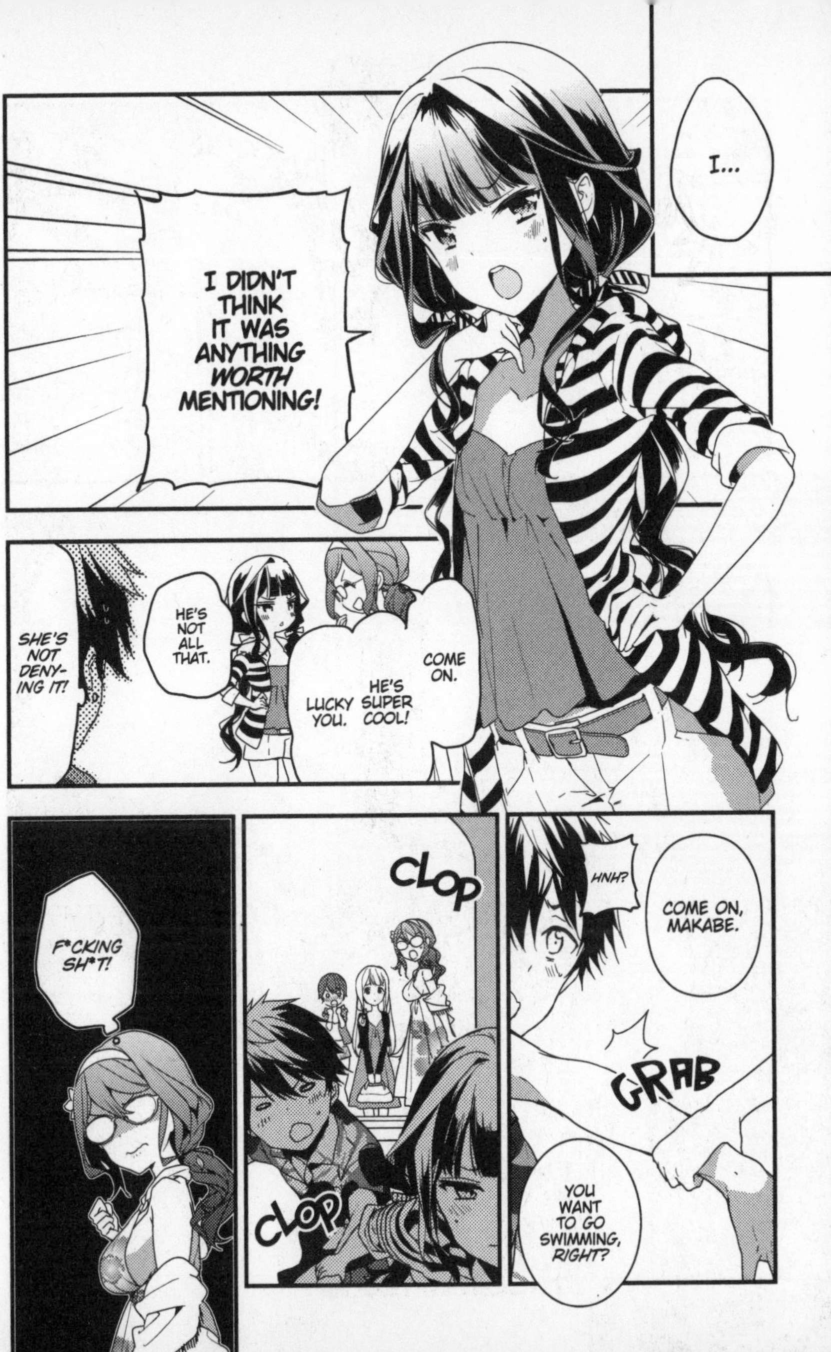
I...
I DIDN'T THINK IT WAS ANYTHING WORTH MENTIONING!
COME ON.
HE'S SUPER COOL!
LUCKY YOU.
HE'S NOT ALL THAT.
SHE'S NOT DENY-ING IT!
HNH?
COME ON, MAKABE.
GRAB
YOU WANT TO GO SWIMMING, RIGHT?
CLOP
CLOP
F*CKING SH*T!

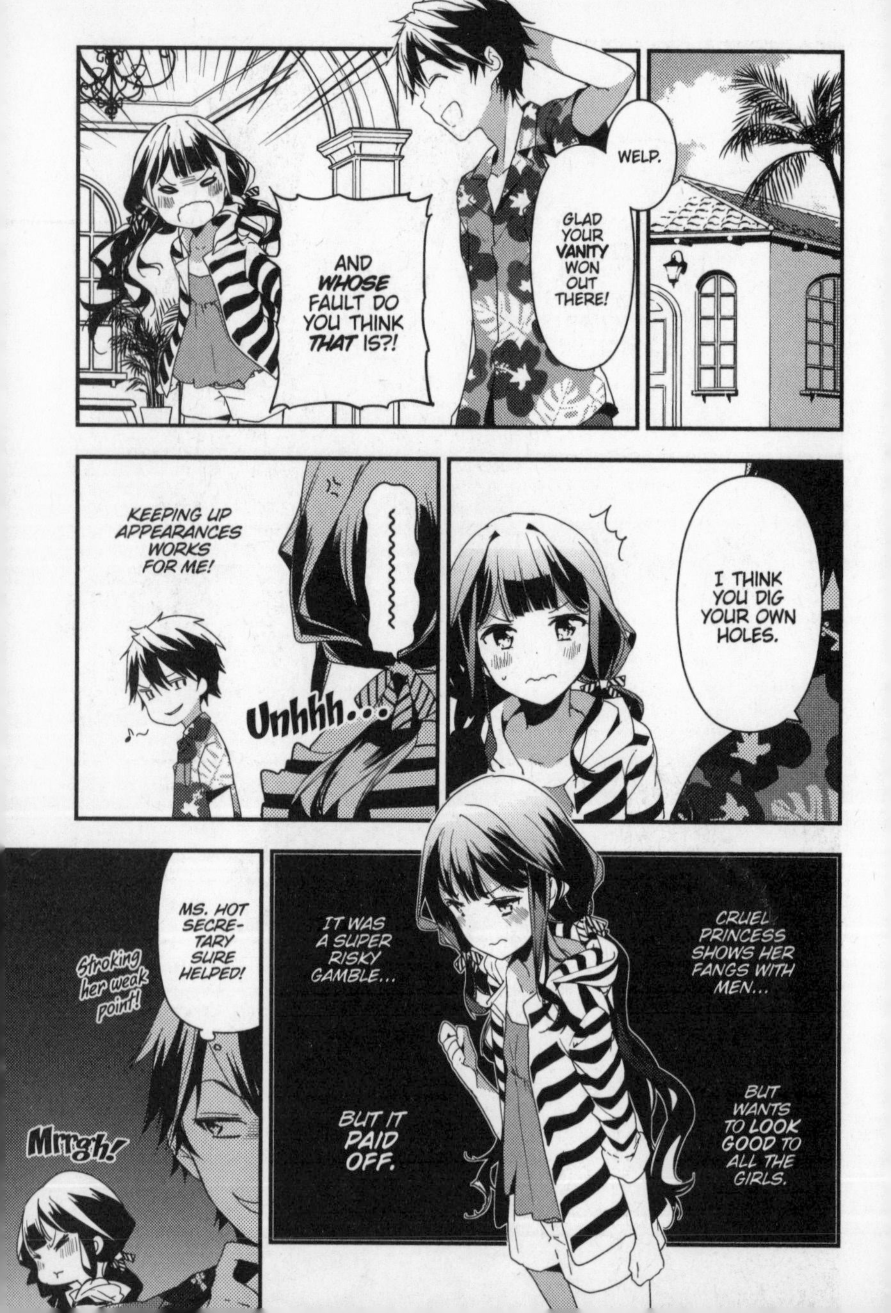
WELP.
GLAD YOUR VANITY WON OUT THERE!
AND WHOSE FAULT DO YOU THINK THAT IS?!
I THINK YOU DIG YOUR OWN HOLES.
KEEPING UP APPEARANCES WORKS FOR ME!
Unhhh...
CRUEL PRINCESS SHOWS HER FANGS WITH MEN...
IT WAS A SUPER RISKY GAMBLE...
BUT WANTS TO LOOK GOOD TO ALL THE GIRLS.
BUT IT PAID OFF.
MS. HOT SECRETARY SURE HELPED!
Stroking her weak point!
Mrrgh!

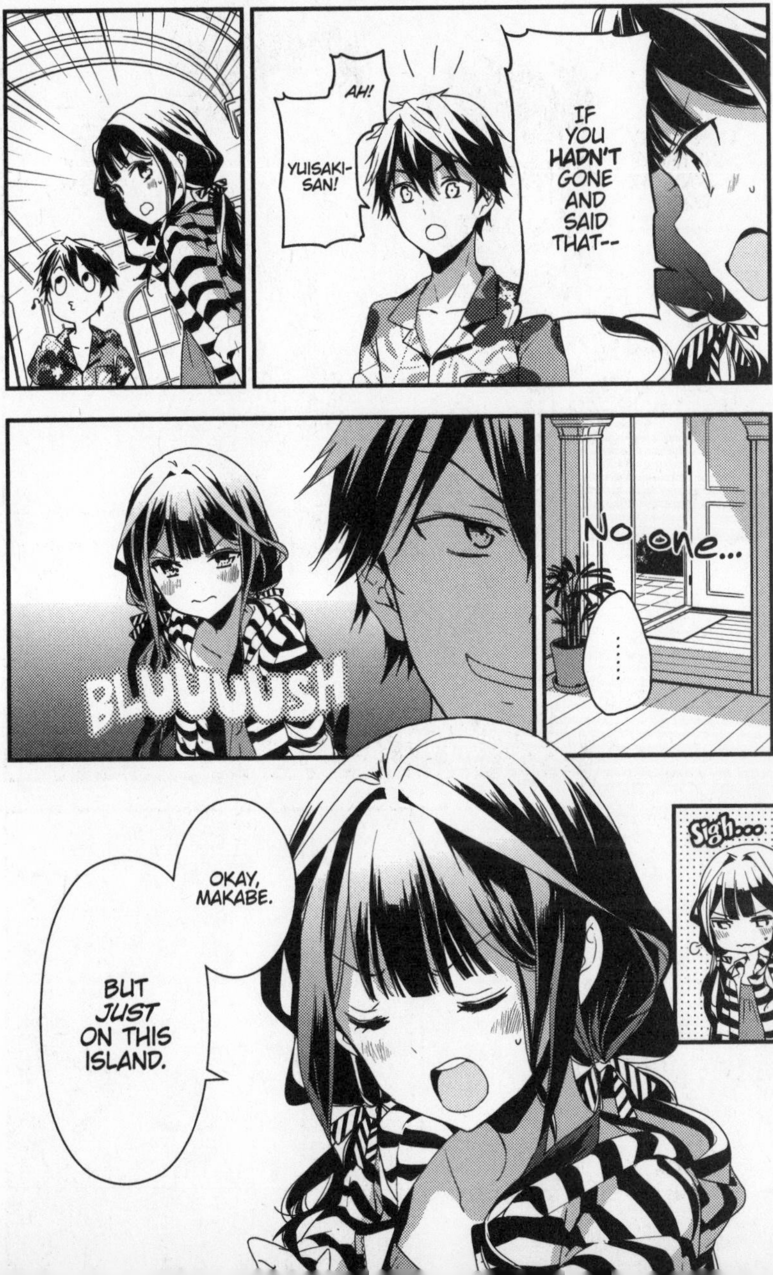
IF YOU HADN'T GONE AND SAID THAT--
AH!
YUISAKI-SAN!
No one...
......
BLUUUUSH
Sighooo
OKAY, MAKABE.
BUT JUST ON THIS ISLAND.

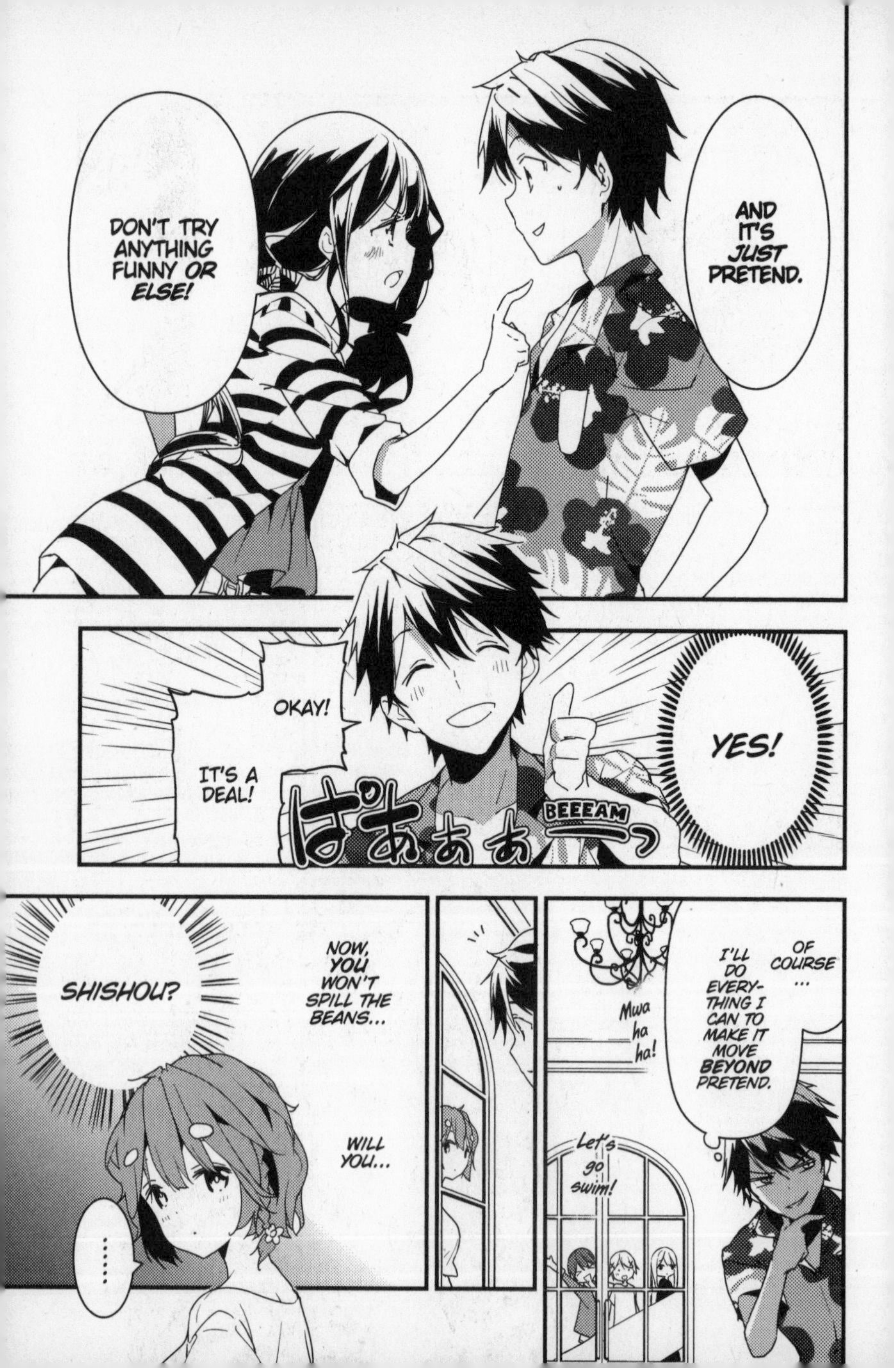
AND IT'S JUST PRETEND.
DON'T TRY ANYTHING FUNNY OR ELSE!
YES!
OKAY!
IT'S A DEAL!
ぱあぁぁー っ
BEEEAM
OF COURSE...
I'LL DO EVERYTHING I CAN TO MAKE IT MOVE BEYOND PRETEND.
Mwa ha ha!
Let's go swim!
NOW, YOU WON'T SPILL THE BEANS...
WILL YOU...
SHISHOU?
......

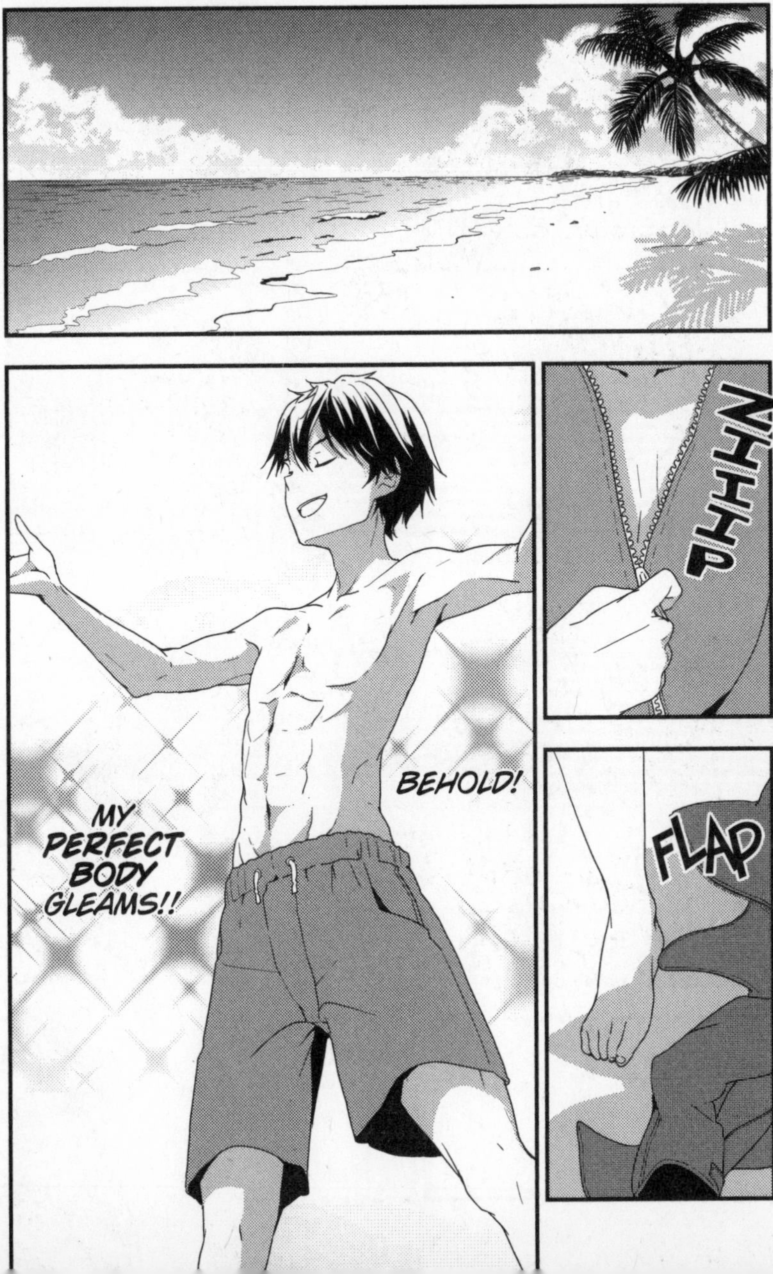
ZIIIIP
FLAP
BEHOLD!
MY PERFECT BODY GLEAMS!!

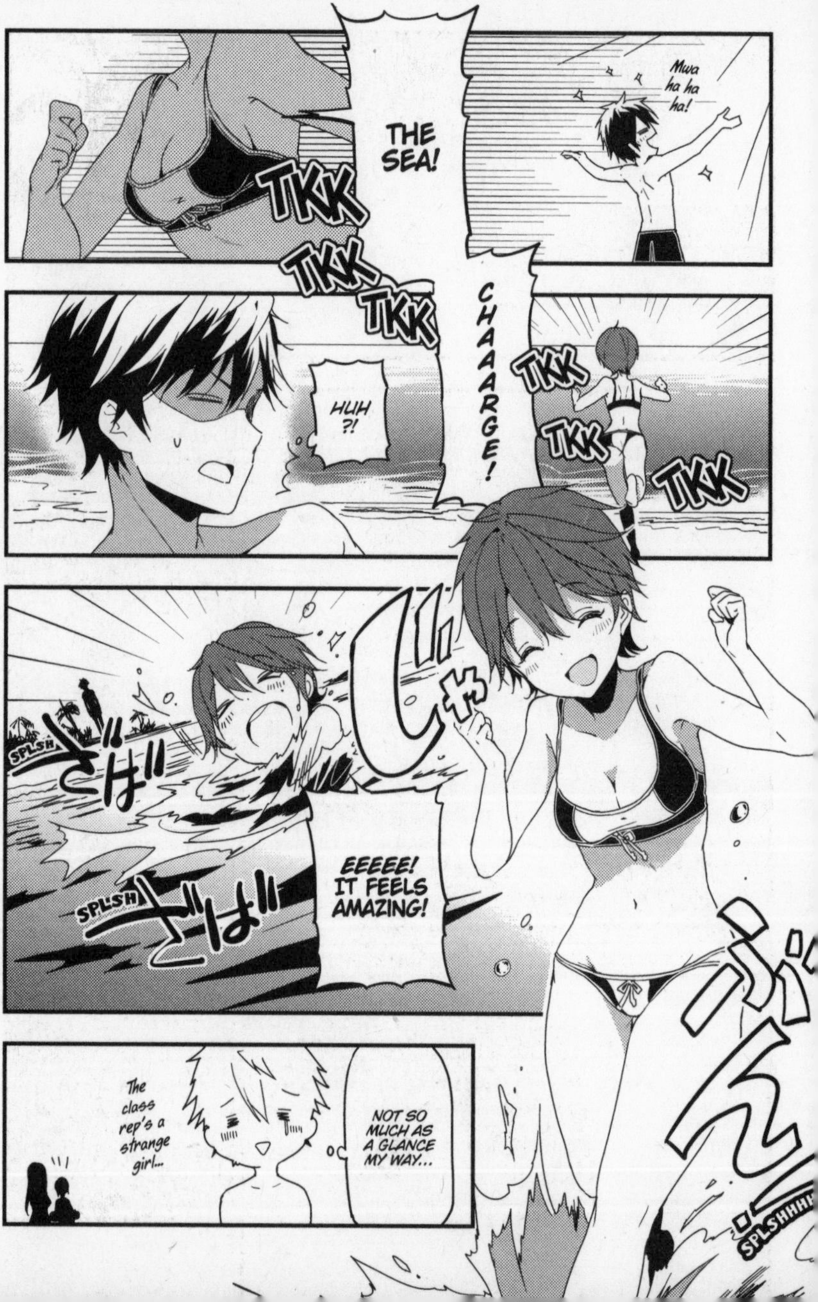
Mwa ha ha ha!
THE SEA!
TKK
TKK
TKK
CHAAARGE!
TKK
TKK
TKK
HUH ?!
EEEEE! IT FEELS AMAZING!
SPLSH
SPLSH
SPLSHHHH
NOT SO MUCH AS A GLANCE MY WAY...
The class rep's a strange girl...

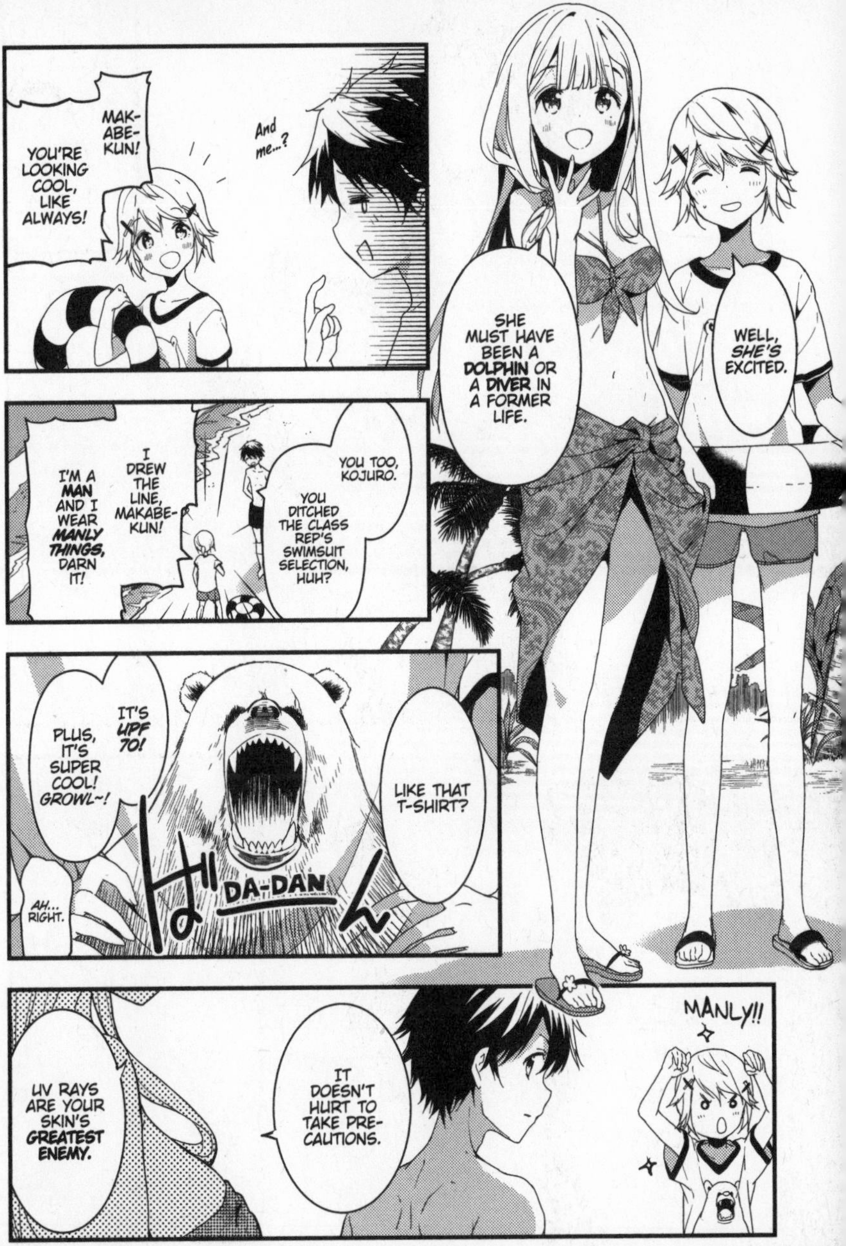
WELL, SHE'S EXCITED.
SHE MUST HAVE BEEN A DOLPHIN OR A DIVER IN A FORMER LIFE.
And me...?
MAK-ABE-KUN!
YOU'RE LOOKING COOL, LIKE ALWAYS!
YOU TOO, KOJURO.
YOU DITCHED THE CLASS REP'S SWIMSUIT SELECTION, HUH?
I DREW THE LINE, MAKABE-KUN!
I'M A MAN AND I WEAR MANLY THINGS, DARN IT!
LIKE THAT T-SHIRT?
DA-DAN
IT'S UPF 70!
PLUS, IT'S SUPER COOL! GROWL~!
AH... RIGHT.
MANLY!!
IT DOESN'T HURT TO TAKE PRE-CAUTIONS.
UV RAYS ARE YOUR SKIN'S GREATEST ENEMY.

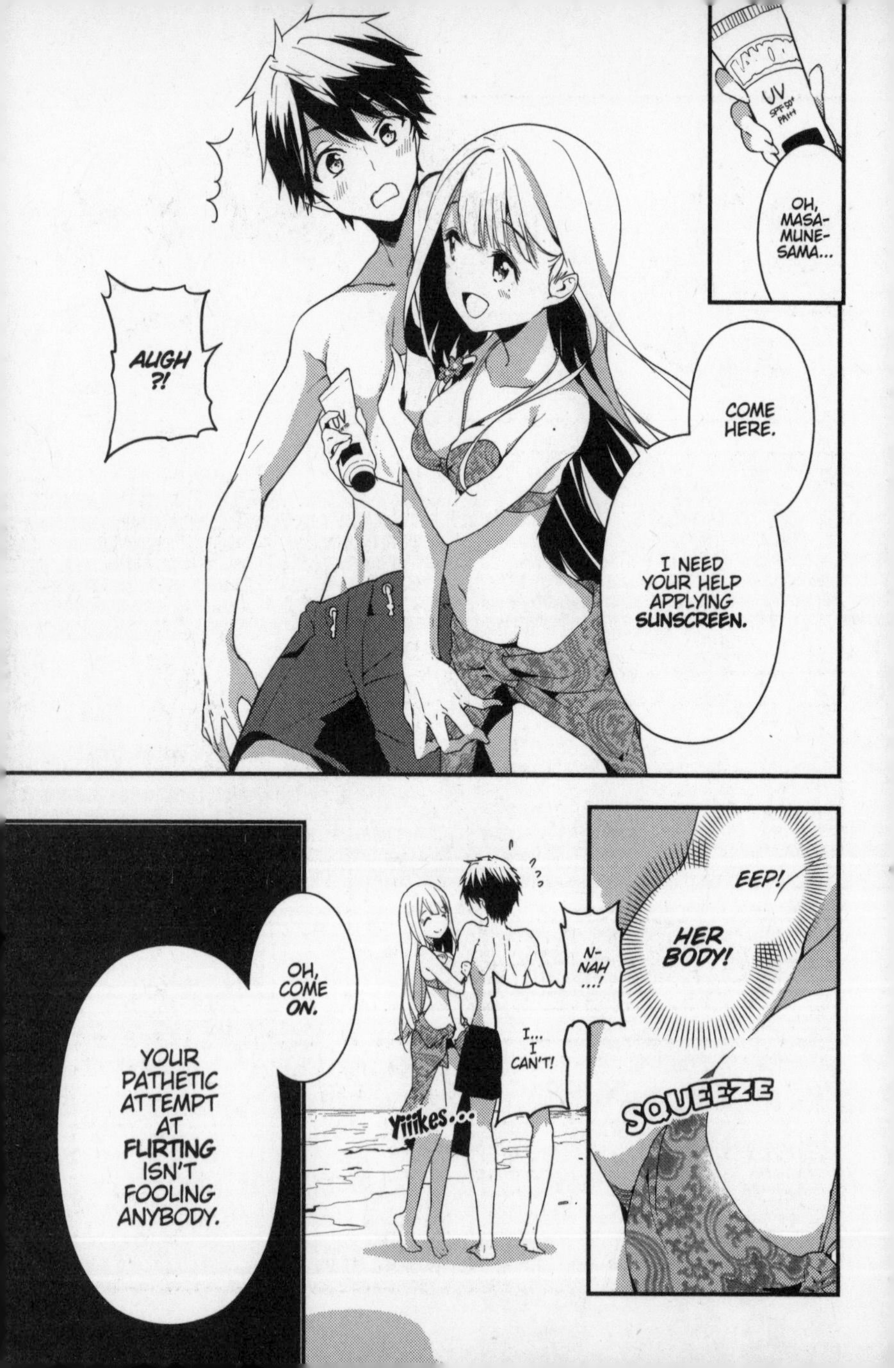
OH, MASA-MUNE-SAMA...
COME HERE.
I NEED YOUR HELP APPLYING SUNSCREEN.
AUGH ?!
EEP!
HER BODY!
SQUEEZE
N-NAH ...!
I... I CAN'T!
OH, COME ON.
YOUR PATHETIC ATTEMPT AT FLIRTING ISN'T FOOLING ANYBODY.
Yiiikes...

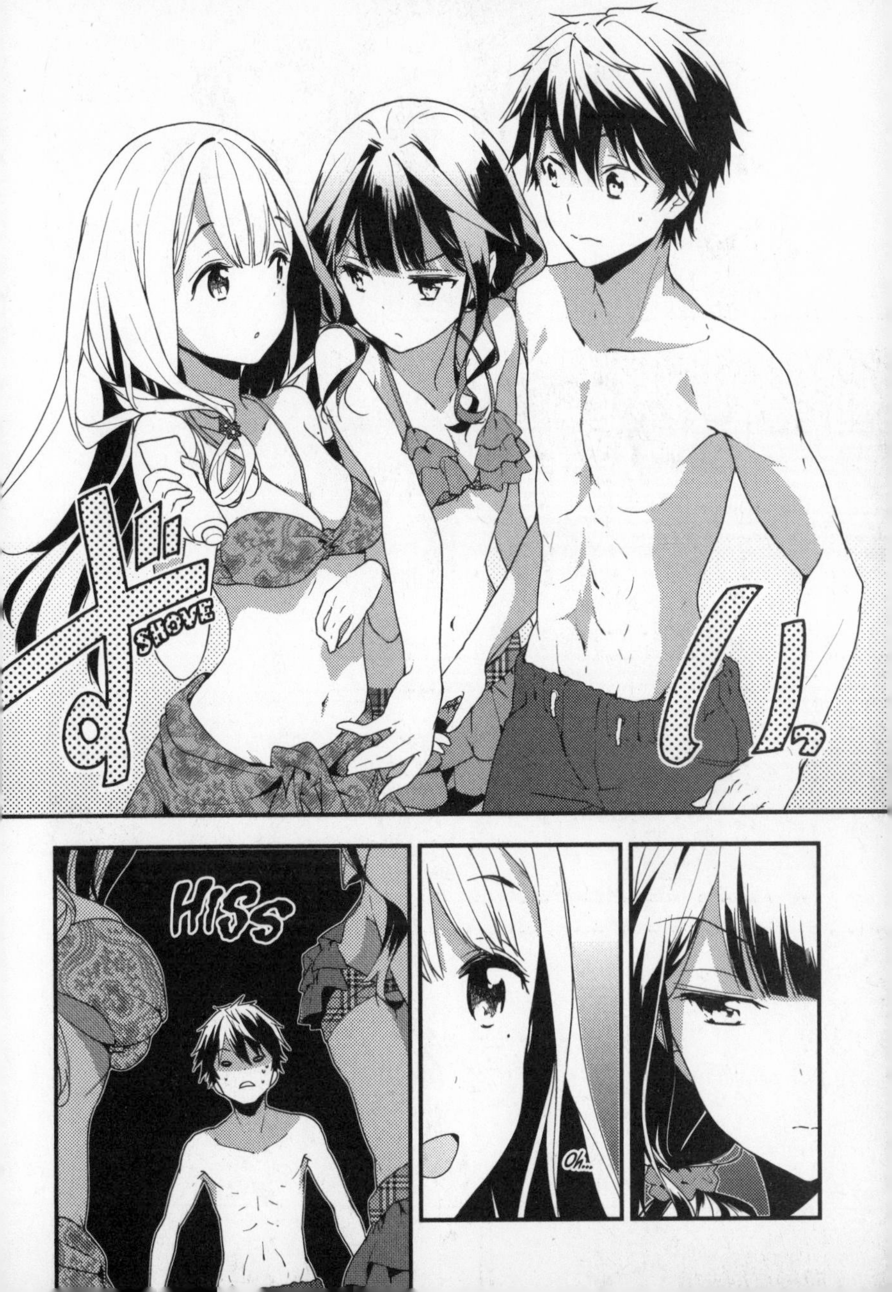
SHOVE
Oh...
HISS

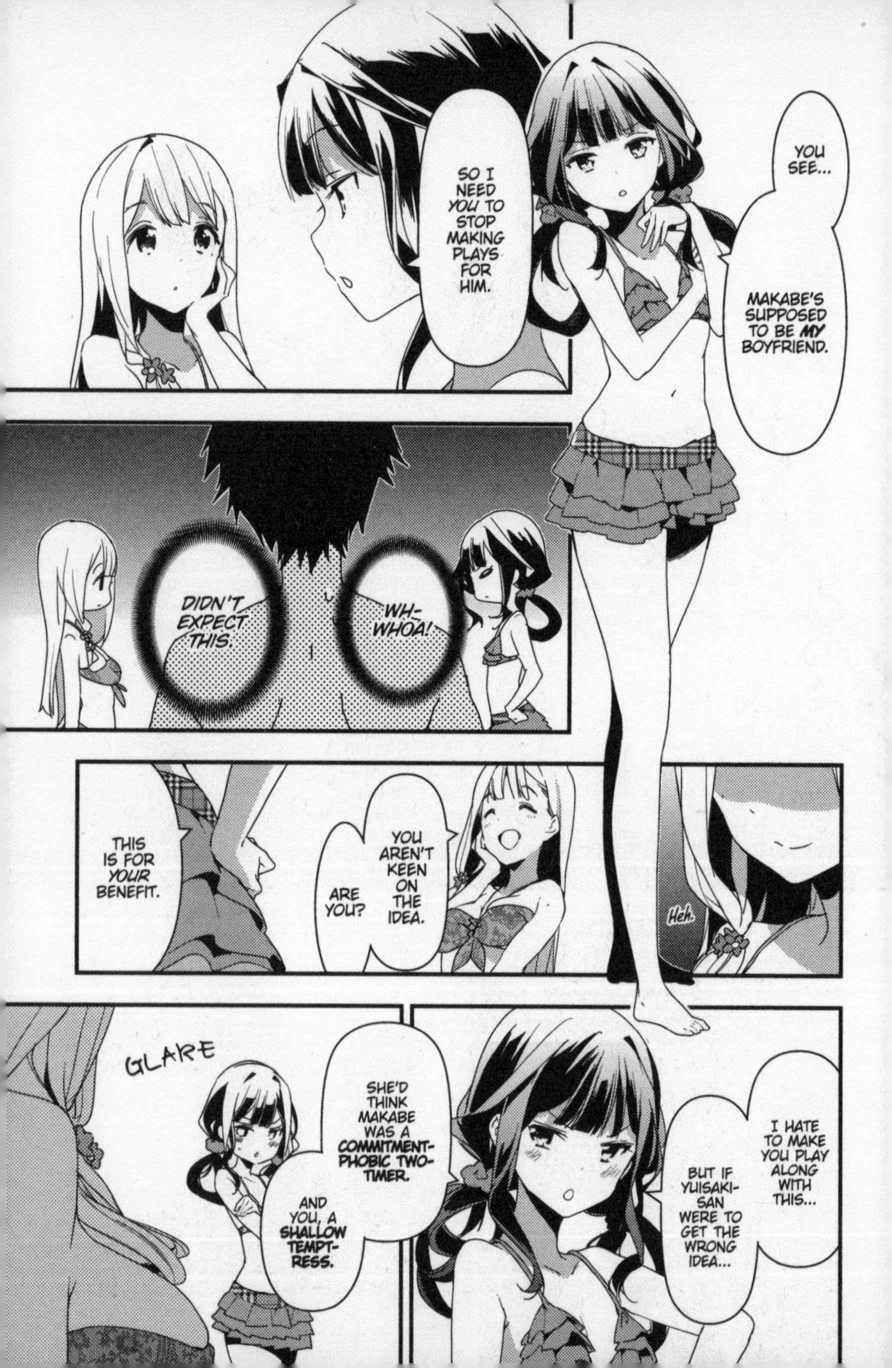
YOU SEE...
MAKABE'S SUPPOSED TO BE *MY* BOYFRIEND.
SO I NEED *YOU* TO STOP MAKING PLAYS FOR HIM.
WH- WHOA!
DIDN'T EXPECT THIS.
Heh.
YOU AREN'T KEEN ON THE IDEA.
ARE YOU?
THIS IS FOR *YOUR* BENEFIT.
I HATE TO MAKE YOU PLAY ALONG WITH THIS...
BUT IF YUISAKI-SAN WERE TO GET THE WRONG IDEA...
SHE'D THINK MAKABE WAS A COMMITMENT-PHOBIC TWO-TIMER.
AND YOU, A SHALLOW TEMPT-RESS.
GLARE

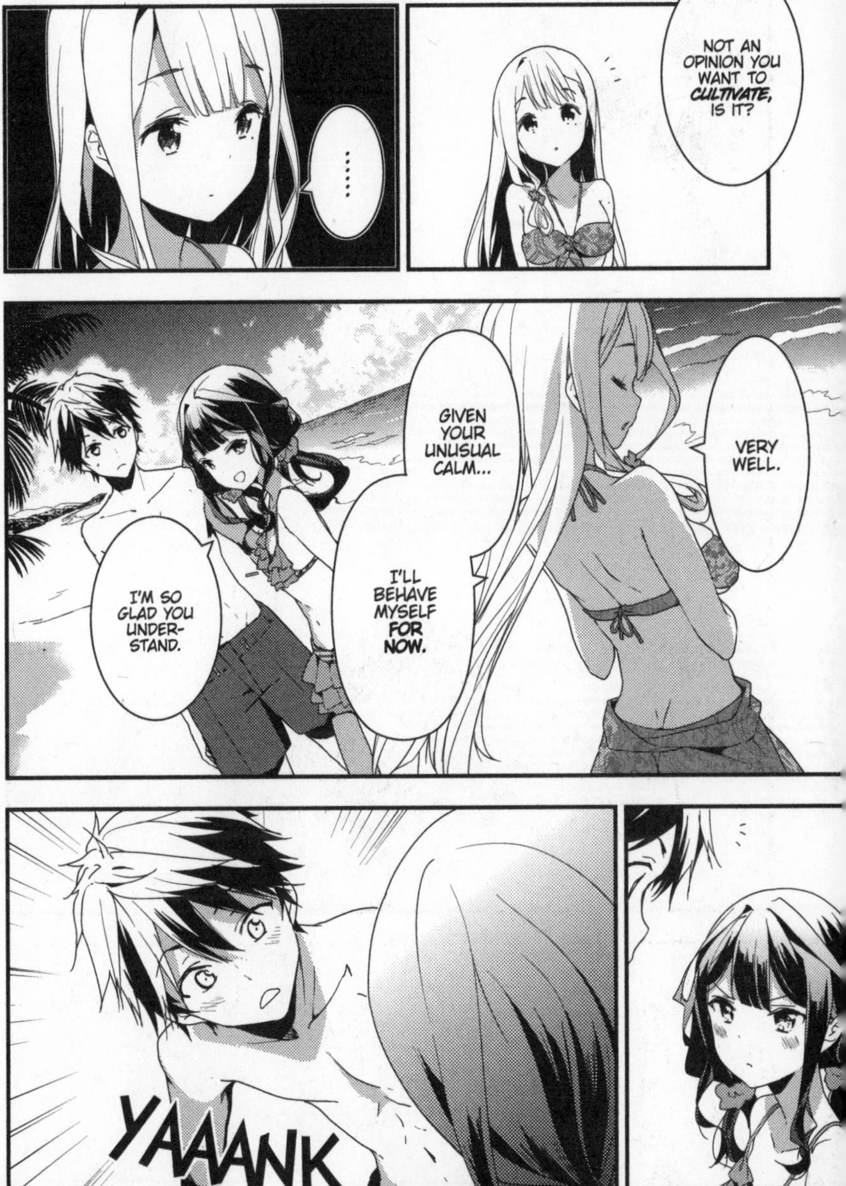
NOT AN OPINION YOU WANT TO CULTIVATE, IS IT?
......
VERY WELL.
GIVEN YOUR UNUSUAL CALM...
I'LL BEHAVE MYSELF FOR NOW.
I'M SO GLAD YOU UNDER-STAND.
YAAANK

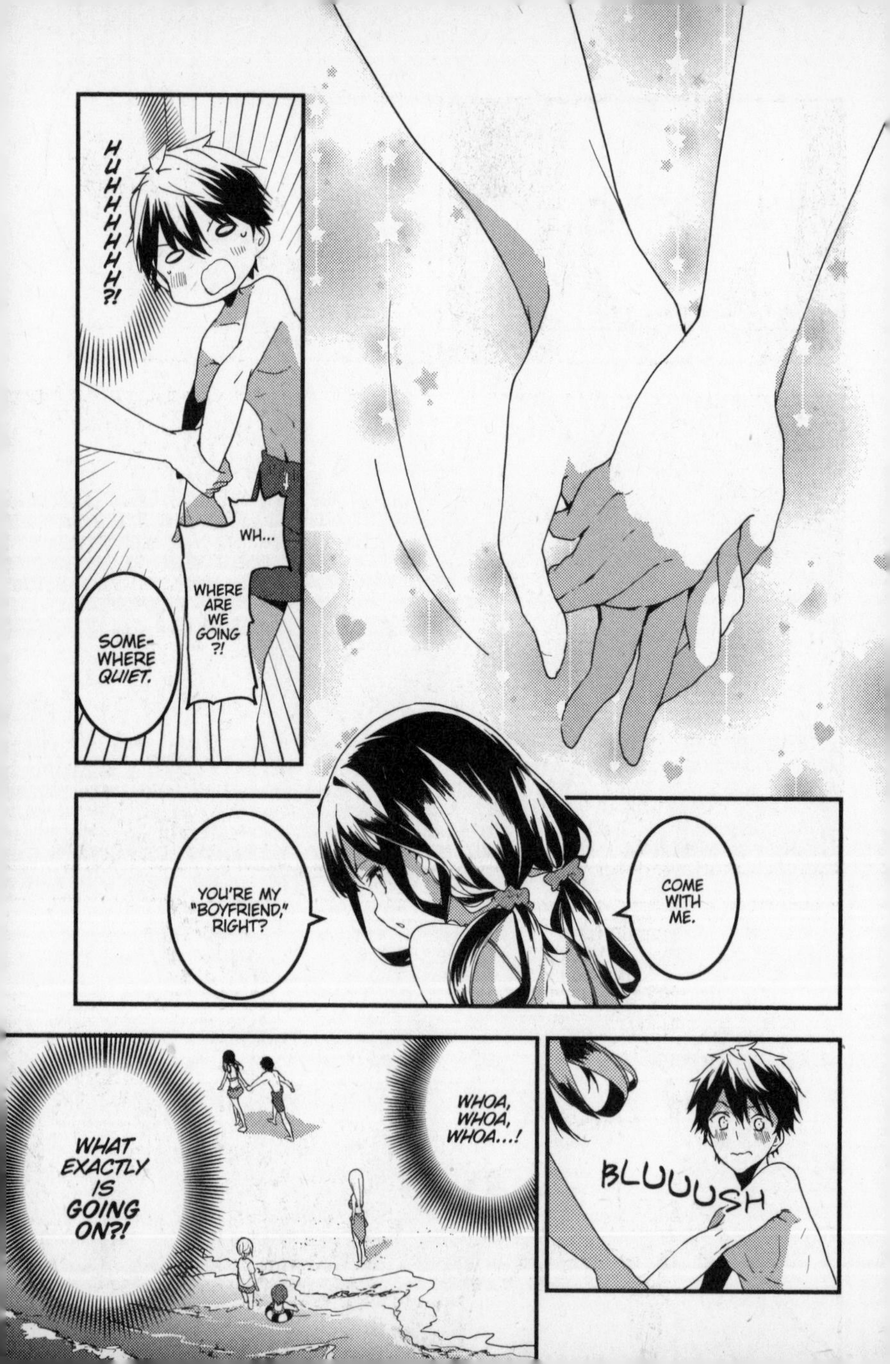
HUHHHHHHH?!
WH...
WHERE ARE WE GOING?!
SOME-WHERE QUIET.
COME WITH ME.
YOU'RE MY "BOYFRIEND," RIGHT?
BLUUUSH
WHOA, WHOA, WHOA...!
WHAT EXACTLY IS GOING ON?!

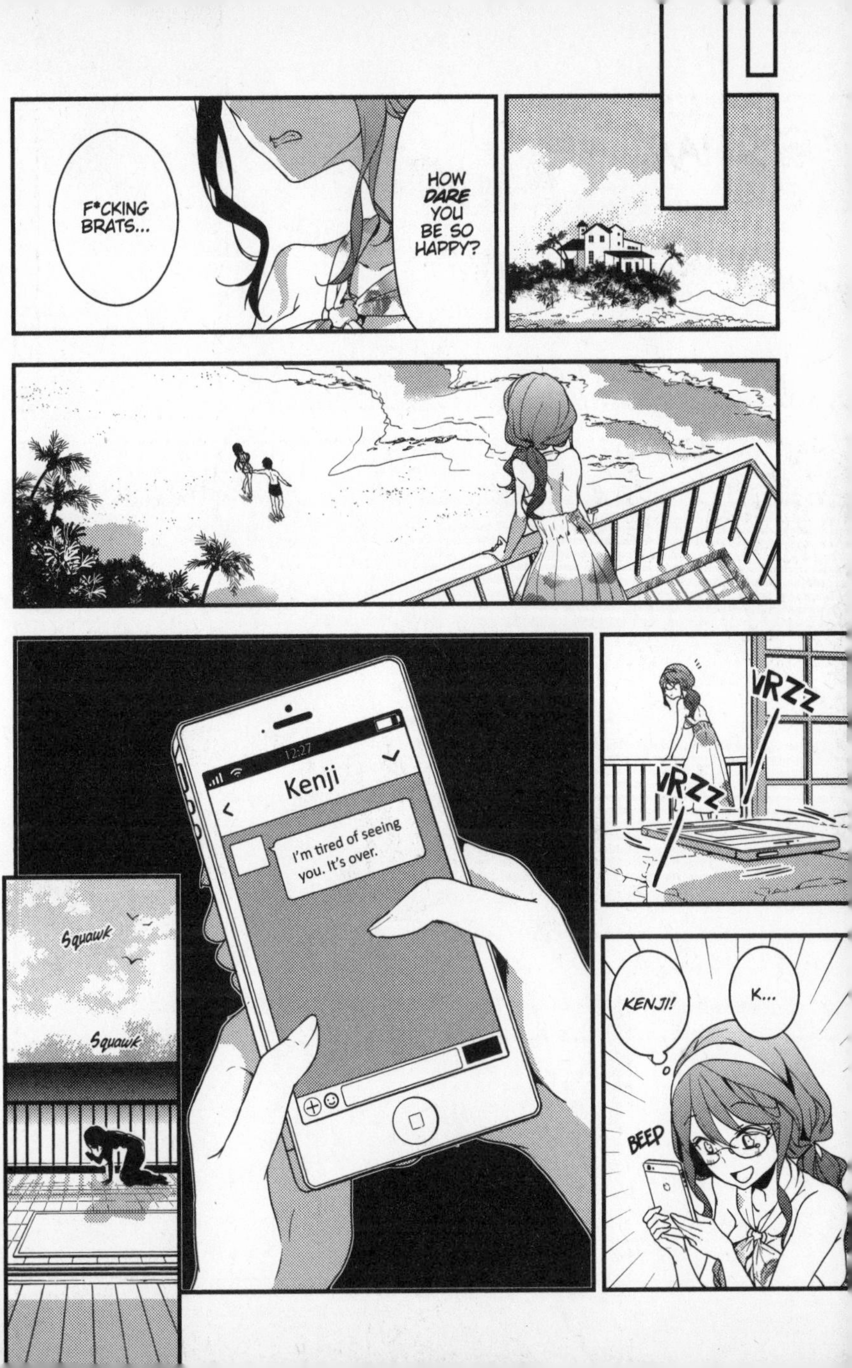
HOW DARE YOU BE SO HAPPY?
F*CKING BRATS...
VRZZ
VRZZ
K...
KENJI!
BEEP
12:27
Kenji
I'm tired of seeing you. It's over.
Squawk
Squawk

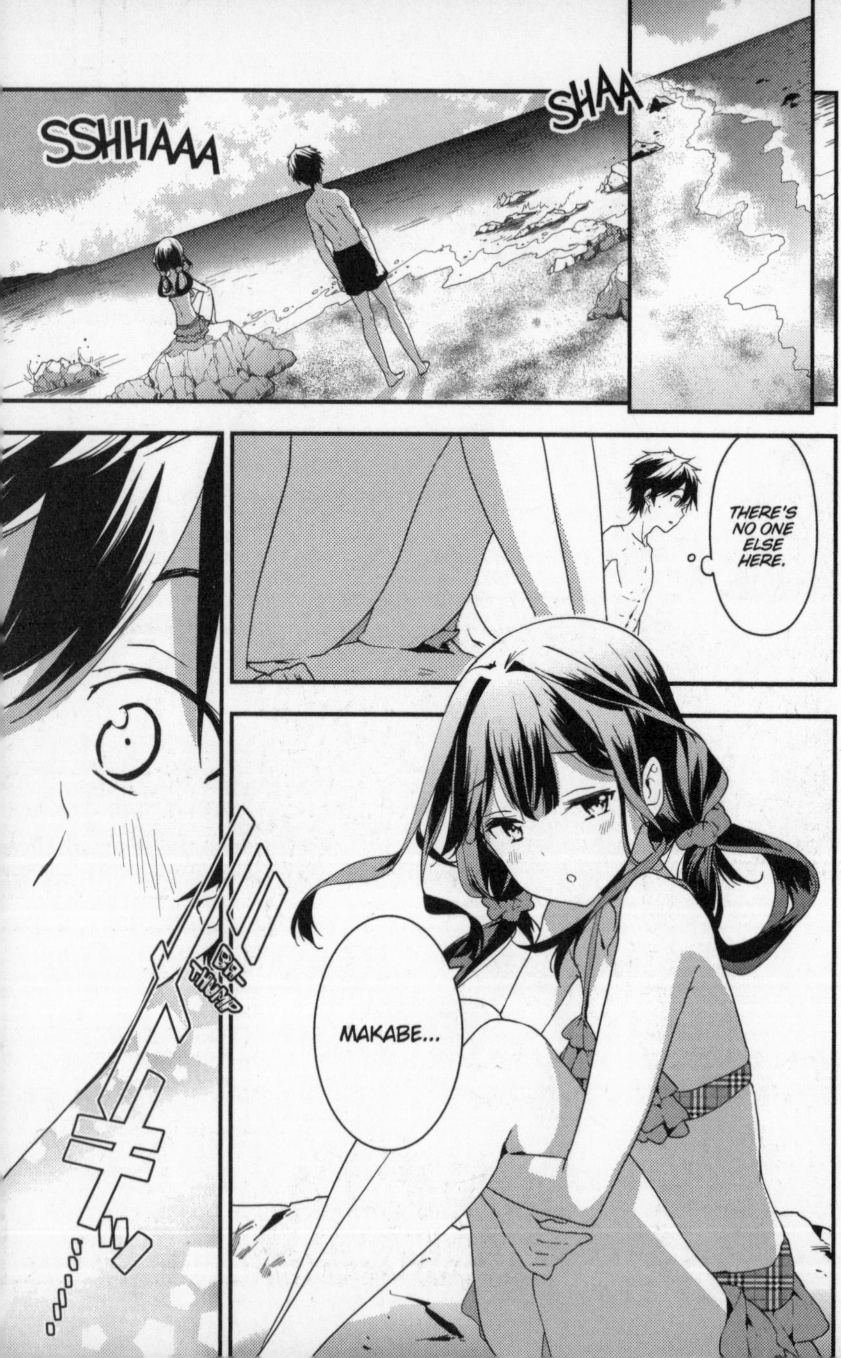
SHAA
SSHHAAA
THERE'S NO ONE ELSE HERE.
MAKABE...
BA-THUMP

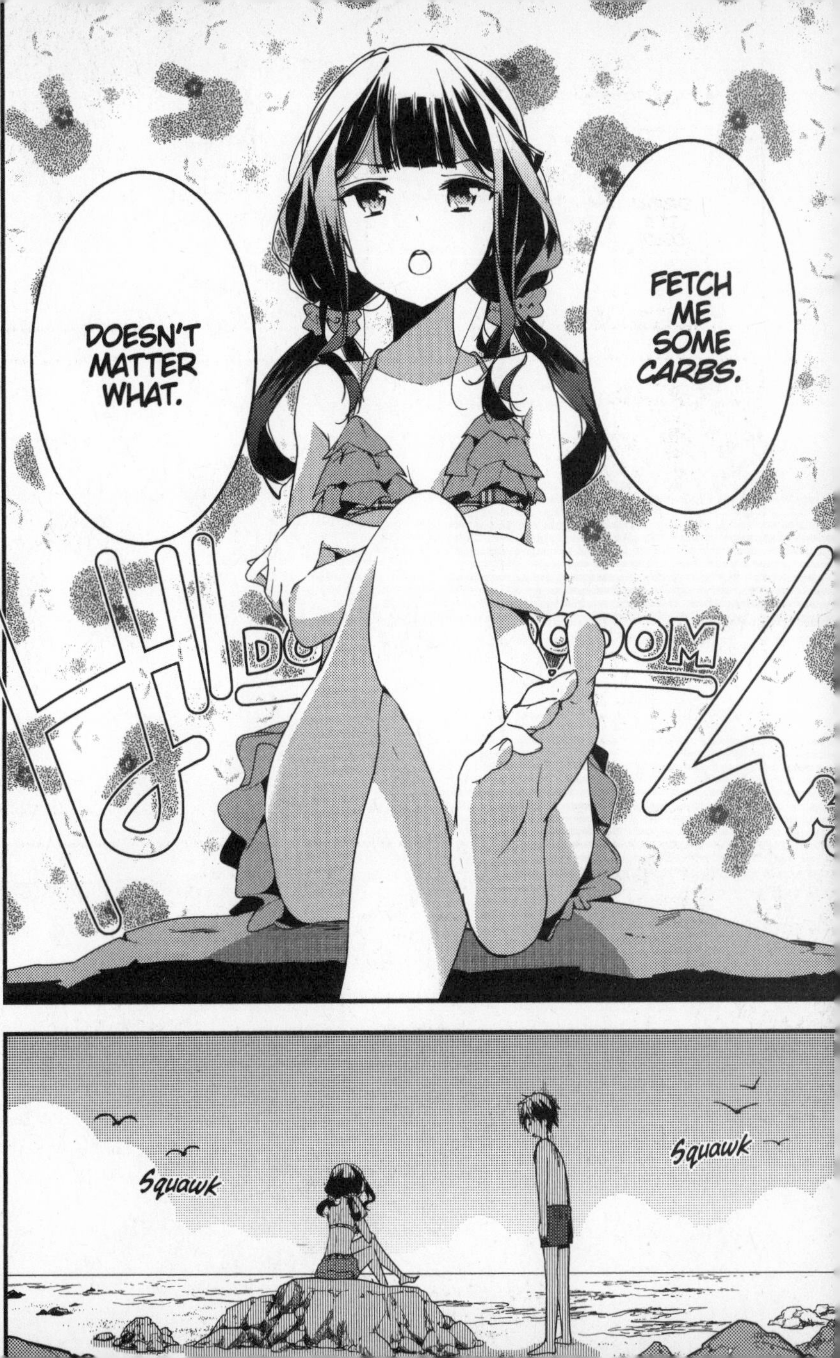
FETCH ME SOME CARBS.
DOESN'T MATTER WHAT.
Squawk
Squawk

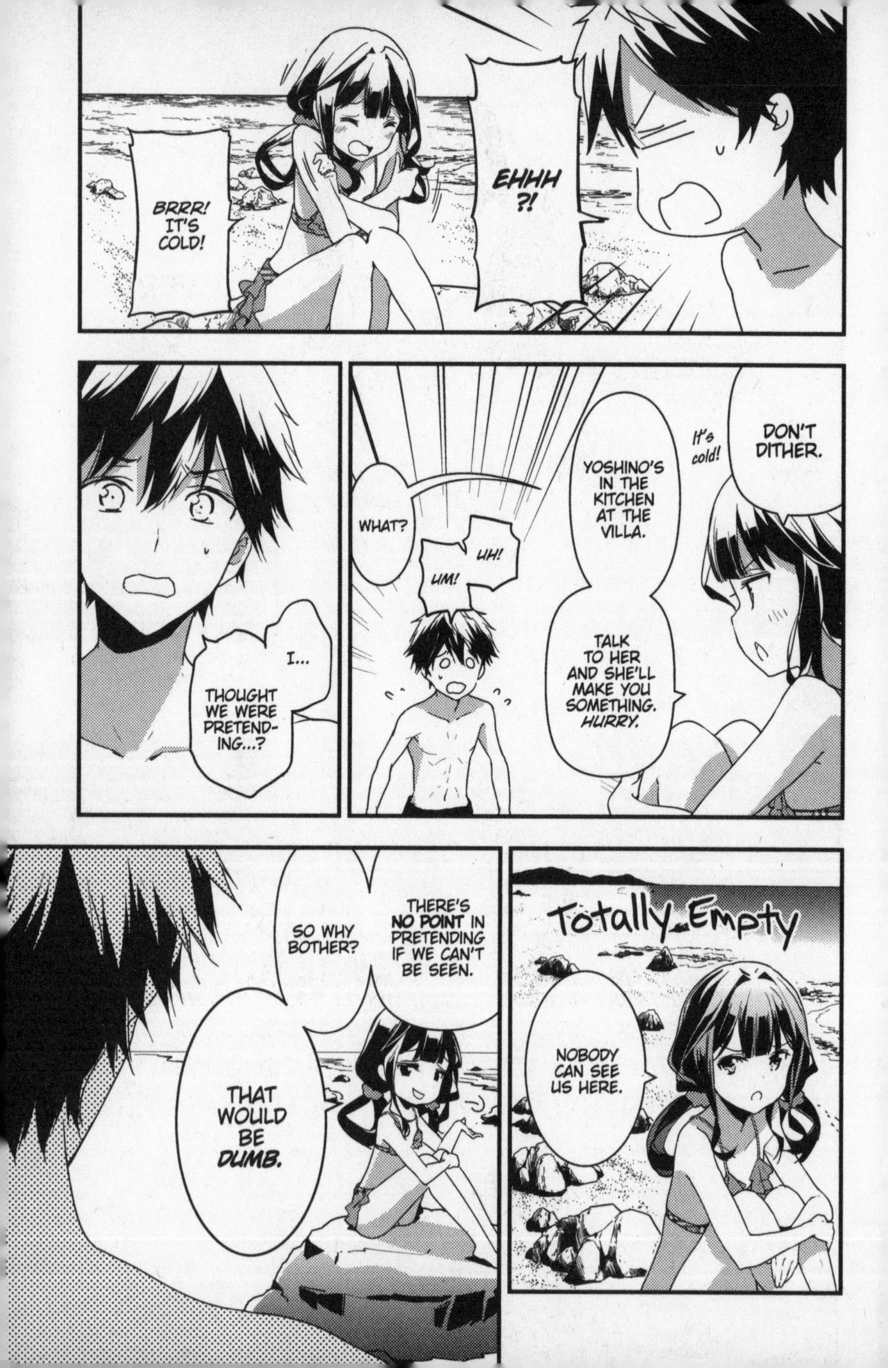
EHHH ?!
BRRR! IT'S COLD!
DON'T DITHER.
It's cold!
YOSHINO'S IN THE KITCHEN AT THE VILLA.
TALK TO HER AND SHE'LL MAKE YOU SOMETHING. HURRY.
UH!
UM!
WHAT?
I...
THOUGHT WE WERE PRETEND-ING...?
Totally Empty
NOBODY CAN SEE US HERE.
THERE'S NO POINT IN PRETENDING IF WE CAN'T BE SEEN.
SO WHY BOTHER?
THAT WOULD BE DUMB.

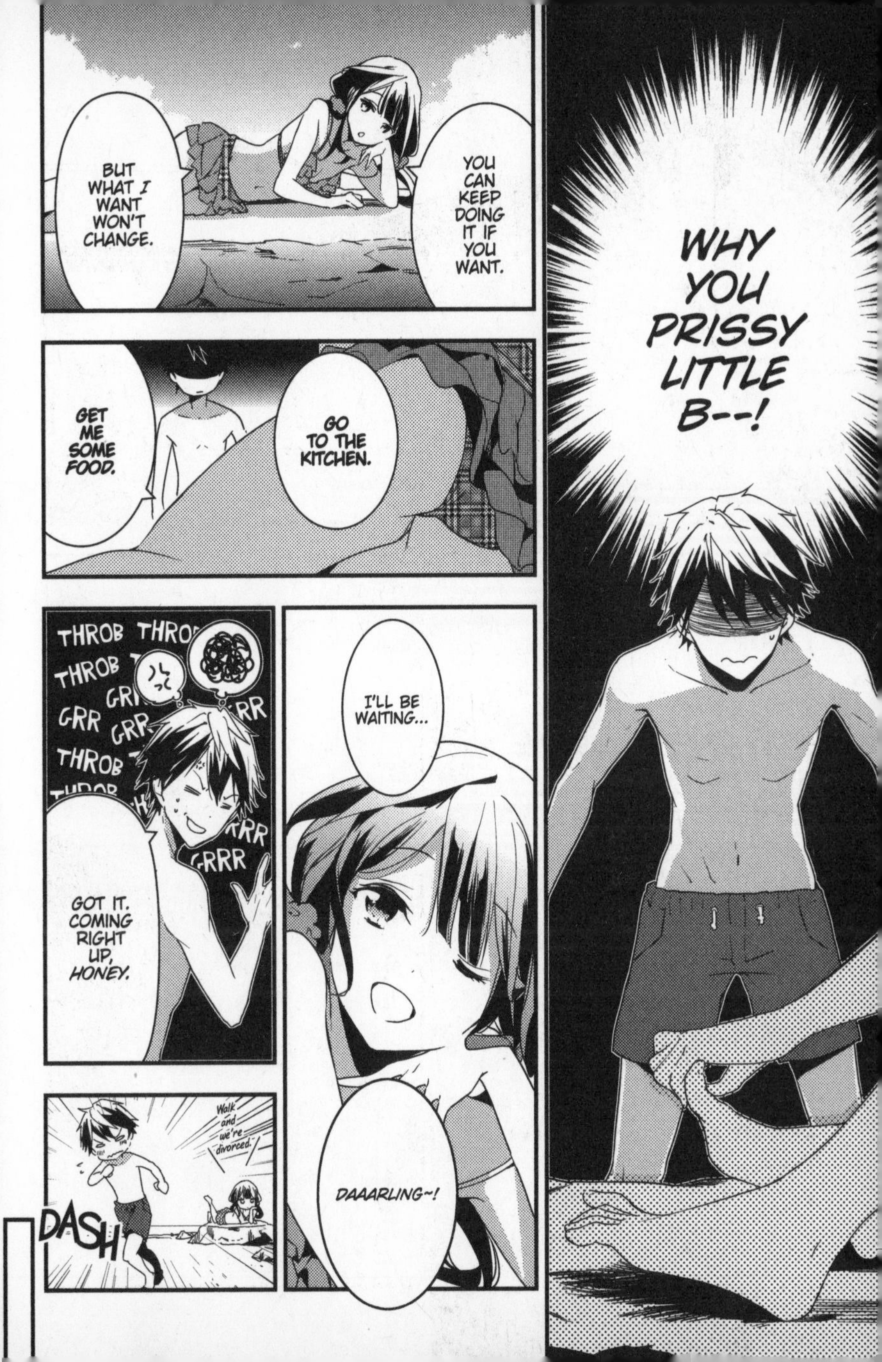
WHY YOU PRISSY LITTLE B--!
YOU CAN KEEP DOING IT IF YOU WANT.
BUT WHAT I WANT WON'T CHANGE.
GO TO THE KITCHEN.
GET ME SOME FOOD.
I'LL BE WAITING...
DAAARLING~!
THROB THROB THROB THROB
GRR GRR GRR GRR GRRR GRRR
GOT IT. COMING RIGHT UP, HONEY.
Walk and we're divorced.
DASH

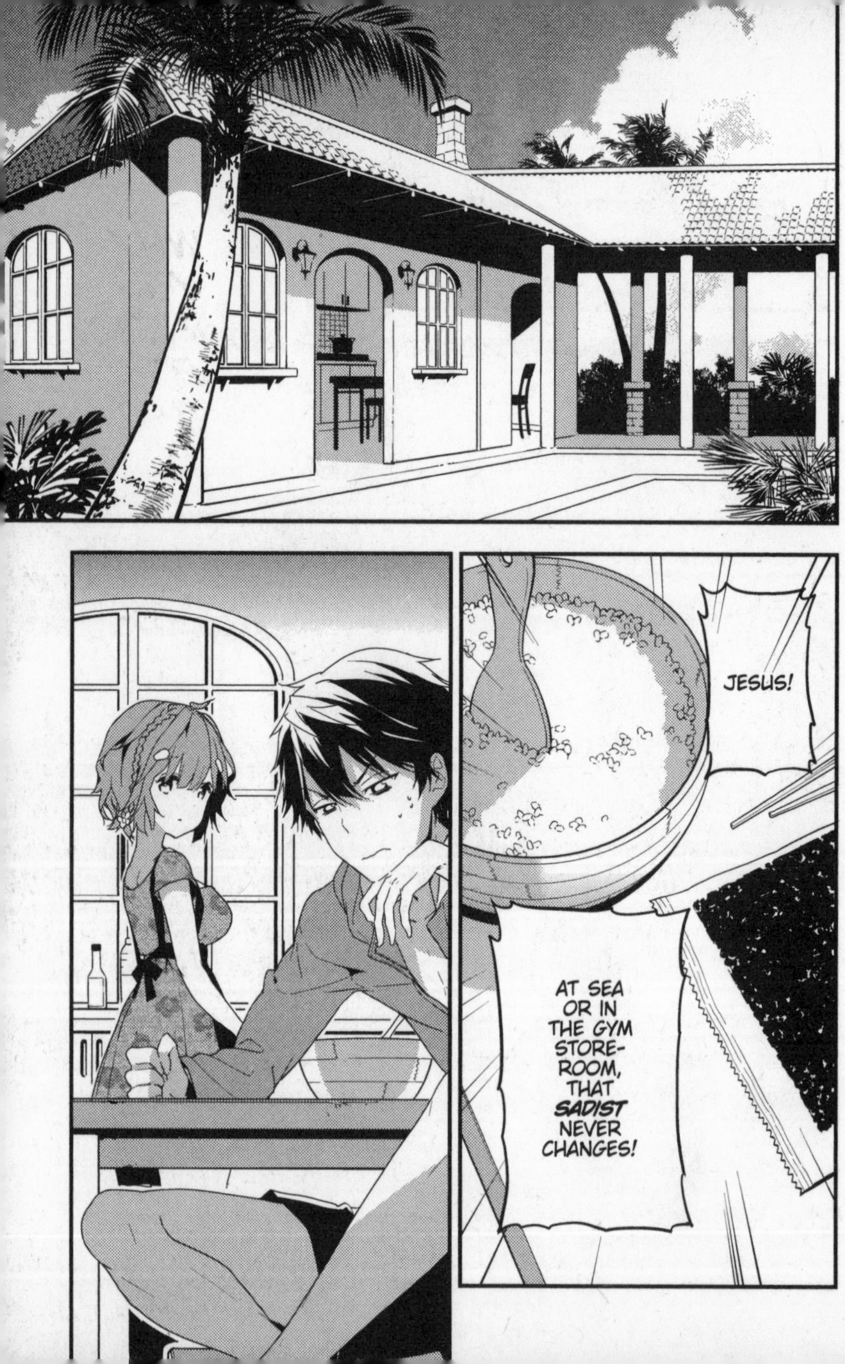
JESUS!
AT SEA OR IN THE GYM STORE-ROOM, THAT SADIST NEVER CHANGES!

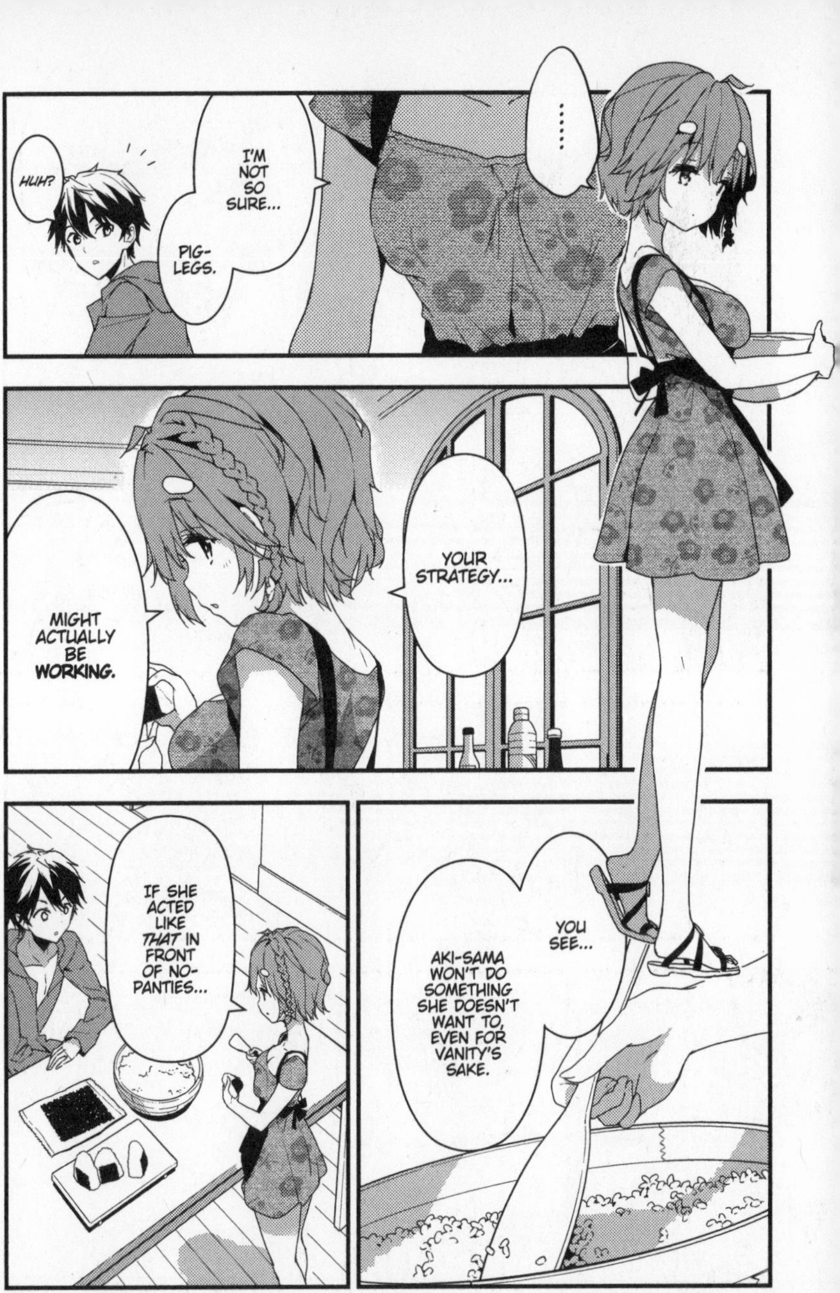
......
I'M NOT SO SURE...
PIG-LEGS.
HUH?
YOUR STRATEGY...
MIGHT ACTUALLY BE WORKING.
YOU SEE...
AKI-SAMA WON'T DO SOMETHING SHE DOESN'T WANT TO, EVEN FOR VANITY'S SAKE.
IF SHE ACTED LIKE *THAT* IN FRONT OF NO-PANTIES...

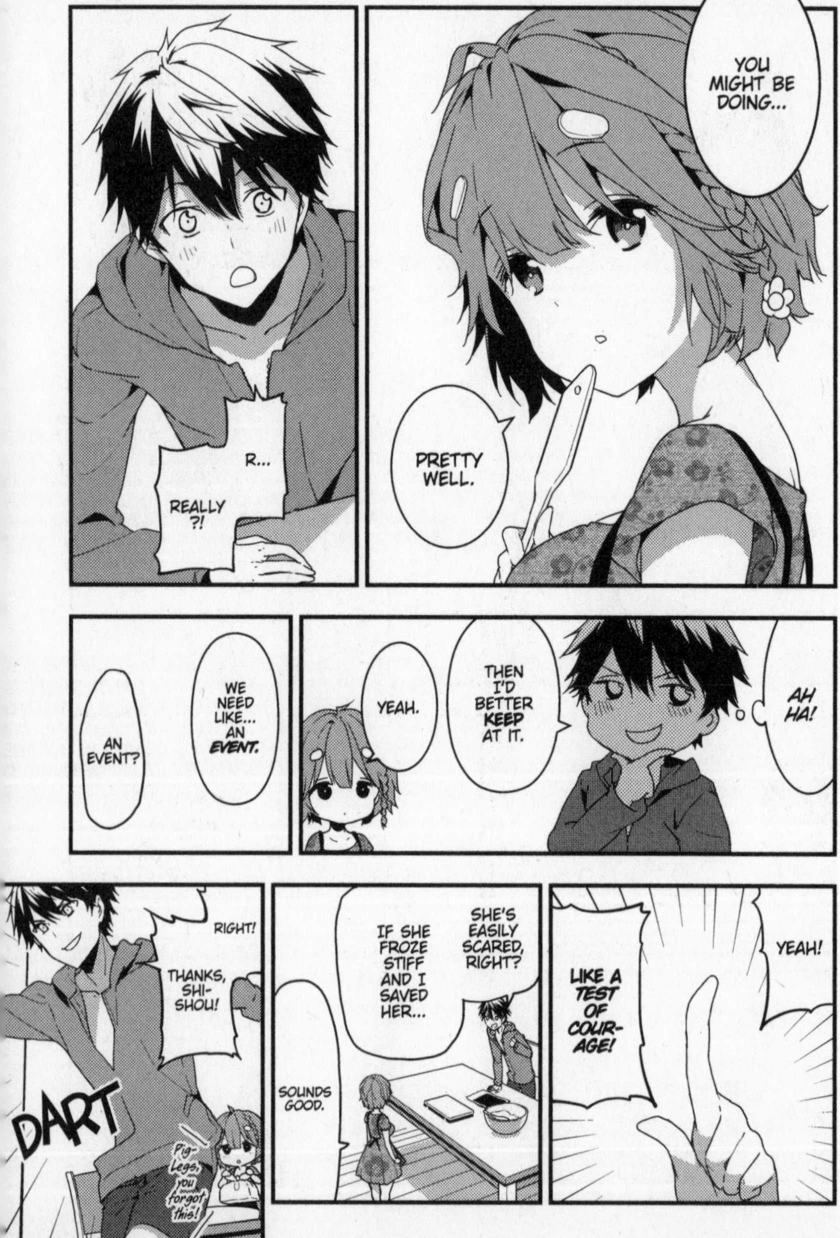
YOU MIGHT BE DOING...
PRETTY WELL.
R...
REALLY?!
AH HA!
THEN I'D BETTER KEEP AT IT.
YEAH.
WE NEED LIKE... AN EVENT.
AN EVENT?
YEAH!
LIKE A TEST OF COUR-AGE!
SHE'S EASILY SCARED, RIGHT?
IF SHE FROZE STIFF AND I SAVED HER...
SOUNDS GOOD.
RIGHT!
THANKS, SHI-SHOU!
DART
Pig-Legs, you forgot this!

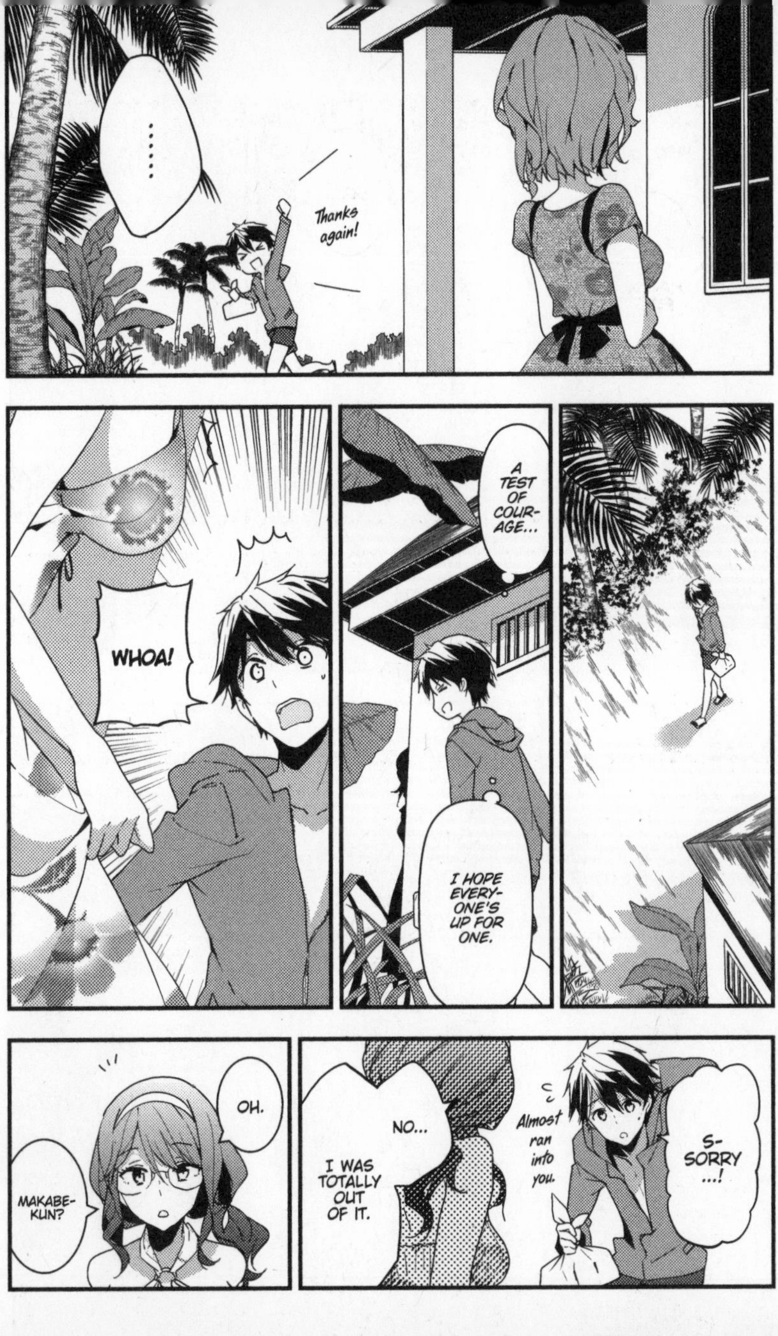
Thanks again!
……
A TEST OF COURAGE…
I HOPE EVERYONE'S UP FOR ONE.
WHOA!
S-SORRY…!
Almost ran into you.
NO…
I WAS TOTALLY OUT OF IT.
OH.
MAKABE-KUN?

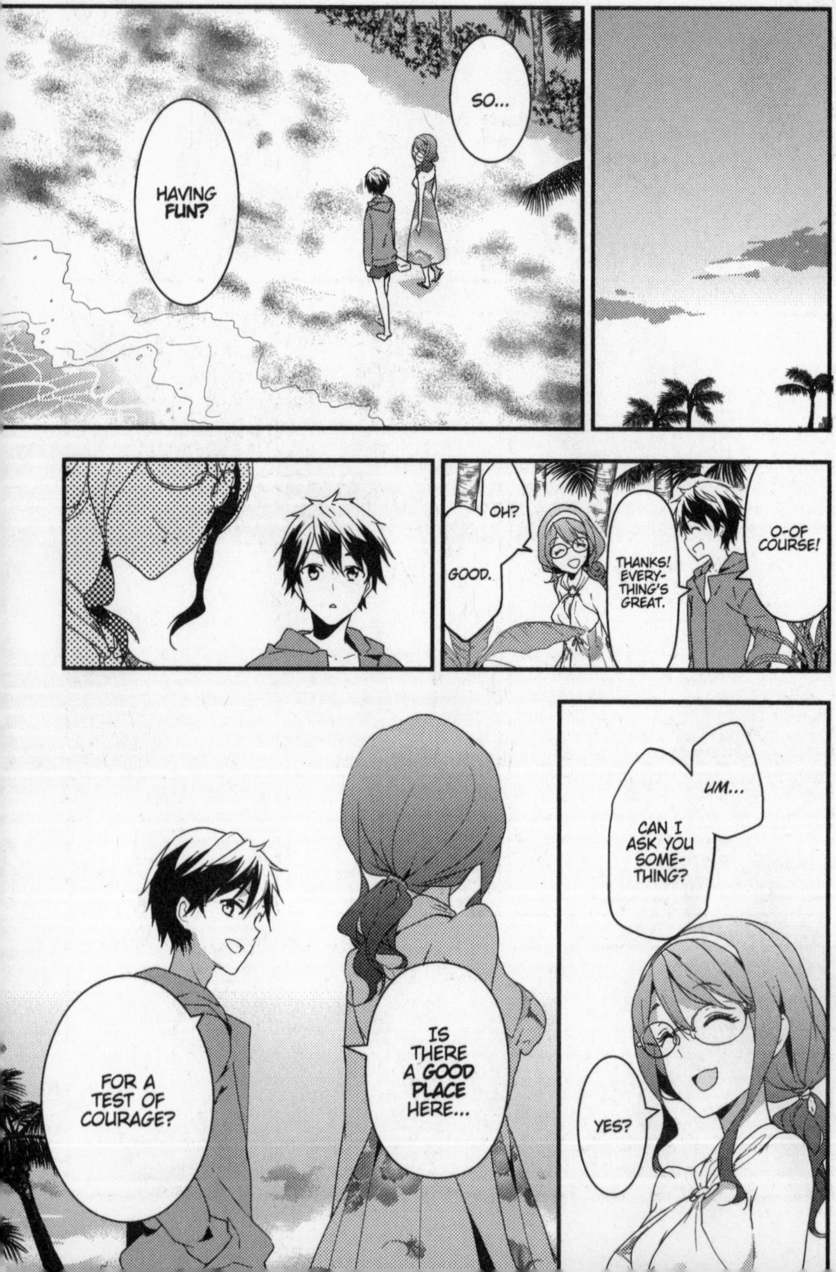
SO...
HAVING FUN?
O-OF COURSE!
THANKS! EVERYTHING'S GREAT.
OH? GOOD.
UM... CAN I ASK YOU SOMETHING?
YES?
IS THERE A GOOD PLACE HERE...
FOR A TEST OF COURAGE?

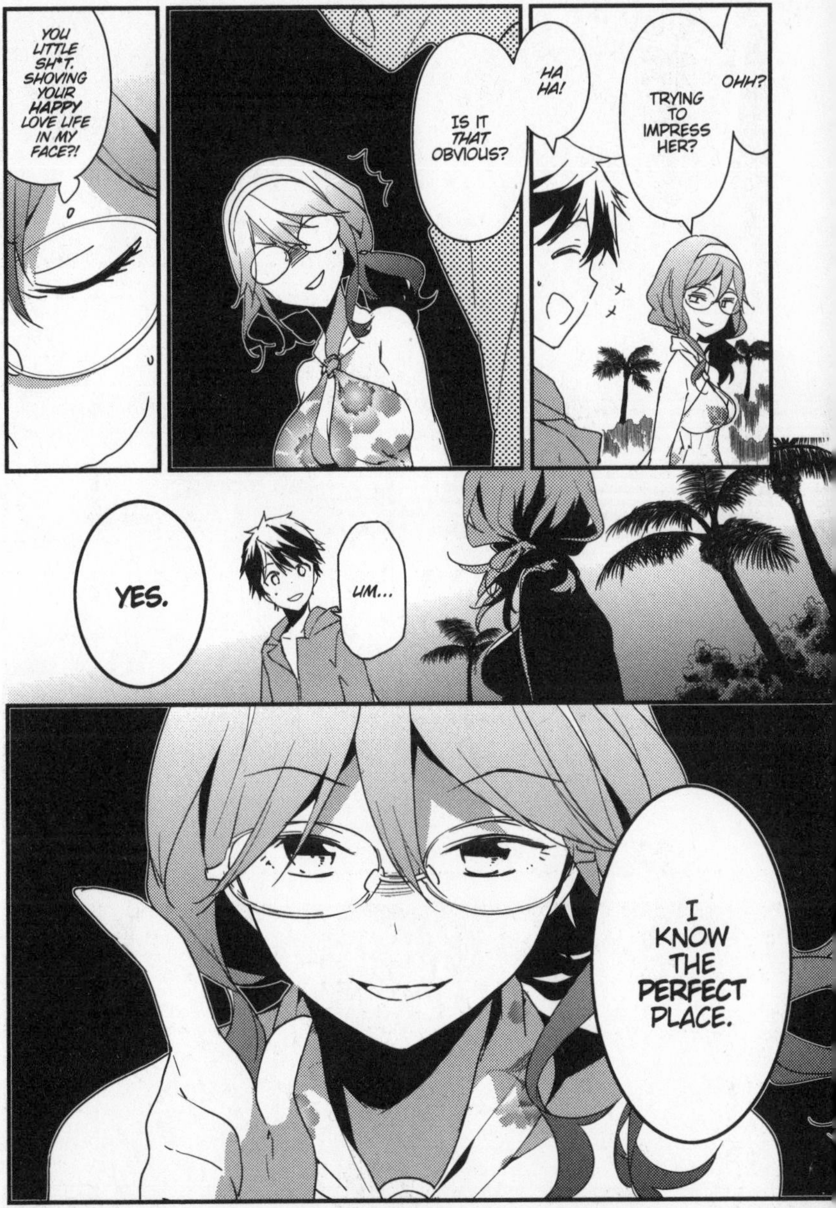
OHH?
TRYING TO IMPRESS HER?
HA HA!
IS IT THAT OBVIOUS?
YOU LITTLE SH*T. SHOVING YOUR HAPPY LOVE LIFE IN MY FACE?!
UM...
YES.
I KNOW THE PERFECT PLACE.

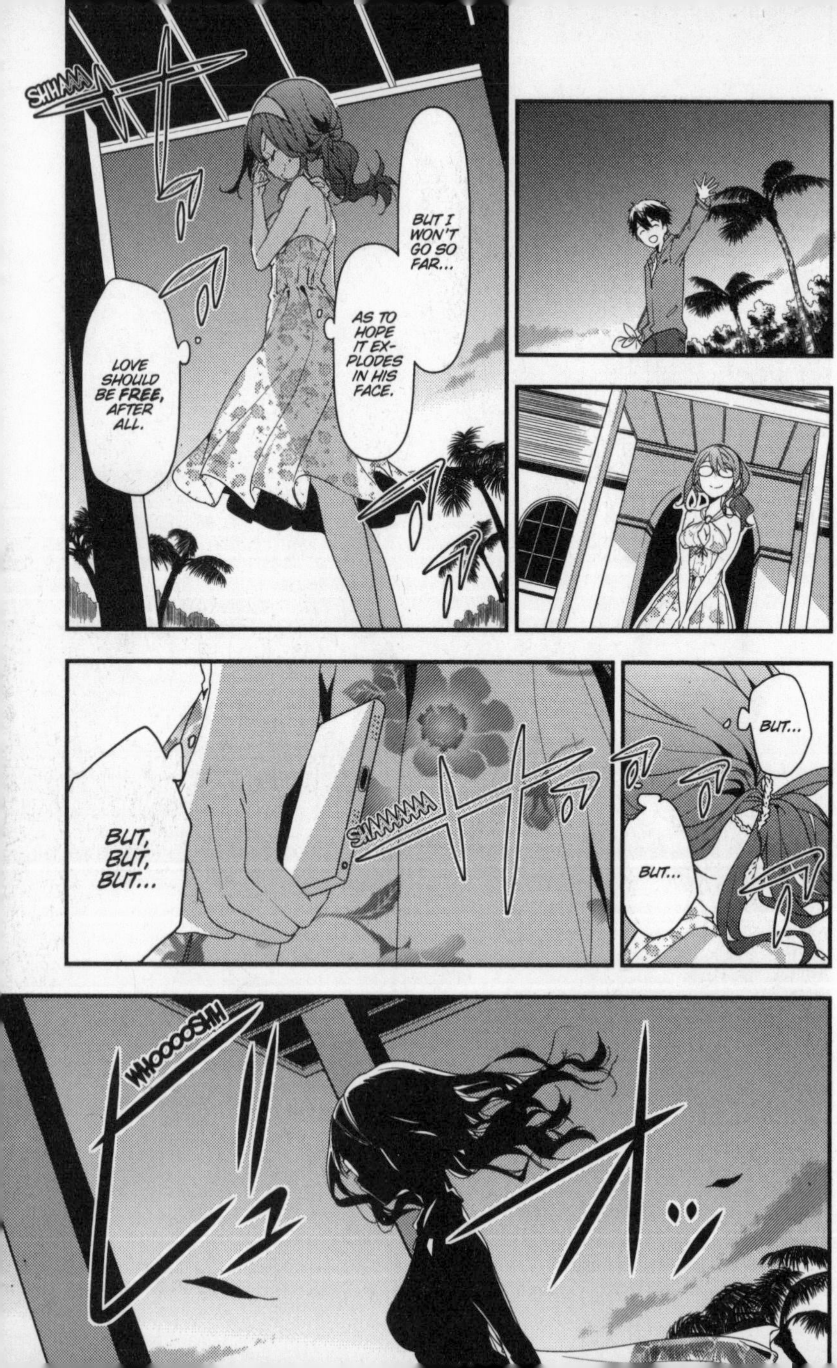
SHHAAA
BUT I WON'T GO SO FAR...
AS TO HOPE IT EXPLODES IN HIS FACE.
LOVE SHOULD BE FREE, AFTER ALL.
BUT...
BUT...
SHAAAAAA
BUT, BUT, BUT...
WHOOOOSH

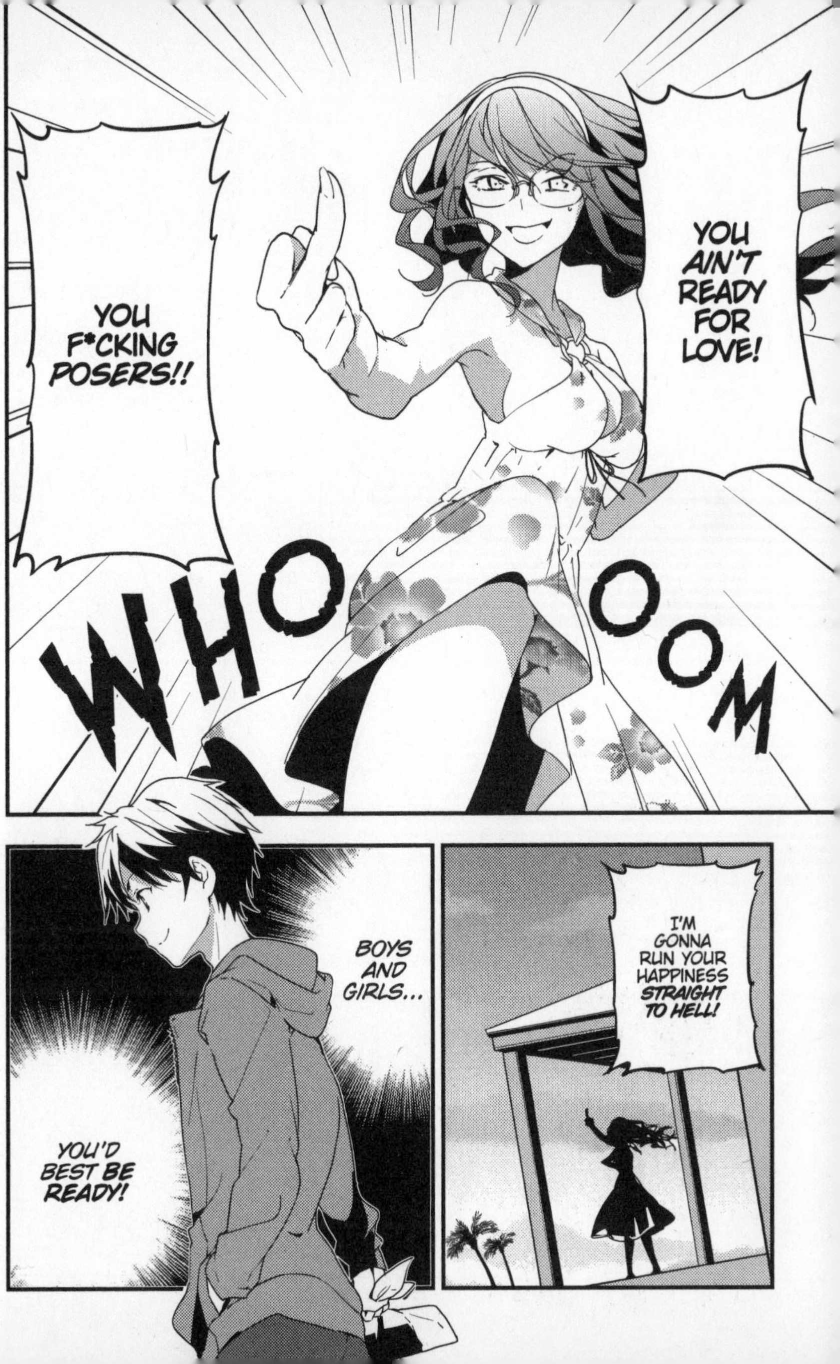
YOU AIN'T READY FOR LOVE!
YOU F*CKING POSERS!!
WHOOOOM
I'M GONNA RUN YOUR HAPPINESS STRAIGHT TO HELL!
BOYS AND GIRLS...
YOU'D BEST BE READY!

Did I eat too much?

4

Masamune-kun's
REVENGE
Presented by Hazuki Takeoka & TIV

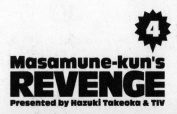

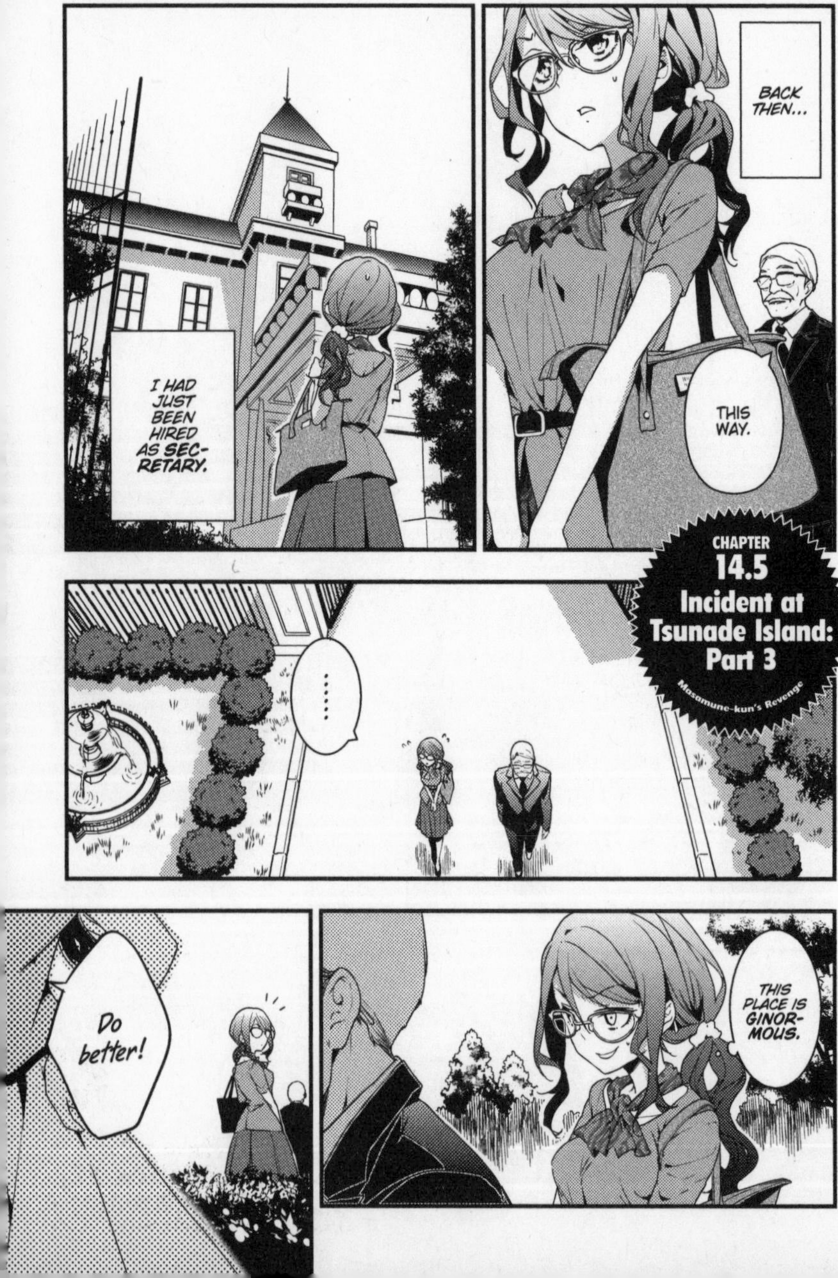
BACK THEN...
THIS WAY.
I HAD JUST BEEN HIRED AS SECRETARY.
CHAPTER 14.5
Incident at Tsunade Island: Part 3
Masamune-kun's Revenge
......
THIS PLACE IS GINORMOUS.
Do better!

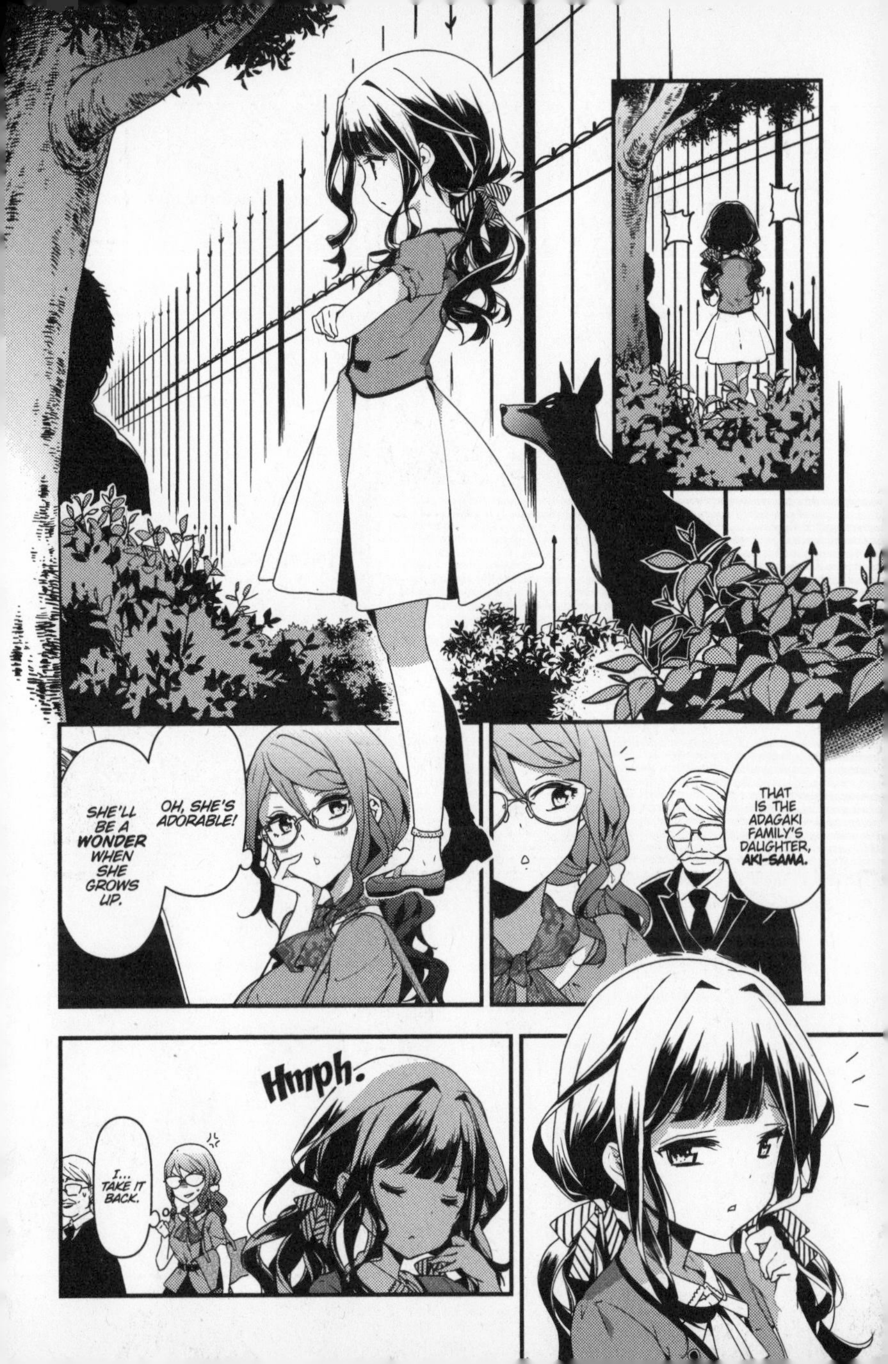

THAT IS THE ADAGAKI FAMILY'S DAUGHTER, AKI-SAMA.
OH, SHE'S ADORABLE!
SHE'LL BE A WONDER WHEN SHE GROWS UP.
Hmph.
I... TAKE IT BACK.

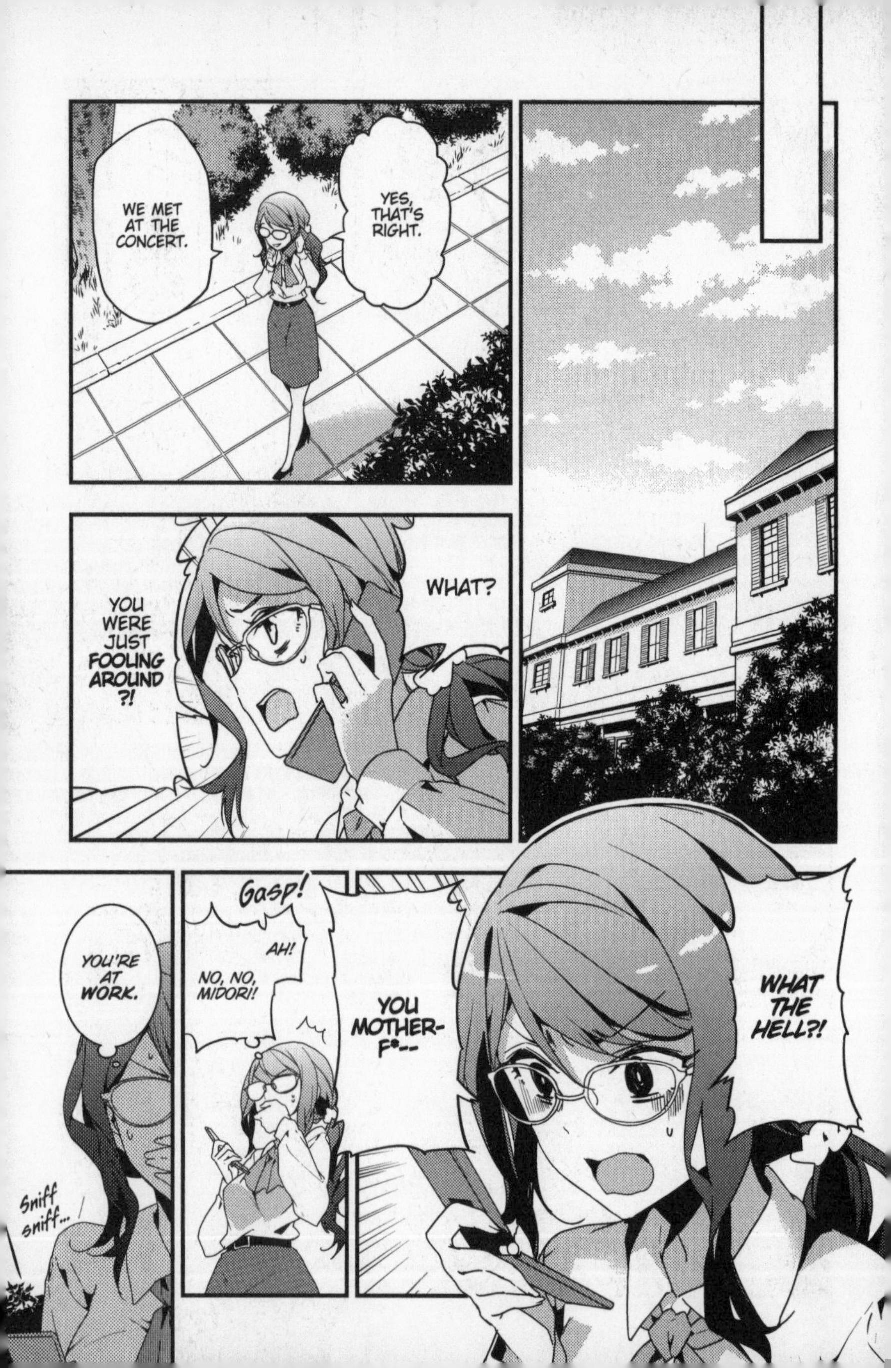
YES, THAT'S RIGHT.
WE MET AT THE CONCERT.
WHAT?
YOU WERE JUST FOOLING AROUND?!
WHAT THE HELL?!
Gasp!
YOU MOTHER-F*--
AH!
NO, NO, MIDORI!
YOU'RE AT WORK.
Sniff sniff...

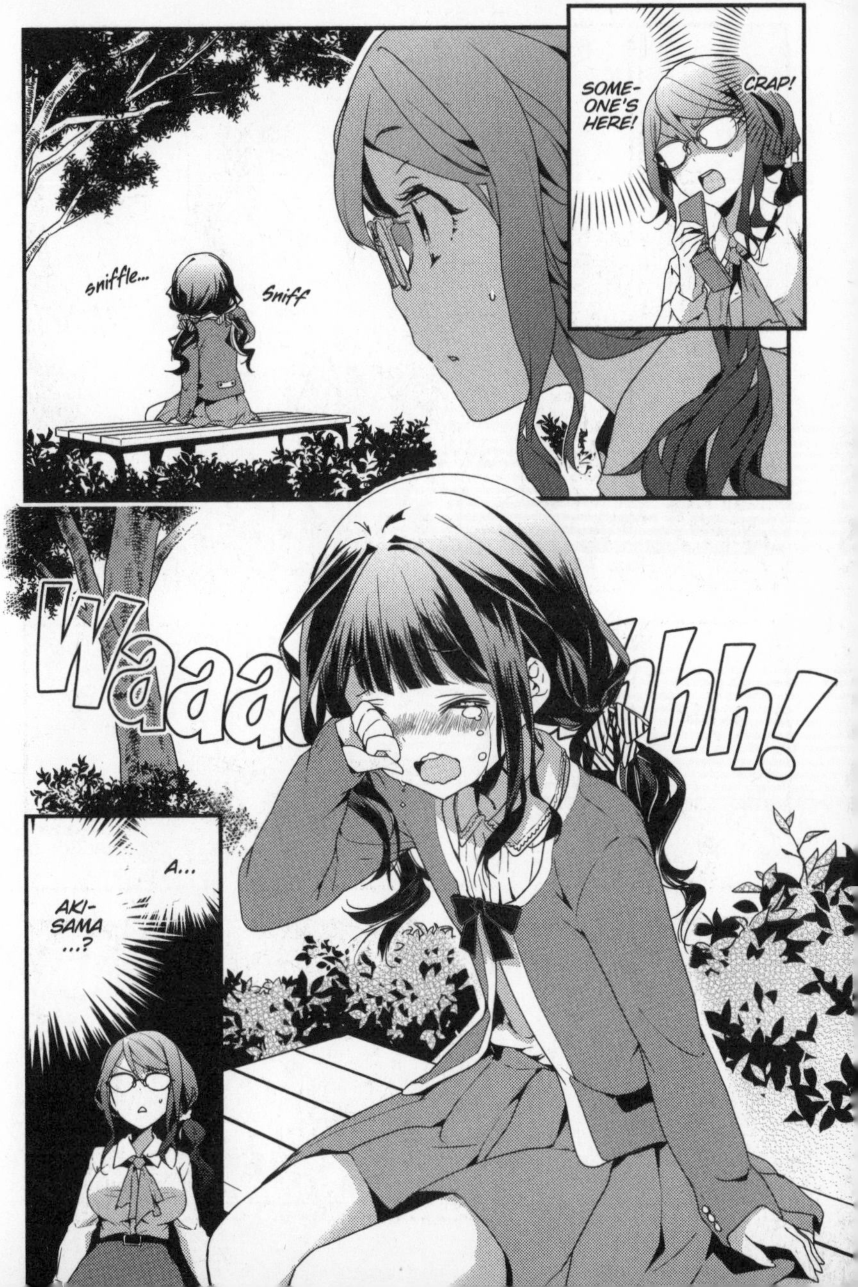
CRAP!
SOME-ONE'S HERE!
Sniff
sniffle...
Waaa
hhh!
A...
AKI-SAMA ...?

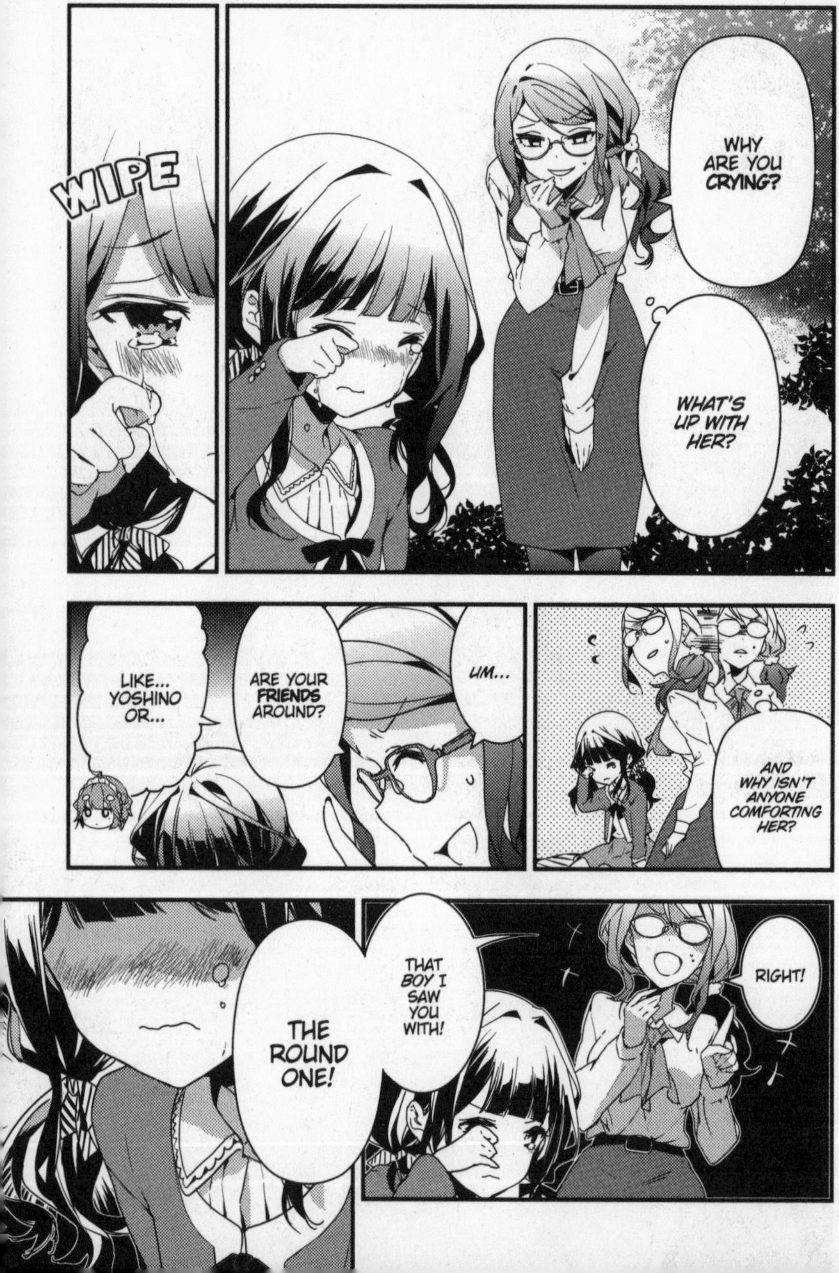
WHY ARE YOU CRYING?
WHAT'S UP WITH HER?
WIPE
AND WHY ISN'T ANYONE COMFORTING HER?
UM...
ARE YOUR FRIENDS AROUND?
LIKE... YOSHINO OR...
RIGHT!
THAT BOY I SAW YOU WITH!
THE ROUND ONE!

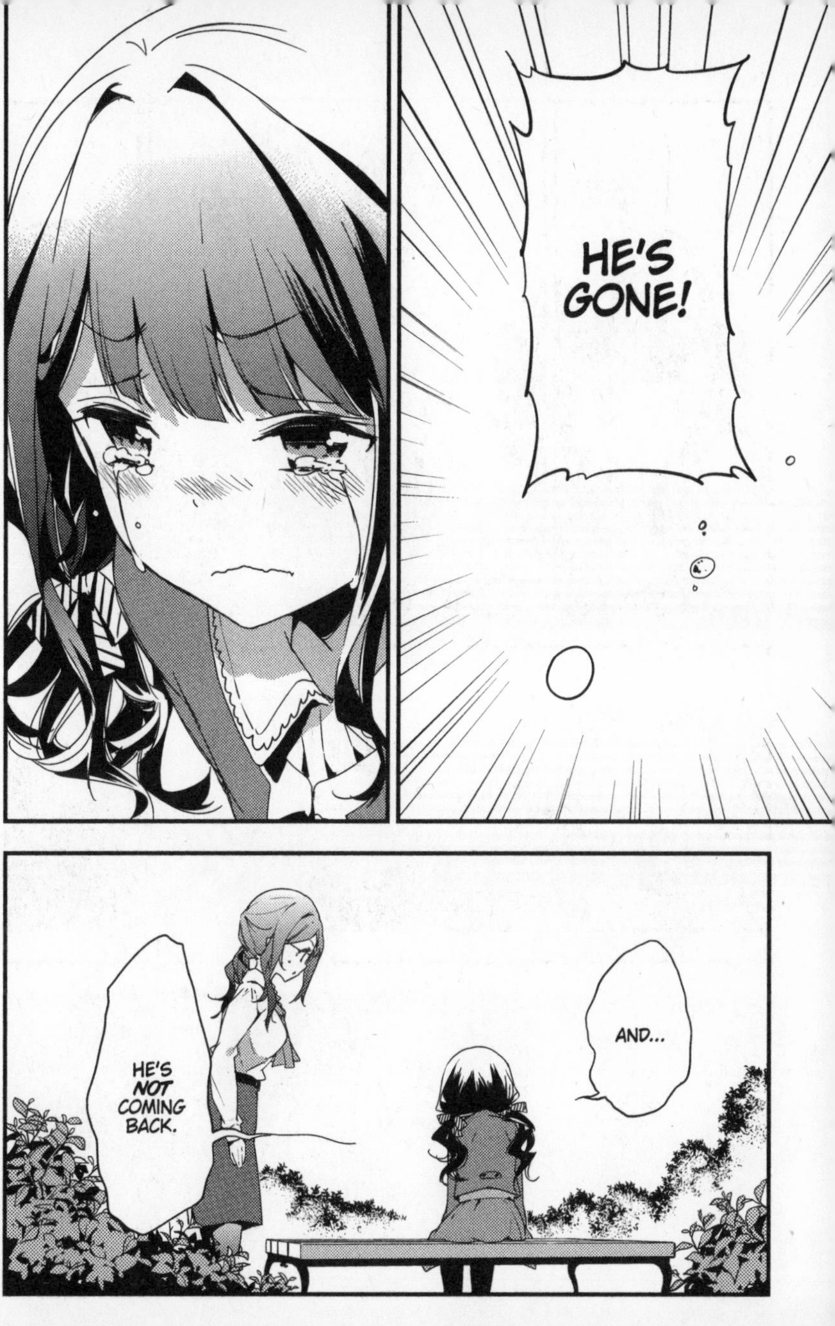
HE'S GONE!
AND...
HE'S *NOT* COMING BACK.

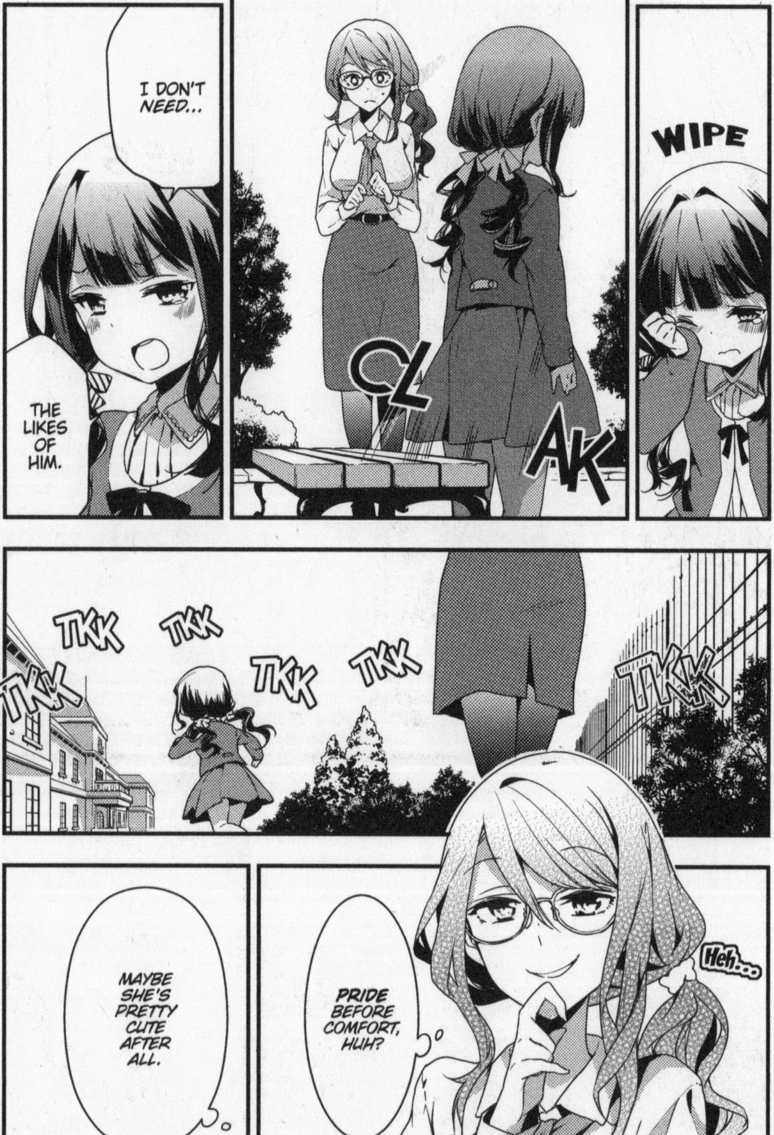
WIPE
CLAK
I DON'T NEED...
THE LIKES OF HIM.
TKK
TKK
TKK
TKK
TKK
TKK
Heh...
PRIDE BEFORE COMFORT, HUH?
MAYBE SHE'S PRETTY CUTE AFTER ALL.

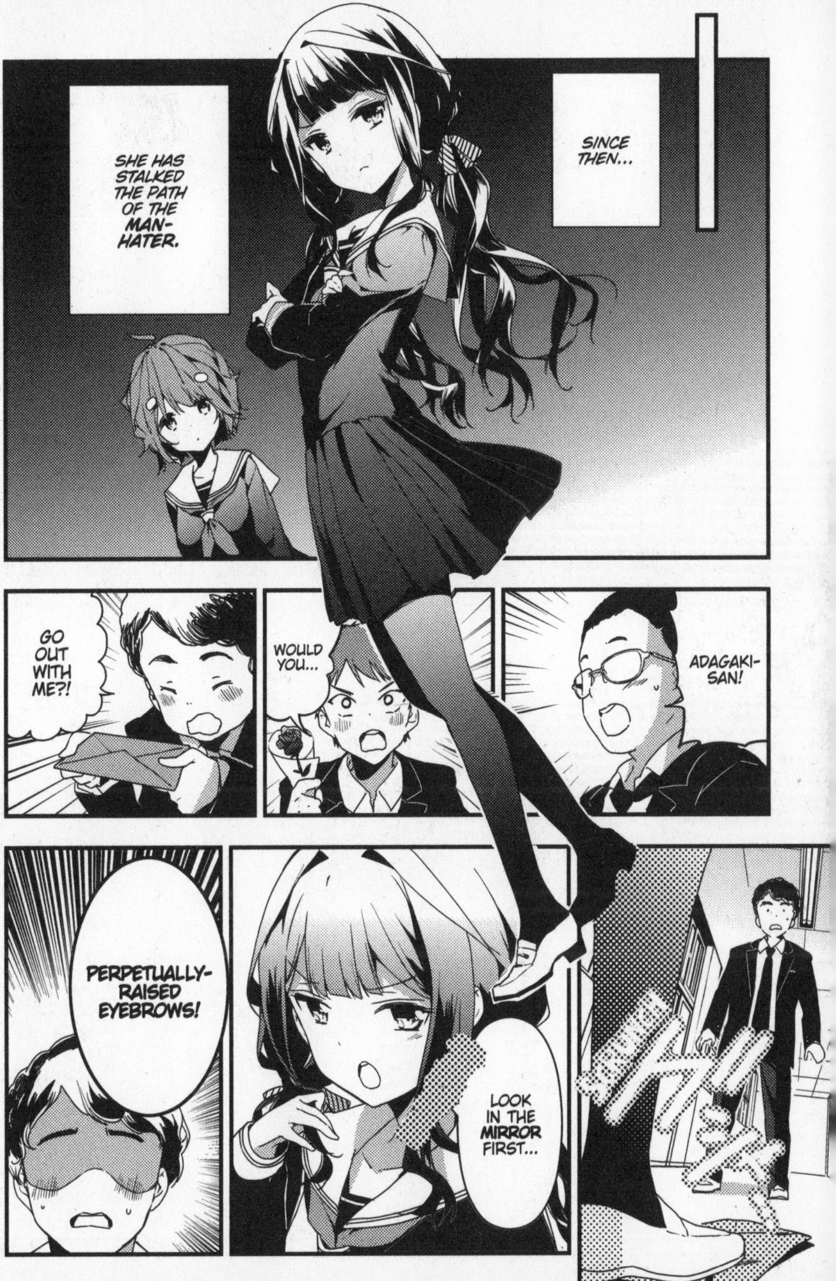
SINCE THEN...
SHE HAS STALKED THE PATH OF THE MAN-HATER.
ADAGAKI-SAN!
WOULD YOU...
GO OUT WITH ME?!
LOOK IN THE MIRROR FIRST...
PERPETUALLY-RAISED EYEBROWS!

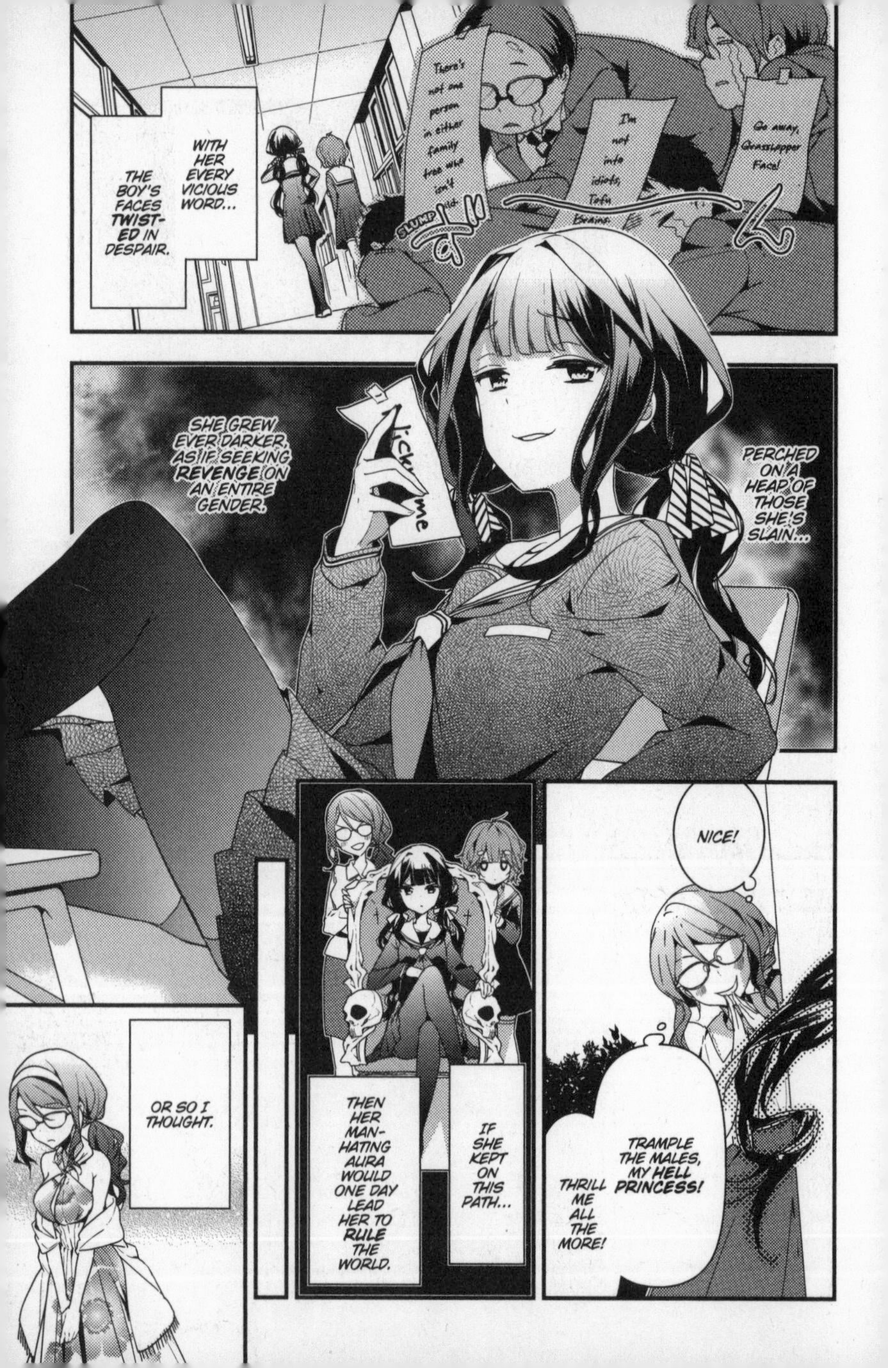
Go away, Grasshopper Face!
I'm not into idiots, Tofu Brains.
There's not one person in either family tree who isn't
SLUMP
WITH HER EVERY VICIOUS WORD...
THE BOY'S FACES TWISTED IN DESPAIR.
PERCHED ON A HEAP OF THOSE SHE'S SLAIN...
SHE GREW EVER DARKER, AS IF SEEKING REVENGE ON AN ENTIRE GENDER.
NICE!
TRAMPLE THE MALES, MY HELL PRINCESS!
THRILL ME ALL THE MORE!
IF SHE KEPT ON THIS PATH...
THEN HER MAN-HATING AURA WOULD ONE DAY LEAD HER TO RULE THE WORLD.
OR SO I THOUGHT.

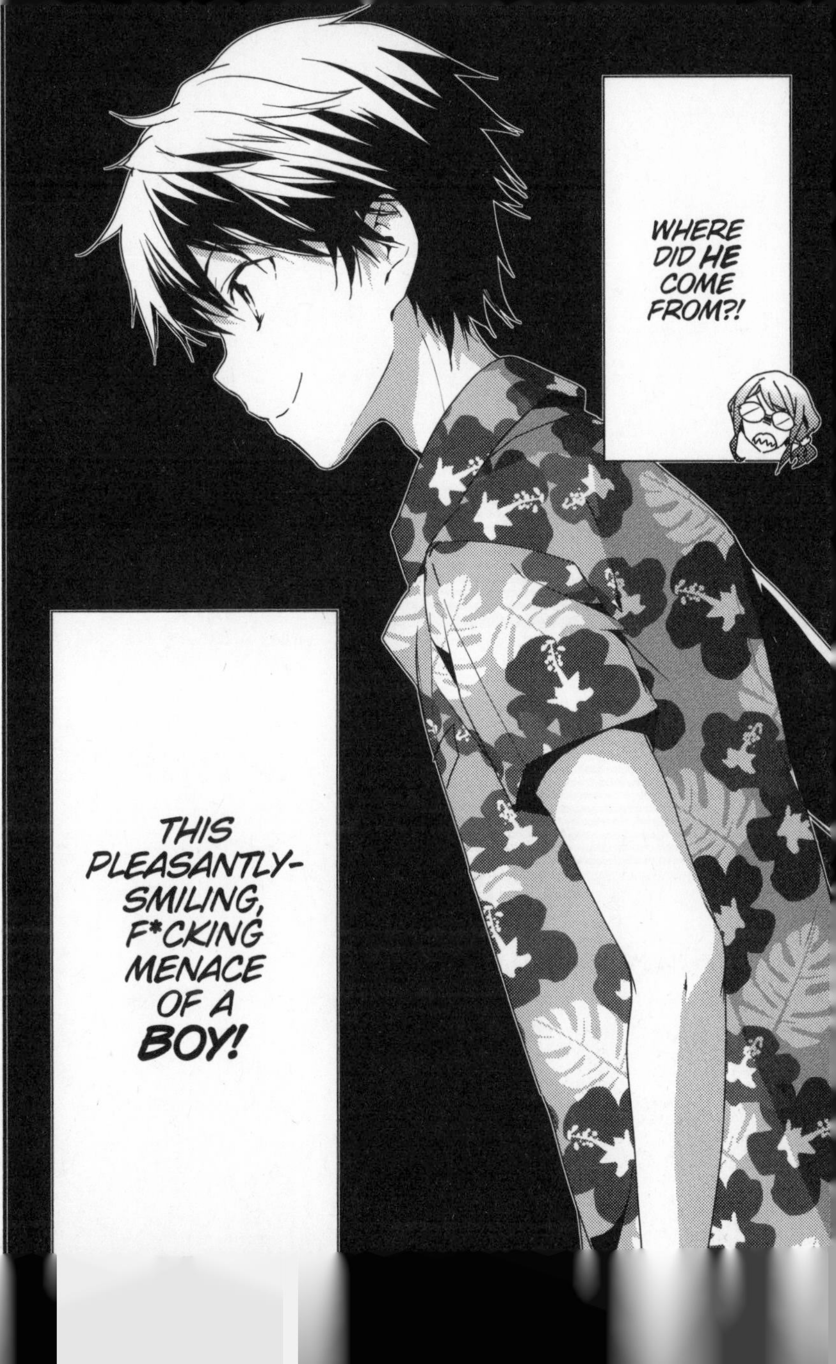
WHERE DID HE COME FROM?!
THIS PLEASANTLY-SMILING, F*CKING MENACE OF A BOY!

Thirty-
something
power!

4

Masamune-kun's

REVENGE

Presented by Hazuki Takeoka & TIV

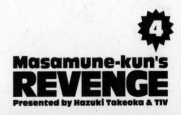

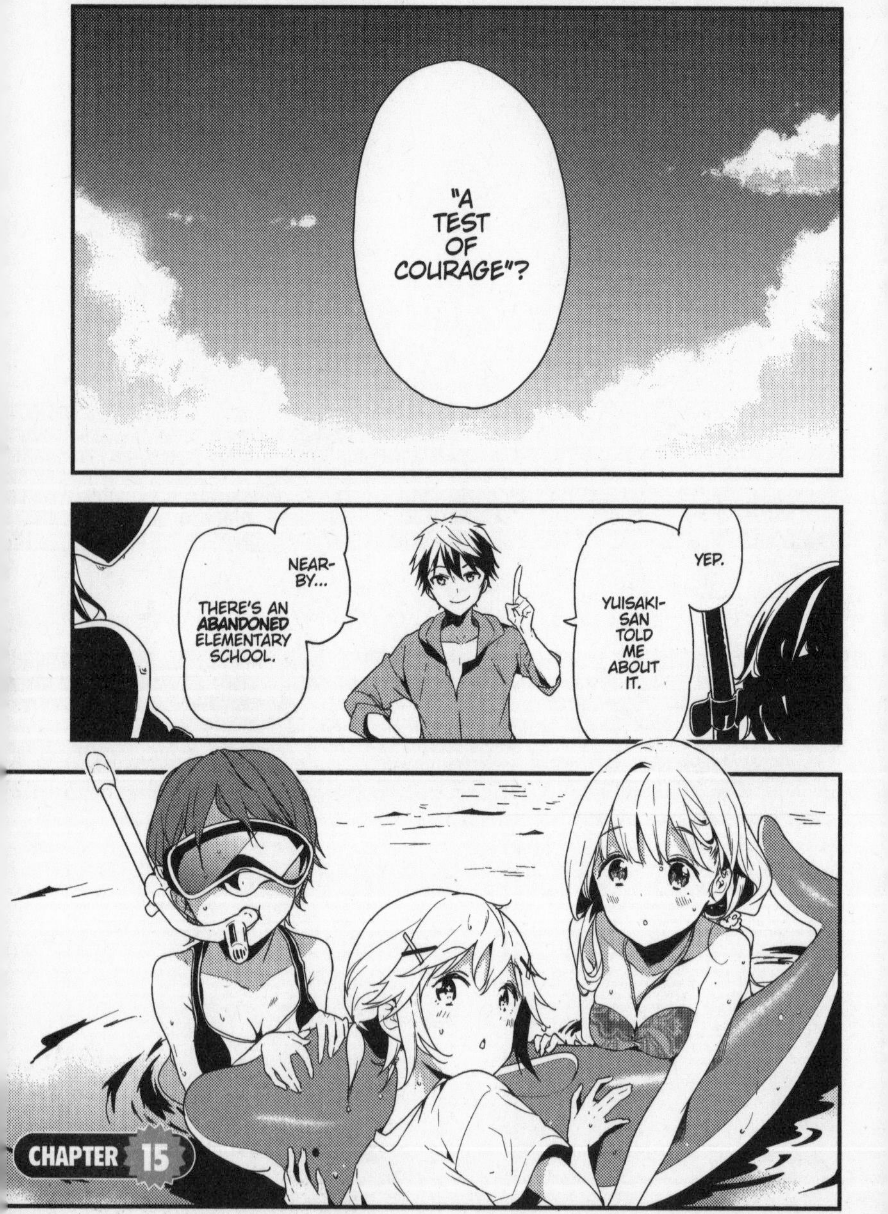
"A TEST OF COURAGE"?
YEP. YUISAKI-SAN TOLD ME ABOUT IT.
NEAR-BY... THERE'S AN ABANDONED ELEMENTARY SCHOOL.
CHAPTER 15

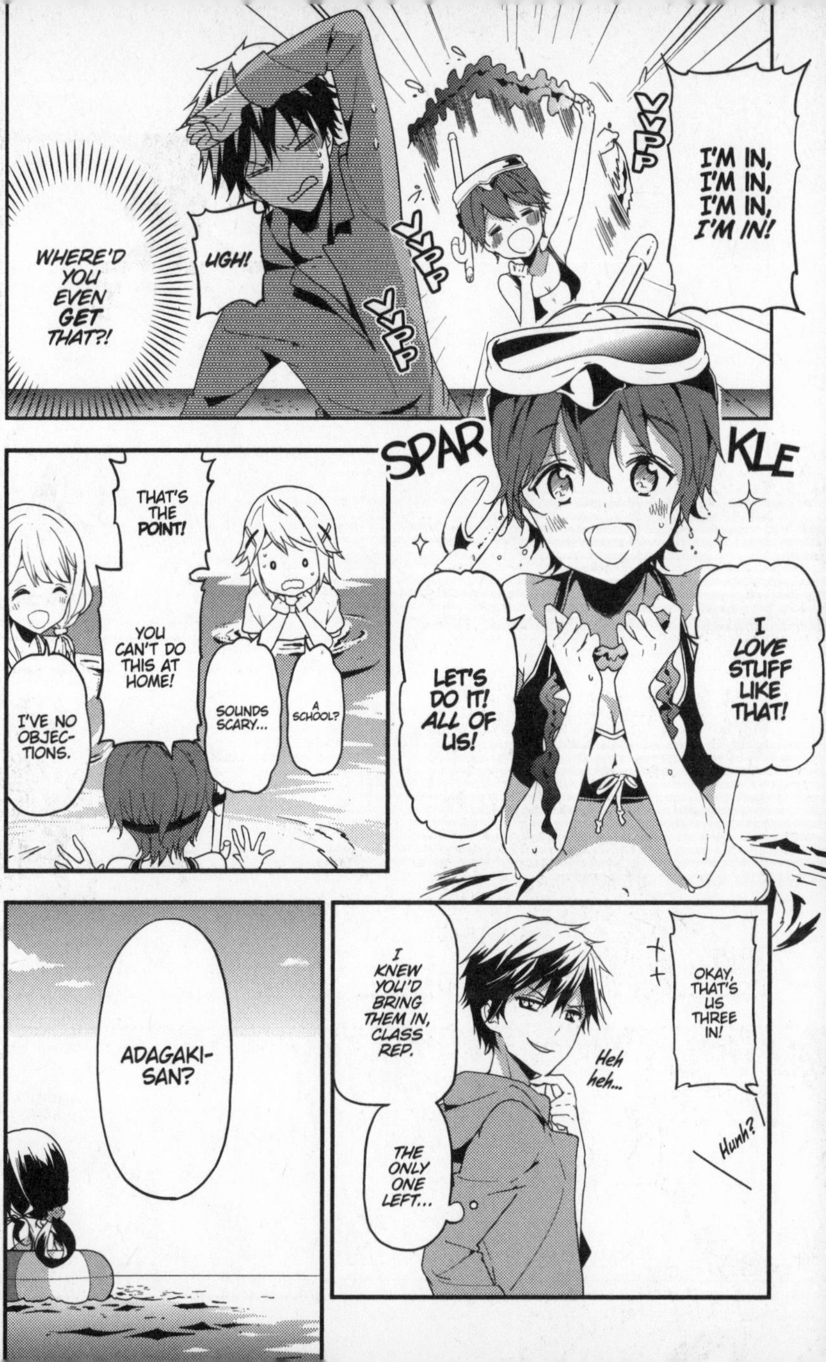
I'M IN, I'M IN, I'M IN, I'M IN!
VVPP
VVPP
VVPP
UGH!
WHERE'D YOU EVEN GET THAT?!
SPARKLE
I LOVE STUFF LIKE THAT!
LET'S DO IT! ALL OF US!
THAT'S THE POINT!
YOU CAN'T DO THIS AT HOME!
A SCHOOL?
SOUNDS SCARY...
I'VE NO OBJECTIONS.
OKAY, THAT'S US THREE IN!
Hunh?
Heh heh...
I KNEW YOU'D BRING THEM IN, CLASS REP.
THE ONLY ONE LEFT...
ADAGAKI-SAN?

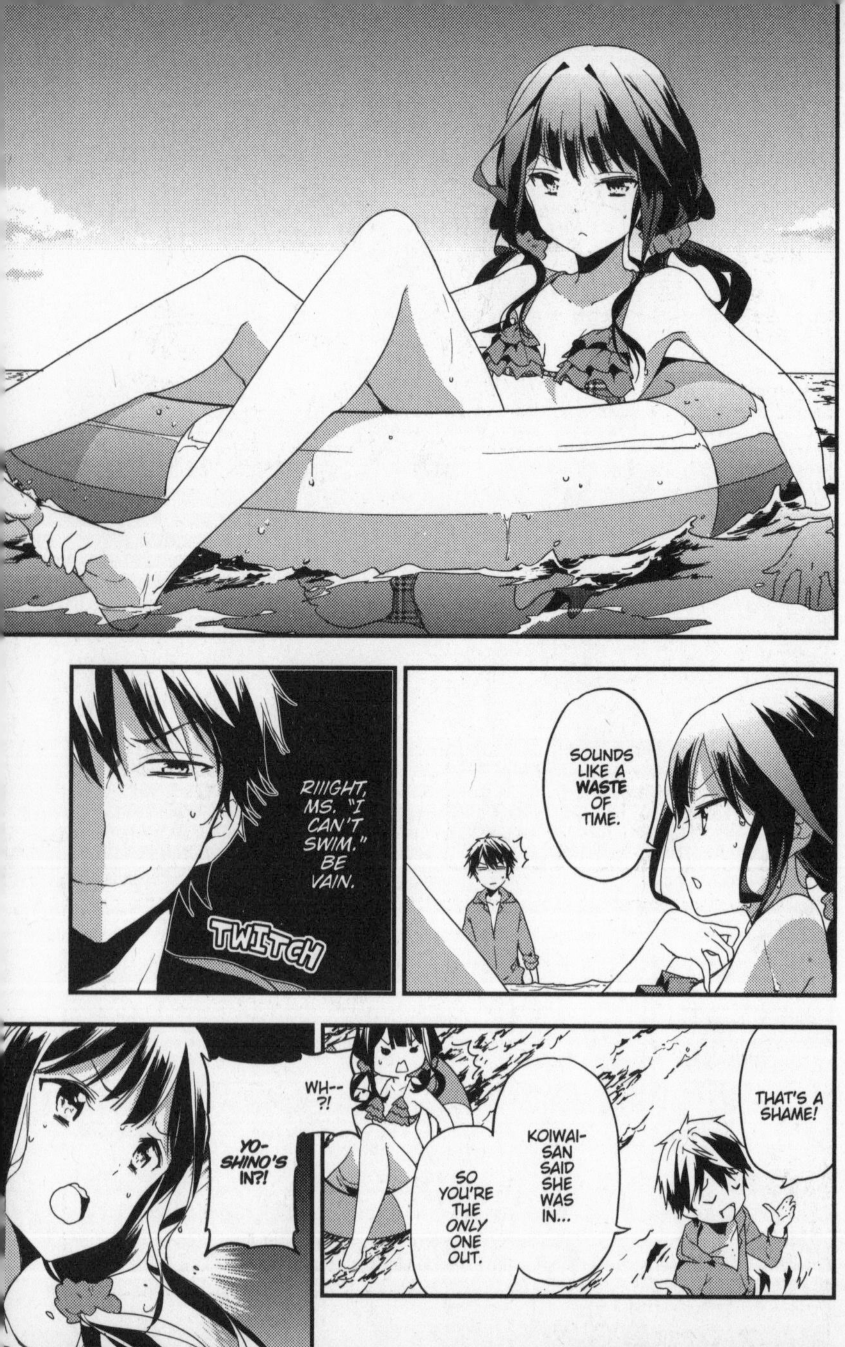
SOUNDS LIKE A WASTE OF TIME.
RIIIGHT, MS. "I CAN'T SWIM." BE VAIN.
TWITCH
THAT'S A SHAME!
KOIWAI-SAN SAID SHE WAS IN...
SO YOU'RE THE ONLY ONE OUT.
WH-- ?!
YO-SHINO'S IN?!

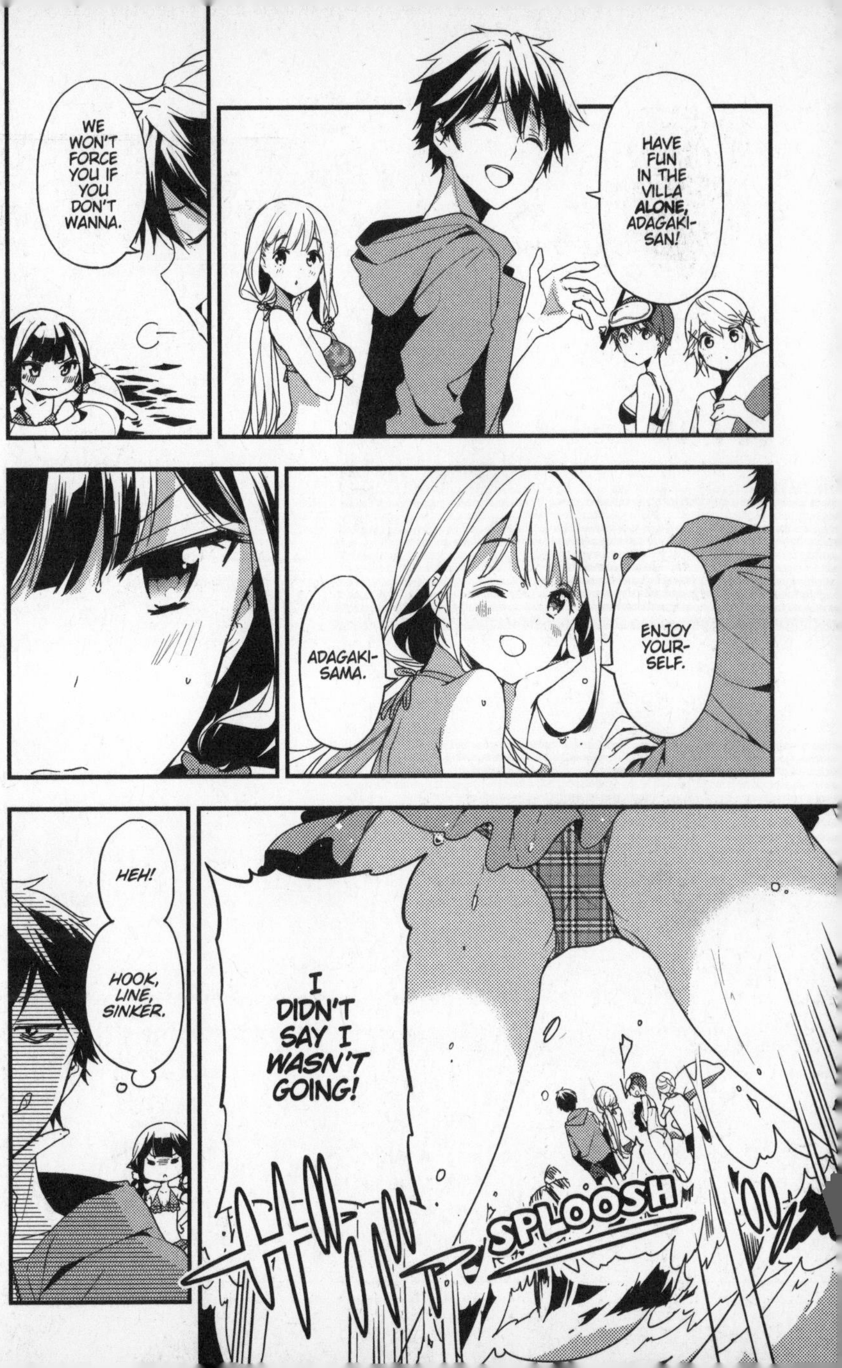
HAVE FUN IN THE VILLA ALONE, ADAGAKI-SAN!
WE WON'T FORCE YOU IF YOU DON'T WANNA.
ENJOY YOUR-SELF.
ADAGAKI-SAMA.
I DIDN'T SAY I WASN'T GOING!
SPLOOSH
HEH!
HOOK, LINE, SINKER.

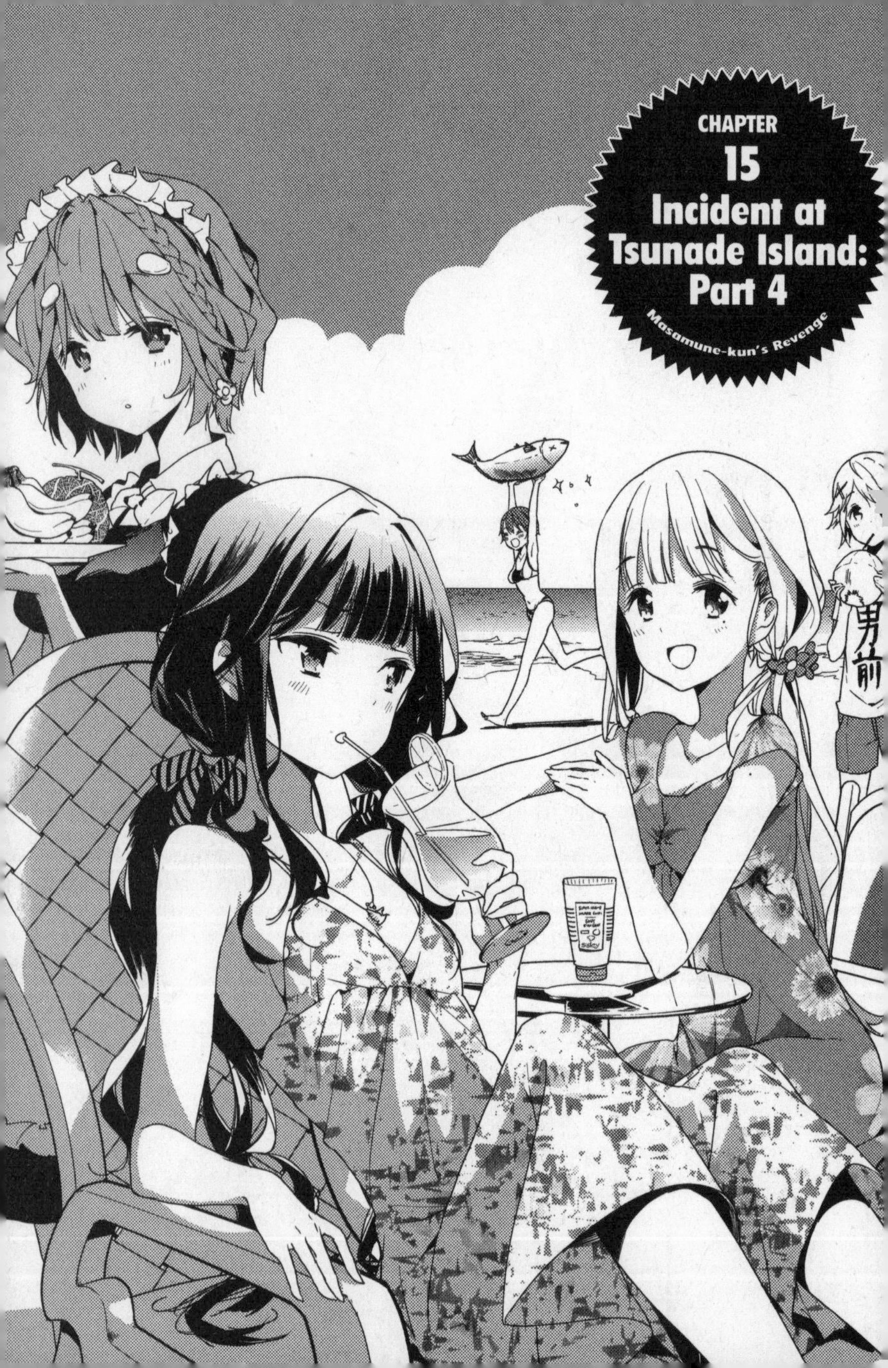
CHAPTER
15
Incident at Tsunade Island: Part 4
Masamune-kun's Revenge
男前

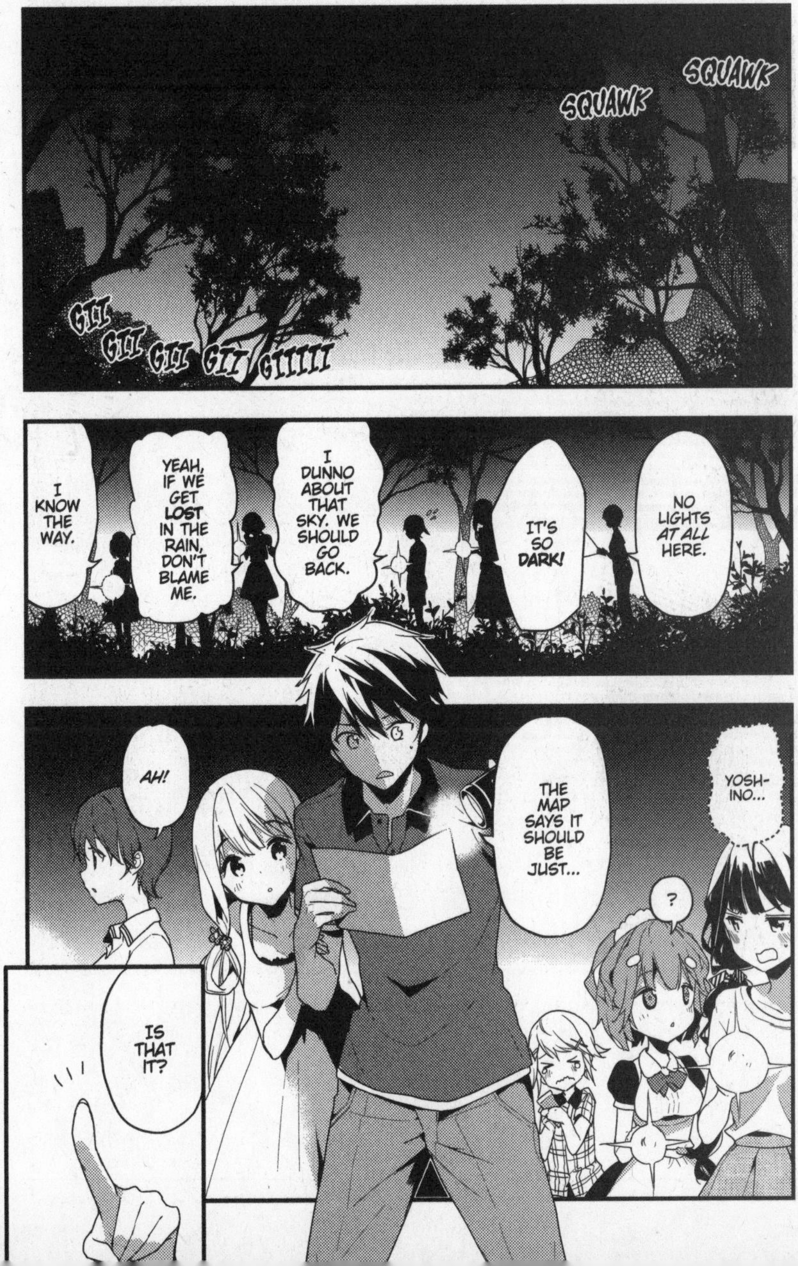
SQUAWK
SQUAWK
GII GII GII GII GIIIII
NO LIGHTS AT ALL HERE.
IT'S SO DARK!
I DUNNO ABOUT THAT SKY. WE SHOULD GO BACK.
YEAH, IF WE GET LOST IN THE RAIN, DON'T BLAME ME.
I KNOW THE WAY.
YOSH-INO...
?
THE MAP SAYS IT SHOULD BE JUST...
AH!
IS THAT IT?

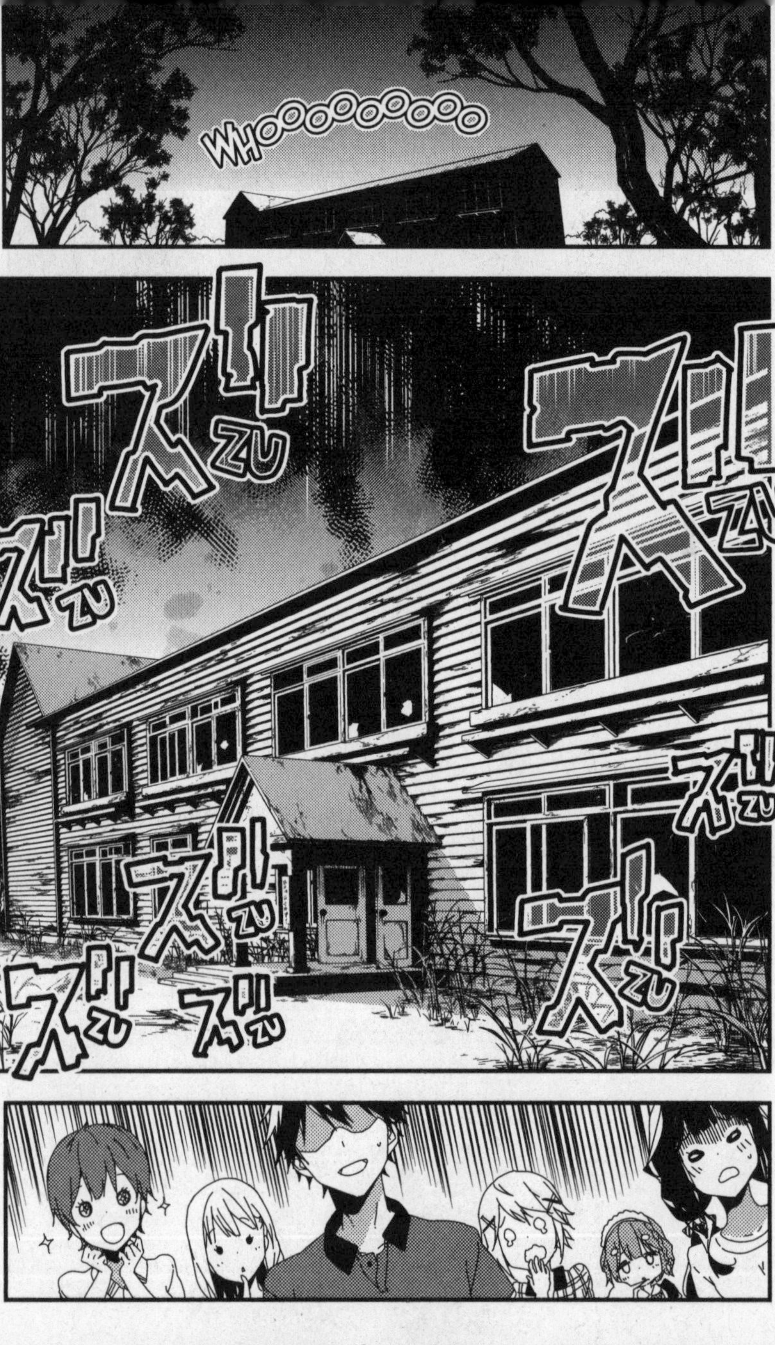
WHOOOOOOOOOO
ZU
ZU
ZU
ZU
ZU
ZU
ZU
ZU

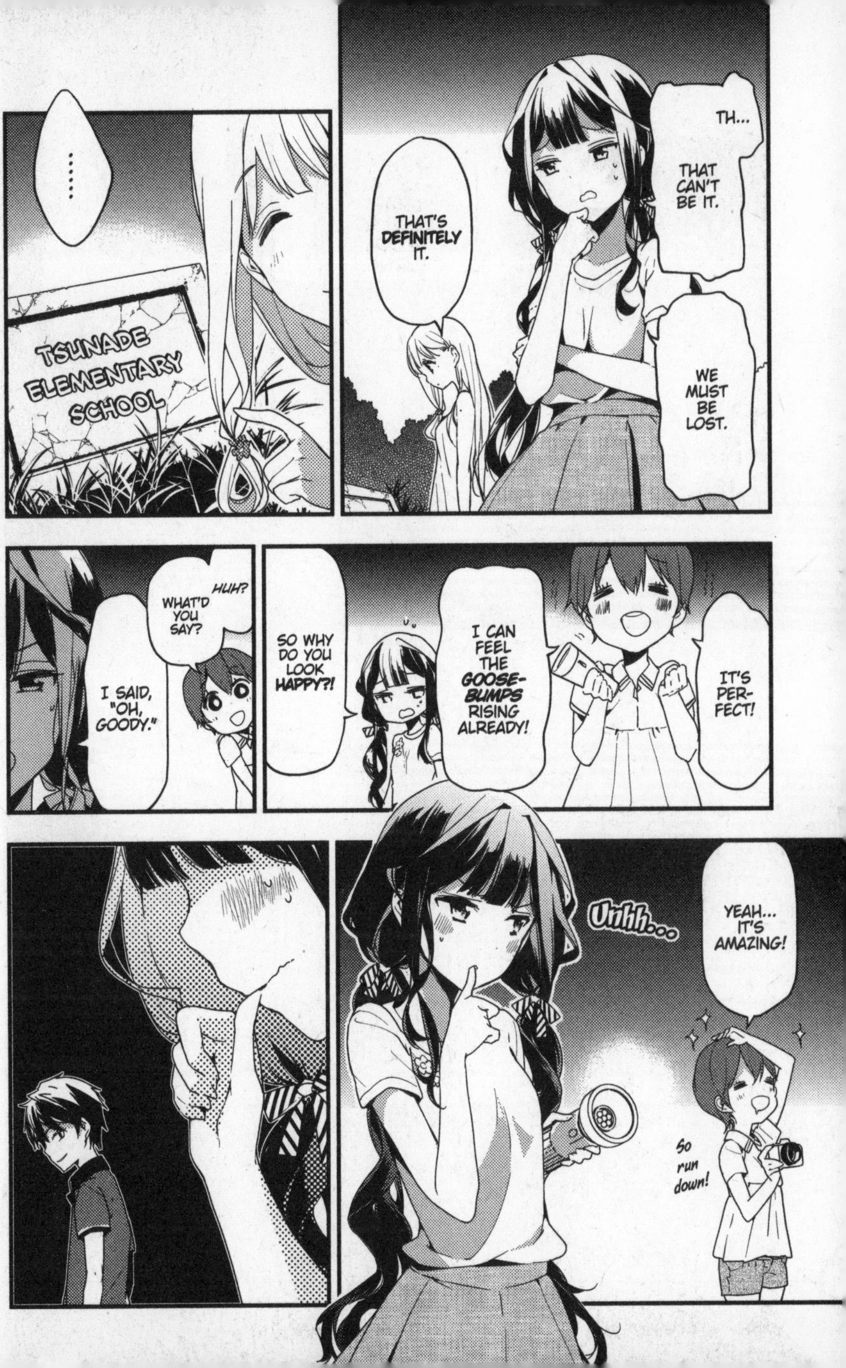
TH... THAT CAN'T BE IT.
WE MUST BE LOST.
THAT'S **DEFINITELY** IT.
......
TSUNADE ELEMENTARY SCHOOL
IT'S PER-FECT!
I CAN FEEL THE **GOOSE-BUMPS** RISING ALREADY!
SO WHY DO YOU LOOK **HAPPY**?!
HUH? WHAT'D YOU SAY?
I SAID, "OH, GOODY."
YEAH... IT'S AMAZING!
Unhh...
So run down!

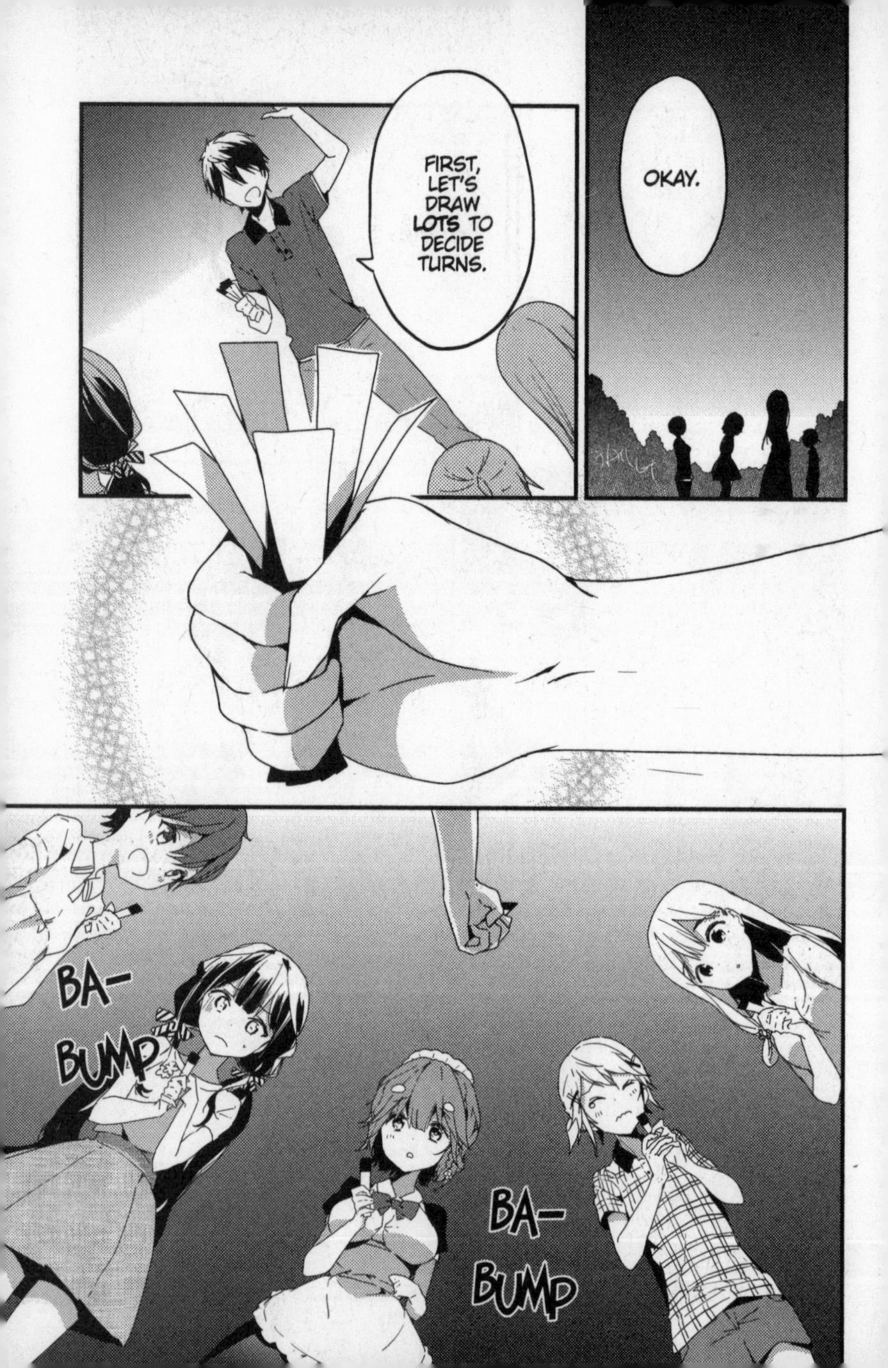
OKAY.
FIRST, LET'S DRAW LOTS TO DECIDE TURNS.
BA-BUMP
BA-BUMP

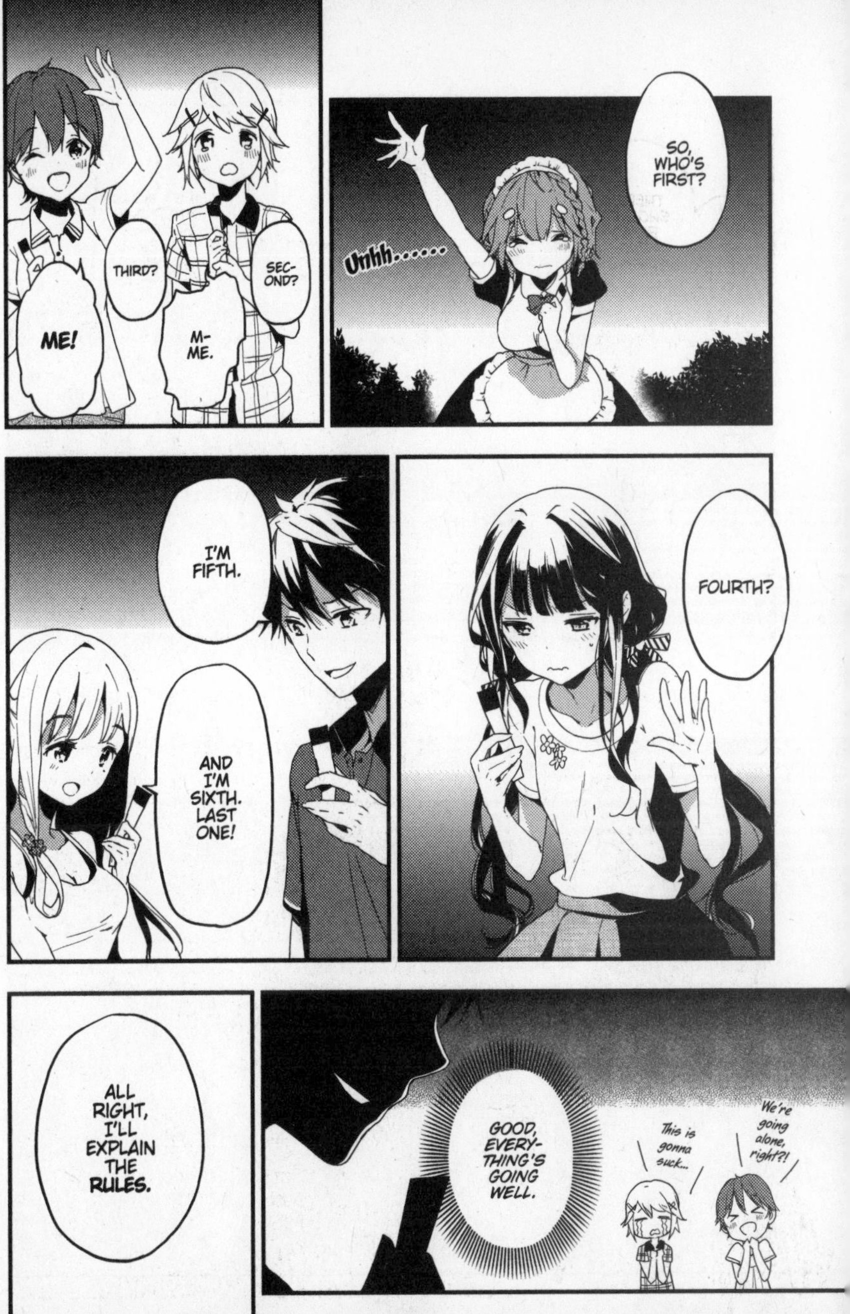
SO, WHO'S FIRST?
Unhh......
SEC-OND?
M-ME.
THIRD?
ME!
FOURTH?
I'M FIFTH.
AND I'M SIXTH. LAST ONE!
GOOD, EVERY-THING'S GOING WELL.
We're going alone, right?!
This is gonna suck...
ALL RIGHT, I'LL EXPLAIN THE RULES.

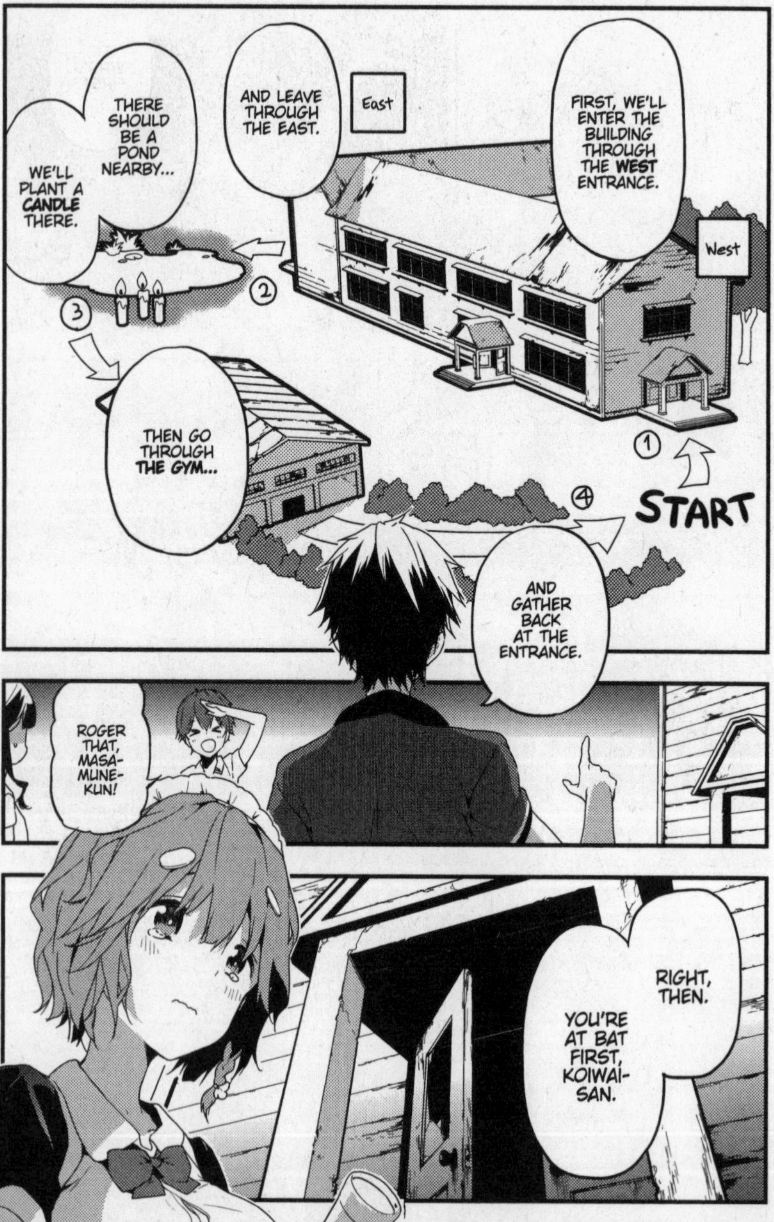
FIRST, WE'LL ENTER THE BUILDING THROUGH THE **WEST** ENTRANCE.
West
East
AND LEAVE THROUGH THE EAST.
THERE SHOULD BE A POND NEARBY...
WE'LL PLANT A **CANDLE** THERE.
THEN GO THROUGH **THE GYM...**
START
AND GATHER BACK AT THE ENTRANCE.
ROGER THAT, MASAMUNE-KUN!
RIGHT, THEN.
YOU'RE AT BAT FIRST, KOIWAI-SAN.

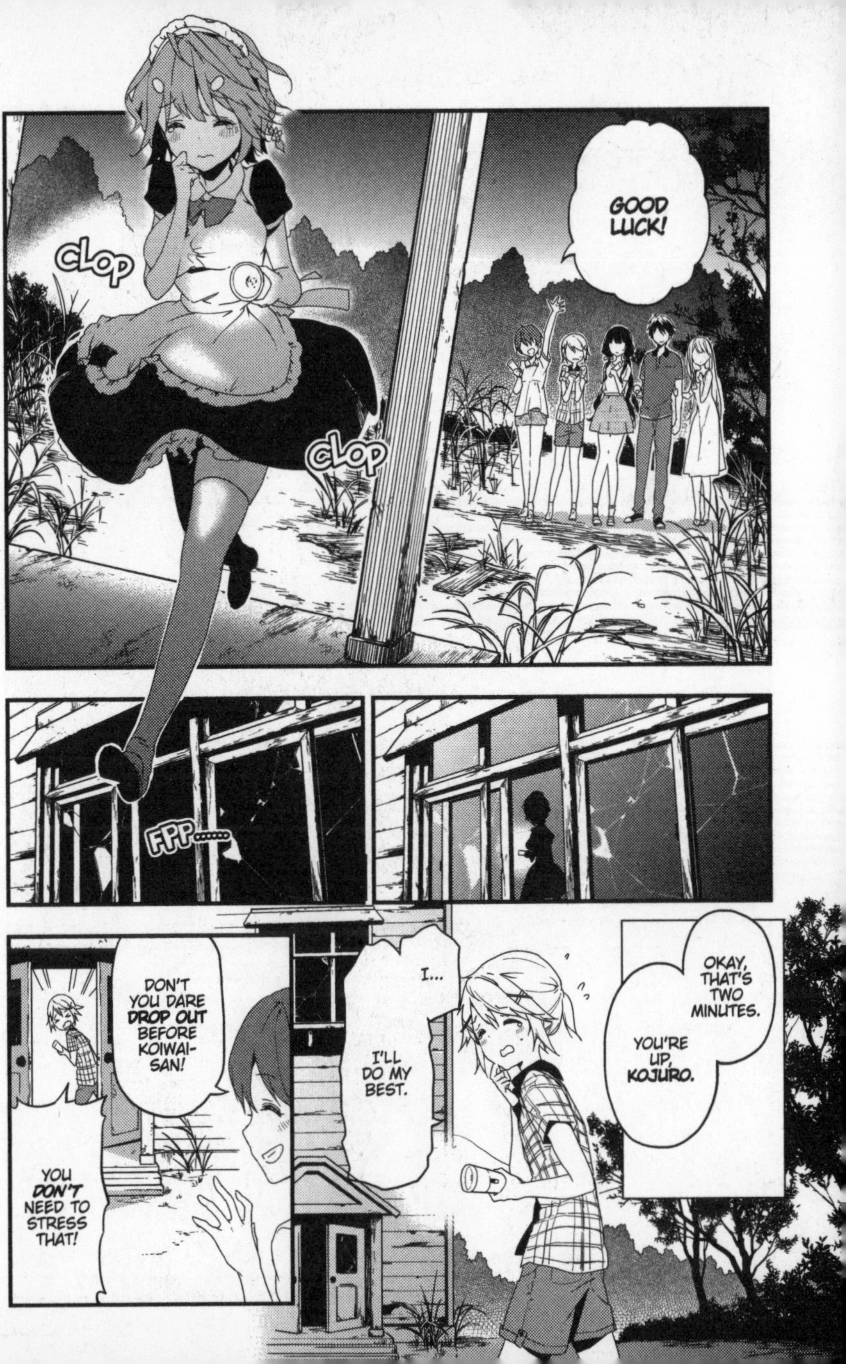
GOOD LUCK!
CLOP
CLOP
FPP......
OKAY, THAT'S TWO MINUTES.
YOU'RE UP, KOJURO.
I...
I'LL DO MY BEST.
DON'T YOU DARE DROP OUT BEFORE KOIWAI-SAN!
YOU DON'T NEED TO STRESS THAT!

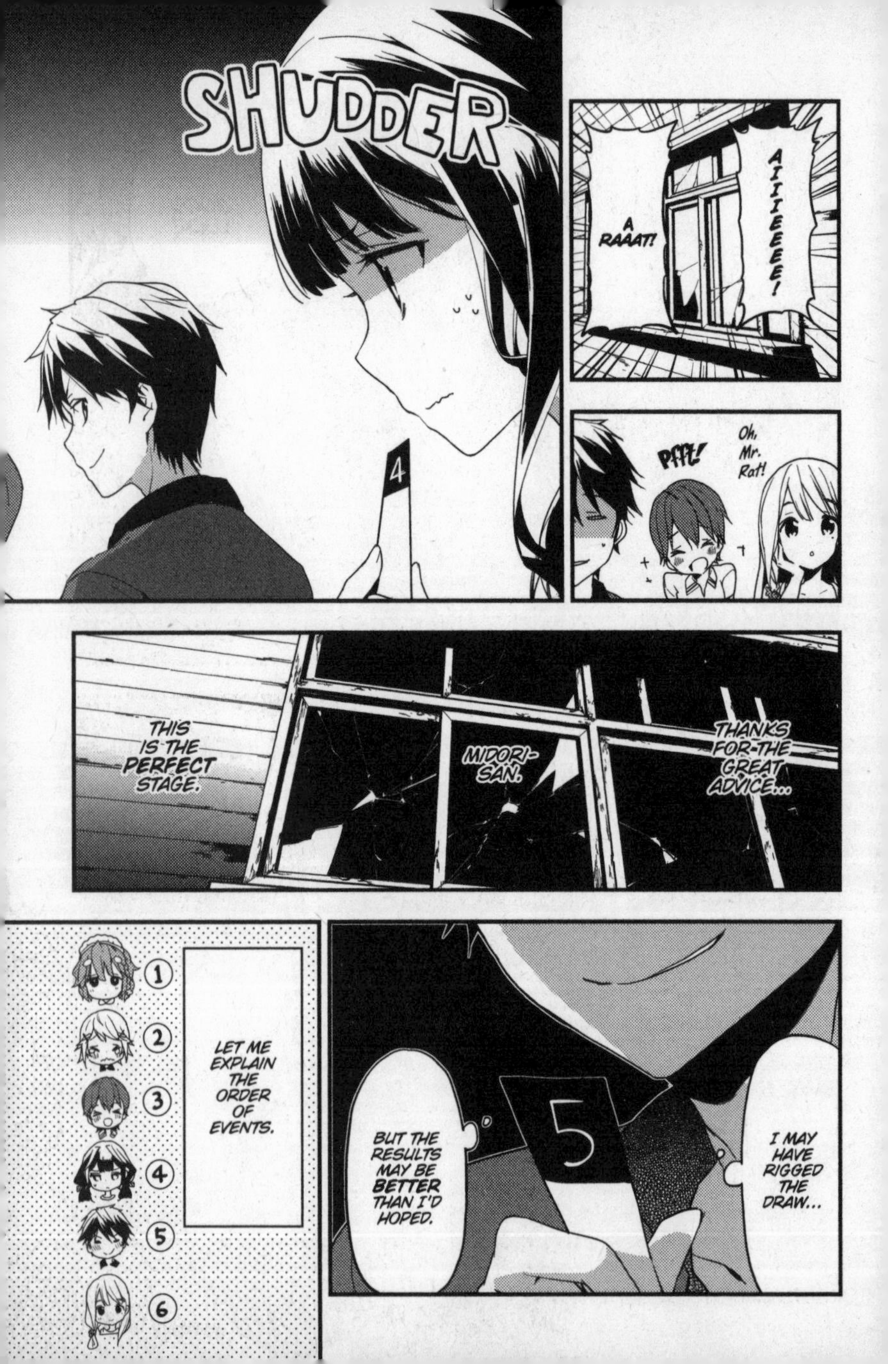
AIIIEEEEE!
A RAAAT!
Oh, Mr. Rat!
PFFT!
SHUDDER
THANKS FOR THE GREAT ADVICE...
MIDORI-SAN.
THIS IS THE PERFECT STAGE.
I MAY HAVE RIGGED THE DRAW...
BUT THE RESULTS MAY BE BETTER THAN I'D HOPED.
LET ME EXPLAIN THE ORDER OF EVENTS.
1
2
3
4
5
6

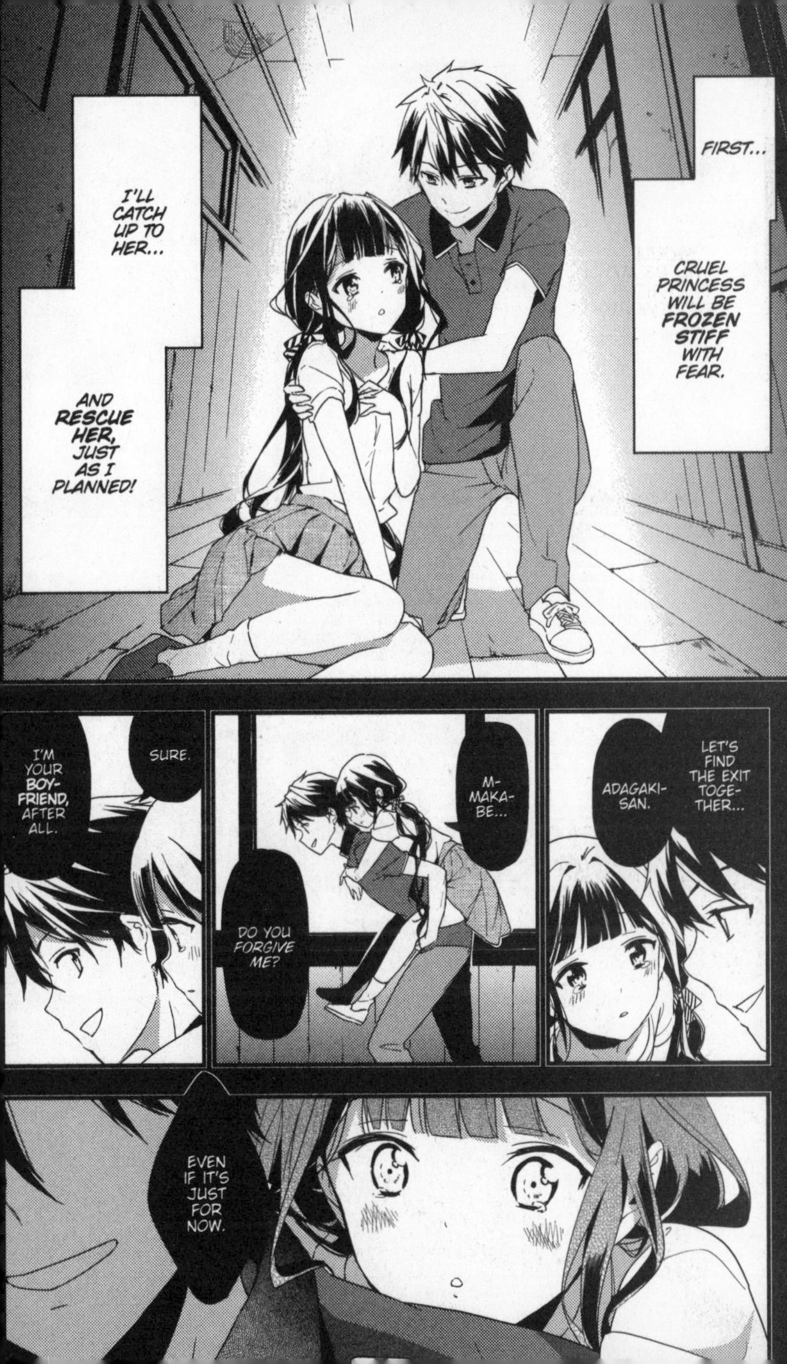
FIRST...
CRUEL PRINCESS WILL BE FROZEN STIFF WITH FEAR.
I'LL CATCH UP TO HER...
AND RESCUE HER, JUST AS I PLANNED!
LET'S FIND THE EXIT TOGETHER...
ADAGAKI-SAN.
M-MAKABE...
DO YOU FORGIVE ME?
SURE.
I'M YOUR BOYFRIEND, AFTER ALL.
EVEN IF IT'S JUST FOR NOW.

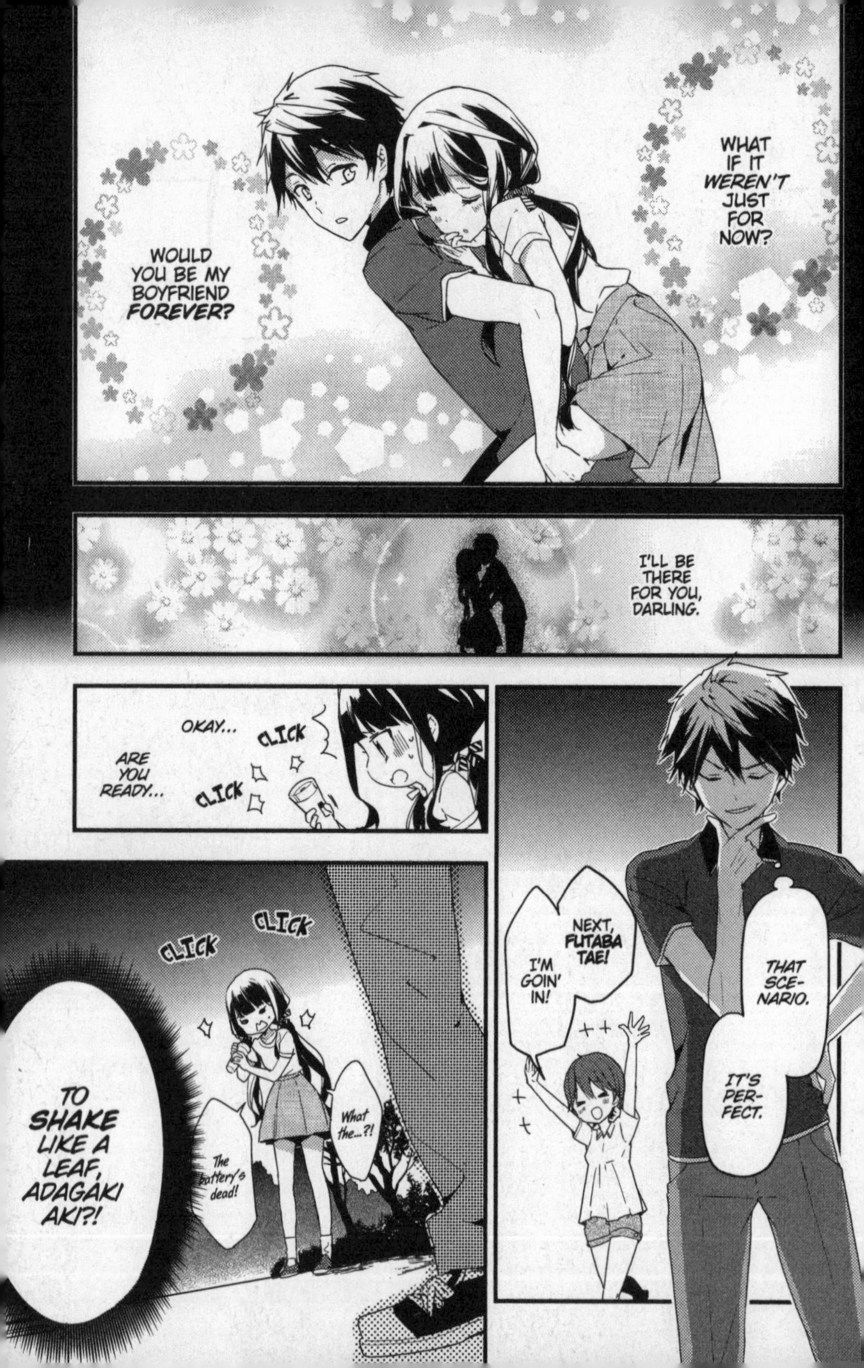
WHAT IF IT WEREN'T JUST FOR NOW?
WOULD YOU BE MY BOYFRIEND FOREVER?
I'LL BE THERE FOR YOU, DARLING.
THAT SCENARIO.
IT'S PERFECT.
NEXT, FUTABA TAE!
I'M GOIN' IN!
OKAY...
CLICK
CLICK
ARE YOU READY...
CLICK
CLICK
What the...?!
The battery's dead!
TO SHAKE LIKE A LEAF, ADAGAKI AKI?!

CREEEEAK

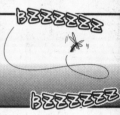

BZZZZZZ

BZZZZZZ

PISSSH

Bug Killer

GOT BIT AGAIN!

SH*T!

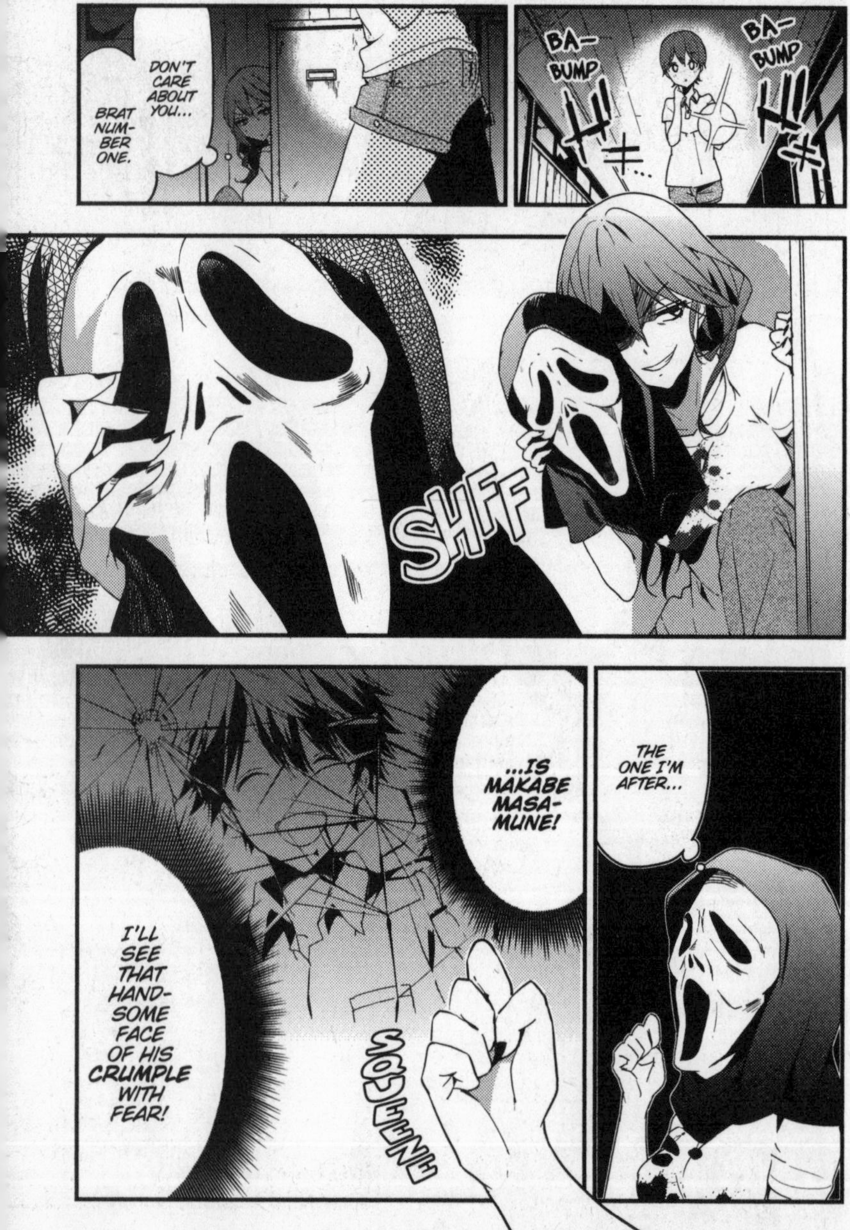
BA-BUMP
BA-BUMP
...
DON'T CARE ABOUT YOU...
BRAT NUMBER ONE.
SHFF
THE ONE I'M AFTER...
...IS MAKABE MASAMUNE!
I'LL SEE THAT HANDSOME FACE OF HIS CRUMPLE WITH FEAR!
SQUEEZE

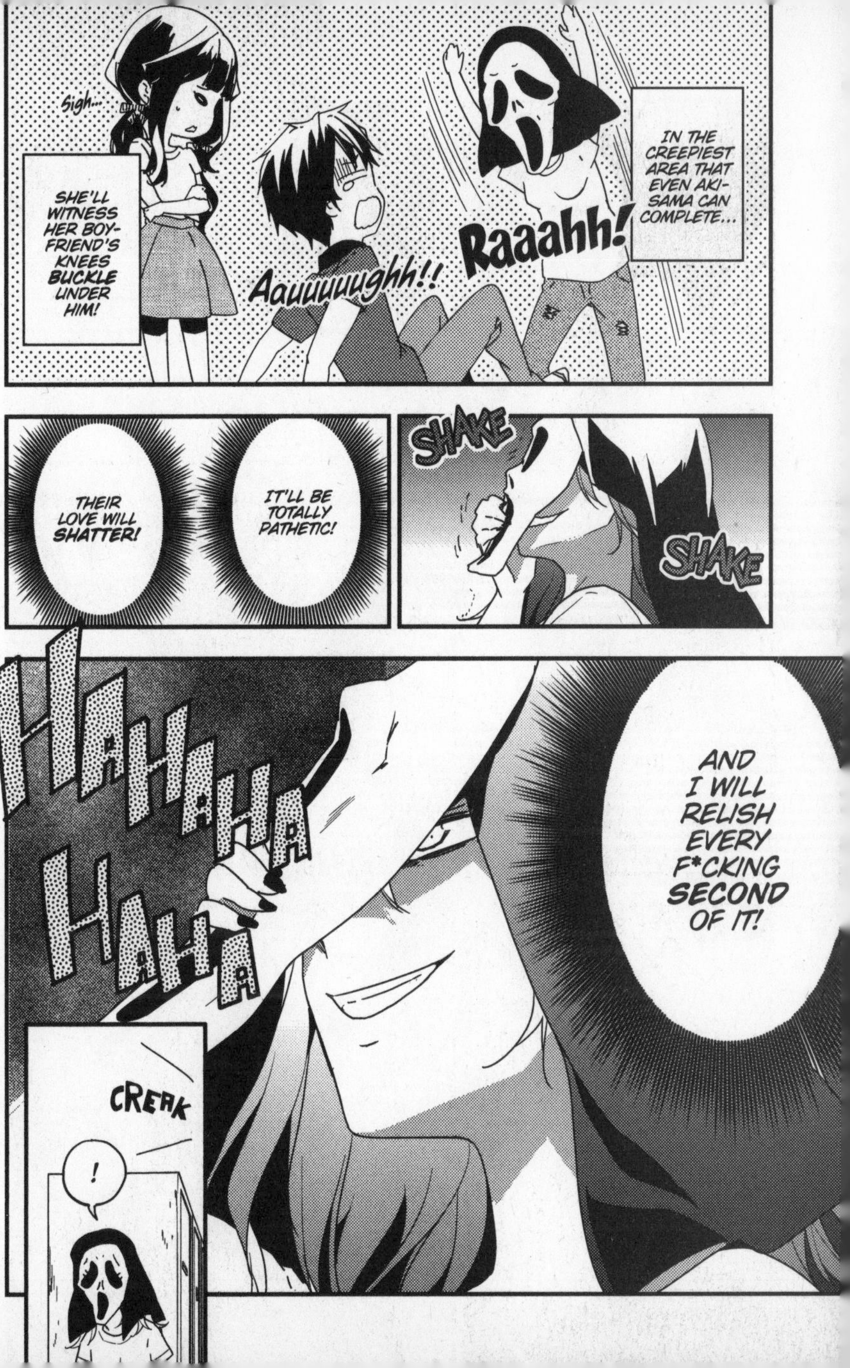
IN THE CREEPIEST AREA THAT EVEN AKI-SAMA CAN COMPLETE...
Raaahh!
Aauuuuughh!!
SHE'LL WITNESS HER BOY-FRIEND'S KNEES BUCKLE UNDER HIM!
Sigh...
SHAKE
SHAKE
IT'LL BE TOTALLY PATHETIC!
THEIR LOVE WILL SHATTER!
AND I WILL RELISH EVERY F*CKING SECOND OF IT!
HAHAHA
HAHAHA
CREAK
!

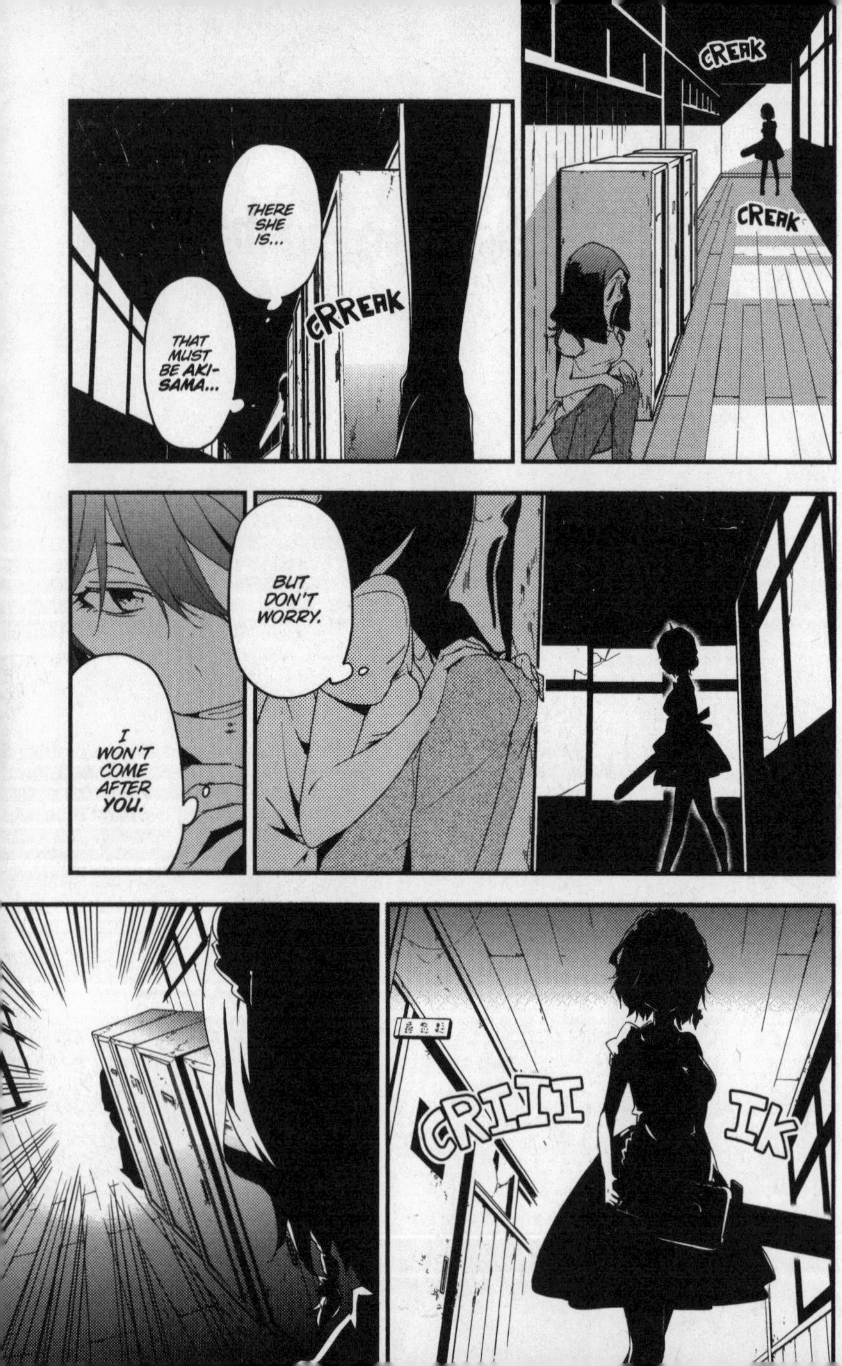
CREAK
CREAK
THERE SHE IS...
THAT MUST BE AKI-SAMA...
CRREAK
BUT DON'T WORRY.
I WON'T COME AFTER YOU.
CRIII IK

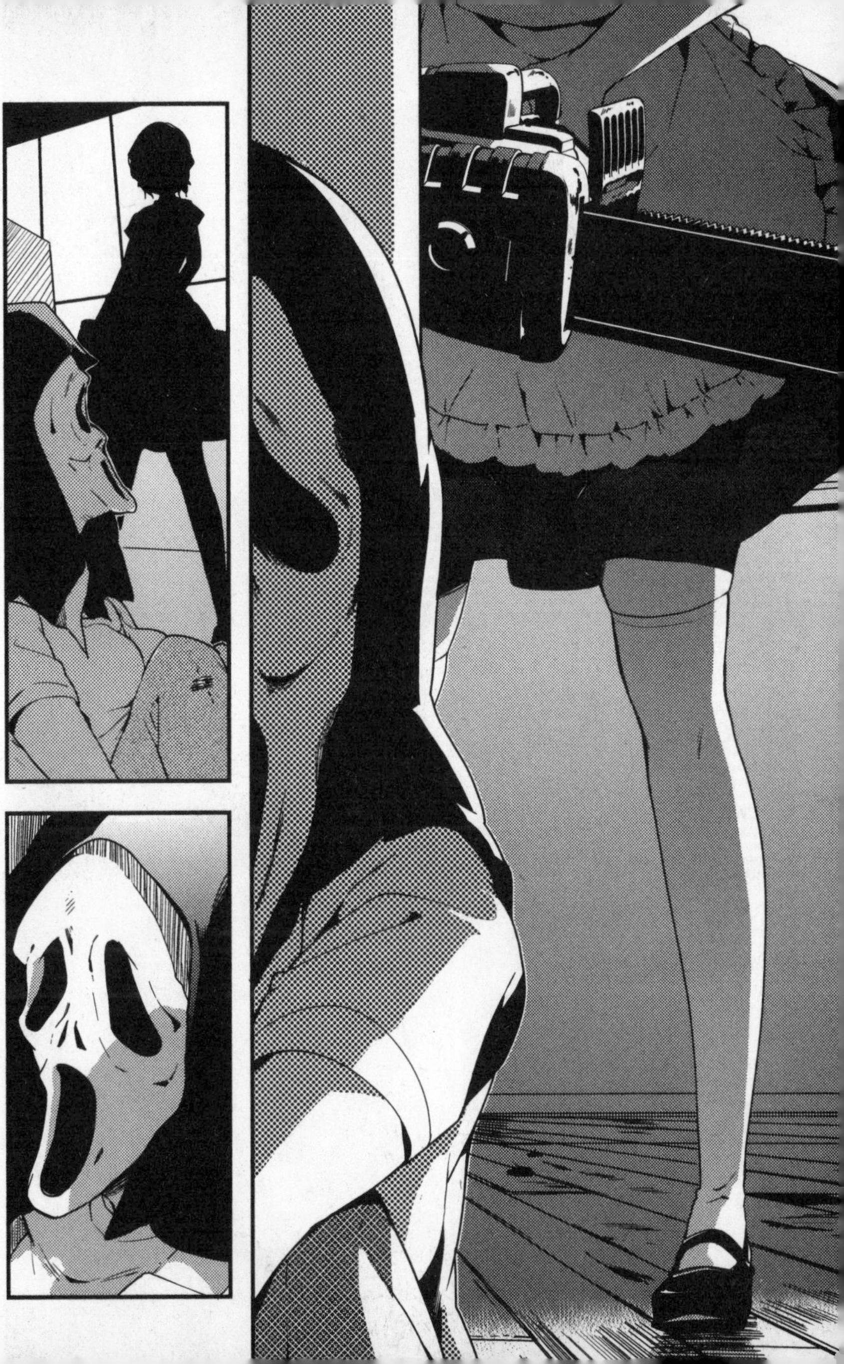

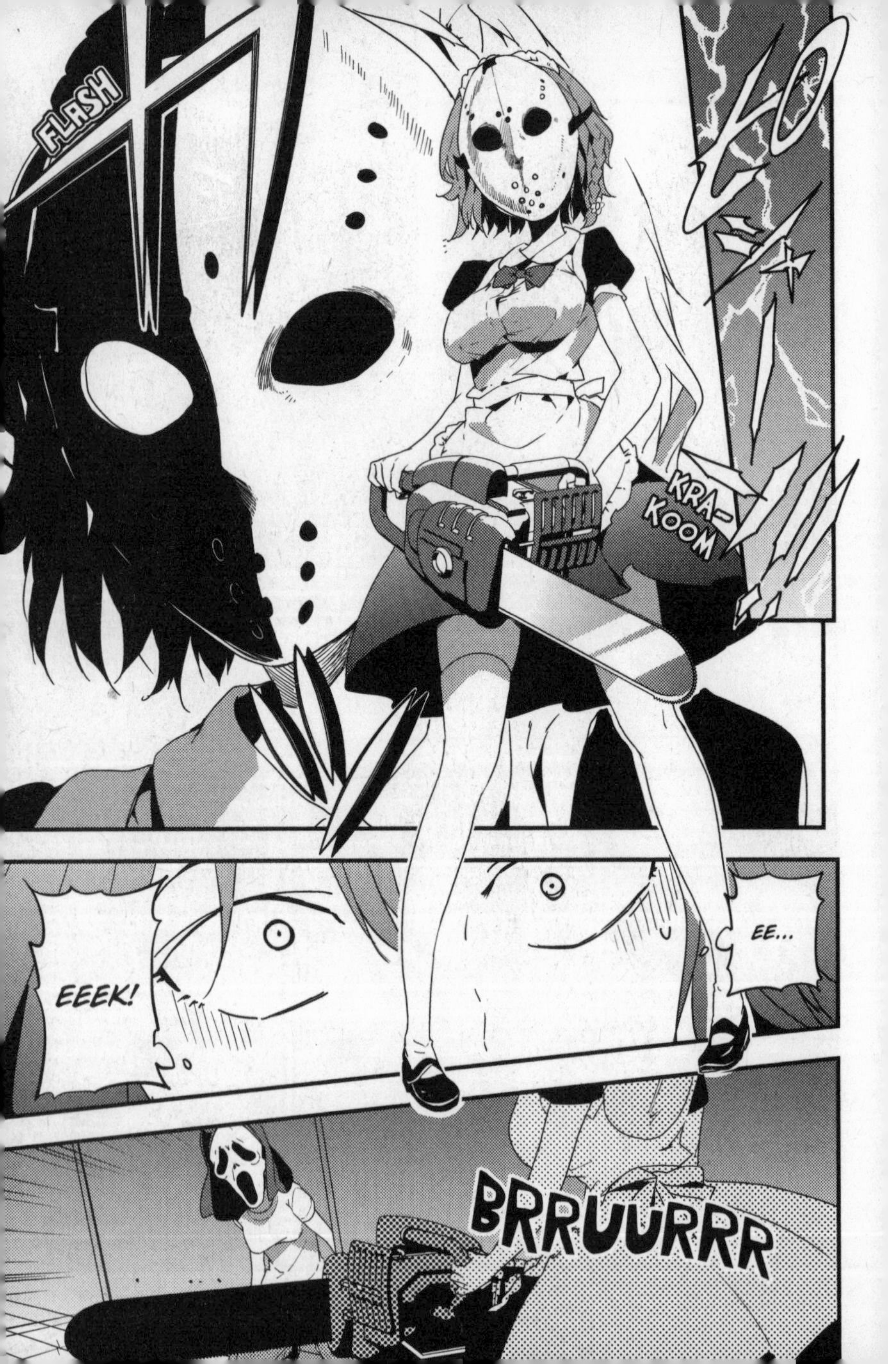
KRA-KOOM
FLASH
EE...
EEEK!
BRRUURRR

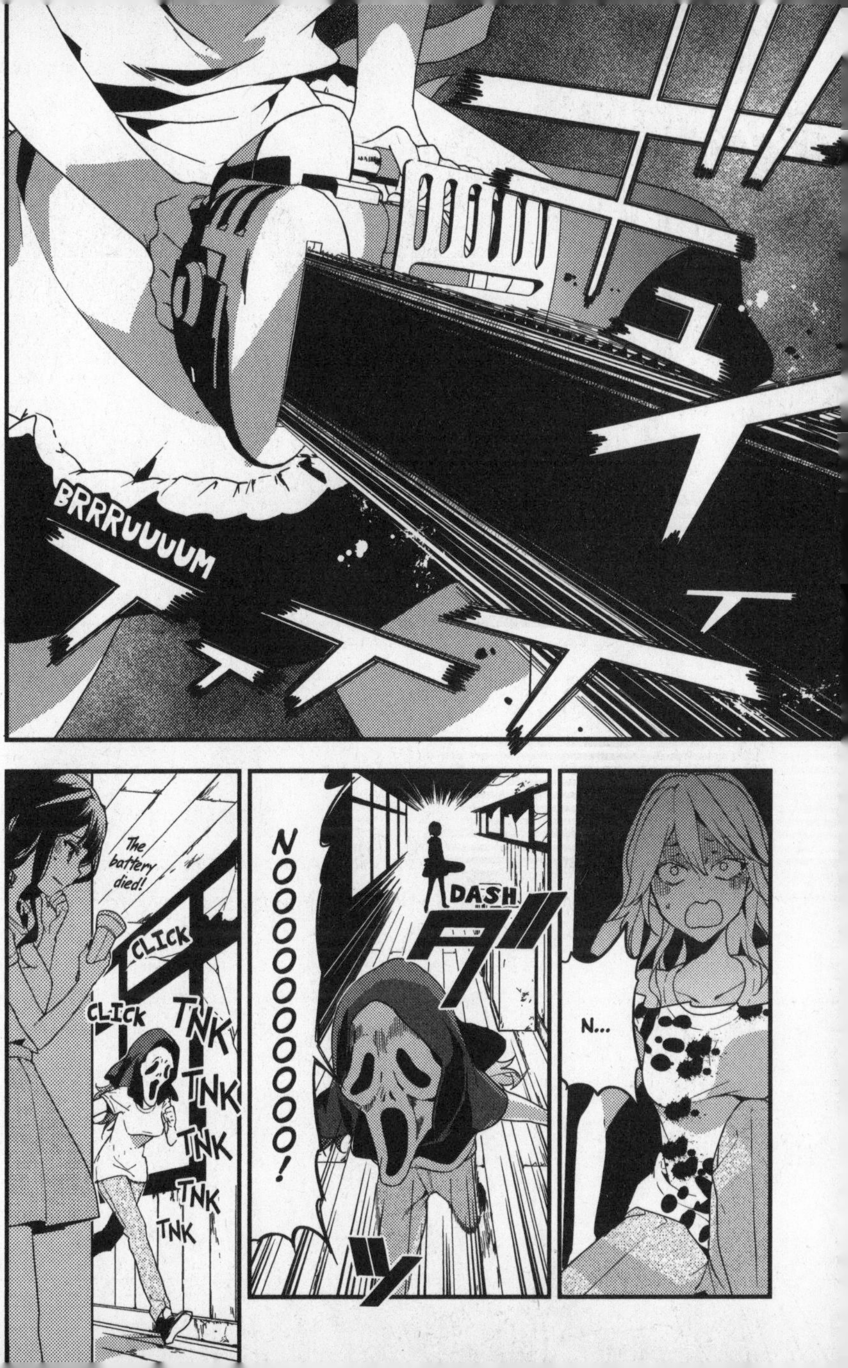
BRRRUUUUM
N...
NOOOOOOOOOOOO!
DASH
The battery died!
CLICK
CLICK
TNK
TNK
TNK
TNK
TNK

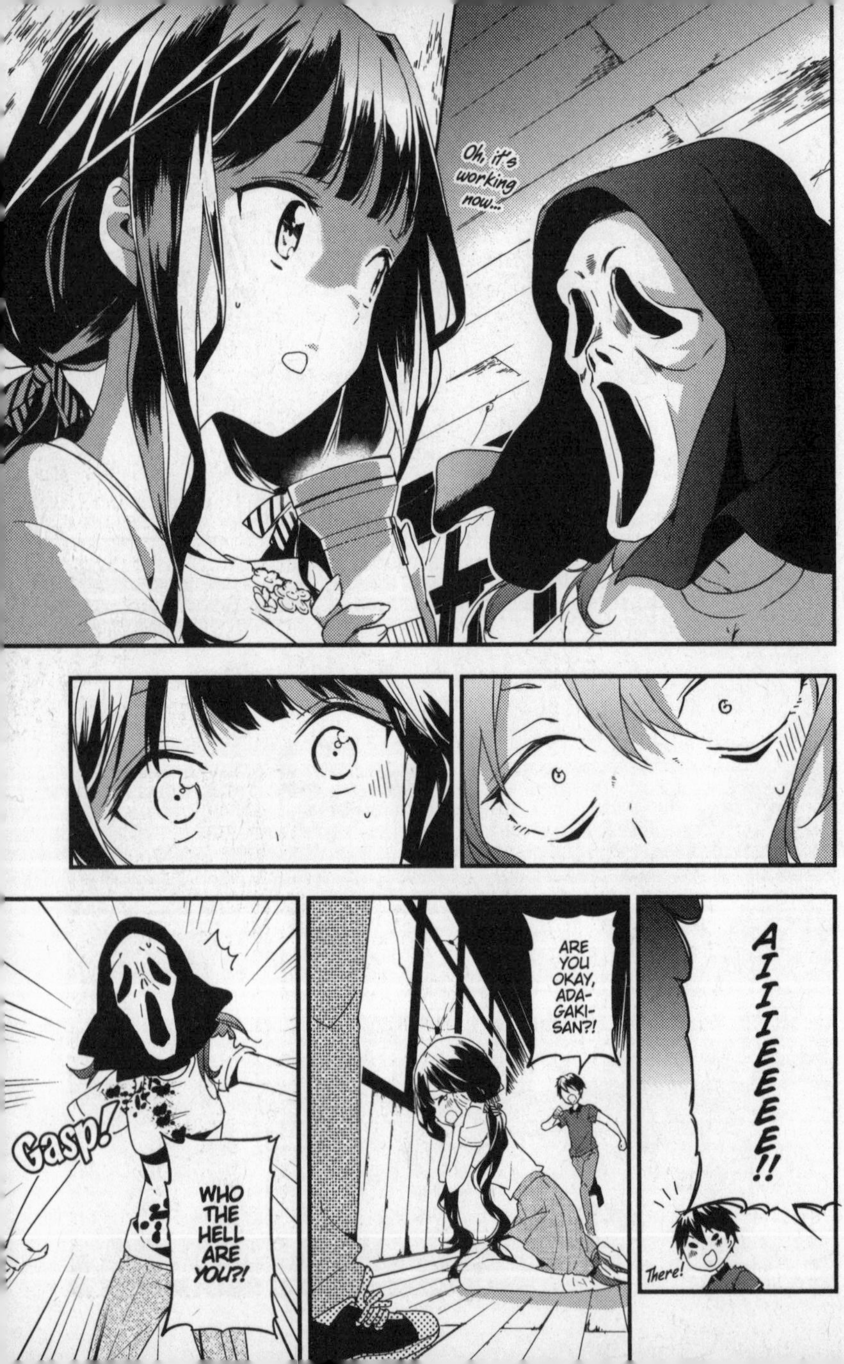
Oh, it's working now...
AIIIEEEEE!!
There!
ARE YOU OKAY, ADAGAKI-SAN?!
Gasp!
WHO THE HELL ARE YOU?!

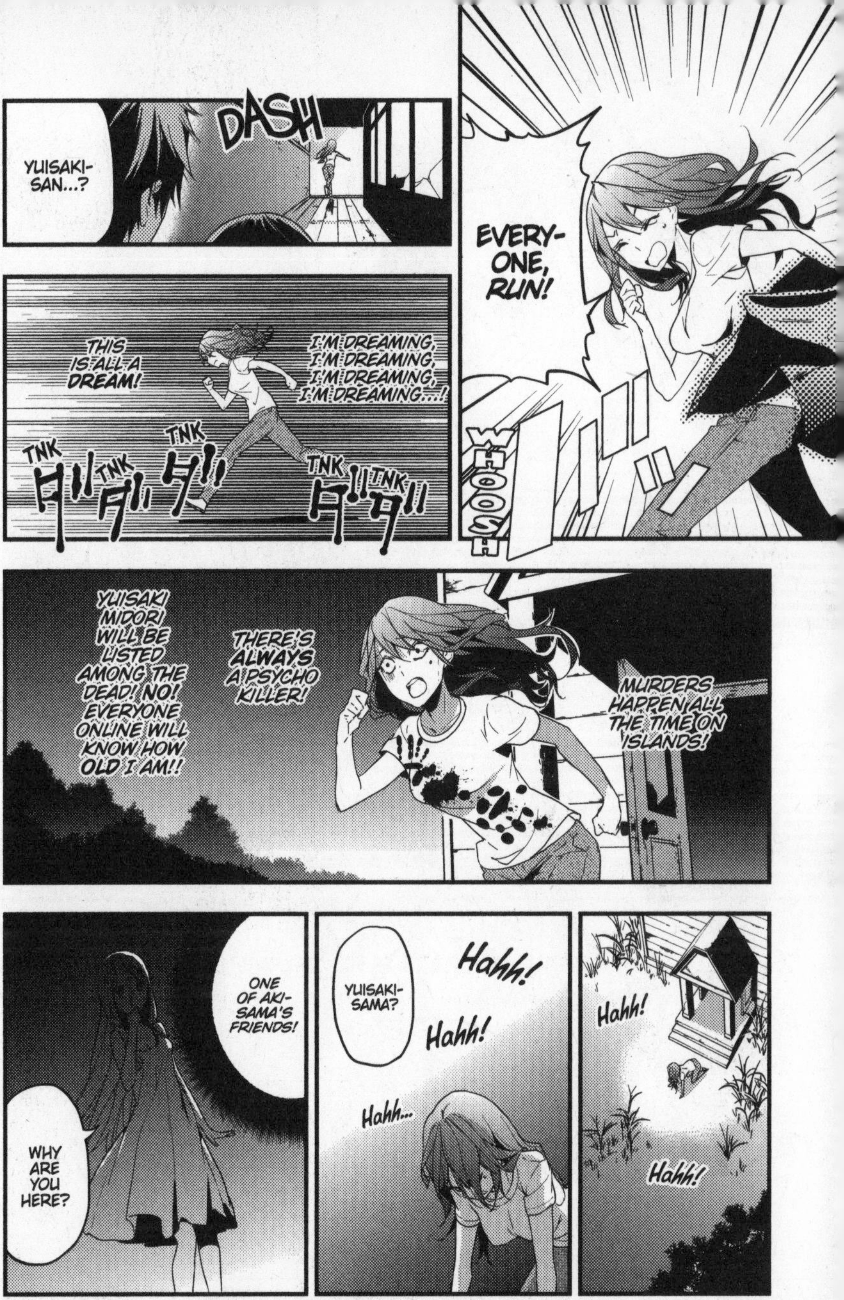
EVERY-ONE, RUN!
WHOOSH
YUISAKI-SAN...?
DASH
I'M DREAMING, I'M DREAMING, I'M DREAMING, I'M DREAMING...!
THIS IS ALL A DREAM!
TNK TNK
TNK TNK
TNK TNK
MURDERS HAPPEN ALL THE TIME ON ISLANDS!
THERE'S ALWAYS A PSYCHO KILLER!
YUISAKI MIDORI WILL BE LISTED AMONG THE DEAD! NO! EVERYONE ONLINE WILL KNOW HOW OLD I AM!!
Hahh!
Hahh!
Hahh!
Hahh!
Hahh!
Hahh...
YUISAKI-SAMA?
ONE OF AKI-SAMA'S FRIENDS!
WHY ARE YOU HERE?

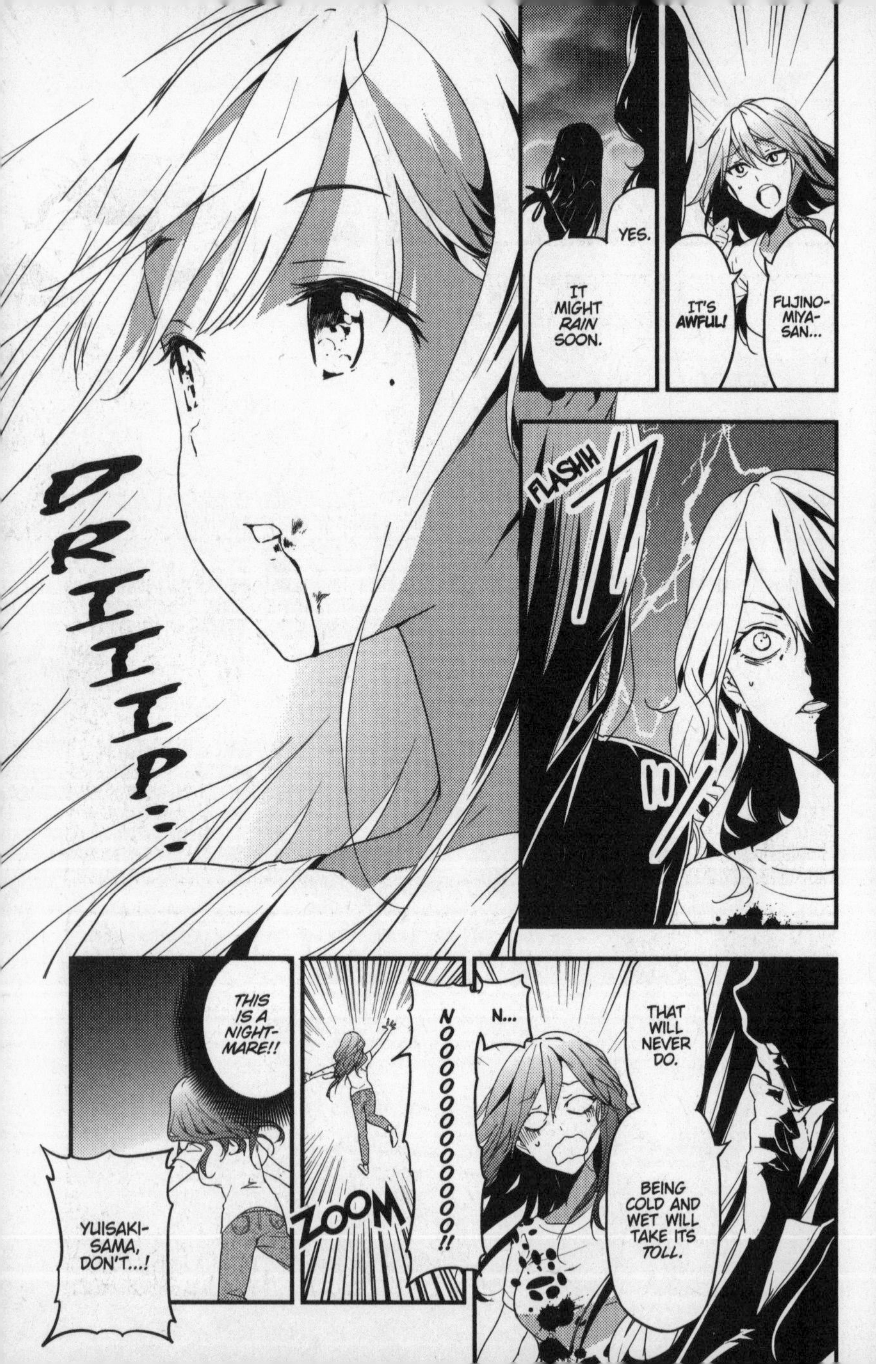
FUJINO-MIYA-SAN...
IT'S AWFUL!
YES.
IT MIGHT RAIN SOON.
FLASHH
DRIIIP...
THAT WILL NEVER DO.
BEING COLD AND WET WILL TAKE ITS TOLL.
N...
NOOOOOOOOOOOOOOO!!
ZOOM
THIS IS A NIGHTMARE!!
YUISAKI-SAMA, DON'T...!

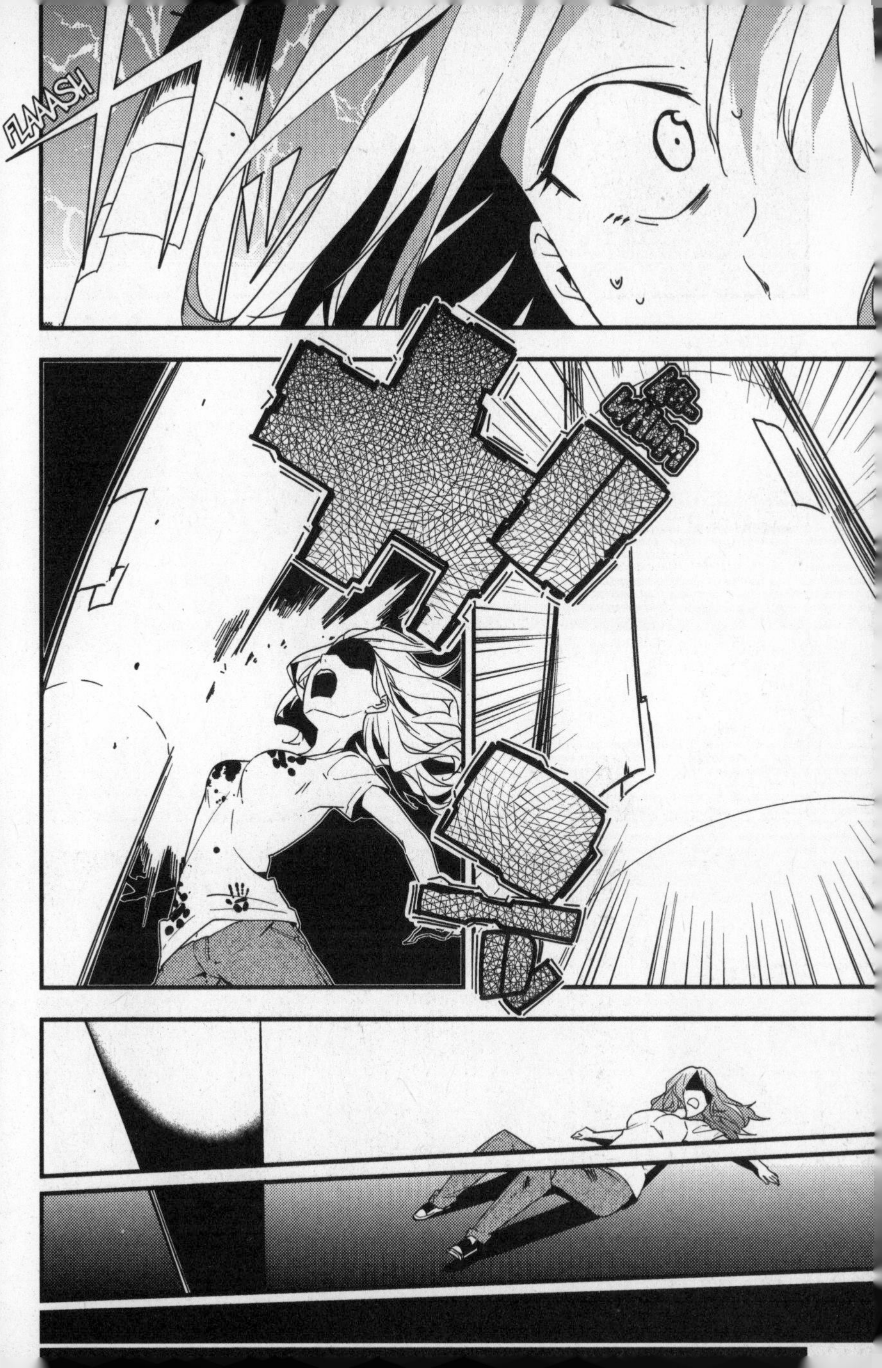
FLAAASH

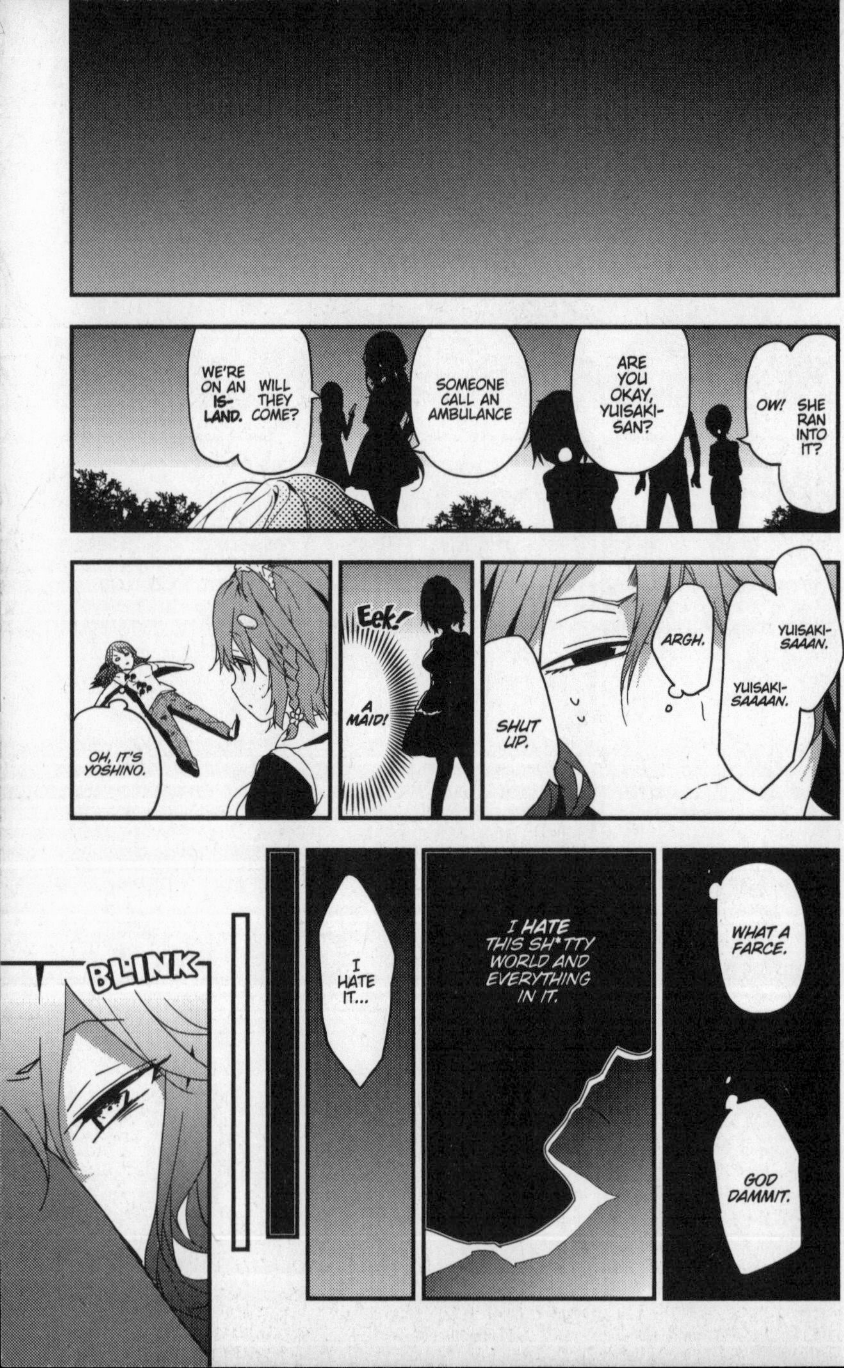
OW! SHE RAN INTO IT?
ARE YOU OKAY, YUISAKI-SAN?
SOMEONE CALL AN AMBULANCE
WE'RE ON AN IS-LAND. WILL THEY COME?
YUISAKI-SAAAN.
YUISAKI-SAAAAN.
ARGH.
SHUT UP.
Eek!
A MAID!
OH, IT'S YOSHINO.
WHAT A FARCE.
GOD DAMMIT.
I HATE THIS SH*TTY WORLD AND EVERYTHING IN IT.
I HATE IT...
BLINK

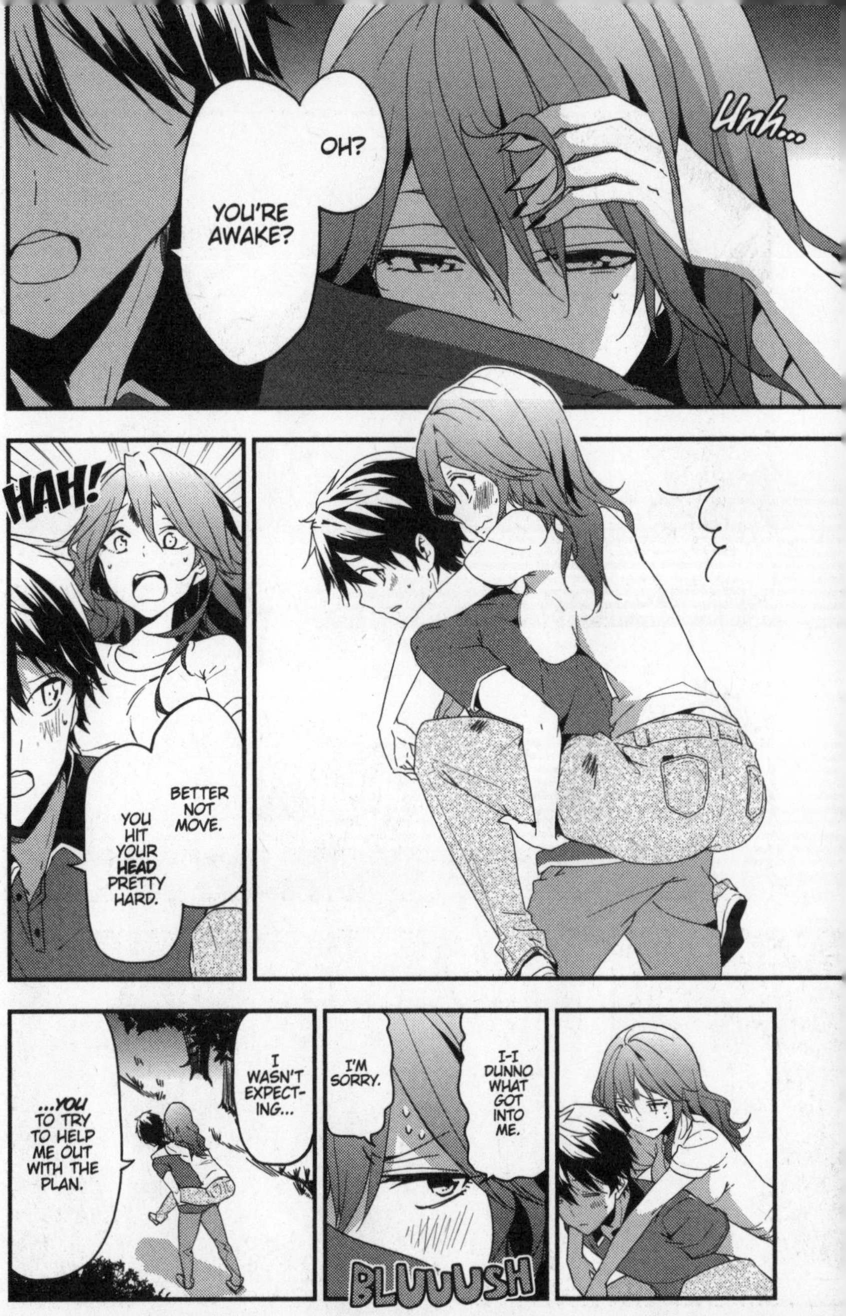
Unh...
OH?
YOU'RE AWAKE?
HAH!
BETTER NOT MOVE.
YOU HIT YOUR HEAD PRETTY HARD.
I-I DUNNO WHAT GOT INTO ME.
I'M SORRY.
BLUUUSH
I WASN'T EXPECT-ING...
...YOU TO TRY TO HELP ME OUT WITH THE PLAN.

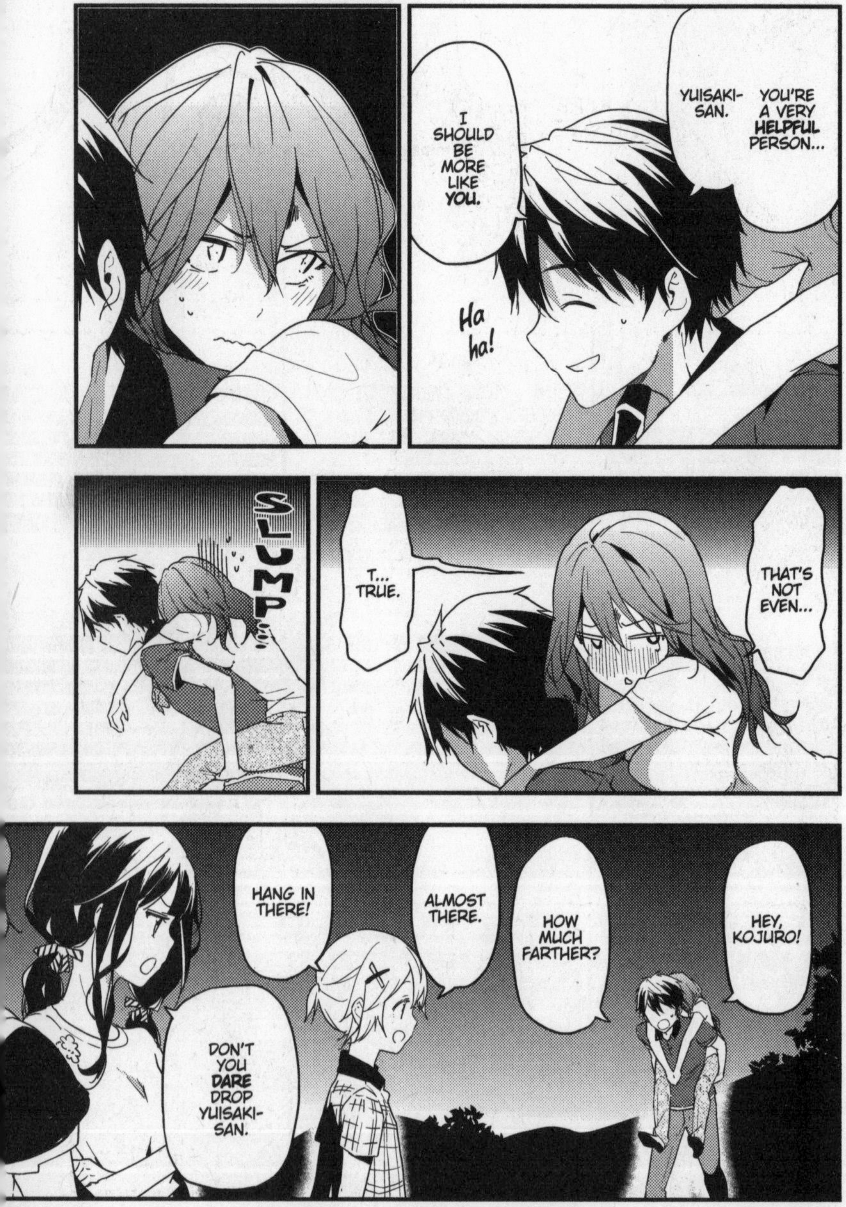
YUISAKI-SAN. YOU'RE A VERY HELPFUL PERSON...
I SHOULD BE MORE LIKE YOU.
Ha ha!
THAT'S NOT EVEN...
T... TRUE.
SLUMP...
HEY, KOJURO!
HOW MUCH FARTHER?
ALMOST THERE.
HANG IN THERE!
DON'T YOU DARE DROP YUISAKI-SAN.

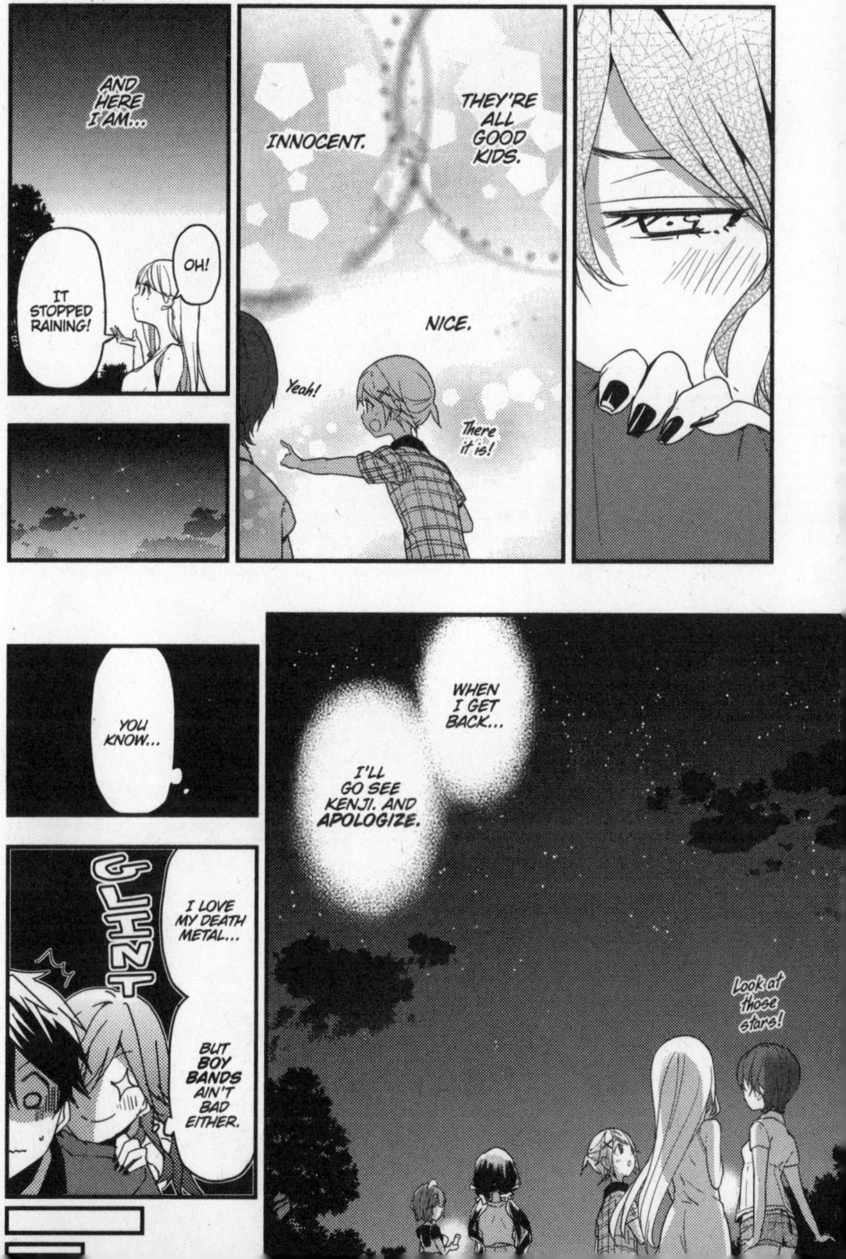
THEY'RE ALL GOOD KIDS.
INNOCENT.
NICE.
There it is!
Yeah!
AND HERE I AM...
OH!
IT STOPPED RAINING!
WHEN I GET BACK...
I'LL GO SEE KENJI. AND APOLOGIZE.
Look at those stars!
YOU KNOW...
GLINT
I LOVE MY DEATH METAL...
BUT BOY BANDS AIN'T BAD EITHER.

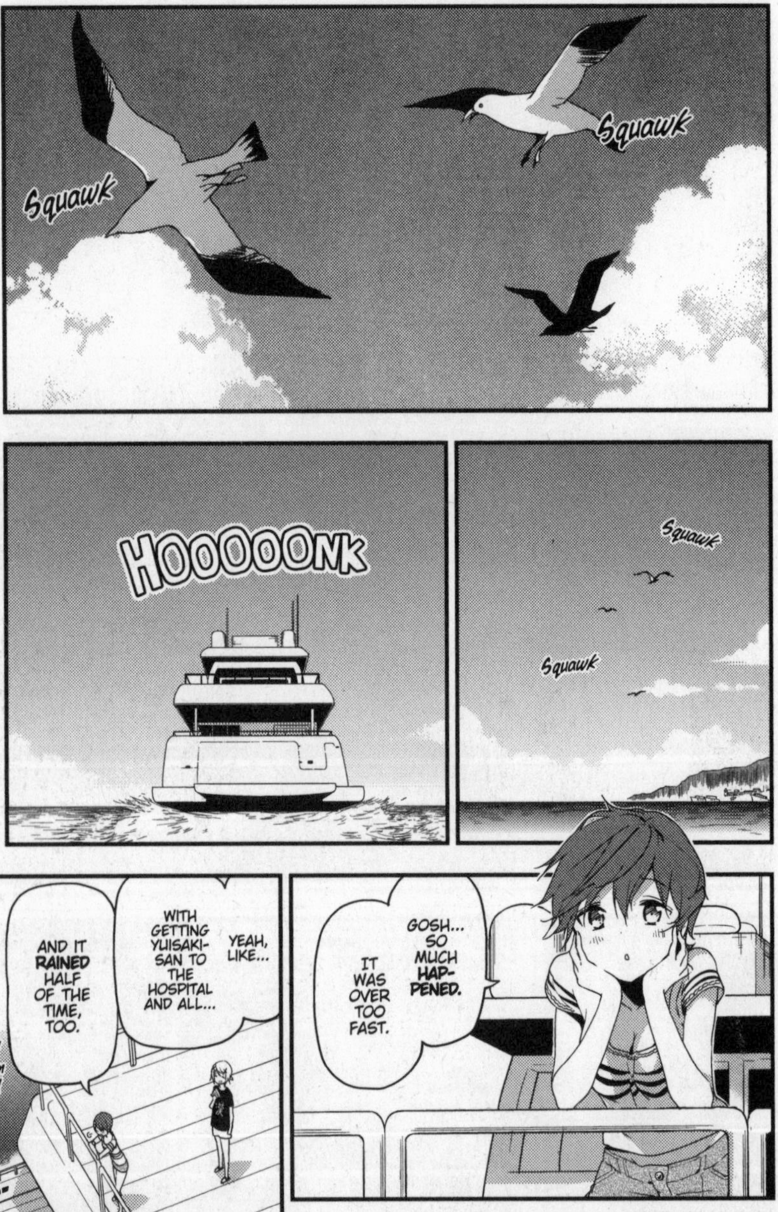
Squawk
Squawk
Squawk
Squawk
HOOOOONK
GOSH... SO MUCH HAPPENED.
IT WAS OVER TOO FAST.
YEAH, LIKE...
WITH GETTING YUISAKI-SAN TO THE HOSPITAL AND ALL...
AND IT RAINED HALF OF THE TIME, TOO.
I wanted to swim more!

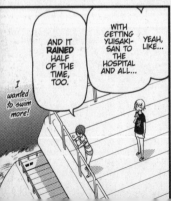

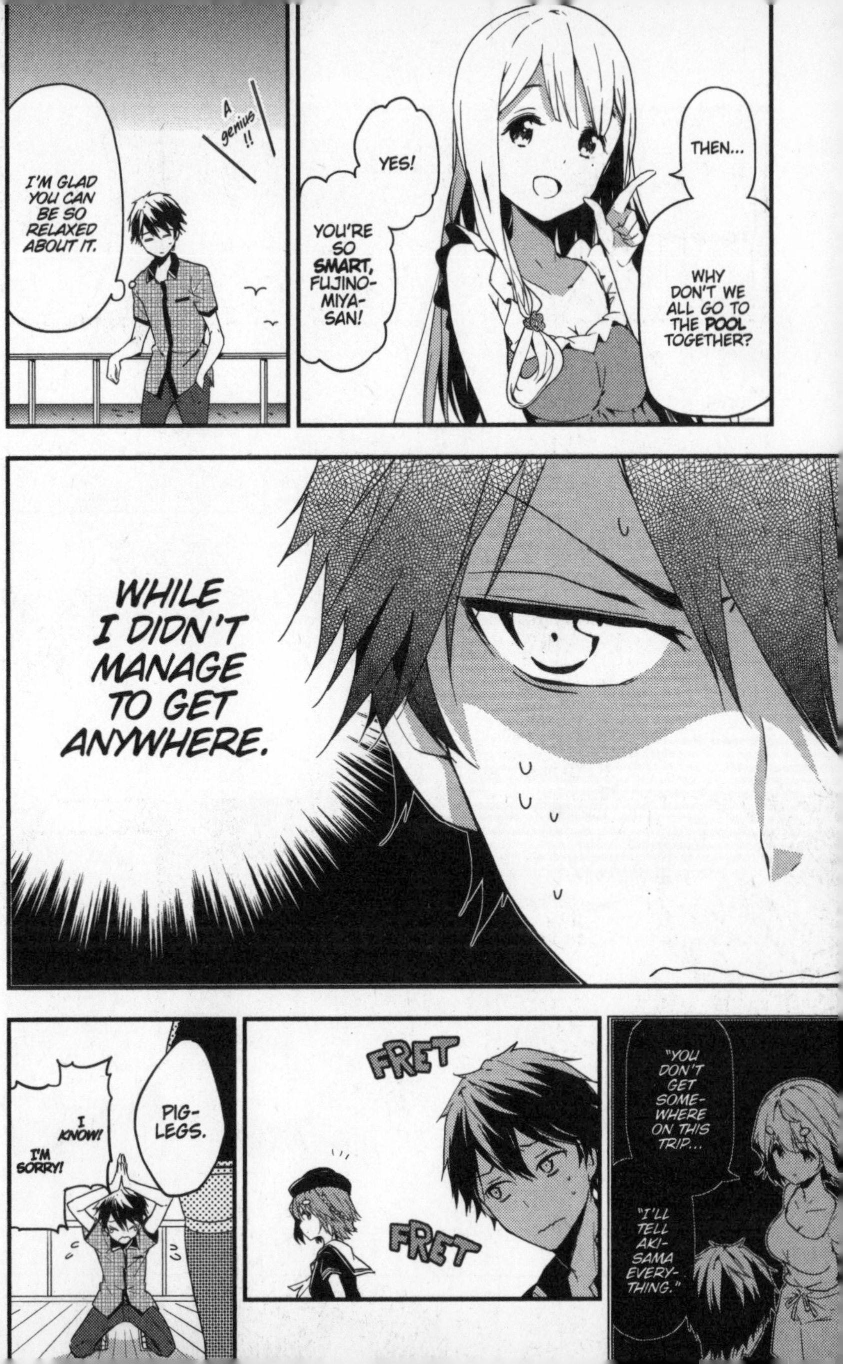
THEN...
WHY DON'T WE ALL GO TO THE POOL TOGETHER?
YES!
YOU'RE SO SMART, FUJINO-MIYA-SAN!
A genius!!
I'M GLAD YOU CAN BE SO RELAXED ABOUT IT.
WHILE I DIDN'T MANAGE TO GET ANYWHERE.
"YOU DON'T GET SOME-WHERE ON THIS TRIP...
"I'LL TELL AKI-SAMA EVERY-THING."
FRET
FRET
PIG-LEGS.
I KNOW!
I'M SORRY!

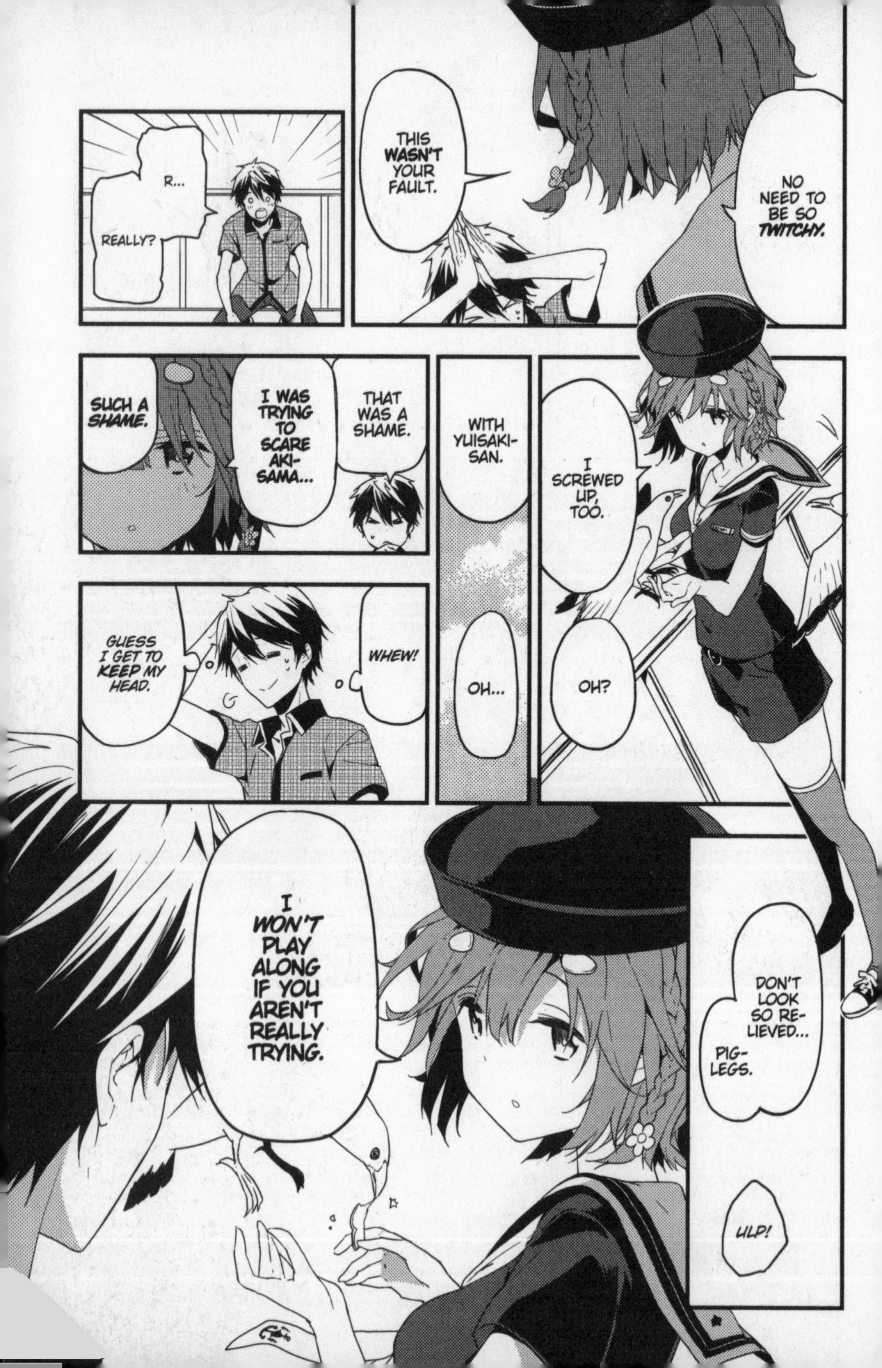
NO NEED TO BE SO *TWITCHY.*
THIS *WASN'T* YOUR FAULT.
R...
REALLY?
I SCREWED UP, TOO.
OH?
WITH YUISAKI-SAN.
OH...
THAT WAS A SHAME.
I WAS TRYING TO SCARE AKI-SAMA...
SUCH A *SHAME.*
WHEW!
GUESS I GET TO KEEP MY HEAD.
DON'T LOOK SO RE-LIEVED...
PIG-LEGS.
I *WON'T* PLAY ALONG IF YOU AREN'T REALLY TRYING.
ULP!

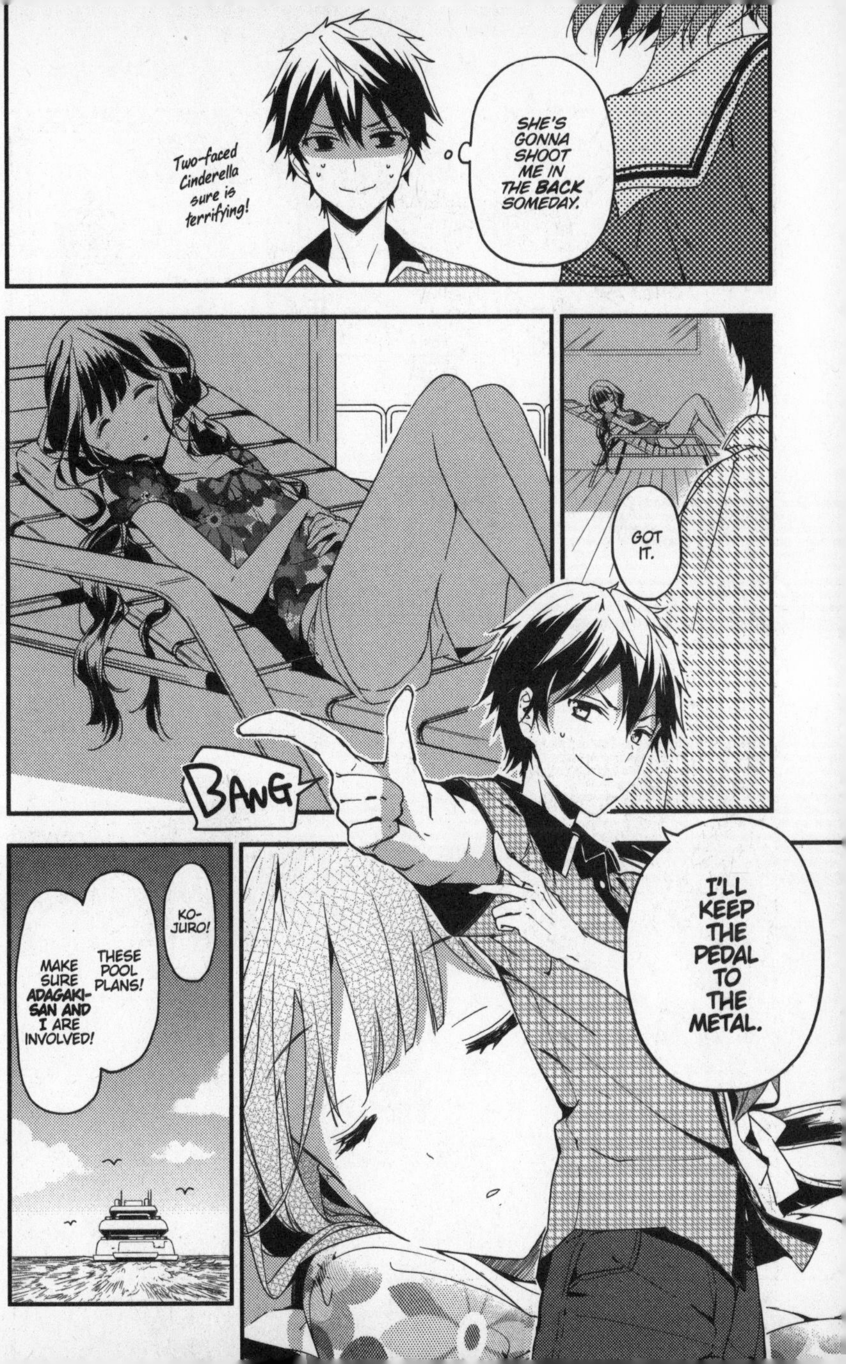
SHE'S GONNA SHOOT ME IN THE BACK SOMEDAY.
Two-faced Cinderella sure is terrifying!
GOT IT.
BANG
I'LL KEEP THE PEDAL TO THE METAL.
KO-JURO!
THESE POOL PLANS!
MAKE SURE ADAGAKI-SAN AND I ARE INVOLVED!

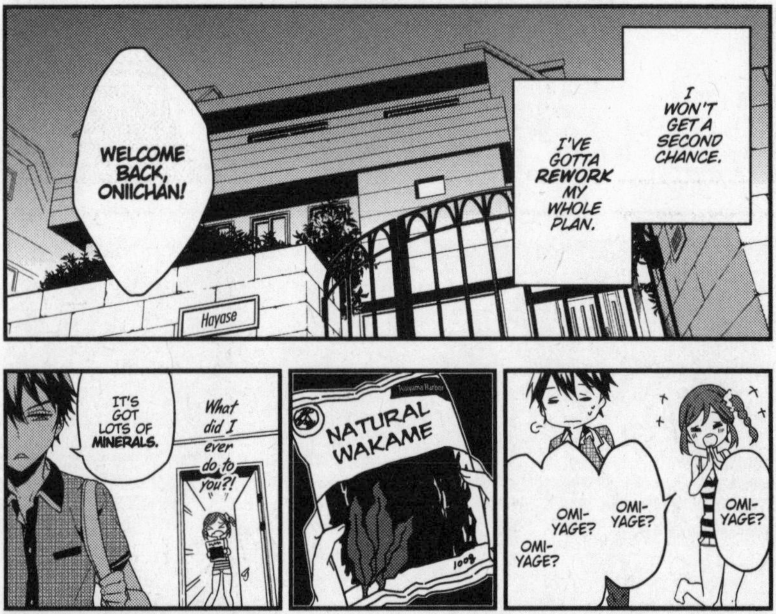
I WON'T GET A SECOND CHANCE.
I'VE GOTTA REWORK MY WHOLE PLAN.
WELCOME BACK, ONIICHAN!
Hayase
OMI-YAGE?
OMI-YAGE?
OMI-YAGE?
OMI-YAGE?
Tsuyama Harbor
NATURAL WAKAME
100g
What did I ever do to you?!
IT'S GOT LOTS OF MINERALS.

*Omiyage are souvenirs, usually food items, the Japanese bring home from their travels.

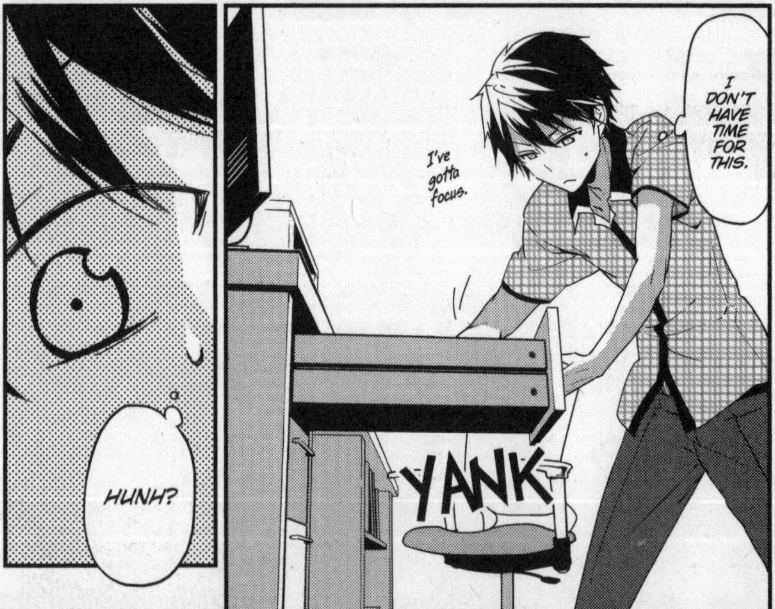
I DON'T HAVE TIME FOR THIS.
I've gotta focus.
YANK
HUNH?

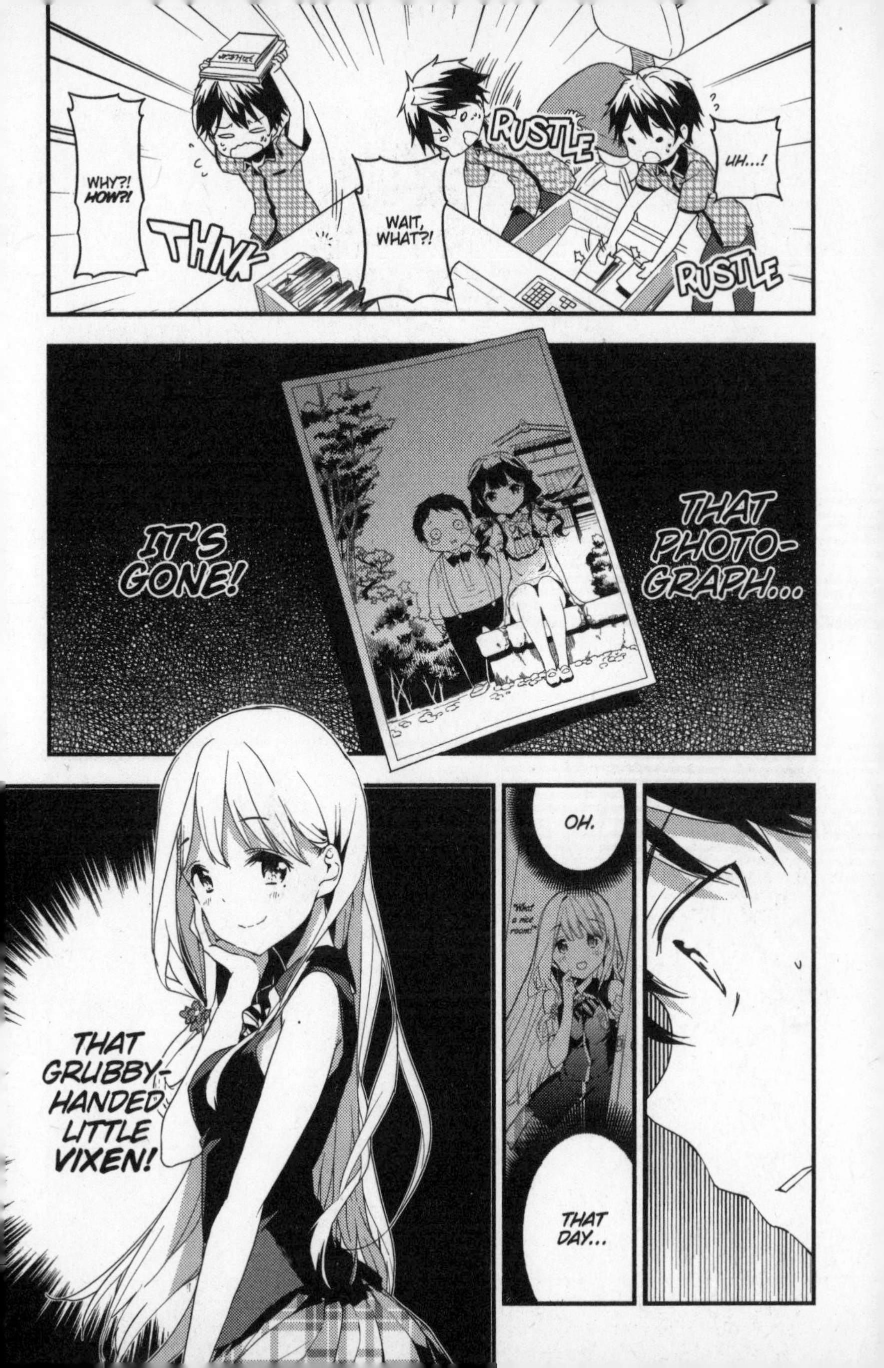
UH...!
RUSTLE
RUSTLE
WAIT, WHAT?!
WHY?! HOW?!
THNK
THAT PHOTOGRAPH...
IT'S GONE!
OH.
"What a nice room!"
THAT DAY...
THAT GRUBBY-HANDED LITTLE VIXEN!

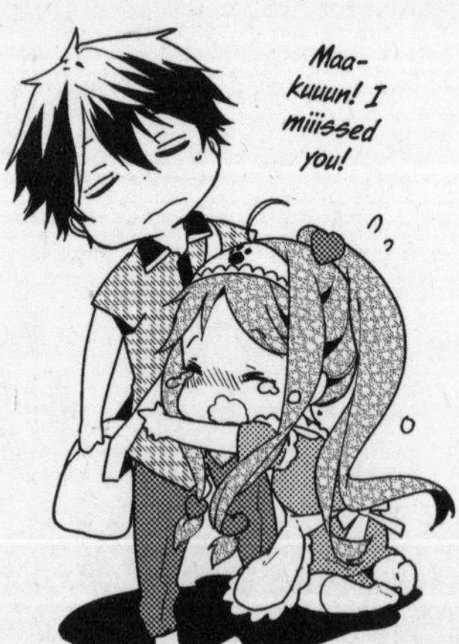
Maa-
kuuun! I
miiissed
you!

4

Masamune-kun's

REVENGE

Presented by Hazuki Takeoka & TIV

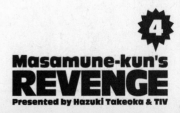

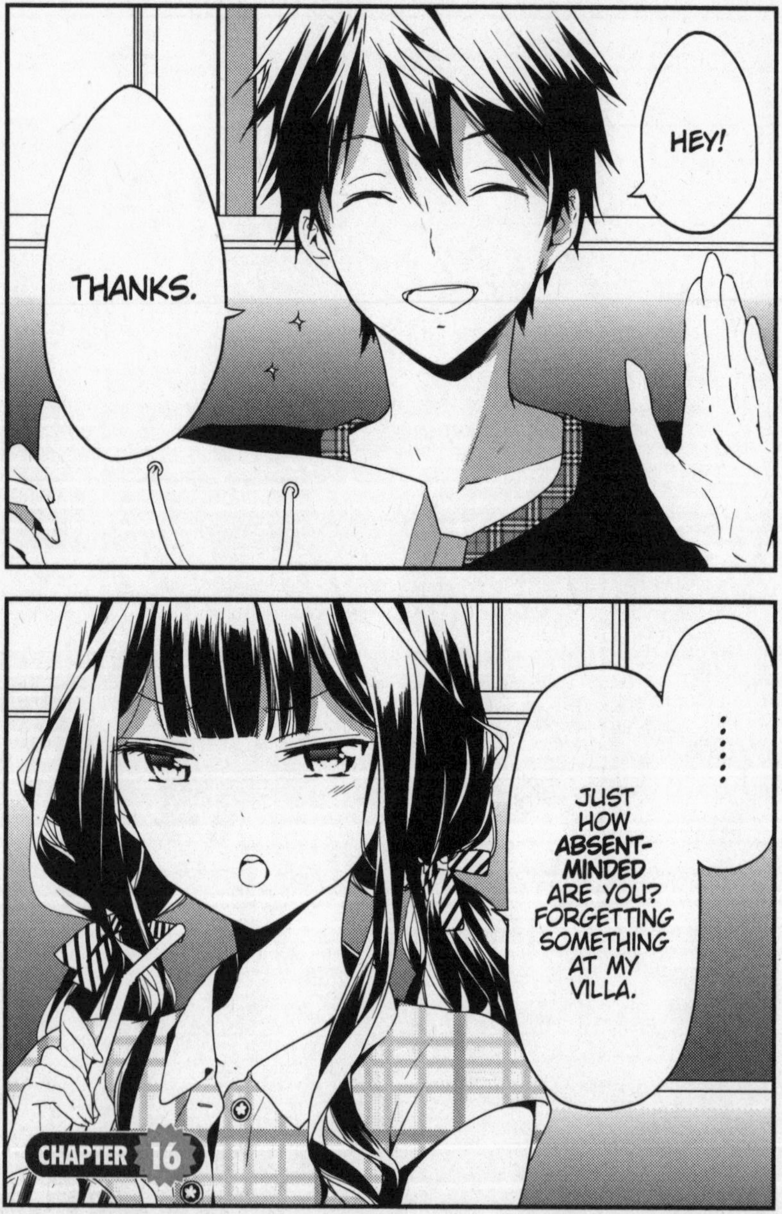
HEY!
THANKS.
……
JUST HOW ABSENT-MINDED ARE YOU? FORGETTING SOMETHING AT MY VILLA.
CHAPTER 16

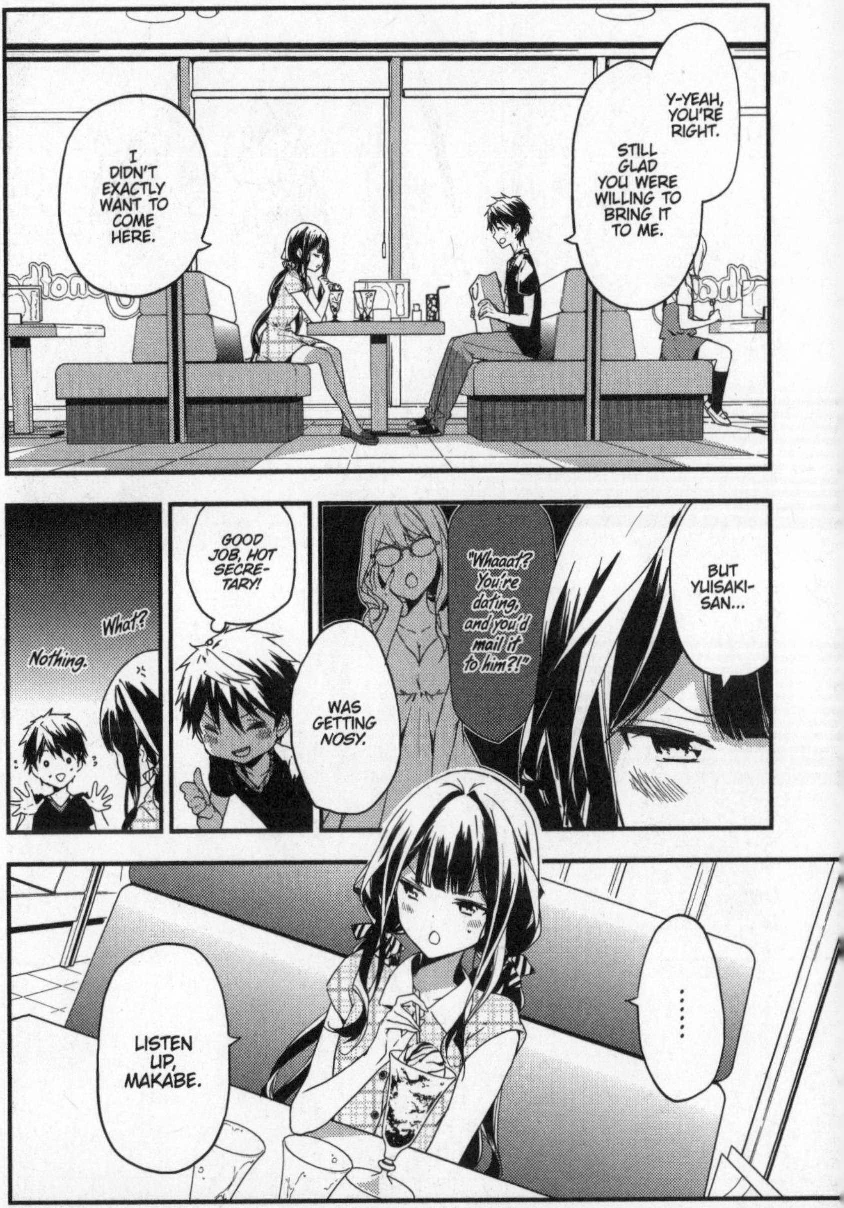
Y-YEAH, YOU'RE RIGHT.
STILL GLAD YOU WERE WILLING TO BRING IT TO ME.
I DIDN'T EXACTLY WANT TO COME HERE.
BUT YUISAKI-SAN...
"Whaaat? You're dating, and you'd mail it to him?!"
WAS GETTING NOSY.
GOOD JOB, HOT SECRETARY!
What?
Nothing.
......
LISTEN UP, MAKABE.

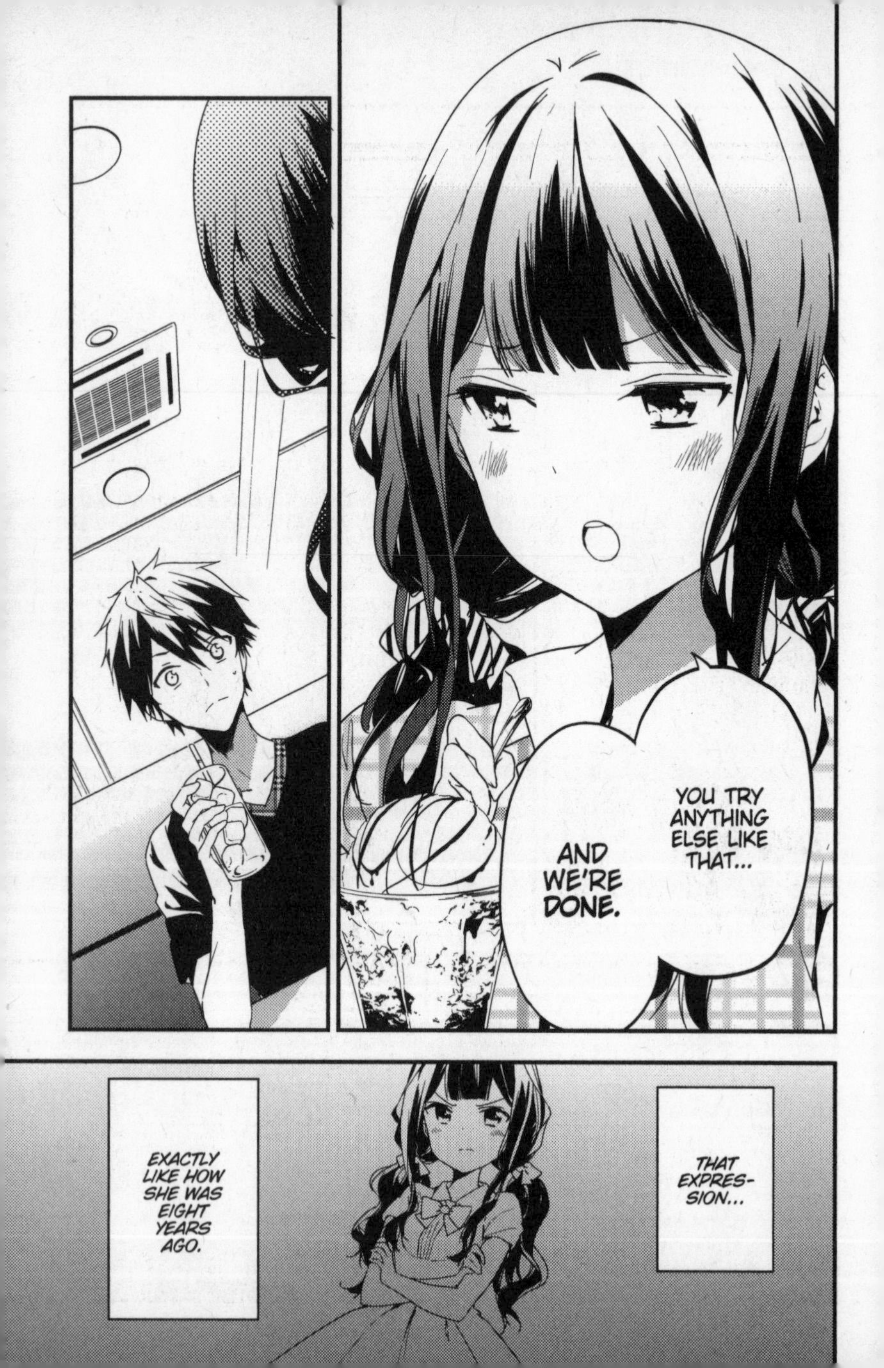
YOU TRY ANYTHING ELSE LIKE THAT...
AND WE'RE DONE.
THAT EXPRES-SION...
EXACTLY LIKE HOW SHE WAS EIGHT YEARS AGO.

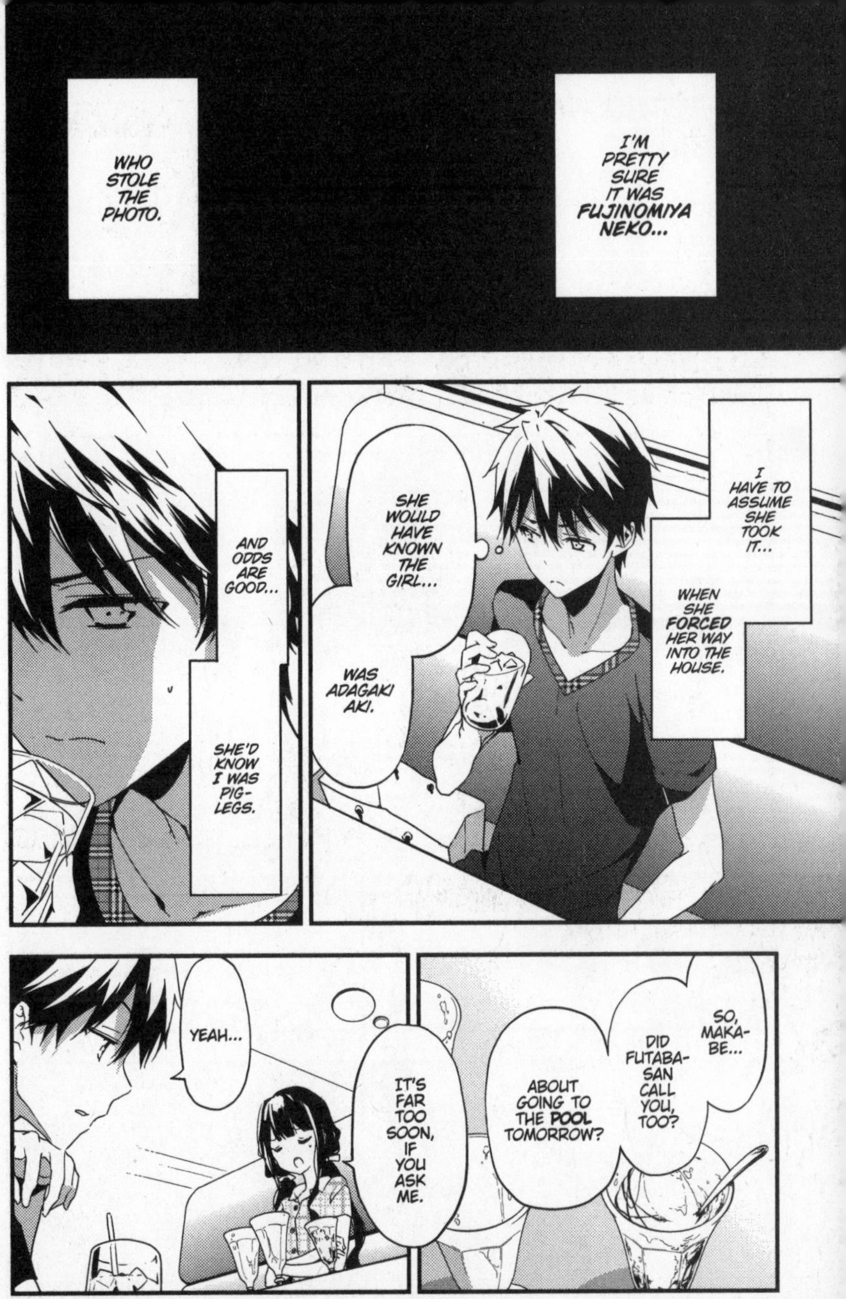
I'M PRETTY SURE IT WAS FUJINOMIYA NEKO...
WHO STOLE THE PHOTO.
I HAVE TO ASSUME SHE TOOK IT...
WHEN SHE FORCED HER WAY INTO THE HOUSE.
SHE WOULD HAVE KNOWN THE GIRL...
WAS ADAGAKI AKI.
AND ODDS ARE GOOD...
SHE'D KNOW I WAS PIG-LEGS.
SO, MAKA-BE...
DID FUTABA-SAN CALL YOU, TOO?
ABOUT GOING TO THE POOL TOMORROW?
IT'S FAR TOO SOON, IF YOU ASK ME.
YEAH...

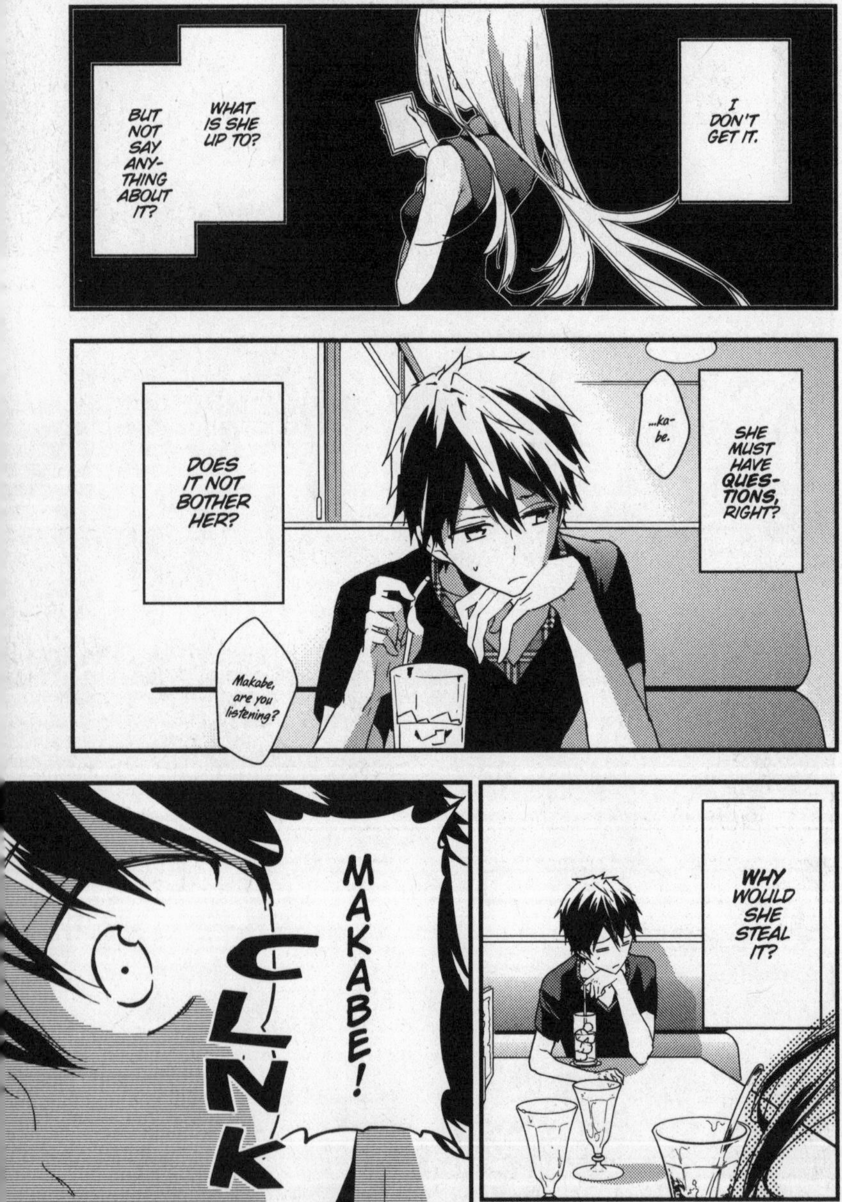
I DON'T GET IT.
WHAT IS SHE UP TO?
BUT NOT SAY ANYTHING ABOUT IT?
SHE MUST HAVE QUESTIONS, RIGHT?
...ka-be.
DOES IT NOT BOTHER HER?
Makabe, are you listening?
WHY WOULD SHE STEAL IT?
MAKABE!
CLNK

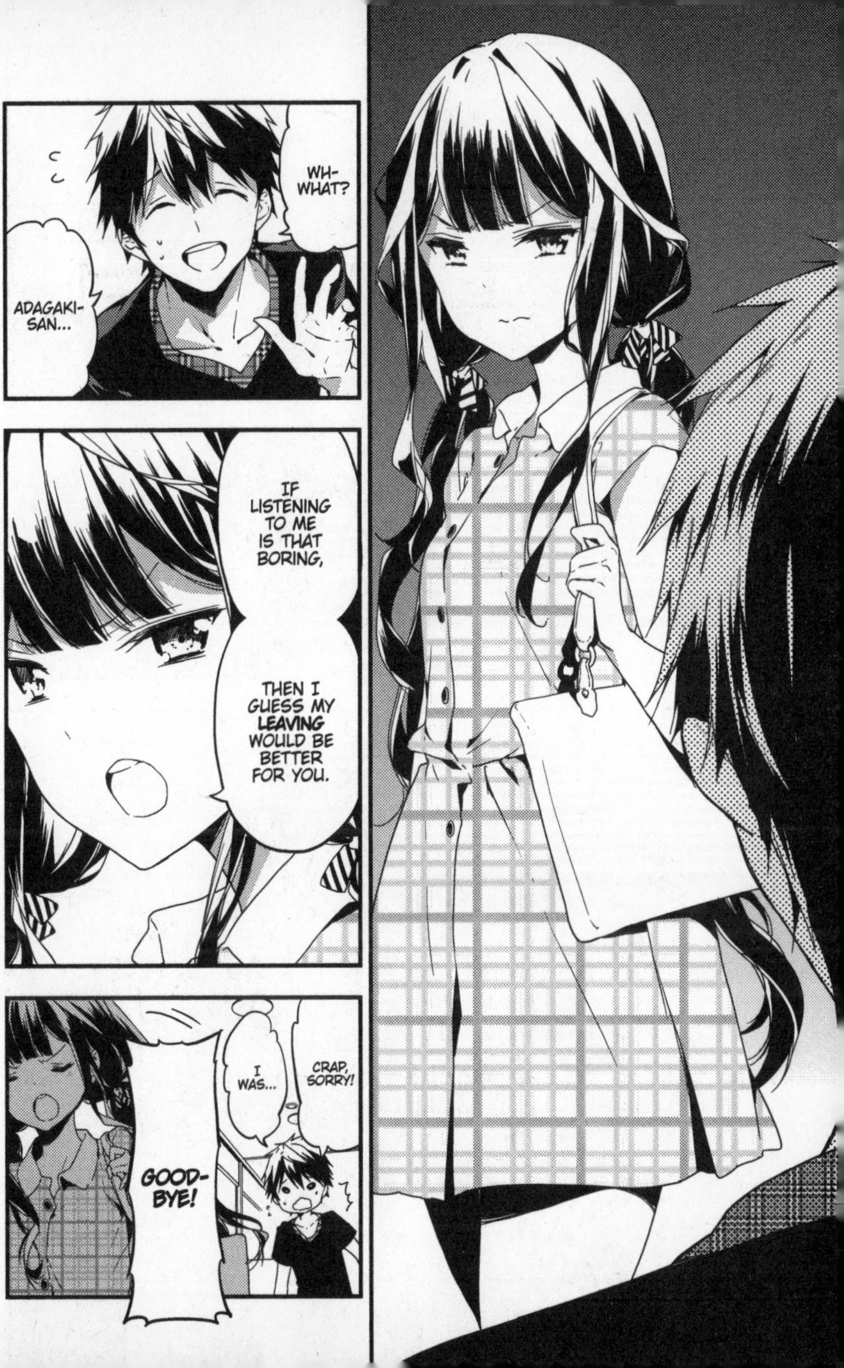
WH-WHAT?
ADAGAKI-SAN...
IF LISTENING TO ME IS THAT BORING,
THEN I GUESS MY **LEAVING** WOULD BE BETTER FOR YOU.
CRAP, SORRY!
I WAS...
GOOD-BYE!

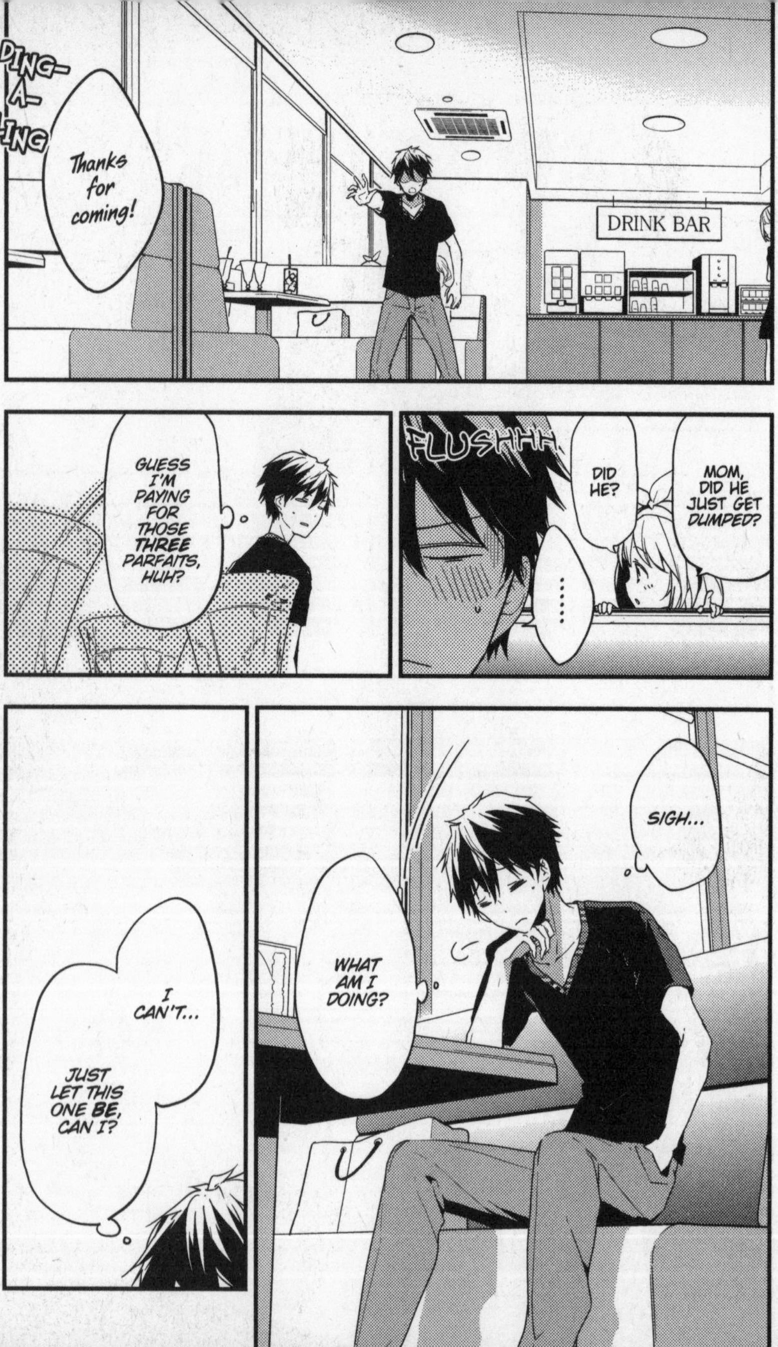
DING-A-LING
Thanks for coming!
MOM, DID HE JUST GET DUMPED?
DID HE?
FLUSHHH
......
GUESS I'M PAYING FOR THOSE THREE PARFAITS, HUH?
SIGH...
WHAT AM I DOING?
I CAN'T...
JUST LET THIS ONE BE, CAN I?

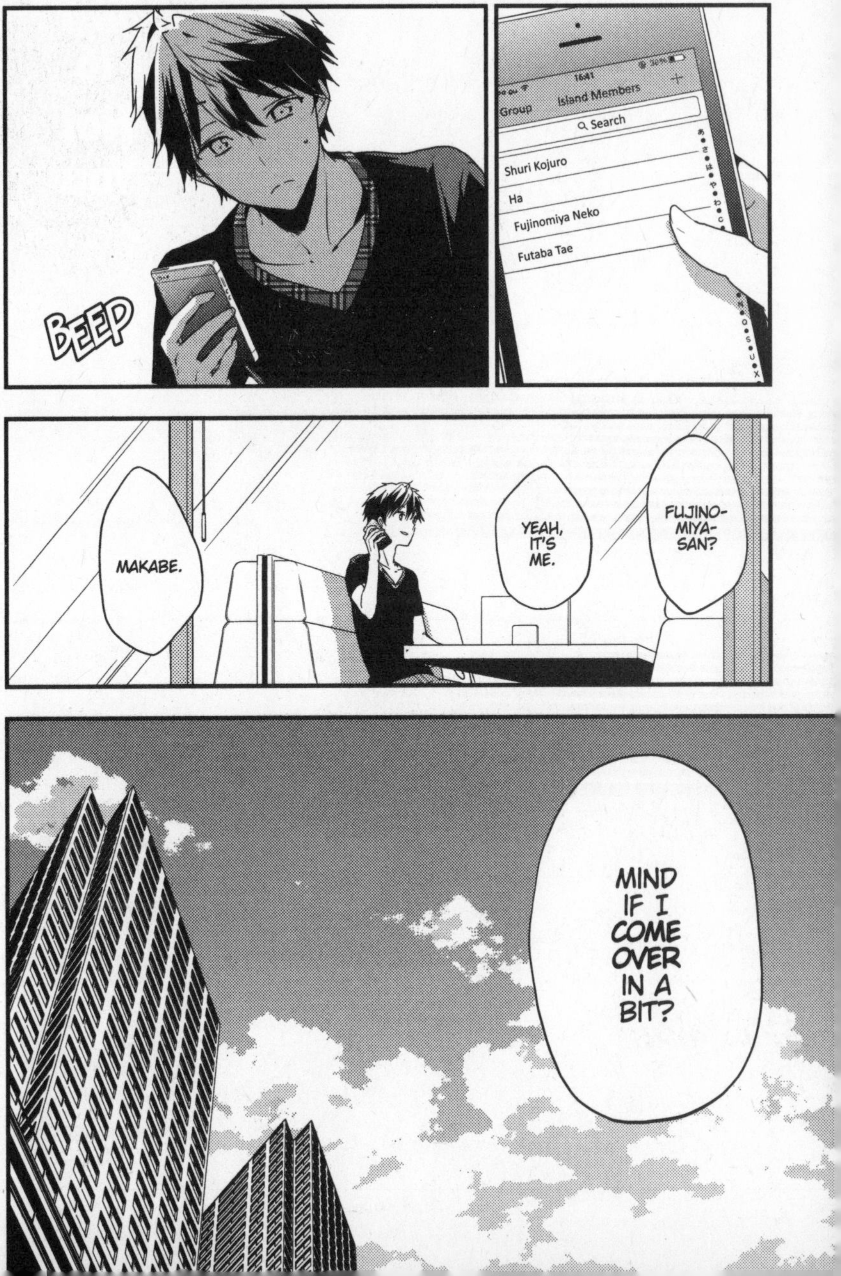

Group
Island Members
Search
Shuri Kojuro
Ha
Fujinomiya Neko
Futaba Tae
BEEP
FUJINO-MIYA-SAN?
YEAH, IT'S ME.
MAKABE.
MIND IF I COME OVER IN A BIT?

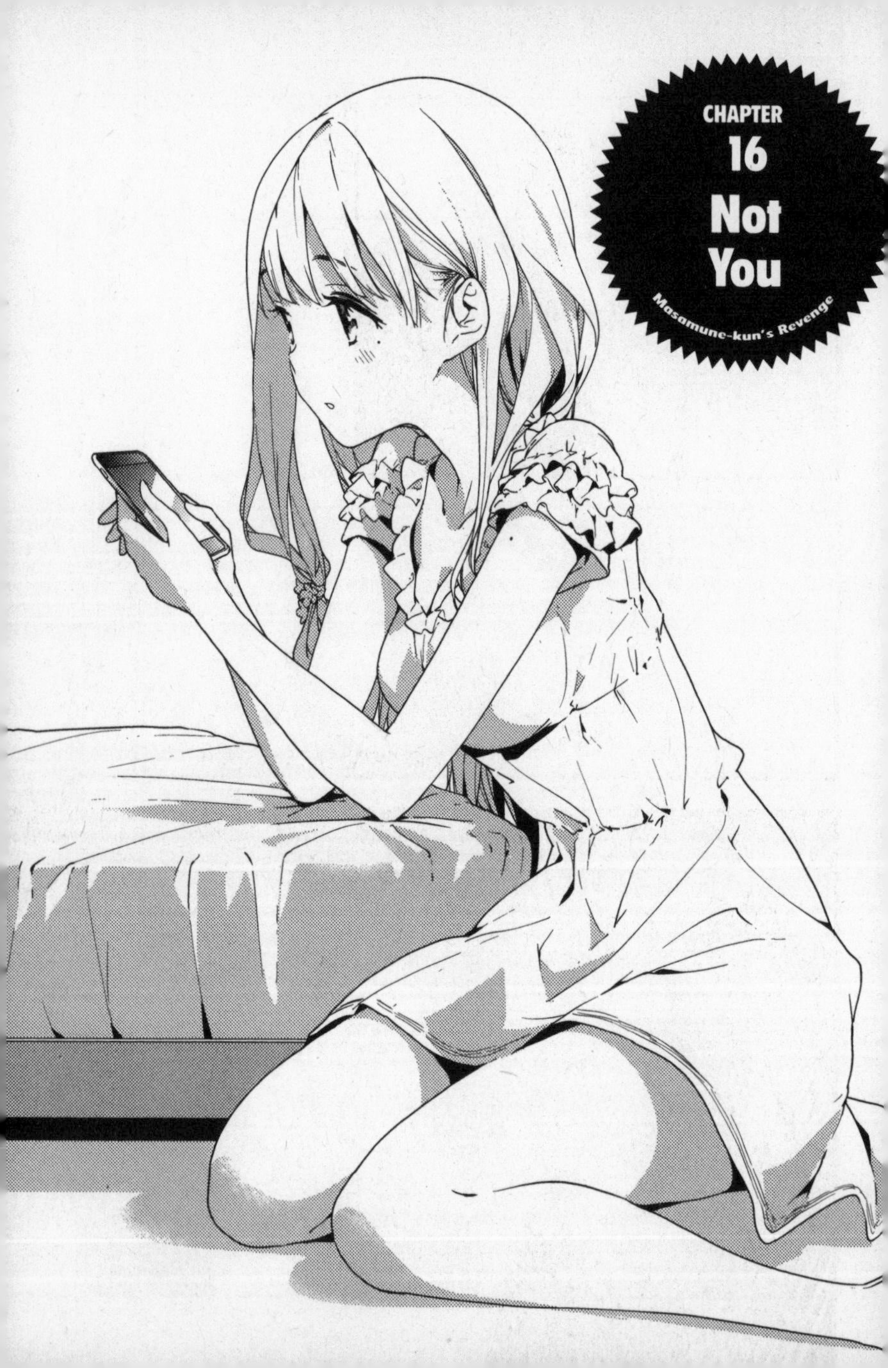
CHAPTER
16
Not
You
Masamune-kun's Revenge

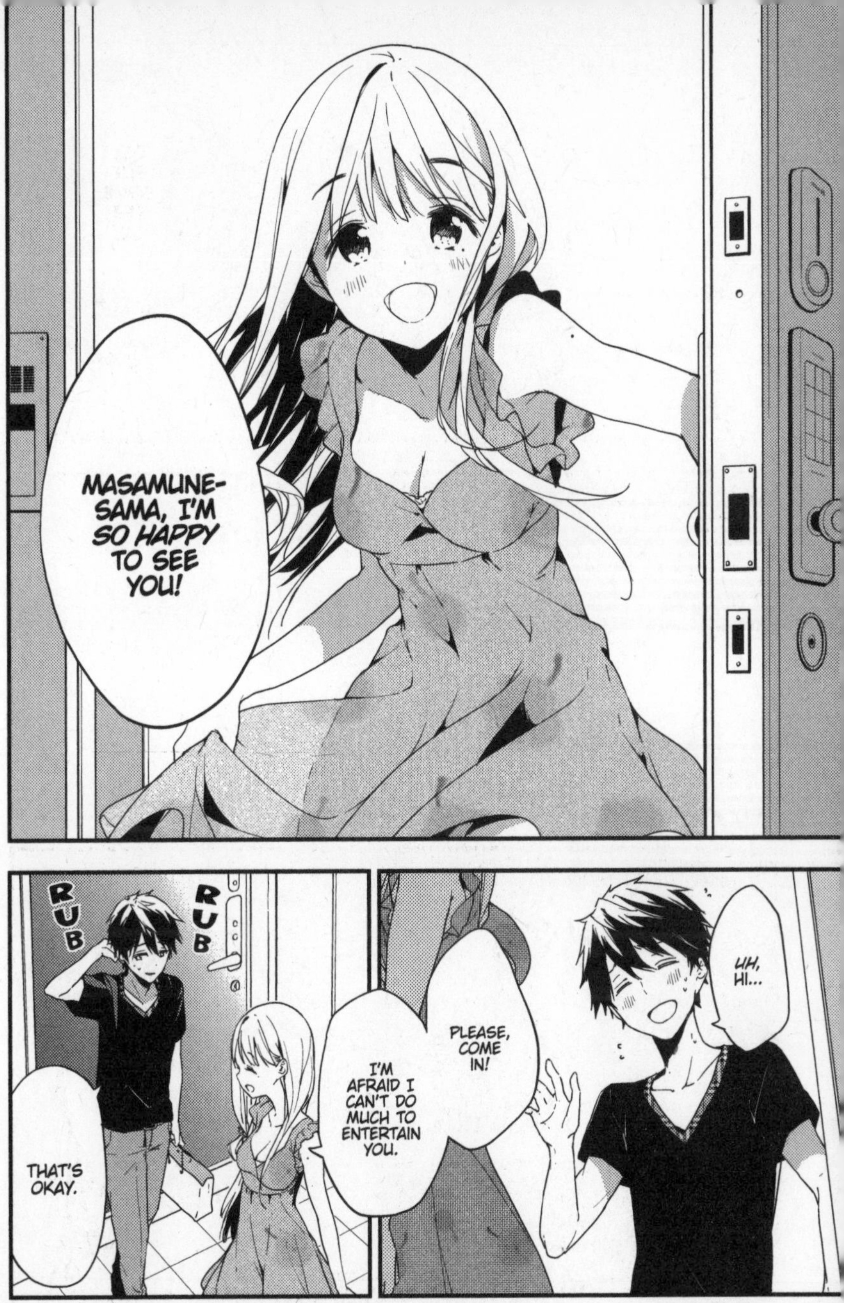
MASAMUNE-SAMA, I'M SO HAPPY TO SEE YOU!
UH, HI...
PLEASE, COME IN!
I'M AFRAID I CAN'T DO MUCH TO ENTERTAIN YOU.
RUB
RUB
THAT'S OKAY.

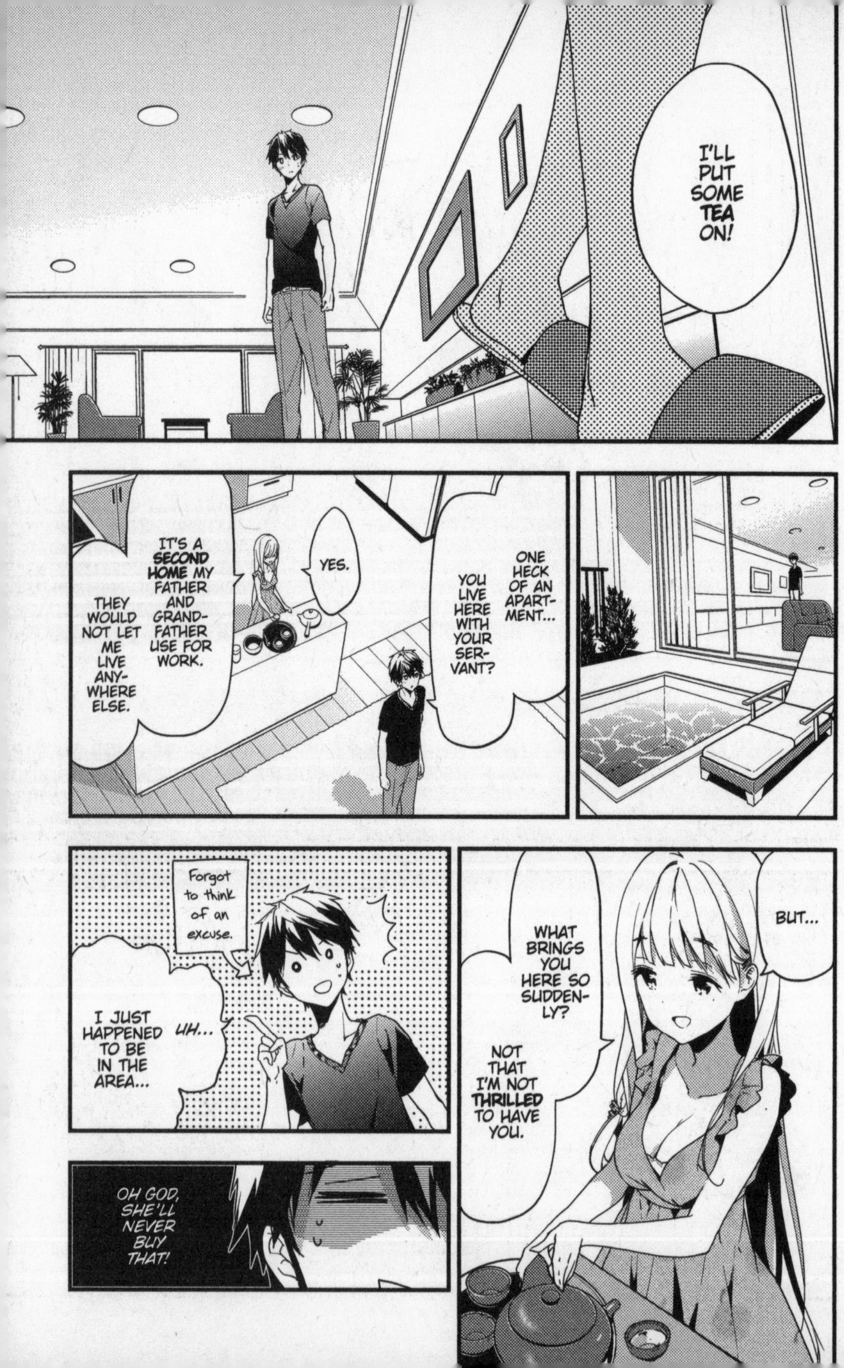
I'LL PUT SOME TEA ON!
ONE HECK OF AN APARTMENT...
YOU LIVE HERE WITH YOUR SERVANT?
YES.
IT'S A **SECOND HOME** MY FATHER AND GRANDFATHER USE FOR WORK.
THEY WOULD NOT LET ME LIVE ANYWHERE ELSE.
BUT...
WHAT BRINGS YOU HERE SO SUDDENLY?
NOT THAT I'M NOT **THRILLED** TO HAVE YOU.
Forgot to think of an excuse.
UH...
I JUST HAPPENED TO BE IN THE AREA...
OH GOD, SHE'LL NEVER BUY THAT!

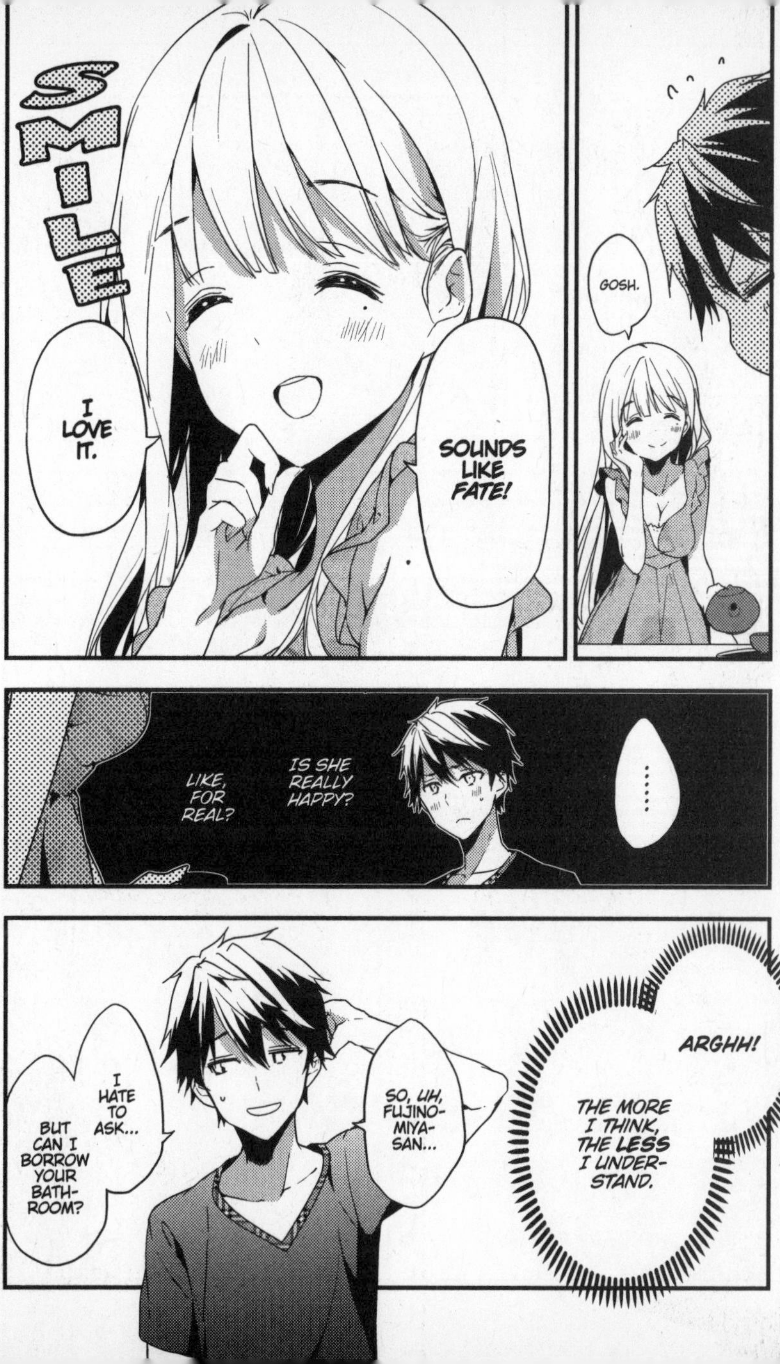
GOSH.
SMILE
SOUNDS LIKE FATE!
I LOVE IT.
......
IS SHE REALLY HAPPY?
LIKE, FOR REAL?
ARGHH!
THE MORE I THINK, THE LESS I UNDER-STAND.
SO, UH, FUJINO-MIYA-SAN...
I HATE TO ASK...
BUT CAN I BORROW YOUR BATH-ROOM?

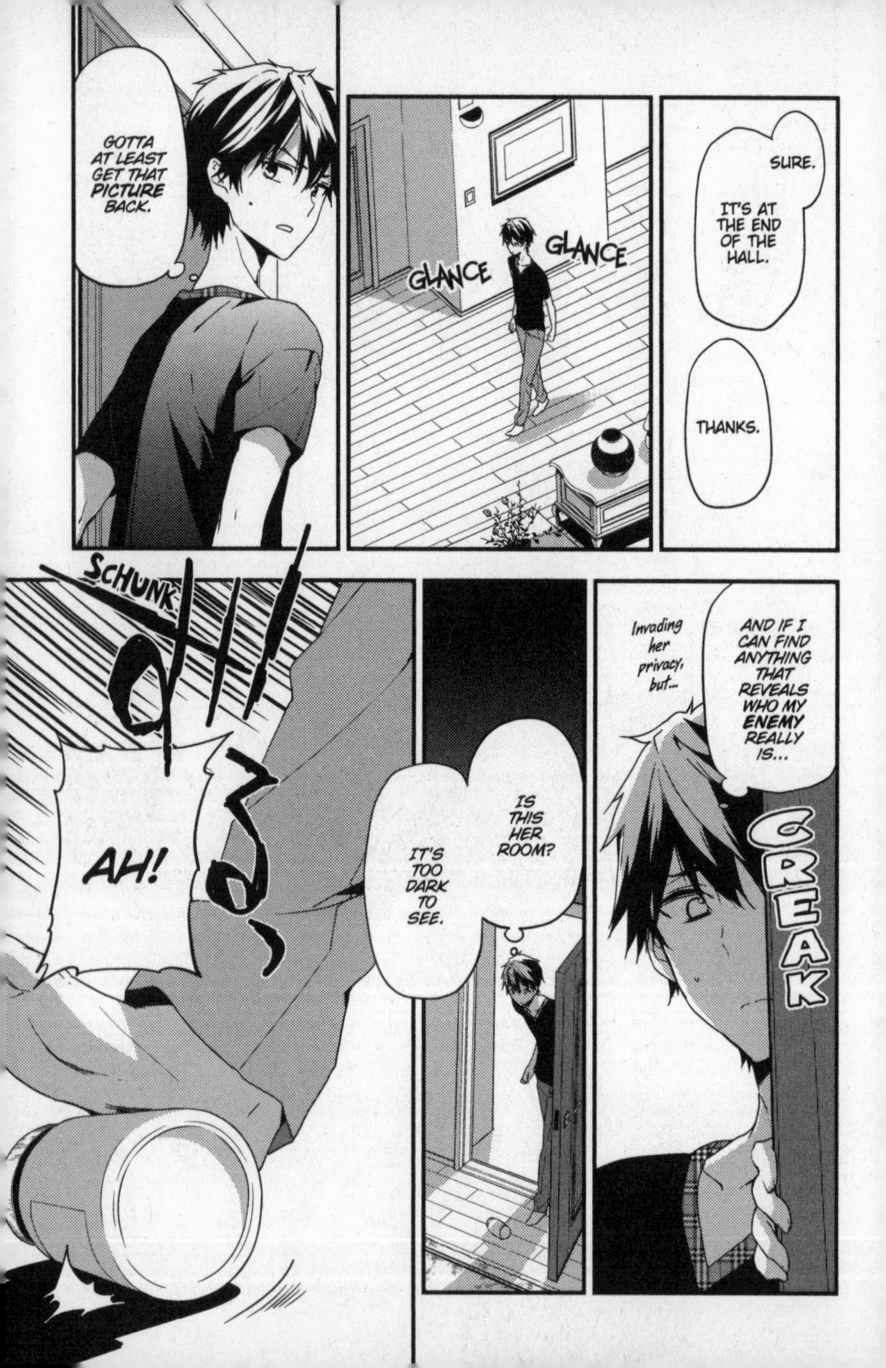

SURE.
IT'S AT THE END OF THE HALL.
THANKS.
GLANCE
GLANCE
GOTTA AT LEAST GET THAT PICTURE BACK.
AND IF I CAN FIND ANYTHING THAT REVEALS WHO MY ENEMY REALLY IS...
Invading her privacy, but...
CREAK
IS THIS HER ROOM?
IT'S TOO DARK TO SEE.
SCHUNK
AH!

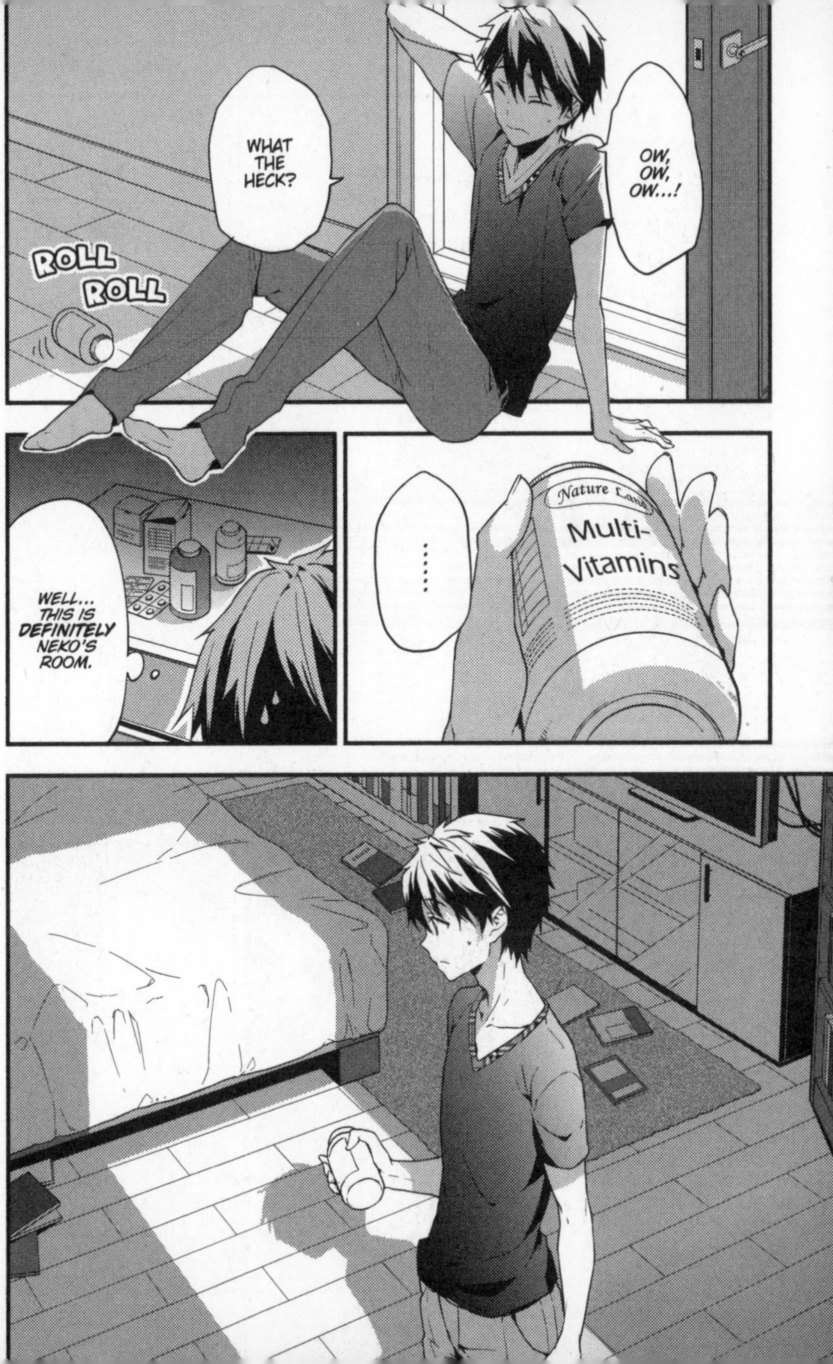
OW, OW, OW...!
WHAT THE HECK?
ROLL ROLL
......
Nature Land
Multi-Vitamins
WELL... THIS IS DEFINITELY NEKO'S ROOM.

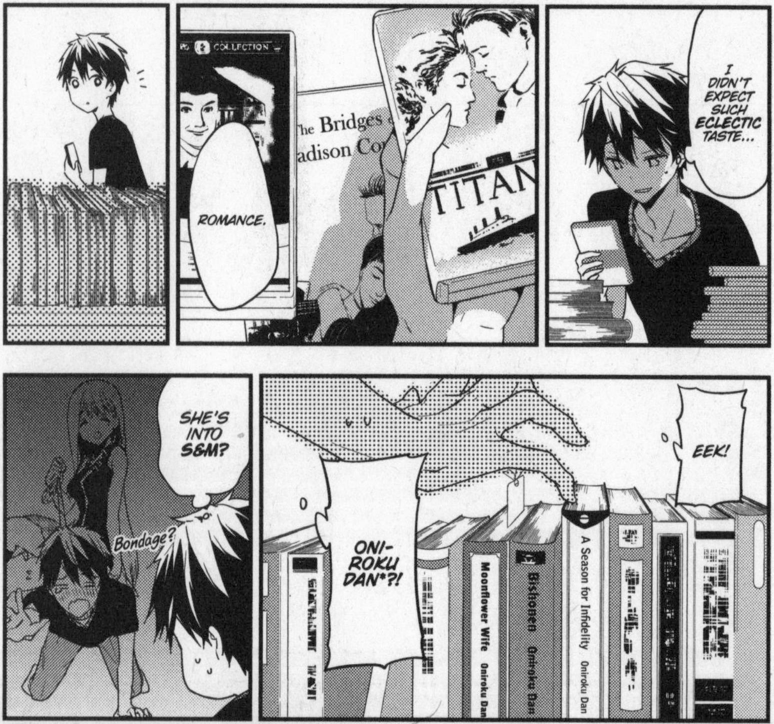
I DIDN'T EXPECT SUCH ECLECTIC TASTE...
ROMANCE.
EEK!
ONI-ROKU DAN*?!
A Season for Infidelity Oniroku Dan
Bishonen Oniroku Dan
Moonflower Wife Oniroku Dan
SHE'S INTO S&M?
Bondage?

*Oniroku Dan is a novelist famous for S&M fantasies, including Futei no Kisetsu, Bishonen, and Yuugao Fujin.

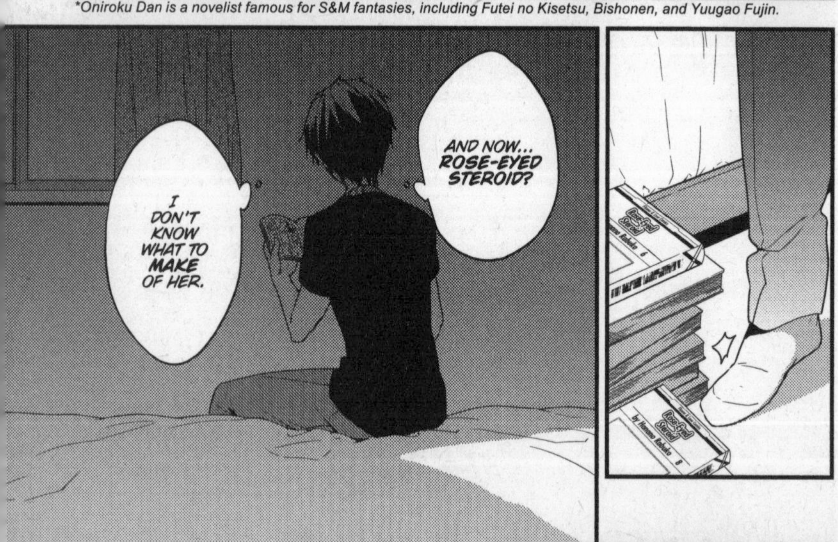
AND NOW... ROSE-EYED STEROID?
I DON'T KNOW WHAT TO MAKE OF HER.

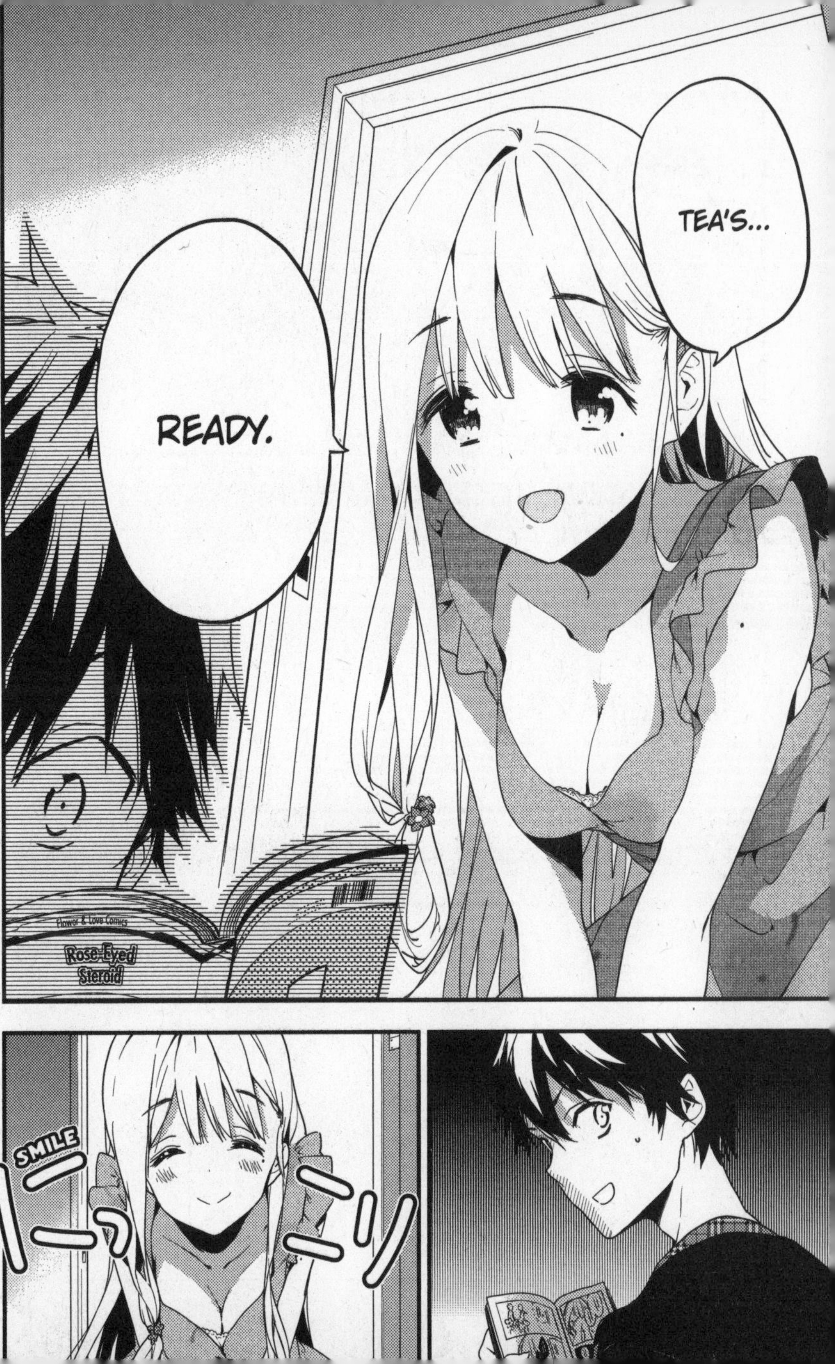
TEA'S...
READY.
Flower & Love Comics
Rose-Eyed Steroid
SMILE

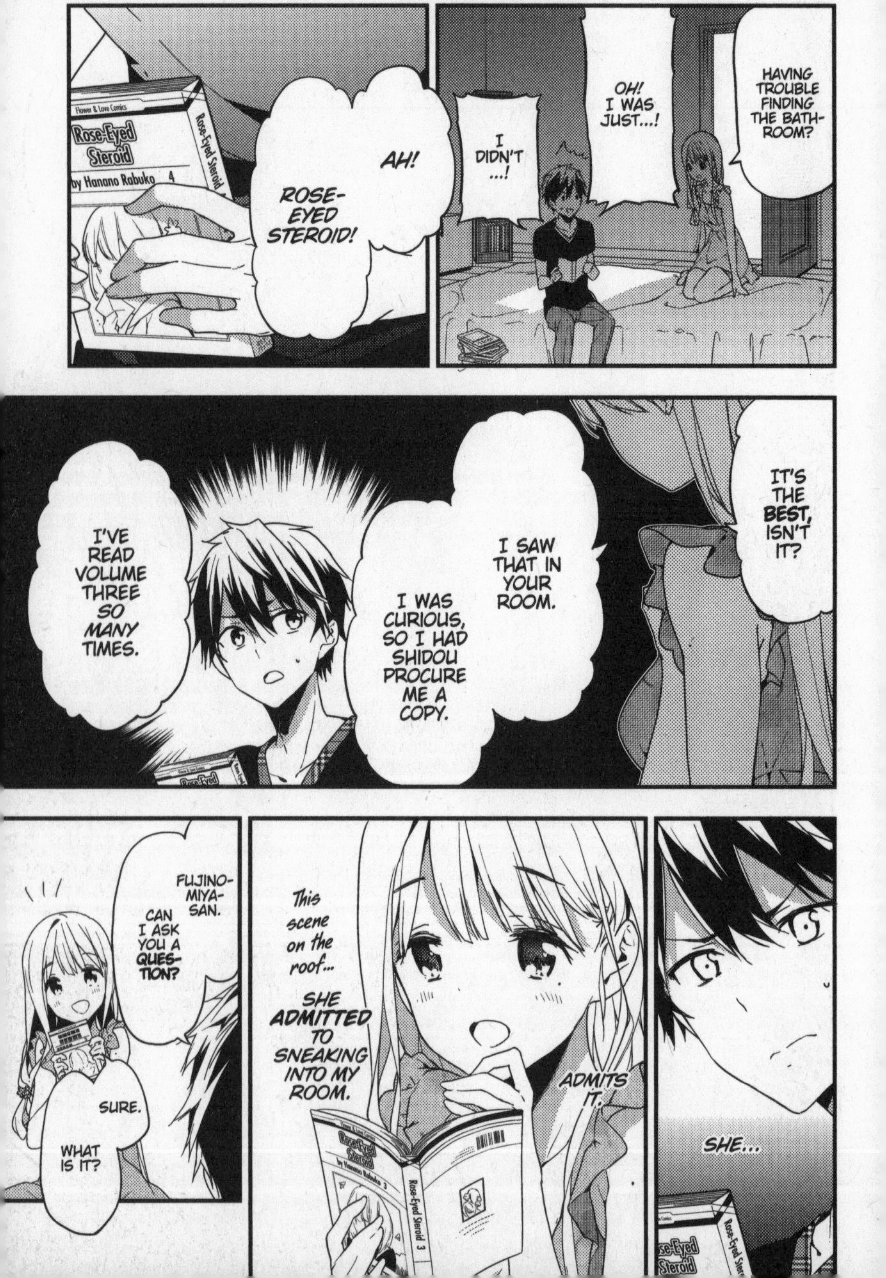
HAVING TROUBLE FINDING THE BATH-ROOM?
OH! I WAS JUST...!
I DIDN'T ...!
Flower & Love Comics
Rose-Eyed Steroid
by Hanano Rabuko 4
AH!
ROSE-EYED STEROID!
IT'S THE BEST, ISN'T IT?
I SAW THAT IN YOUR ROOM.
I WAS CURIOUS, SO I HAD SHIDOU PROCURE ME A COPY.
I'VE READ VOLUME THREE SO MANY TIMES.
SHE...
ADMITS IT.
This scene on the roof...
SHE ADMITTED TO SNEAKING INTO MY ROOM.
Rose-Eyed Steroid
by Hanano Rabuko 3
FUJINO-MIYA-SAN.
CAN I ASK YOU A QUES-TION?
SURE.
WHAT IS IT?

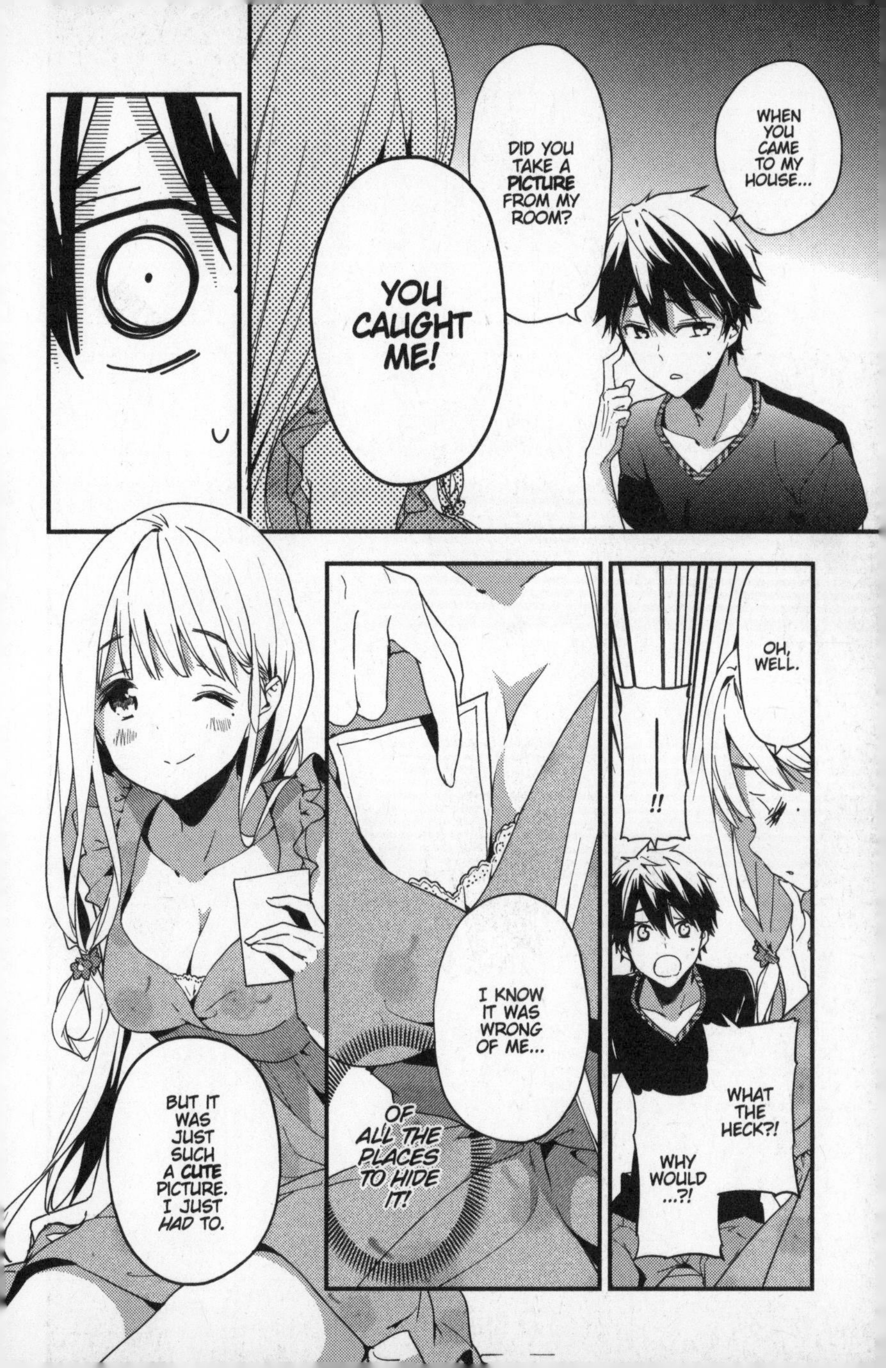
WHEN YOU CAME TO MY HOUSE...
DID YOU TAKE A PICTURE FROM MY ROOM?
YOU CAUGHT ME!
OH, WELL.
!!
WHAT THE HECK?!
WHY WOULD ...?!
I KNOW IT WAS WRONG OF ME...
OF ALL THE PLACES TO HIDE IT!
BUT IT WAS JUST SUCH A CUTE PICTURE. I JUST HAD TO.

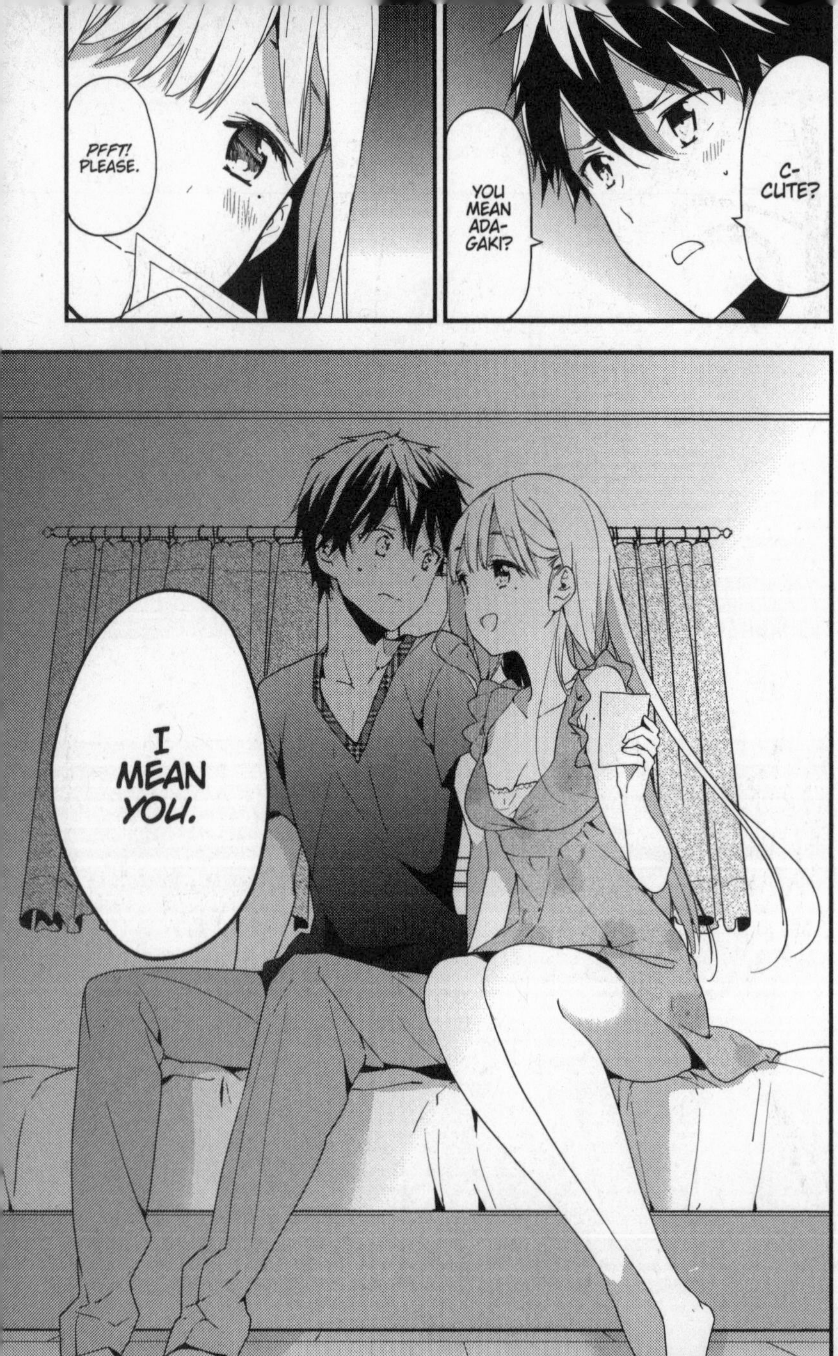
C-CUTE?
YOU MEAN ADA-GAKI?
PFFT! PLEASE.
I MEAN YOU.

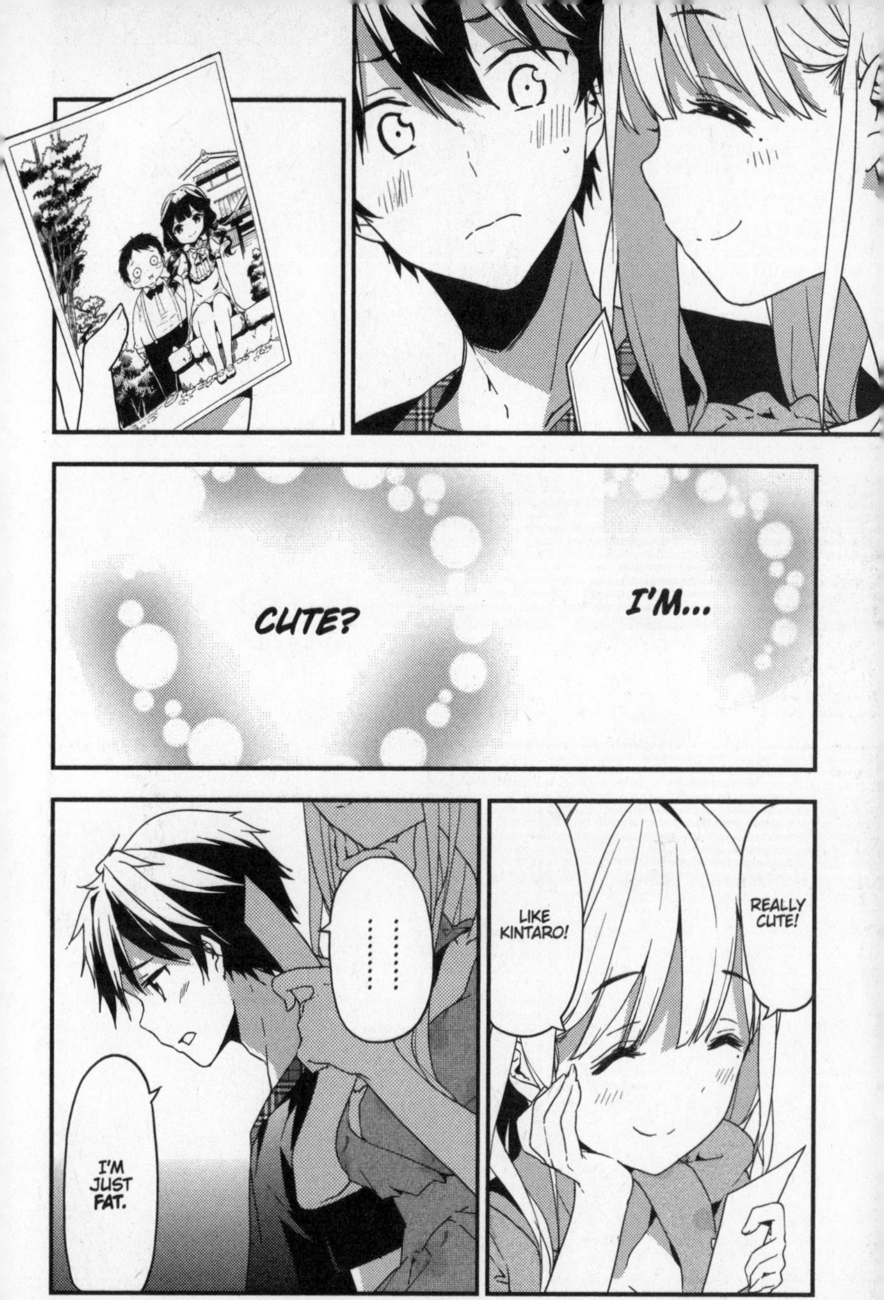
I'M...
CUTE?
REALLY CUTE!
LIKE KINTARO!
......
I'M JUST FAT.

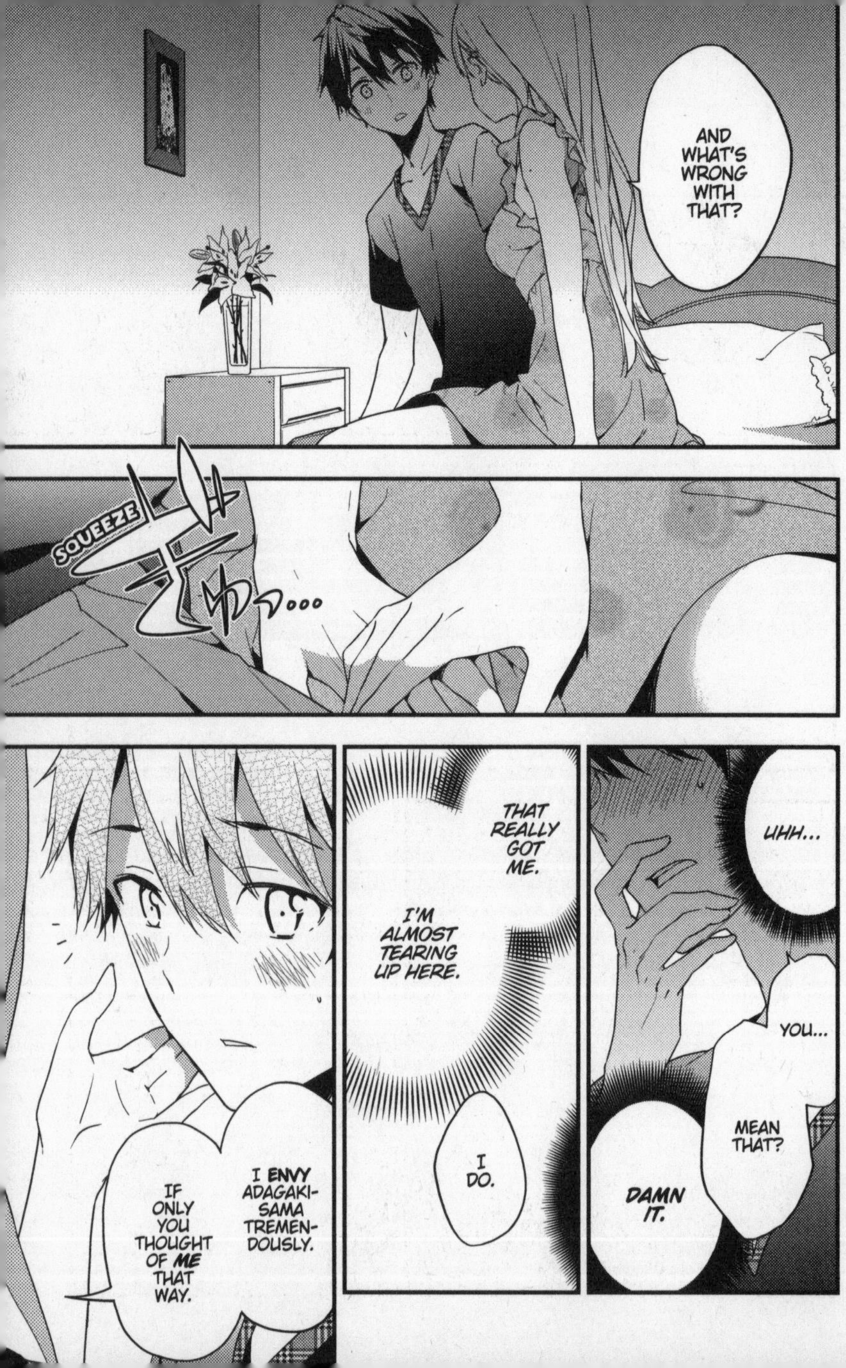
AND WHAT'S WRONG WITH THAT?
SQUEEZE
UHH...
YOU...
MEAN THAT?
DAMN IT.
THAT REALLY GOT ME.
I'M ALMOST TEARING UP HERE.
I DO.
I ENVY ADAGAKI-SAMA TREMENDOUSLY.
IF ONLY YOU THOUGHT OF ME THAT WAY.

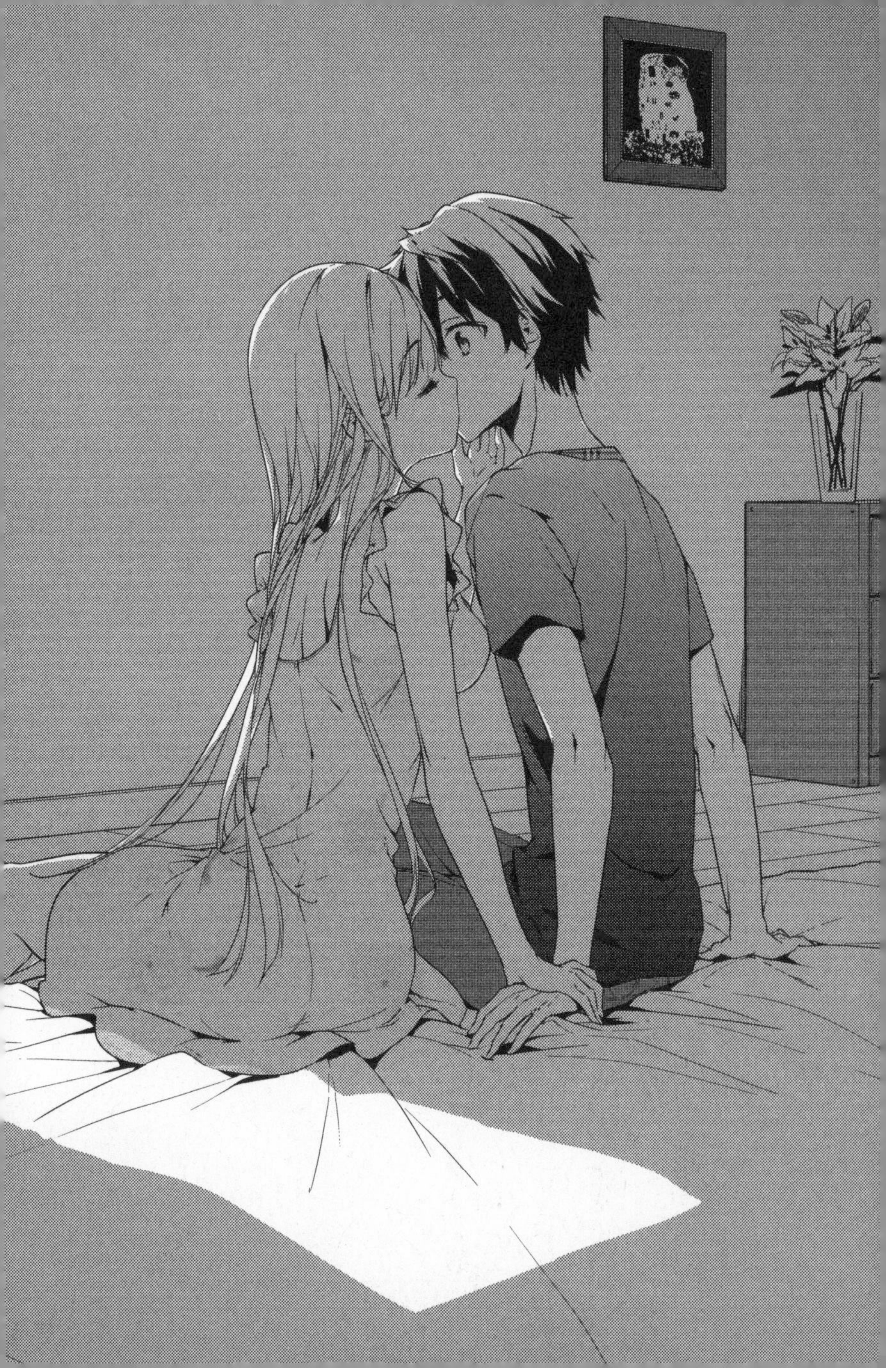

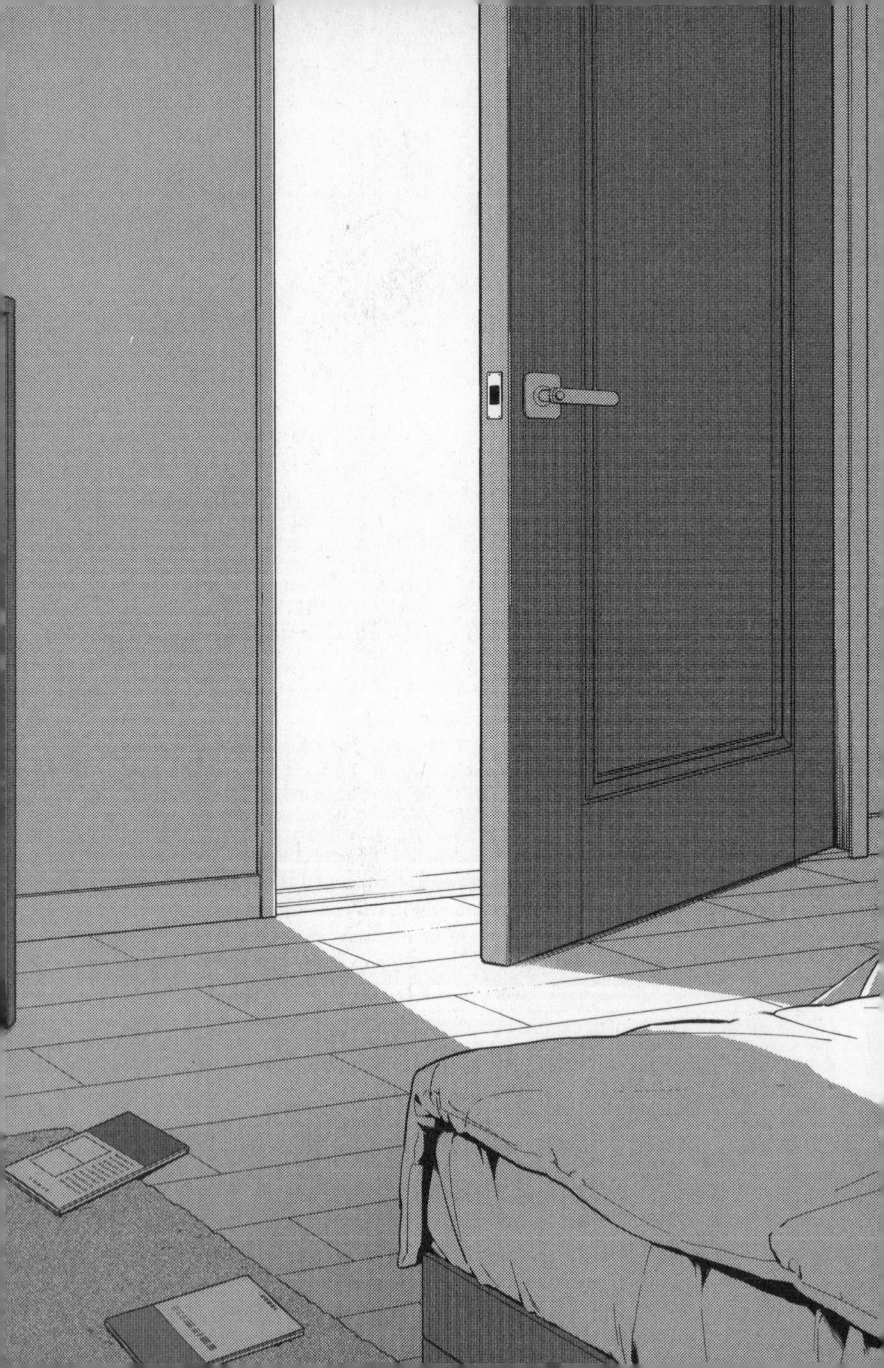

GIRL'S LIPS...

PRESSED AGAINST MINE...

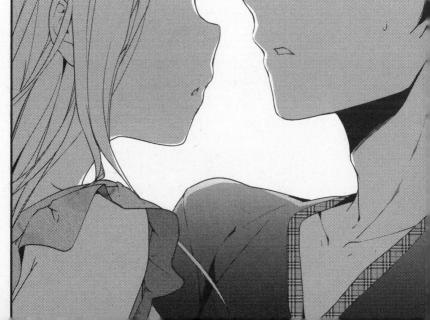

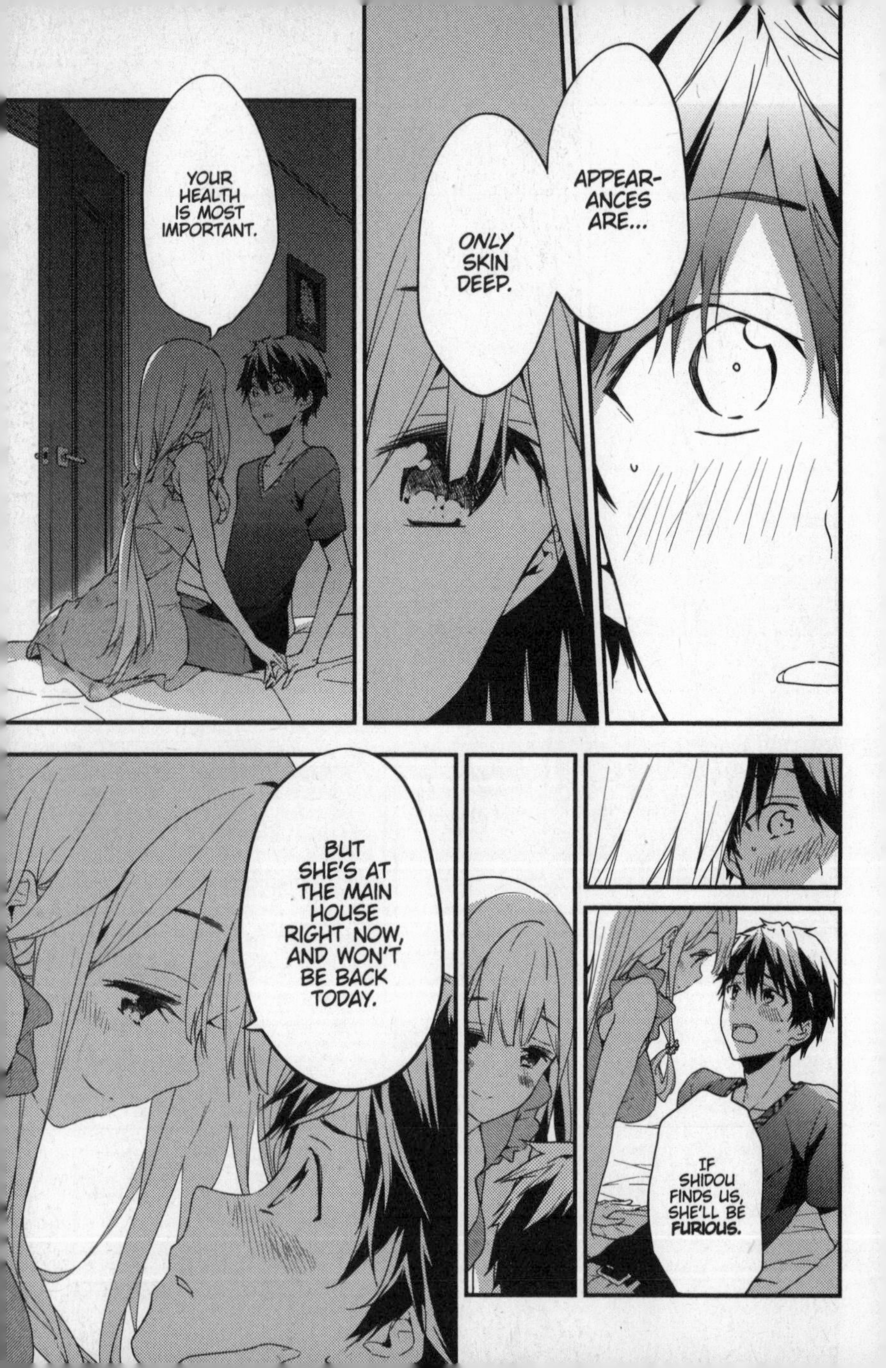
APPEARANCES ARE...
ONLY SKIN DEEP.
YOUR HEALTH IS MOST IMPORTANT.
IF SHIDOU FINDS US, SHE'LL BE **FURIOUS**.
BUT SHE'S AT THE MAIN HOUSE RIGHT NOW, AND WON'T BE BACK TODAY.

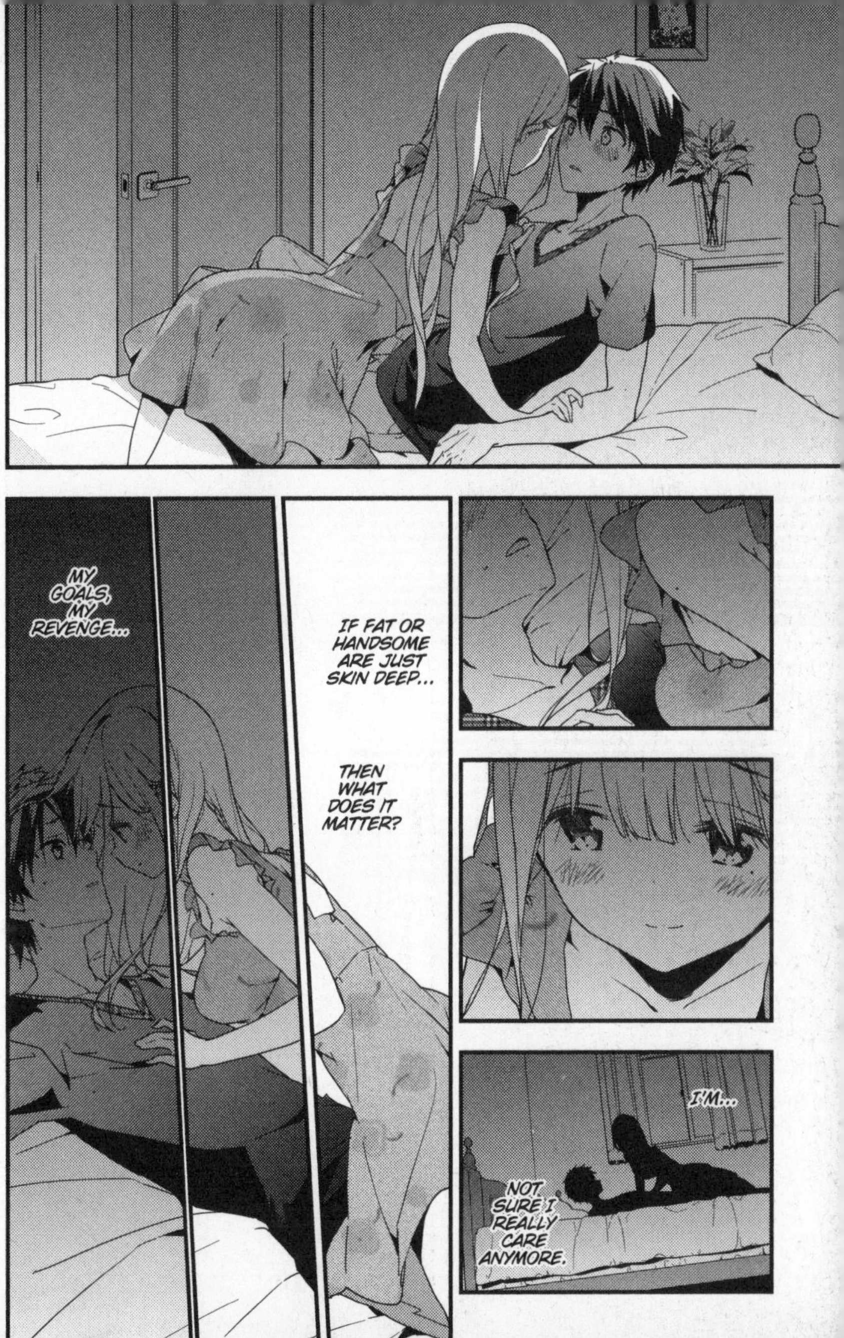
I'M...
NOT SURE I REALLY CARE ANYMORE.
IF FAT OR HANDSOME ARE JUST SKIN DEEP...
THEN WHAT DOES IT MATTER?
MY GOALS, MY REVENGE...

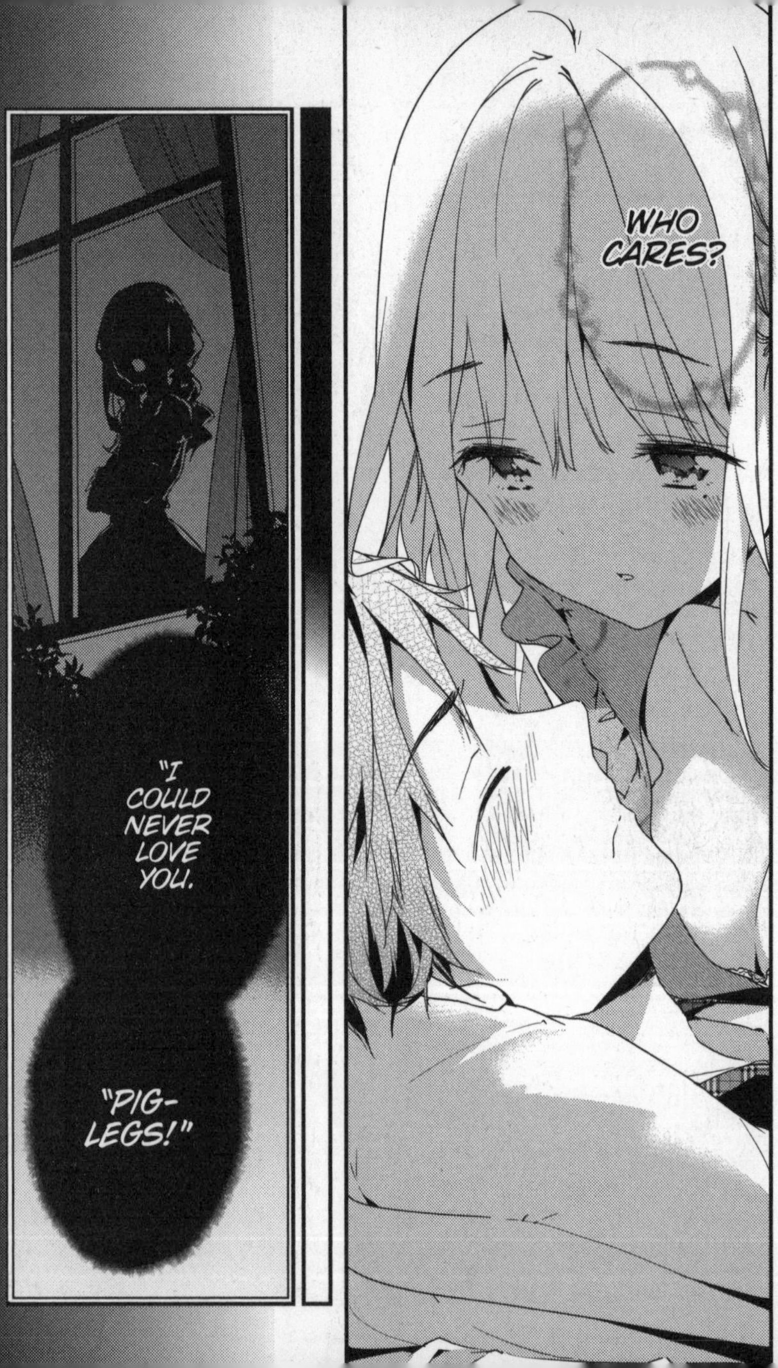
WHO CARES?
"I COULD NEVER LOVE YOU.
"PIG-LEGS!"

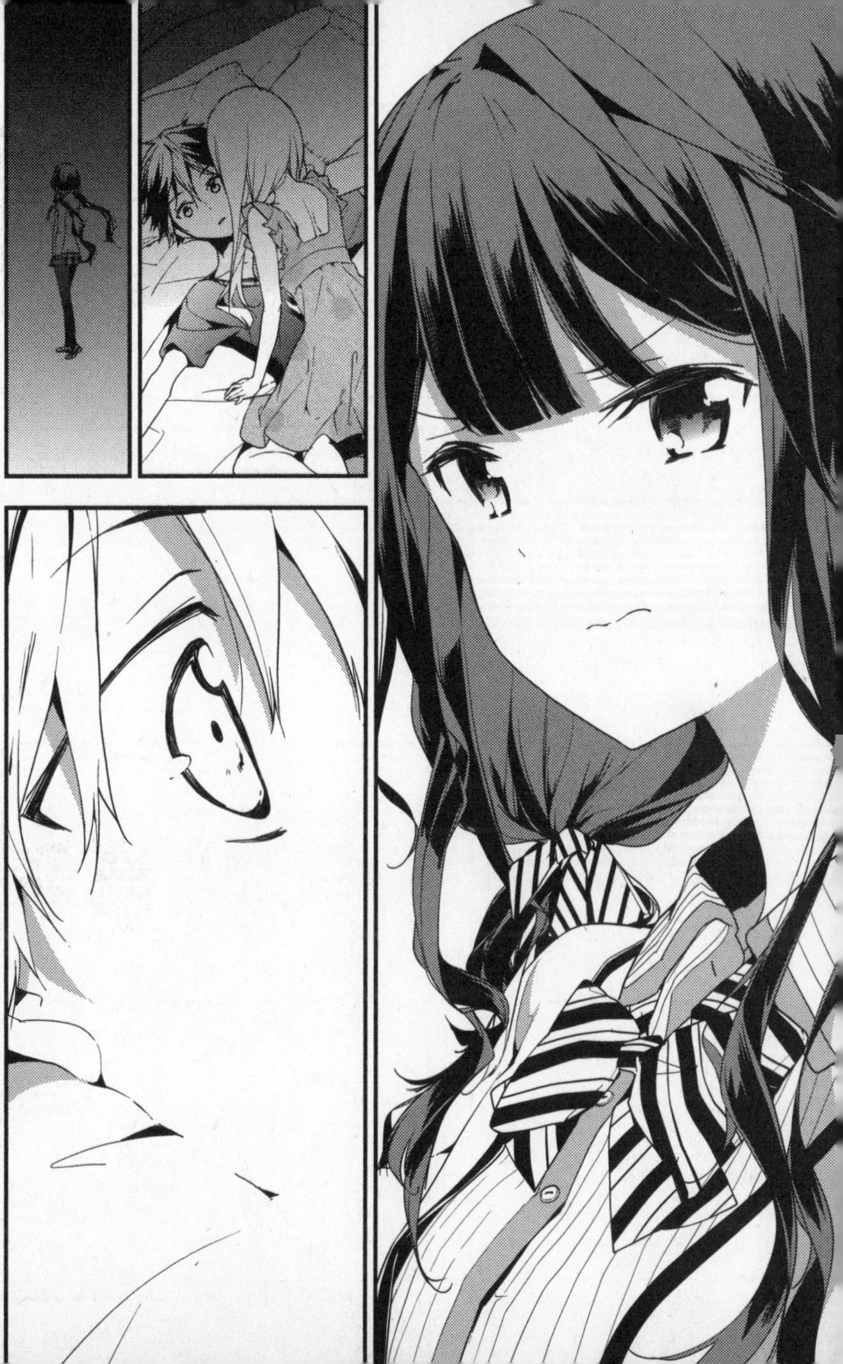

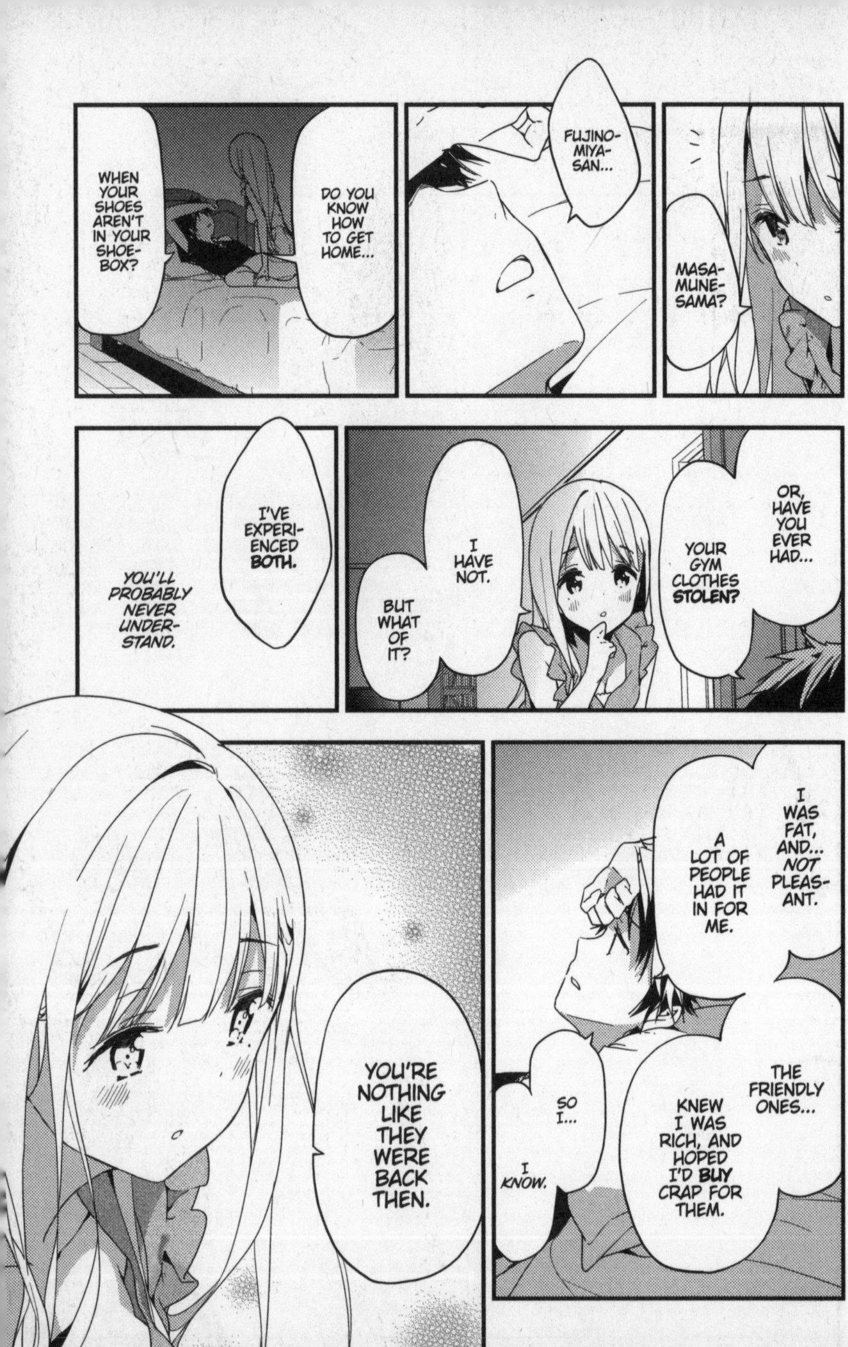
MASA-MUNE-SAMA?
FUJINO-MIYA-SAN...
DO YOU KNOW HOW TO GET HOME...
WHEN YOUR SHOES AREN'T IN YOUR SHOE-BOX?
OR, HAVE YOU EVER HAD...
YOUR GYM CLOTHES **STOLEN?**
I HAVE NOT.
BUT WHAT OF IT?
I'VE EXPERIENCED **BOTH.**
YOU'LL PROBABLY NEVER UNDER-STAND.
I WAS FAT, AND... *NOT* PLEAS-ANT.
A LOT OF PEOPLE HAD IT IN FOR ME.
THE FRIENDLY ONES...
KNEW I WAS RICH, AND HOPED I'D **BUY** CRAP FOR THEM.
SO I...
I *KNOW.*
YOU'RE NOTHING LIKE THEY WERE BACK THEN.

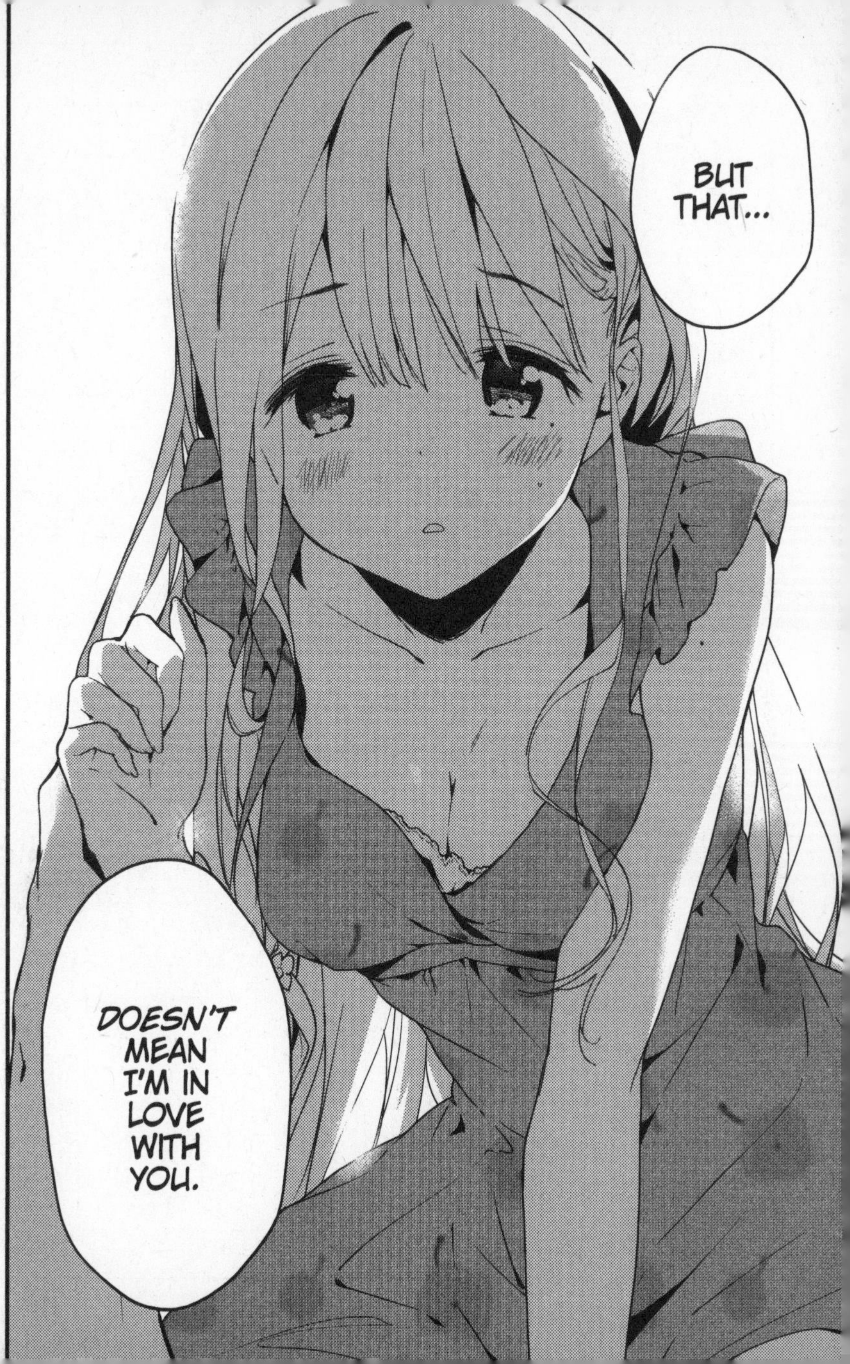
BUT THAT...
DOESN'T MEAN I'M IN LOVE WITH YOU.

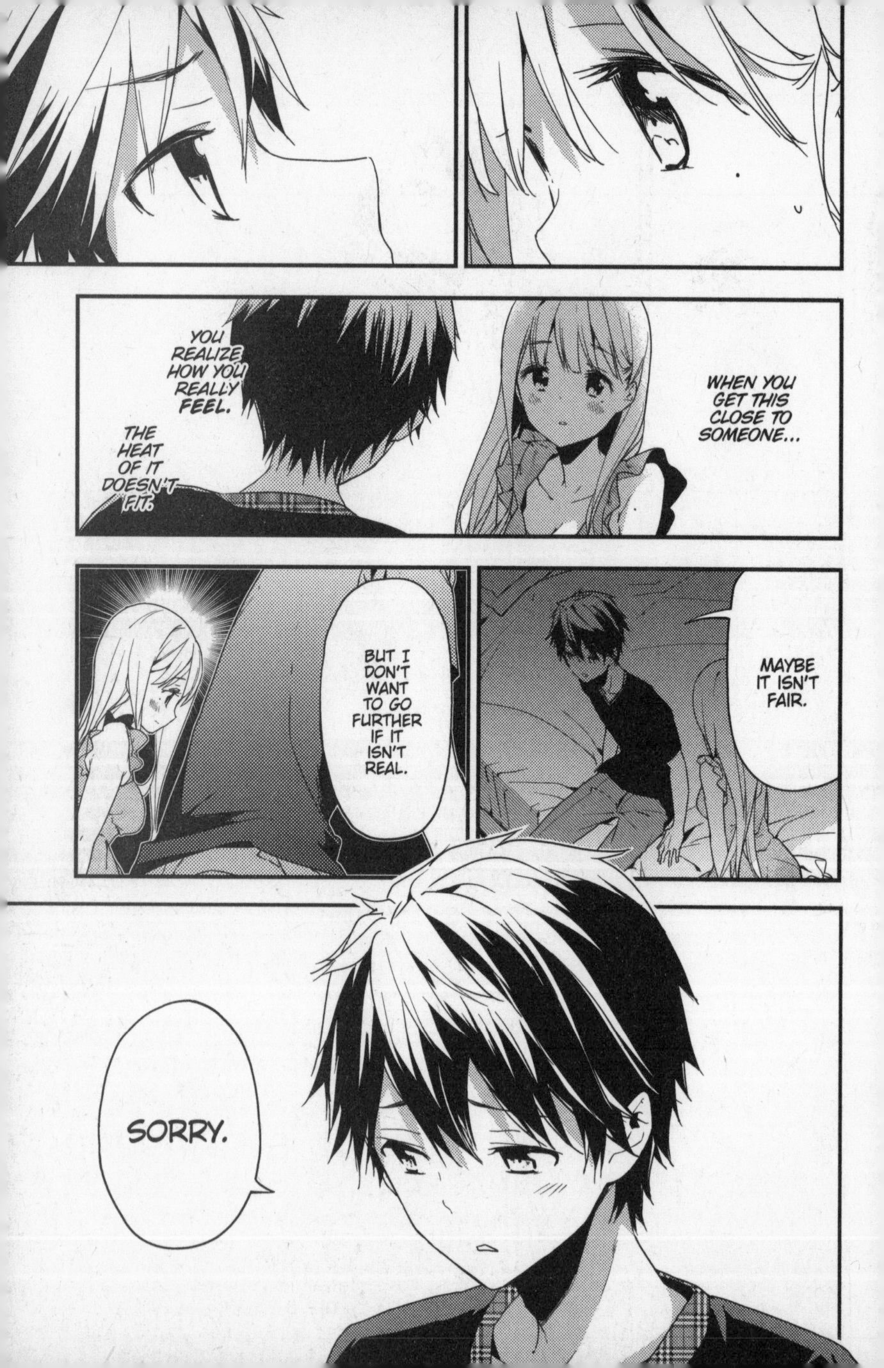
WHEN YOU GET THIS CLOSE TO SOMEONE...
YOU REALIZE HOW YOU REALLY FEEL.
THE HEAT OF IT DOESN'T FIT.
MAYBE IT ISN'T FAIR.
BUT I DON'T WANT TO GO FURTHER IF IT ISN'T REAL.
SORRY.

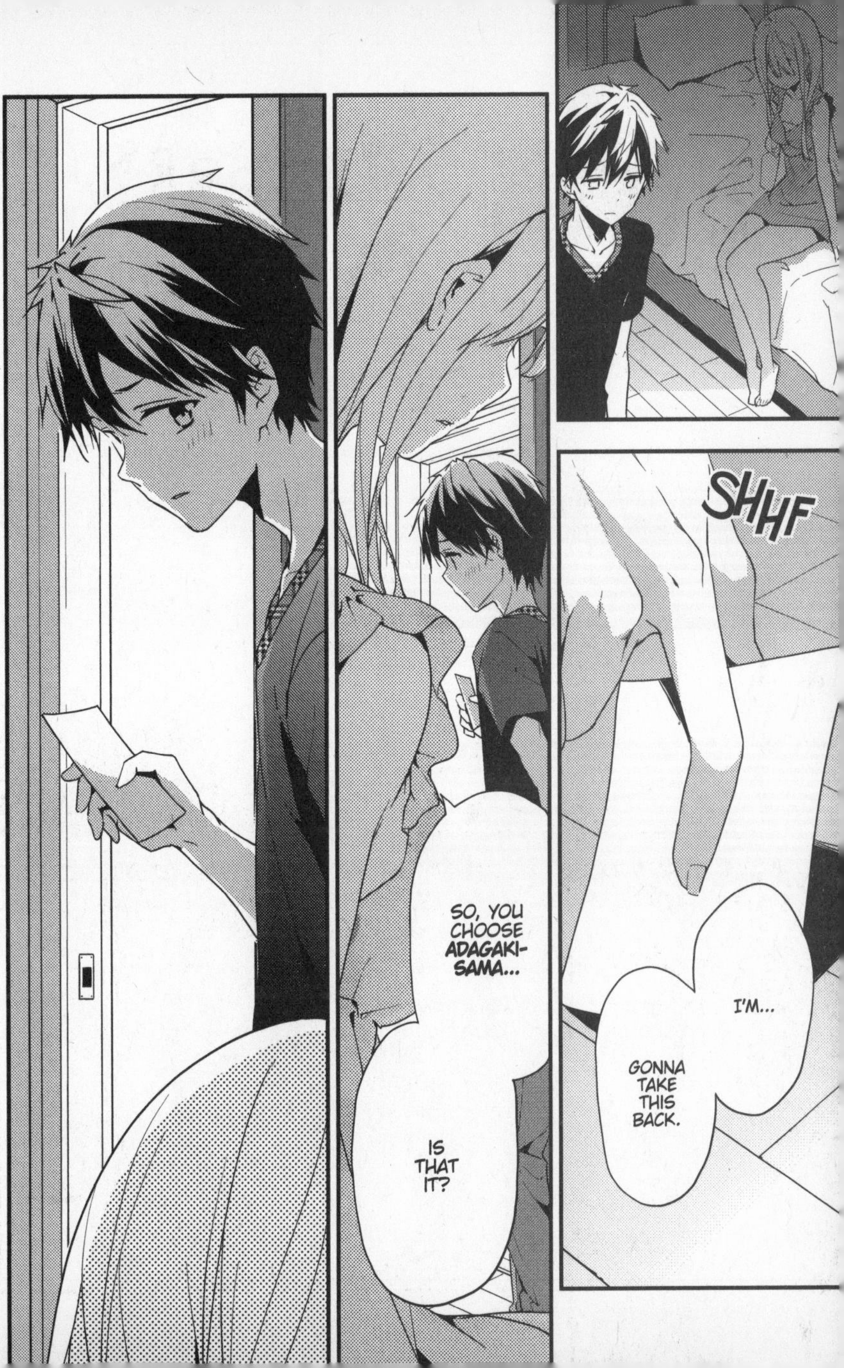
SHHF
I'M...
GONNA TAKE THIS BACK.
SO, YOU CHOOSE ADAGAKI-SAMA...
IS THAT IT?

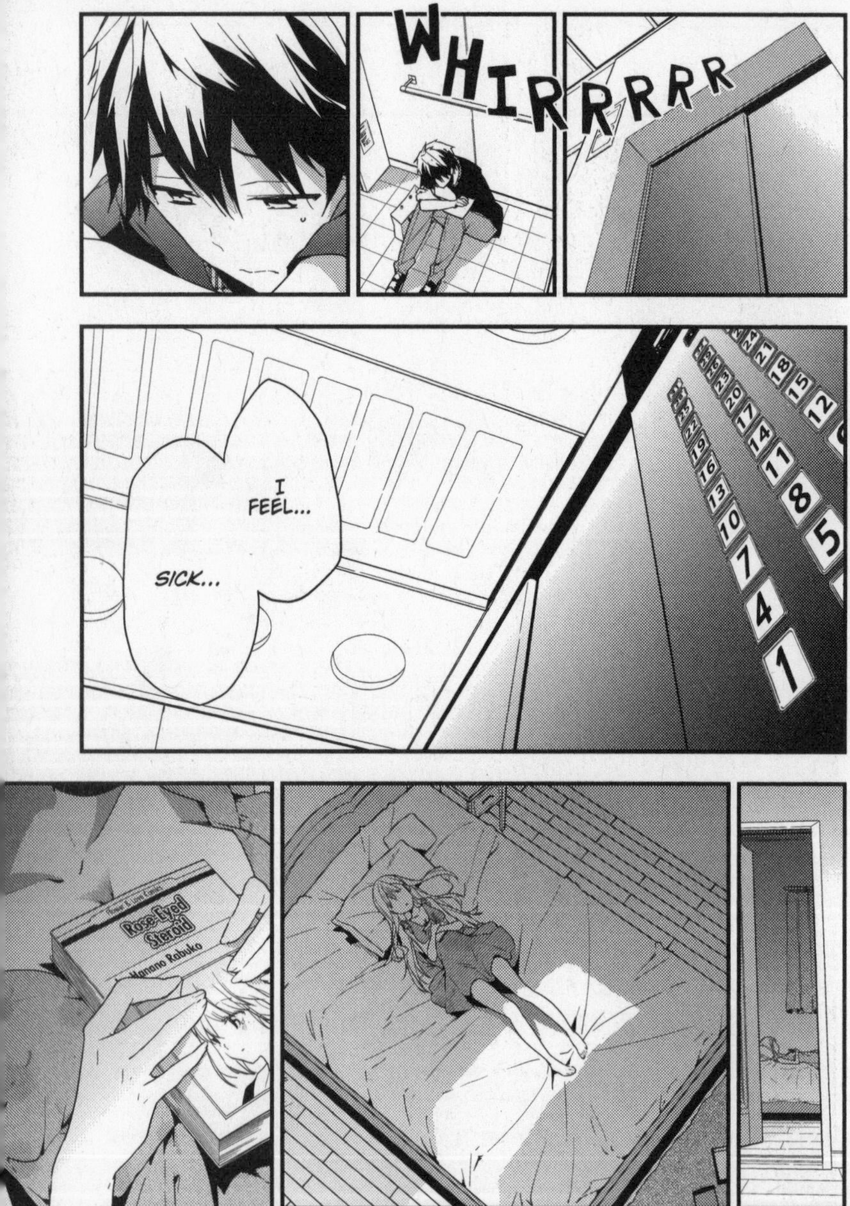
WHIRRRRR
I FEEL...
SICK...
Rose-Eyed Steroid
Hanano Rabuko

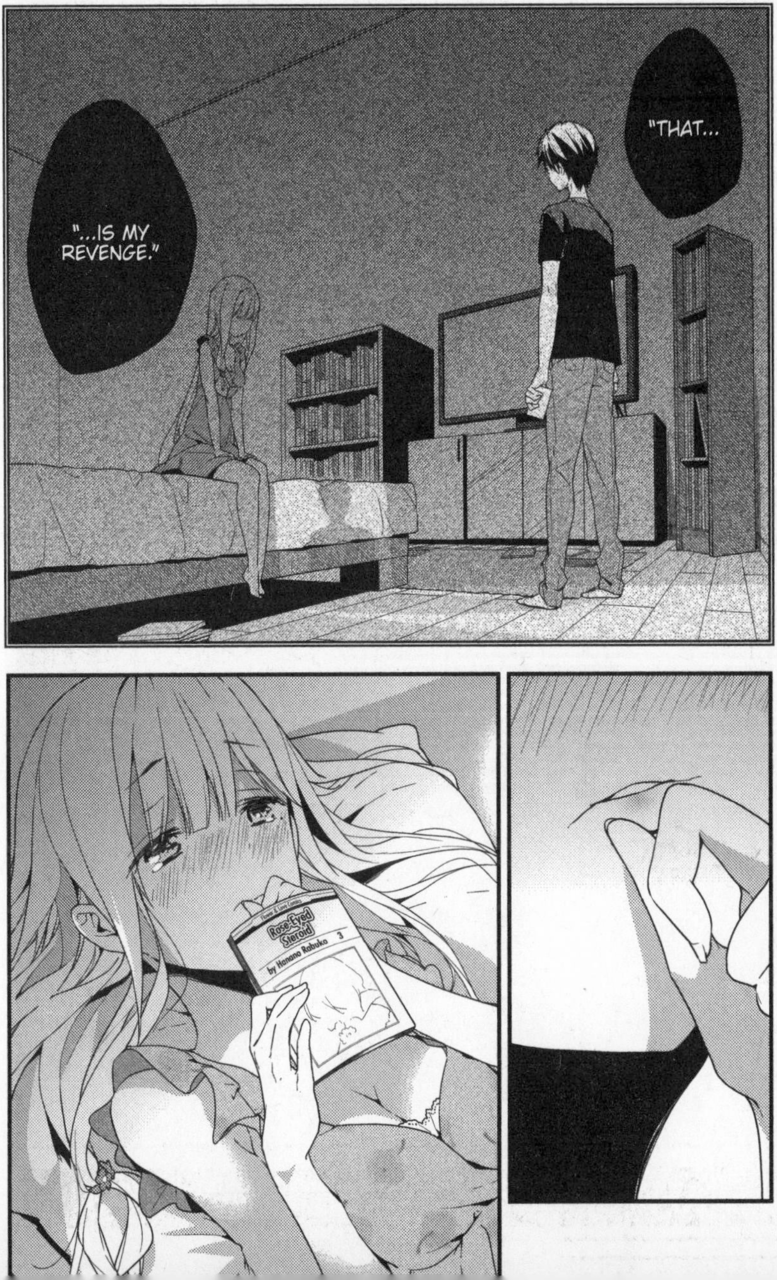
"THAT...
"...IS MY REVENGE."
Rose-Eyed Steroid
3
by Hanano Rabuko

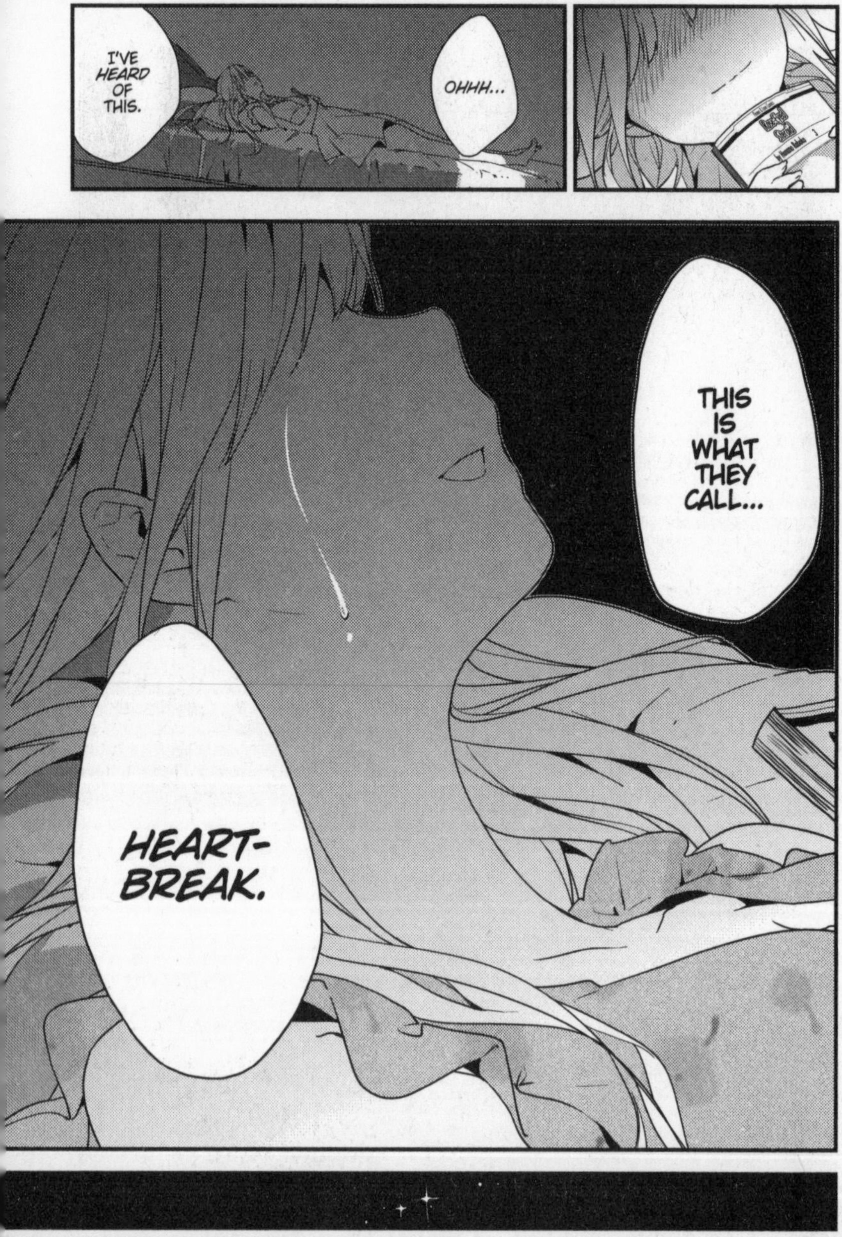
OHHH...
I'VE HEARD OF THIS.
THIS IS WHAT THEY CALL...
HEART-BREAK.

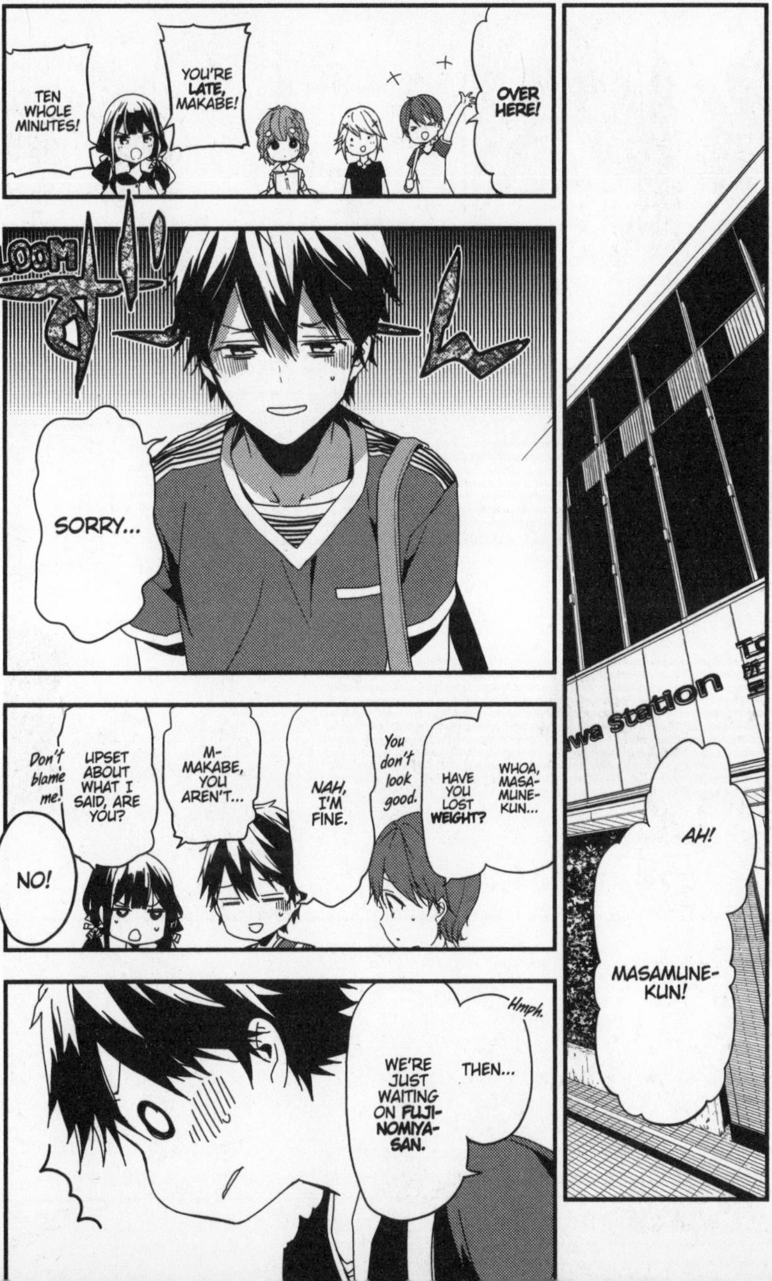
wa Station
AH!
MASAMUNE-KUN!
OVER HERE!
YOU'RE LATE, MAKABE!
TEN WHOLE MINUTES!
GLOOM
SORRY...
WHOA, MASAMUNE-KUN...
HAVE YOU LOST WEIGHT?
You don't look good.
NAH, I'M FINE.
M-MAKABE, YOU AREN'T...
UPSET ABOUT WHAT I SAID, ARE YOU?
Don't blame me!
NO!
Hmph.
THEN...
WE'RE JUST WAITING ON FUJINOMIYA-SAN.

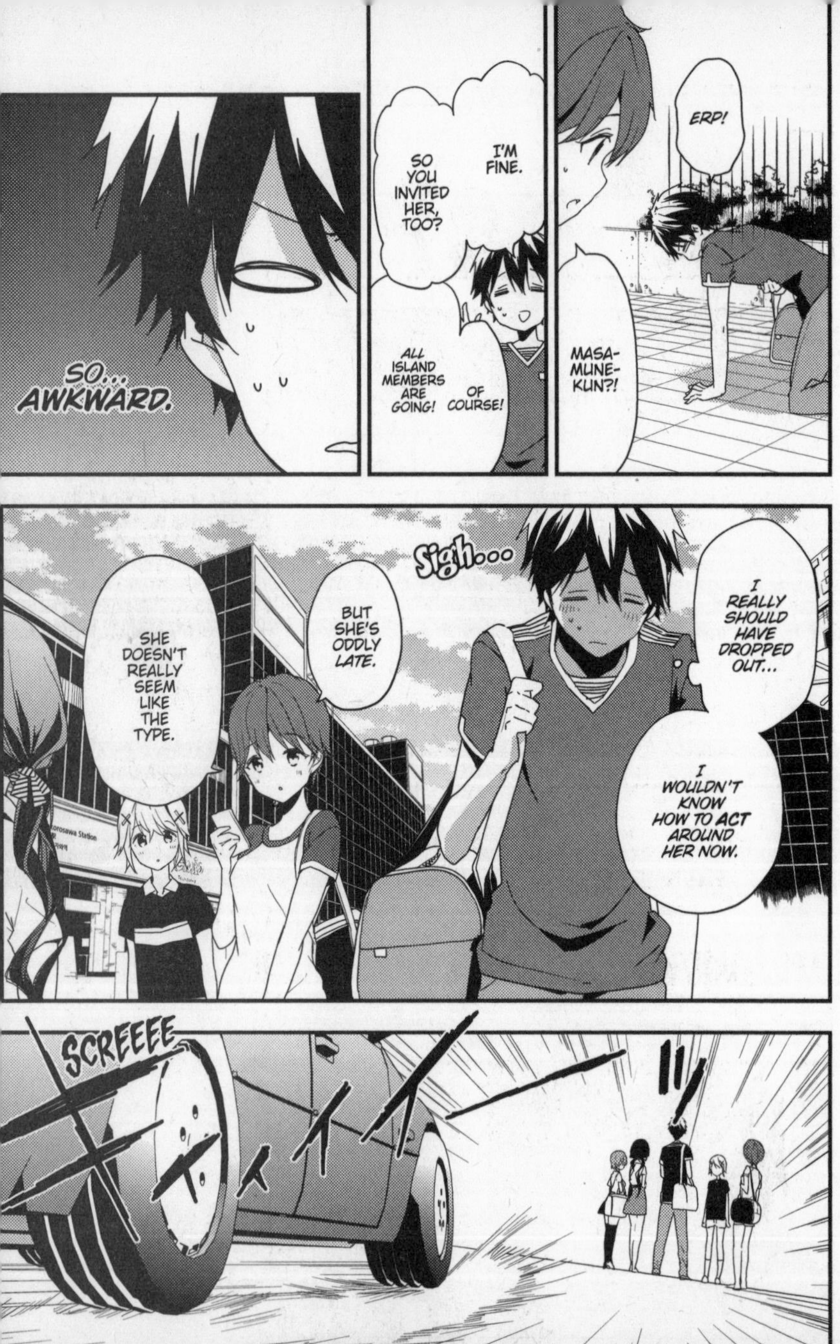
ERP!
MASA-MUNE-KUN?!
I'M FINE.
SO YOU INVITED HER, TOO?
OF COURSE!
ALL ISLAND MEMBERS ARE GOING!
SO... AWKWARD.
I REALLY SHOULD HAVE DROPPED OUT...
I WOULDN'T KNOW HOW TO ACT AROUND HER NOW.
Sigh...
BUT SHE'S ODDLY LATE.
SHE DOESN'T REALLY SEEM LIKE THE TYPE.
!!
SCREEEE

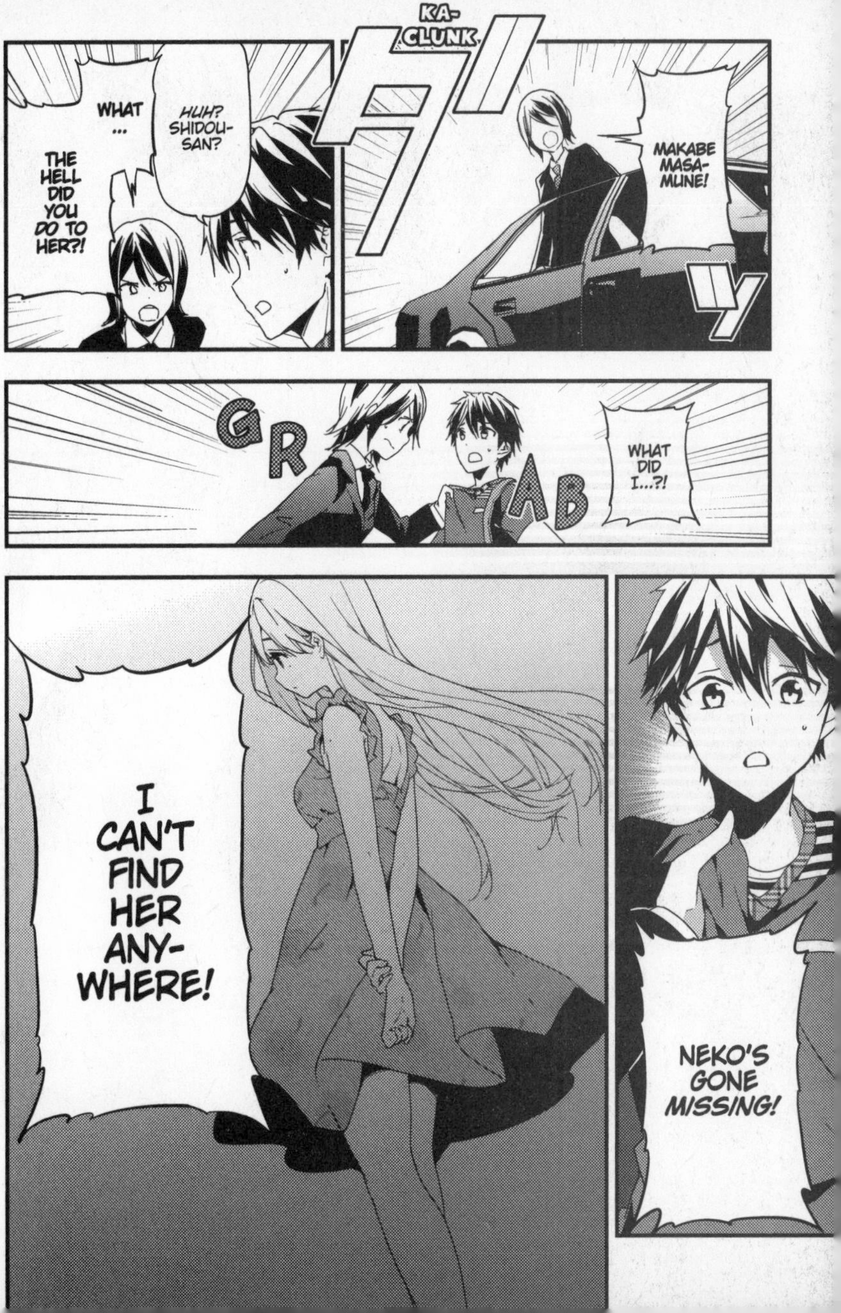
KA-CLUNK
MAKABE MASAMUNE!
HUH? SHIDOU-SAN?
WHAT ... THE HELL DID YOU DO TO HER?!
GRAB
WHAT DID I...?!
NEKO'S GONE MISSING!
I CAN'T FIND HER ANY-WHERE!

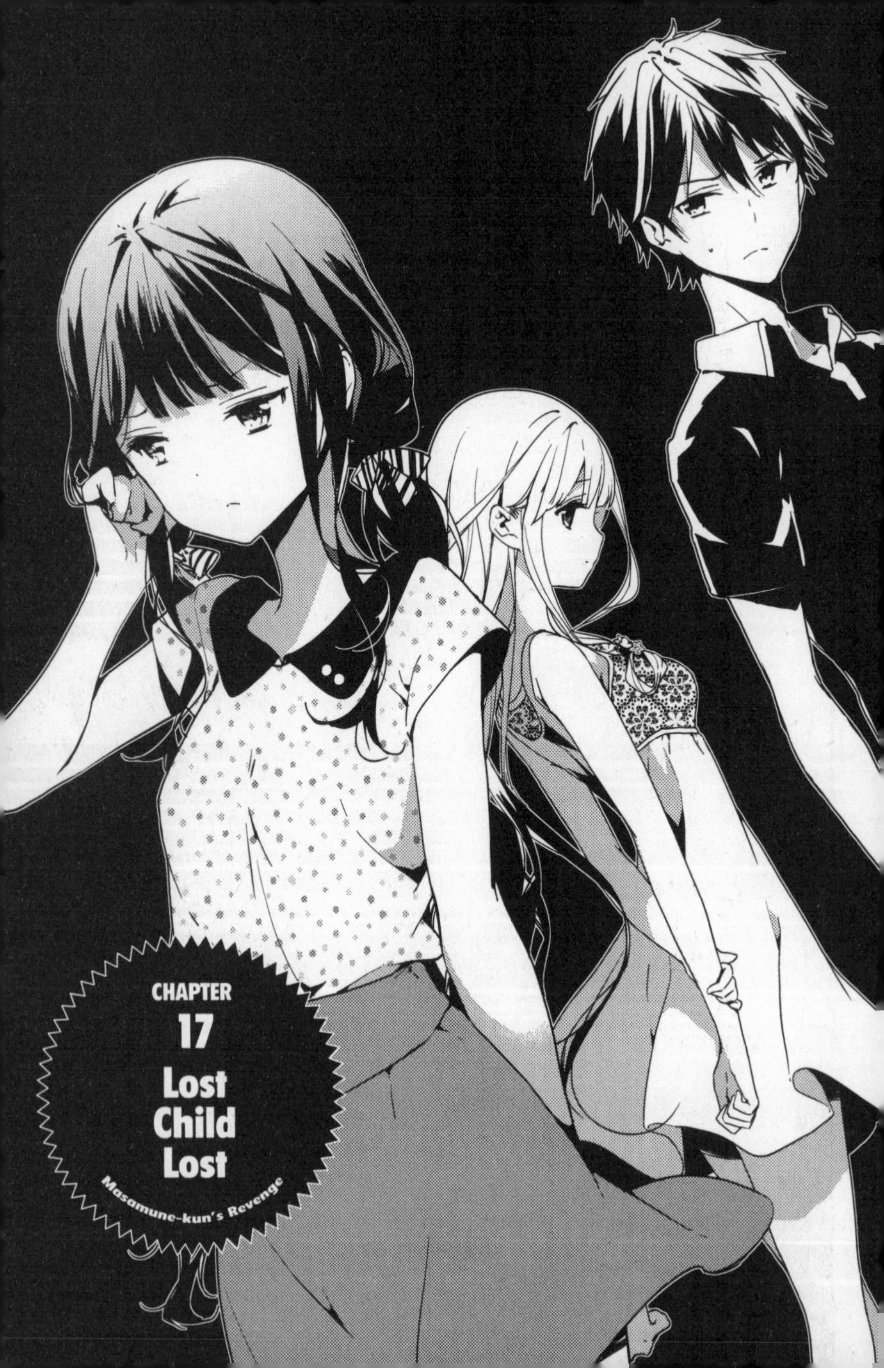
CHAPTER
17
Lost
Child
Lost
Masamune-kun's Revenge

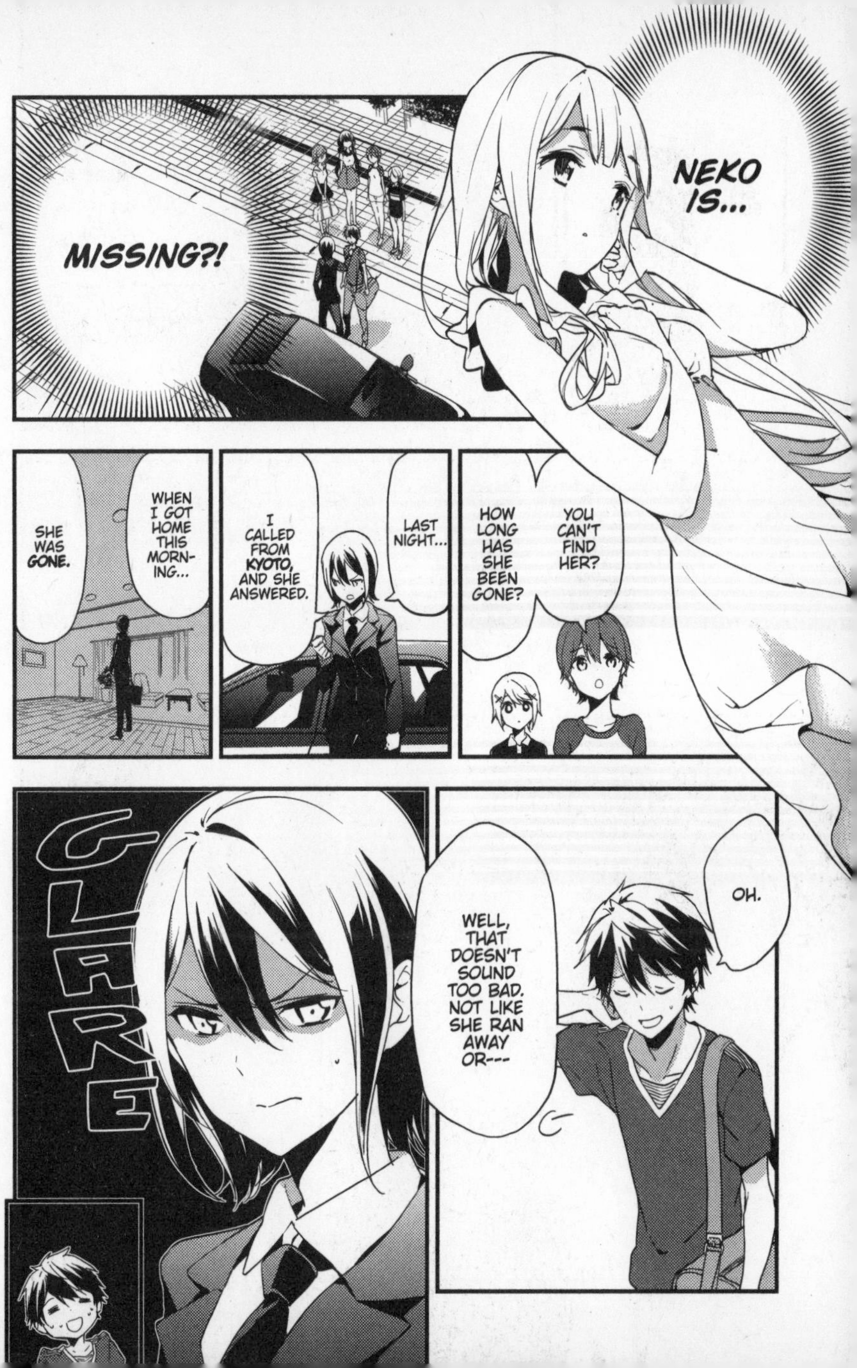
NEKO IS...
MISSING?!
YOU CAN'T FIND HER?
HOW LONG HAS SHE BEEN GONE?
LAST NIGHT...
I CALLED FROM KYOTO, AND SHE ANSWERED.
WHEN I GOT HOME THIS MORNING...
SHE WAS GONE.
OH.
WELL, THAT DOESN'T SOUND TOO BAD. NOT LIKE SHE RAN AWAY OR---
GLARE

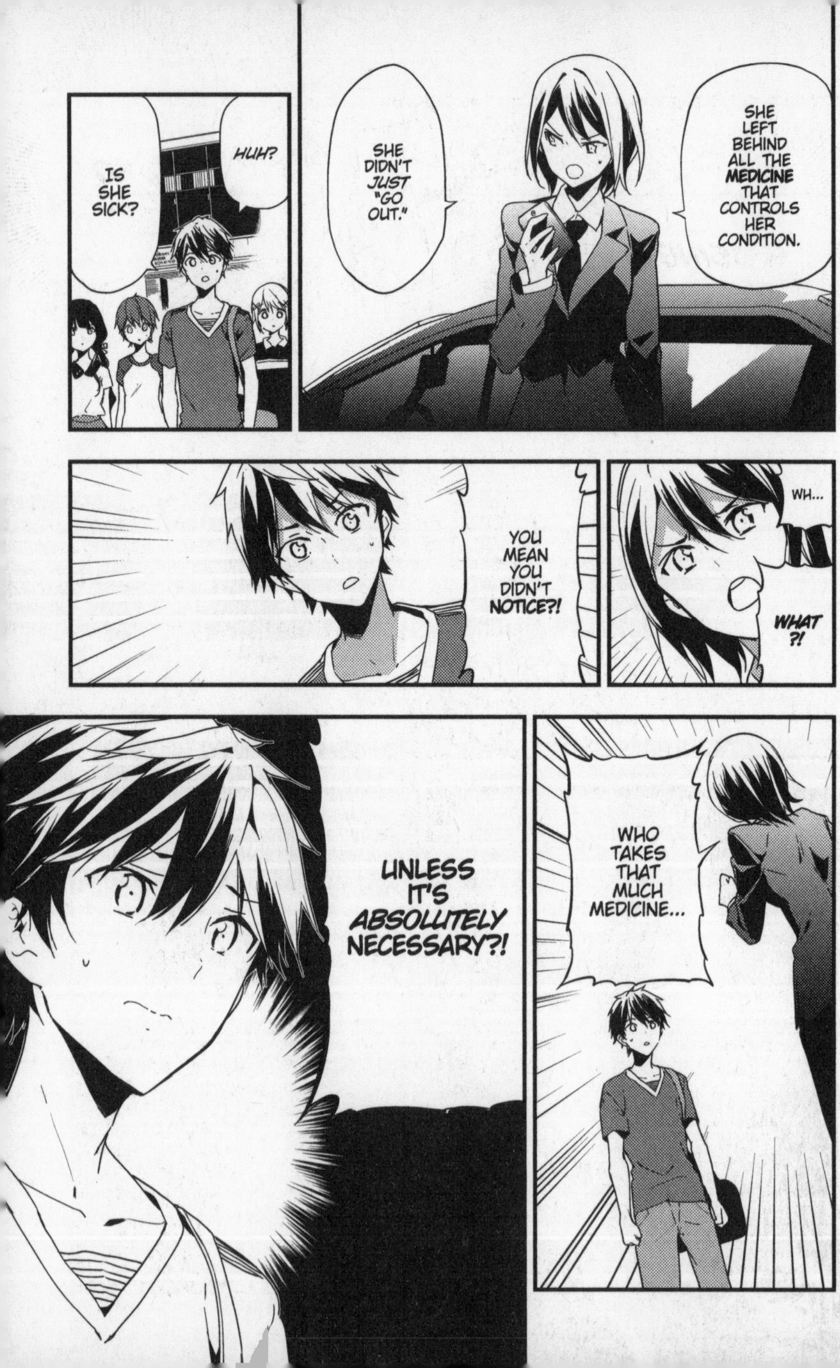
SHE LEFT BEHIND ALL THE MEDICINE THAT CONTROLS HER CONDITION.
SHE DIDN'T JUST "GO OUT."
HUH?
IS SHE SICK?
WH...
WHAT?!
YOU MEAN YOU DIDN'T NOTICE?!
WHO TAKES THAT MUCH MEDICINE...
UNLESS IT'S ABSOLUTELY NECESSARY?!

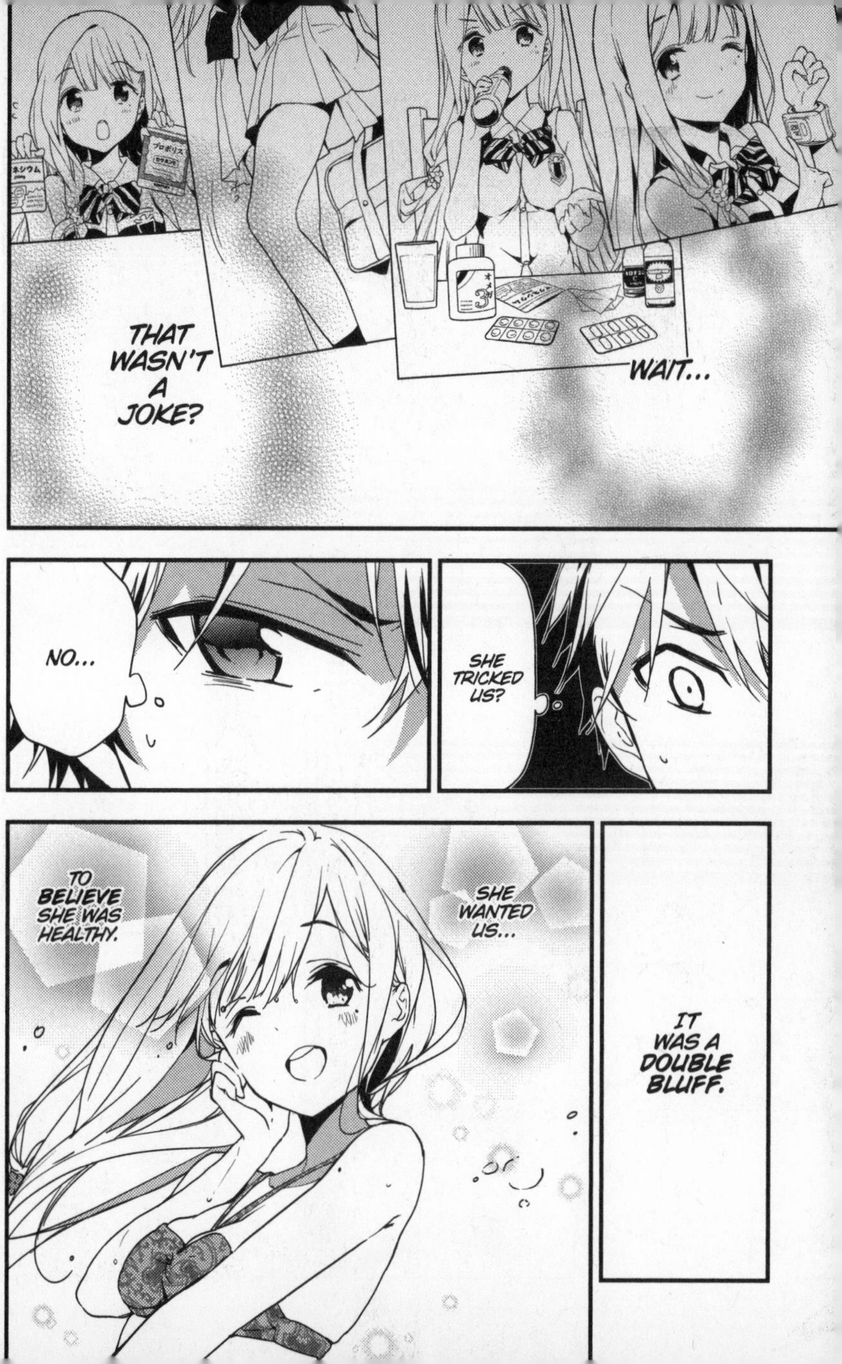
WAIT...
THAT WASN'T A JOKE?
SHE TRICKED US?
NO...
IT WAS A DOUBLE BLUFF.
SHE WANTED US...
TO BELIEVE SHE WAS HEALTHY.

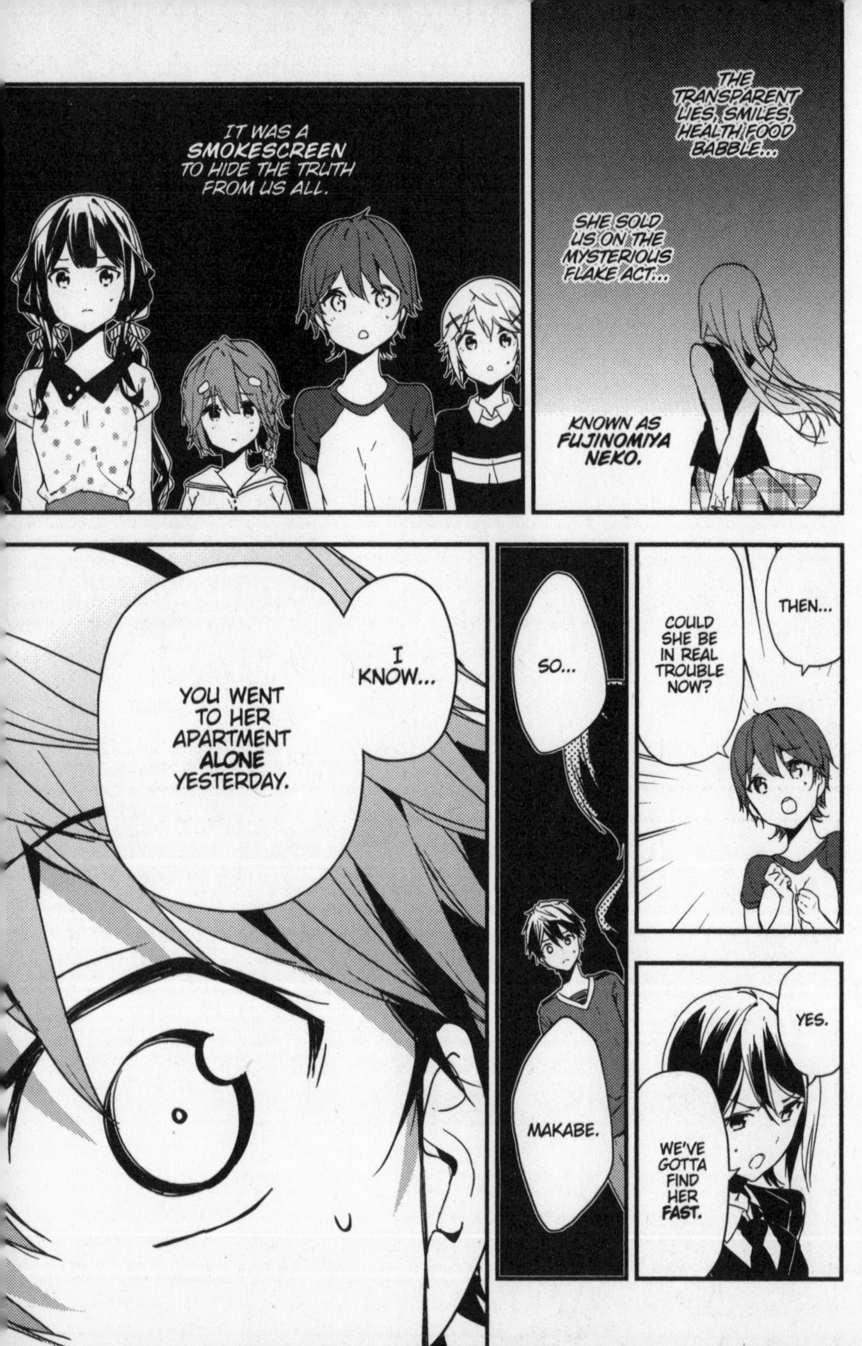
THE TRANSPARENT LIES, SMILES, HEALTH FOOD BABBLE...
SHE SOLD US ON THE MYSTERIOUS FLAKE ACT...
KNOWN AS FUJINOMIYA NEKO.
IT WAS A SMOKESCREEN TO HIDE THE TRUTH FROM US ALL.
THEN...
COULD SHE BE IN REAL TROUBLE NOW?
YES.
WE'VE GOTTA FIND HER FAST.
SO...
MAKABE.
I KNOW...
YOU WENT TO HER APARTMENT ALONE YESTERDAY.

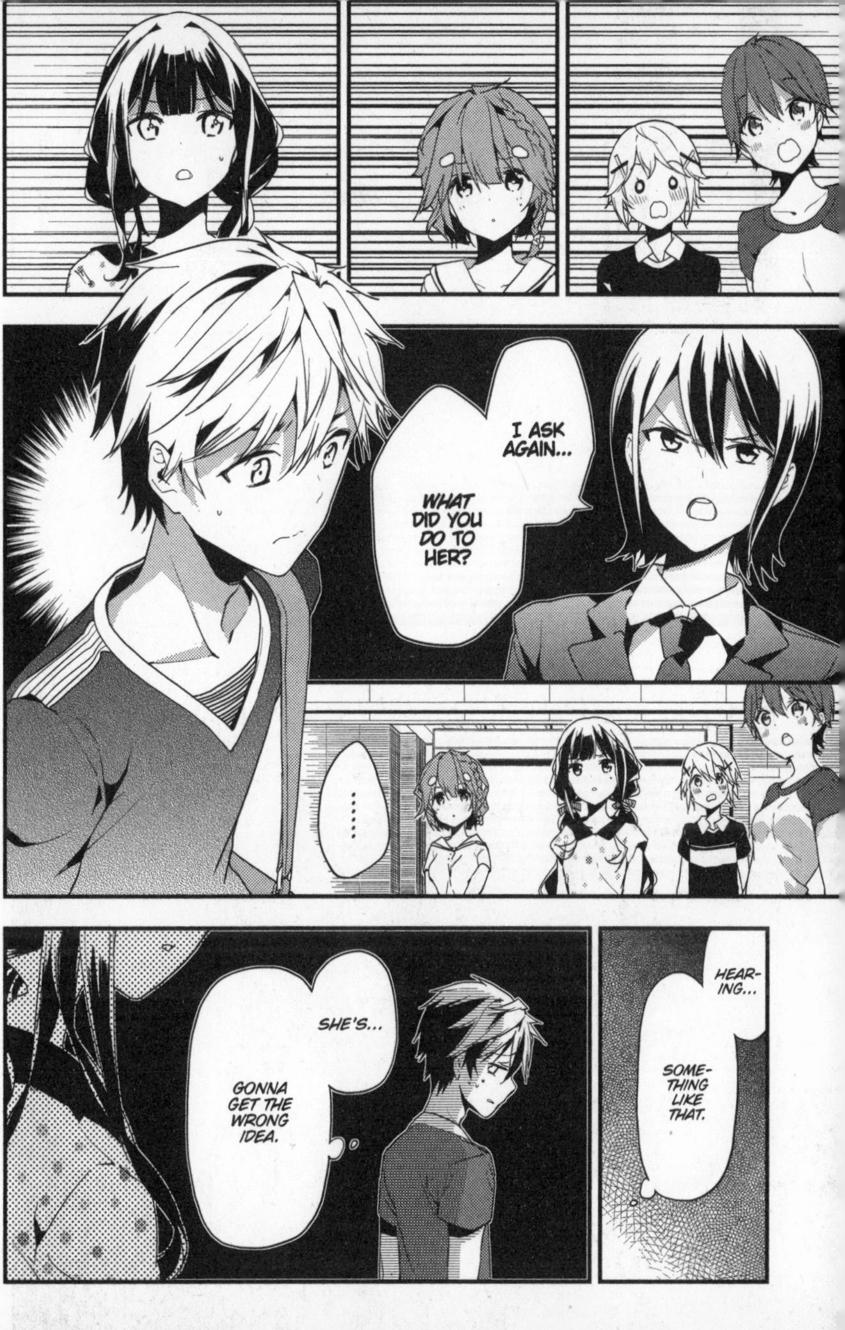
I ASK AGAIN...
WHAT DID YOU DO TO HER?
......
HEARING...
SOMETHING LIKE THAT.
SHE'S...
GONNA GET THE WRONG IDEA.

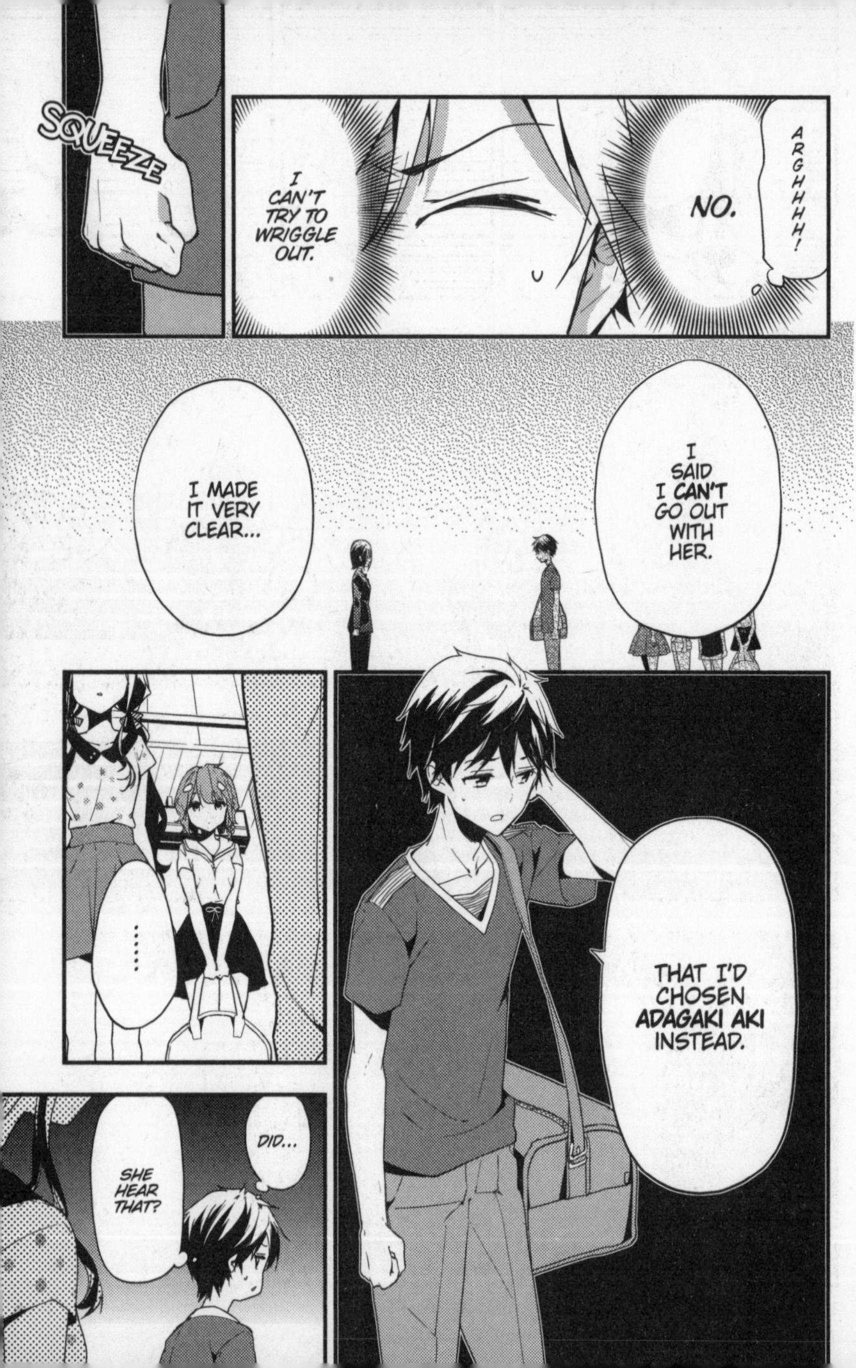
ARGHHHH!
NO.
I CAN'T TRY TO WRIGGLE OUT.
SQUEEZE
I SAID I CAN'T GO OUT WITH HER.
I MADE IT VERY CLEAR...
THAT I'D CHOSEN ADAGAKI AKI INSTEAD.
......
DID...
SHE HEAR THAT?

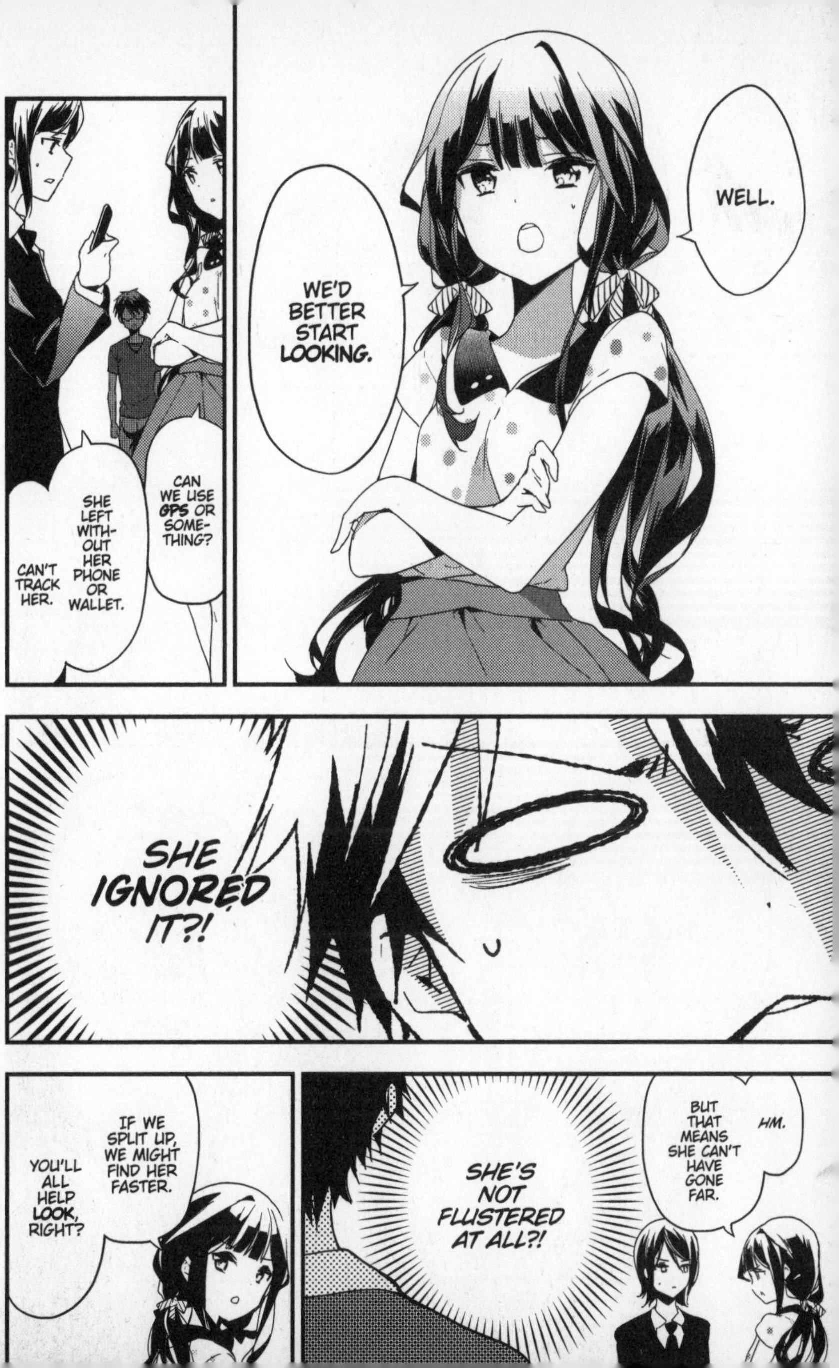
WELL.
WE'D BETTER START LOOKING.
CAN WE USE GPS OR SOMETHING?
SHE LEFT WITHOUT HER PHONE OR WALLET.
CAN'T TRACK HER.
SHE IGNORED IT?!
HM.
BUT THAT MEANS SHE CAN'T HAVE GONE FAR.
SHE'S NOT FLUSTERED AT ALL?!
IF WE SPLIT UP, WE MIGHT FIND HER FASTER.
YOU'LL ALL HELP LOOK, RIGHT?

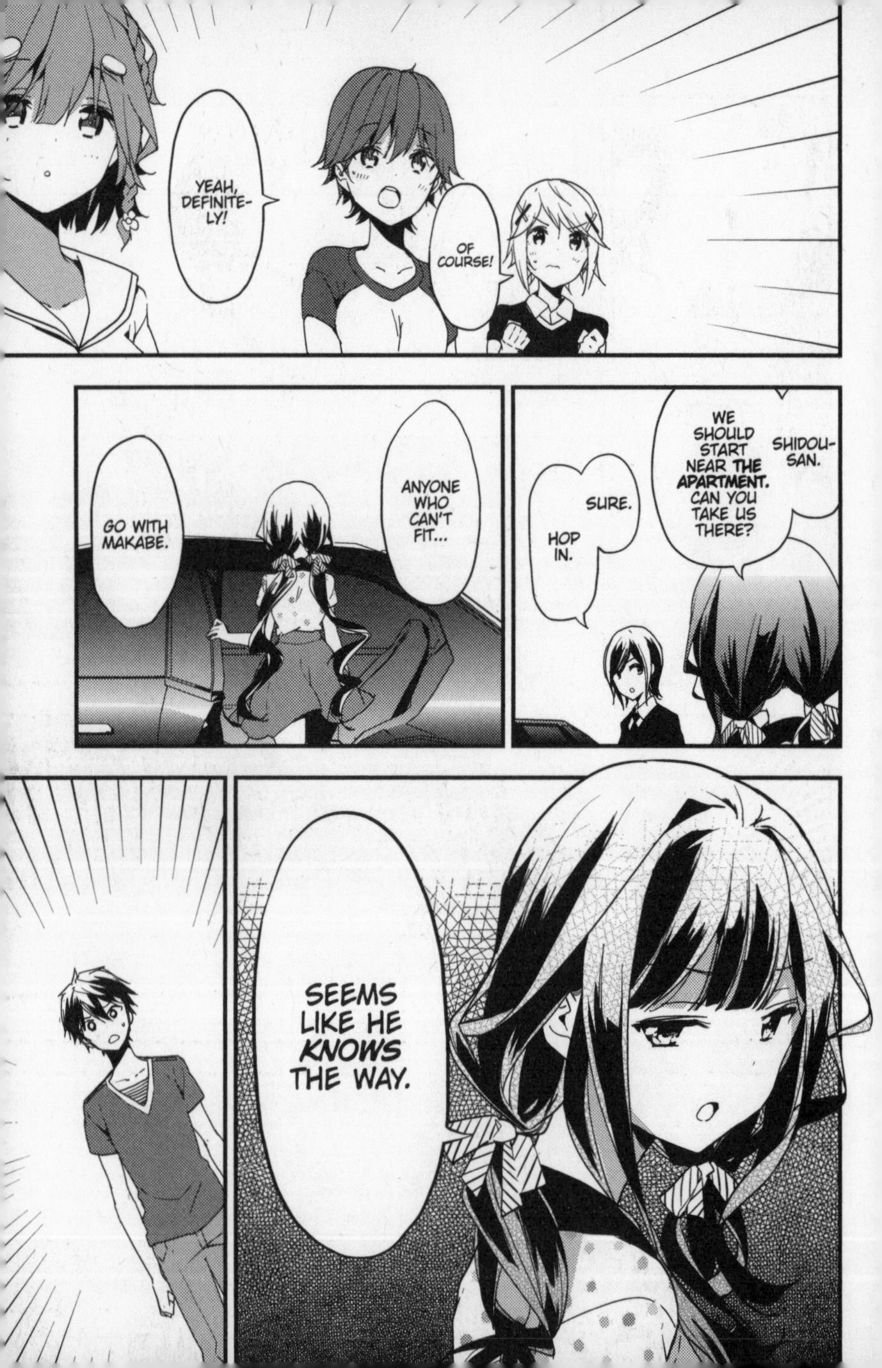
OF COURSE!
YEAH, DEFINITE-LY!
SHIDOU-SAN.
WE SHOULD START NEAR THE APARTMENT. CAN YOU TAKE US THERE?
SURE. HOP IN.
ANYONE WHO CAN'T FIT...
GO WITH MAKABE.
SEEMS LIKE HE *KNOWS* THE WAY.

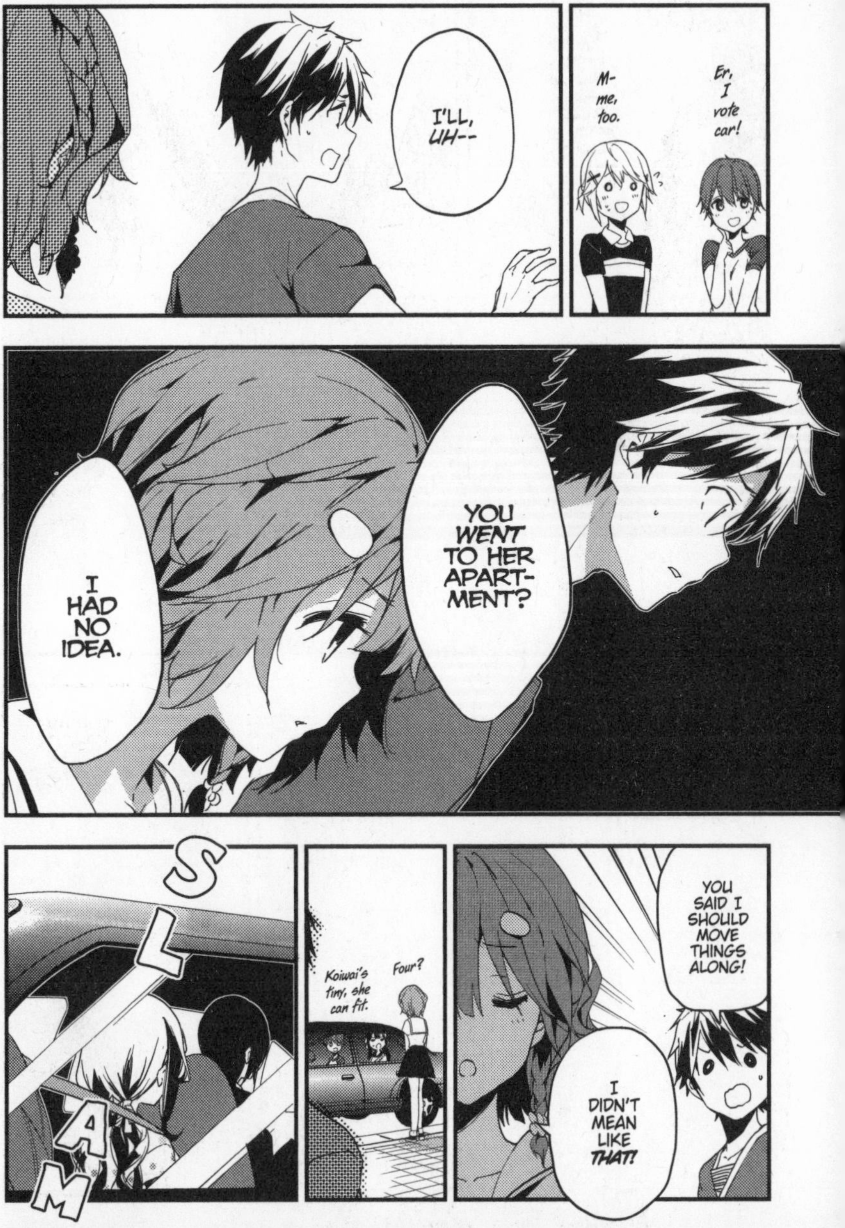
Er, I vote car!
M-me, too.
I'LL, UH--
YOU *WENT* TO HER APARTMENT?
I HAD NO IDEA.
YOU SAID I SHOULD MOVE THINGS ALONG!
I DIDN'T MEAN LIKE *THAT!*
Four?
Koiwai's tiny, she can fit.
SLAM

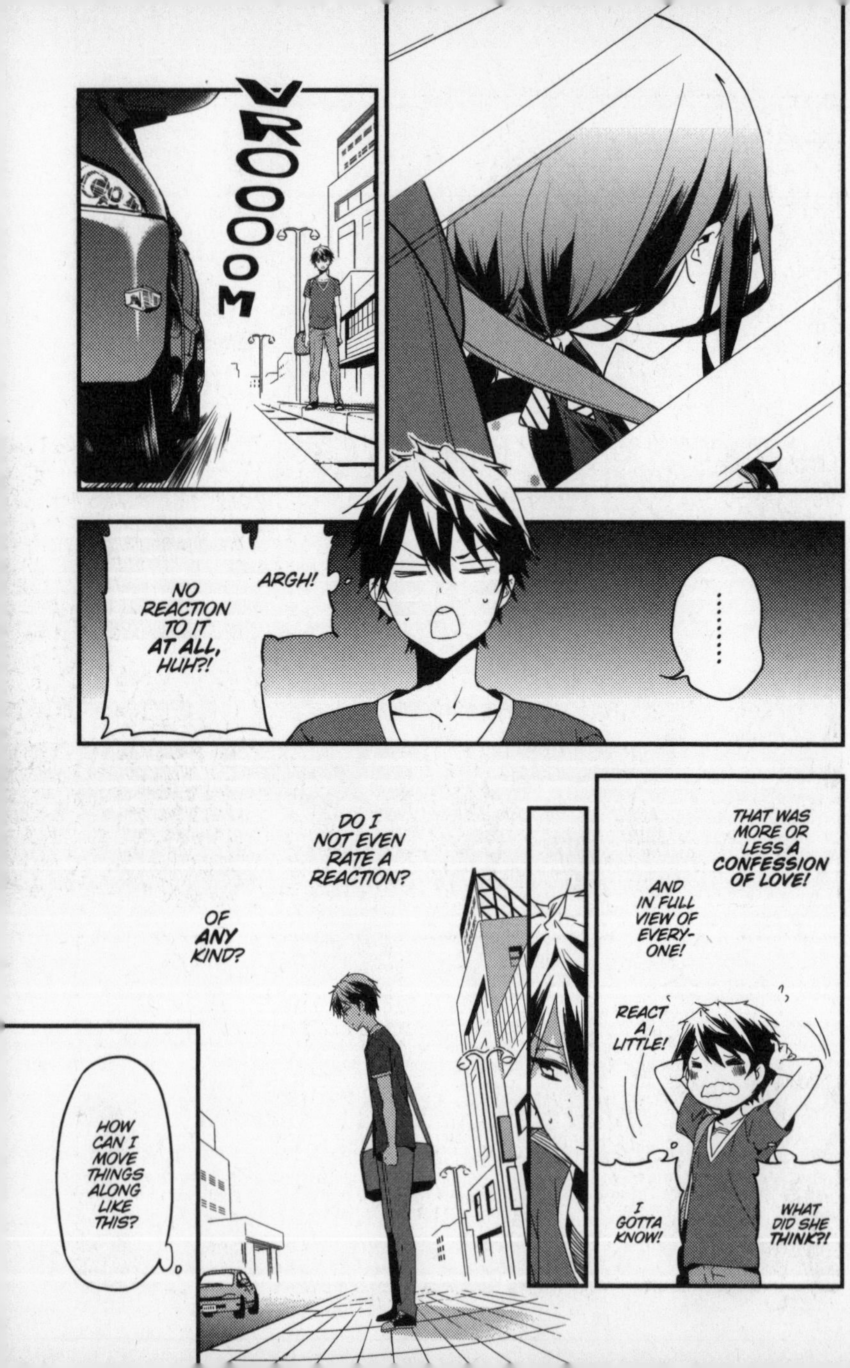
VROOOOOM
......
ARGH!
NO REACTION TO IT AT ALL, HUH?!
THAT WAS MORE OR LESS A CONFESSION OF LOVE!
AND IN FULL VIEW OF EVERYONE!
REACT A LITTLE!
WHAT DID SHE THINK?!
I GOTTA KNOW!
DO I NOT EVEN RATE A REACTION?
OF ANY KIND?
HOW CAN I MOVE THINGS ALONG LIKE THIS?

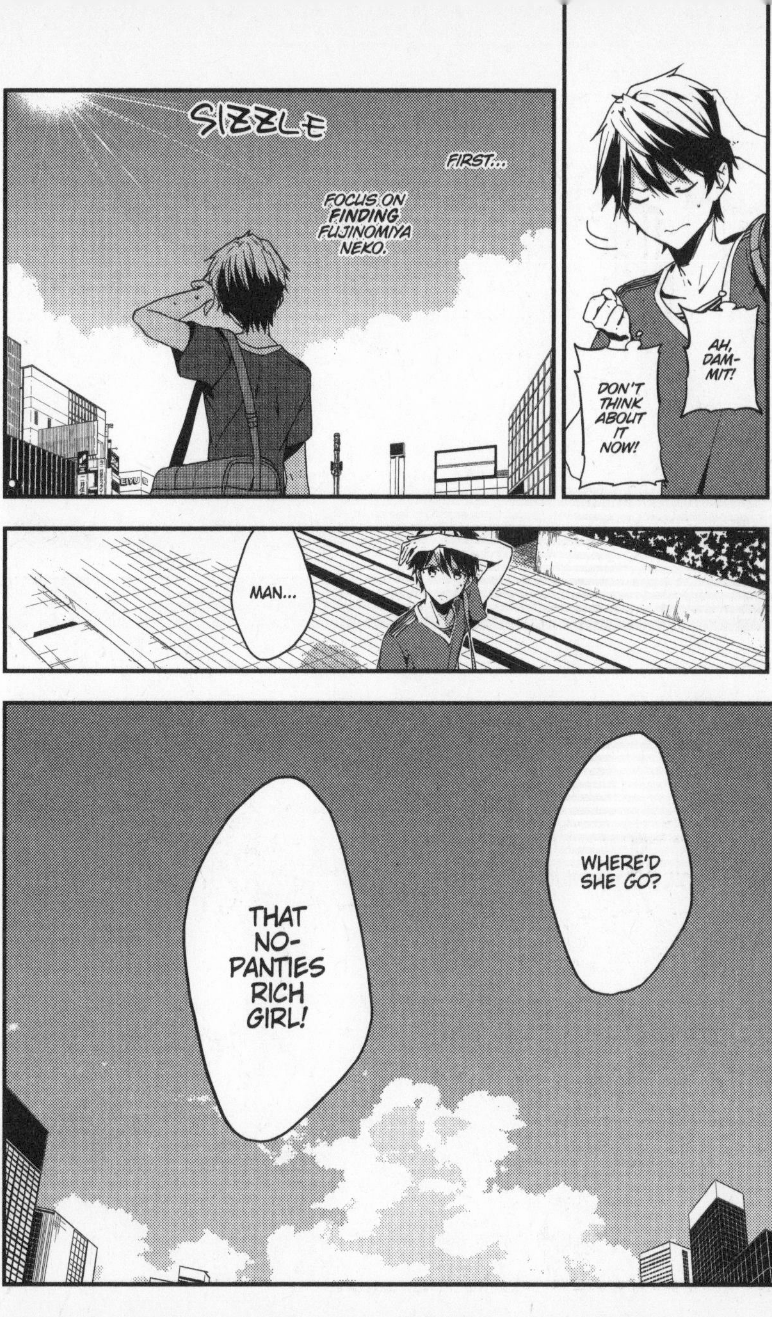
AH, DAM-MIT!
DON'T THINK ABOUT IT NOW!
SIZZLE
FIRST...
FOCUS ON FINDING FUJINOMIYA NEKO.
MAN...
WHERE'D SHE GO?
THAT NO-PANTIES RICH GIRL!

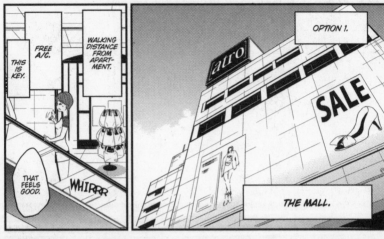

THIS IS KEY.

FREE A/C.

WALKING DISTANCE FROM APARTMENT.

THAT FEELS GOOD.

WHIRRR

OPTION 1.

atro

SALE

THE MALL.

YAKISOBA

I LOOKED EVERYWHERE, BUT SHE'S NOT HERE.

NOPE.

Hnnn...

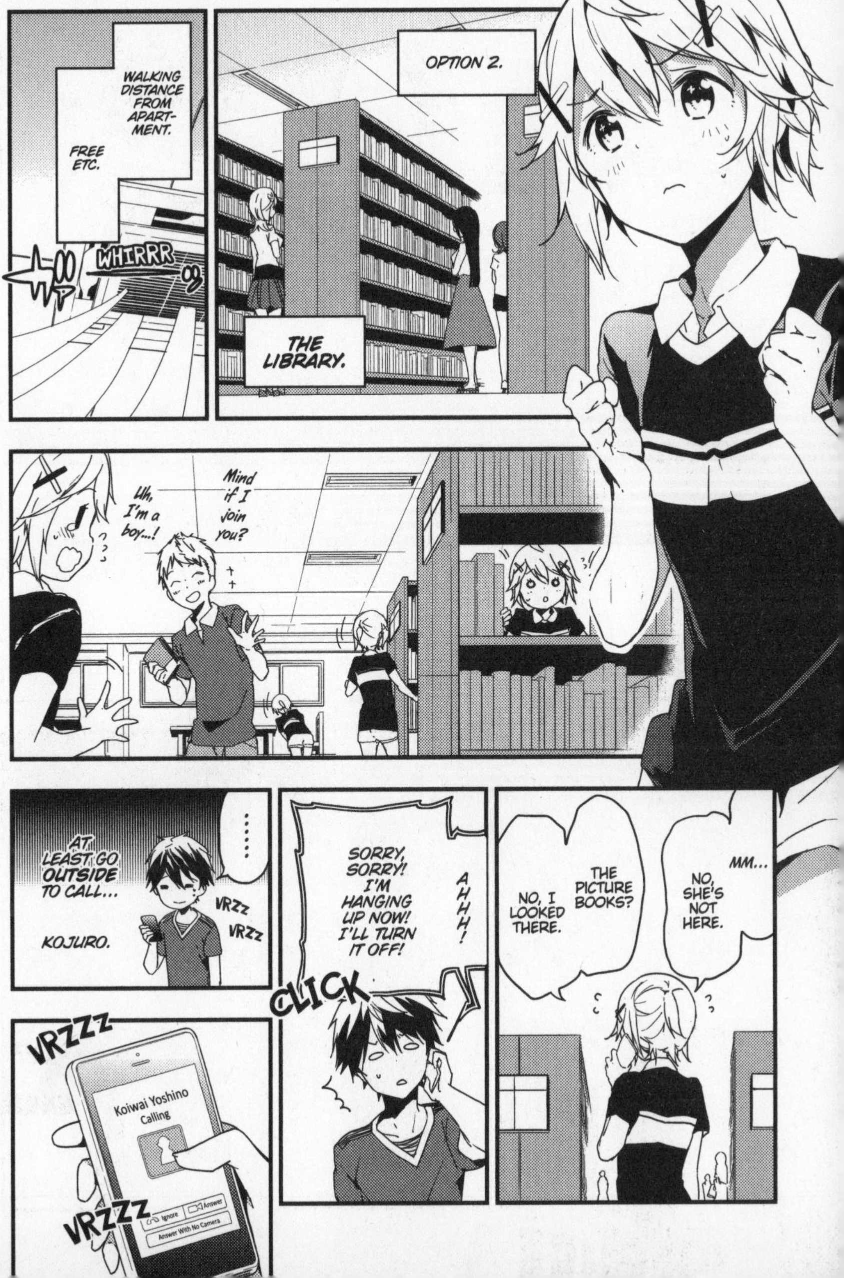
OPTION 2.
THE LIBRARY.
WALKING DISTANCE FROM APART-MENT.
FREE ETC.
WHIRRR
Mind if I join you?
Uh, I'm a boy...!
MM...
NO, SHE'S NOT HERE.
THE PICTURE BOOKS?
NO, I LOOKED THERE.
AHHH!
SORRY, SORRY! I'M HANGING UP NOW! I'LL TURN IT OFF!
CLICK
......
AT LEAST GO OUTSIDE TO CALL...
KOJURO.
VRZz
VRZz
VRZZZ
Koiwai Yoshino Calling
Ignore
Answer
Answer With No Camera
VRZZZ

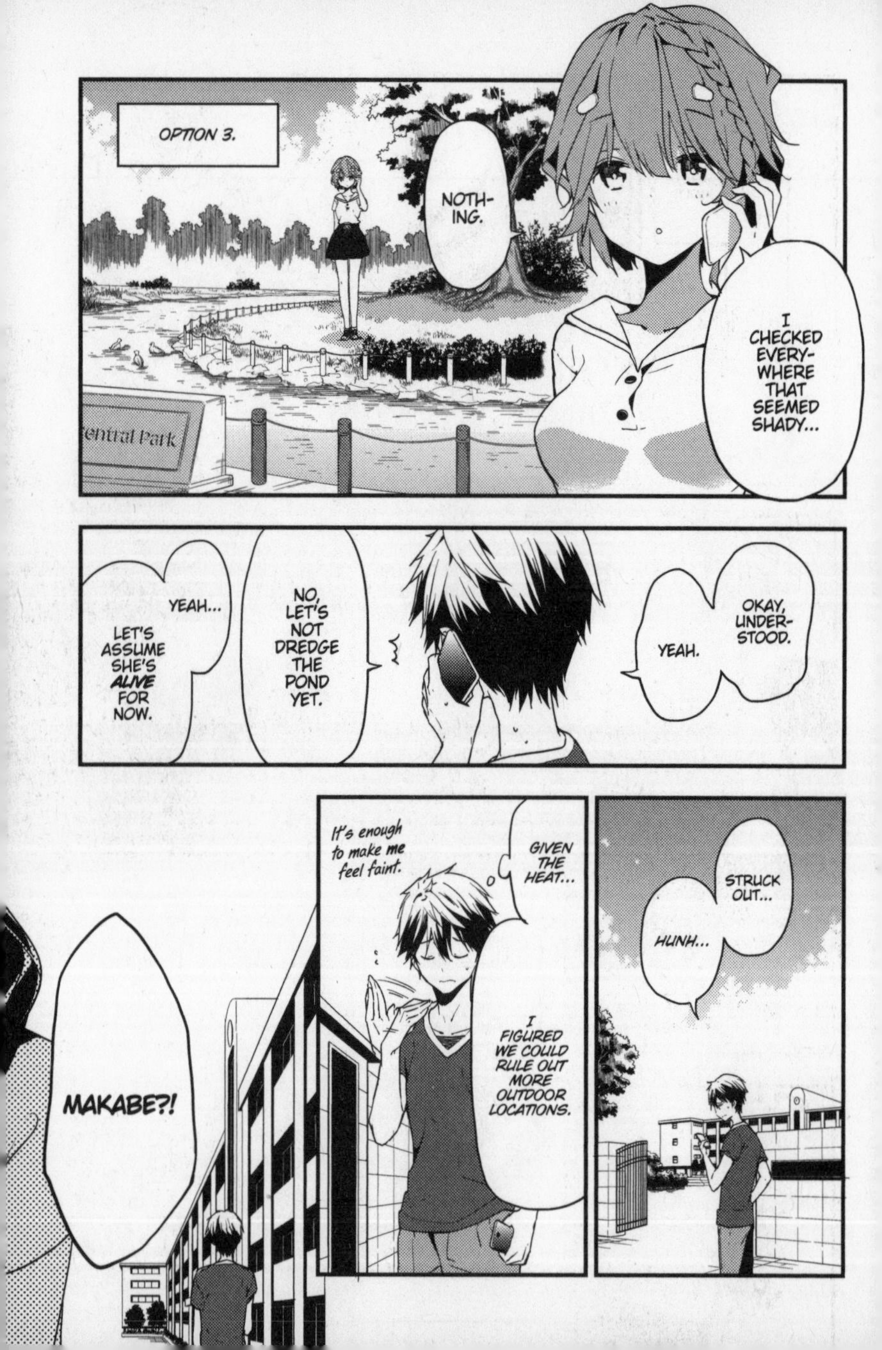
OPTION 3.
I CHECKED EVERY-WHERE THAT SEEMED SHADY...
NOTH-ING.
entral Park
OKAY, UNDER-STOOD.
YEAH.
NO, LET'S NOT DREDGE THE POND YET.
YEAH...
LET'S ASSUME SHE'S ***ALIVE*** FOR NOW.
STRUCK OUT...
HUNH...
GIVEN THE HEAT...
I FIGURED WE COULD RULE OUT MORE OUTDOOR LOCATIONS.
It's enough to make me feel faint.
MAKABE?!

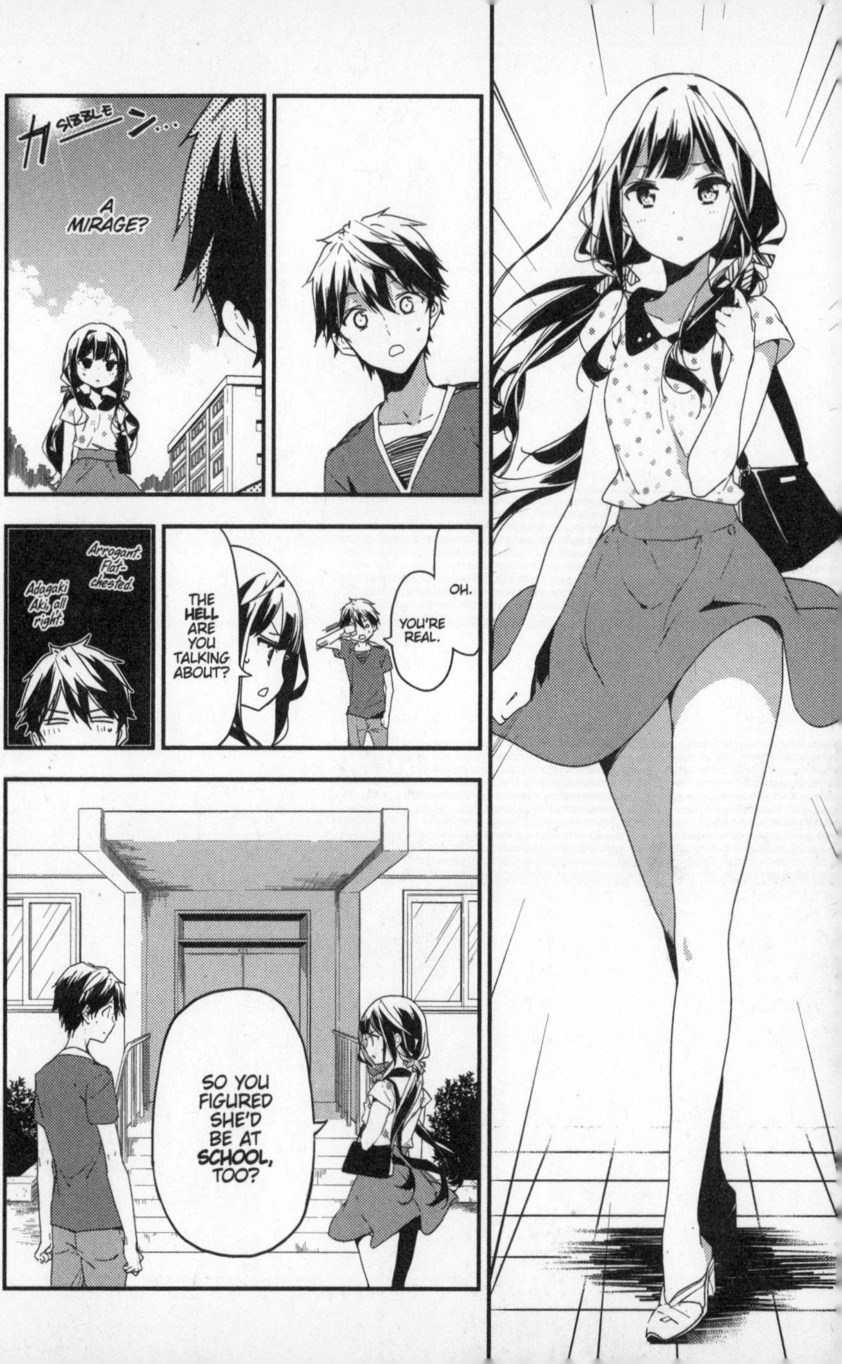

SIBBLE...
A MIRAGE?
OH. YOU'RE REAL.
THE HELL ARE YOU TALKING ABOUT?
Arrogant. Flat-chested.
Adagaki Aki, all right.
SO YOU FIGURED SHE'D BE AT SCHOOL, TOO?

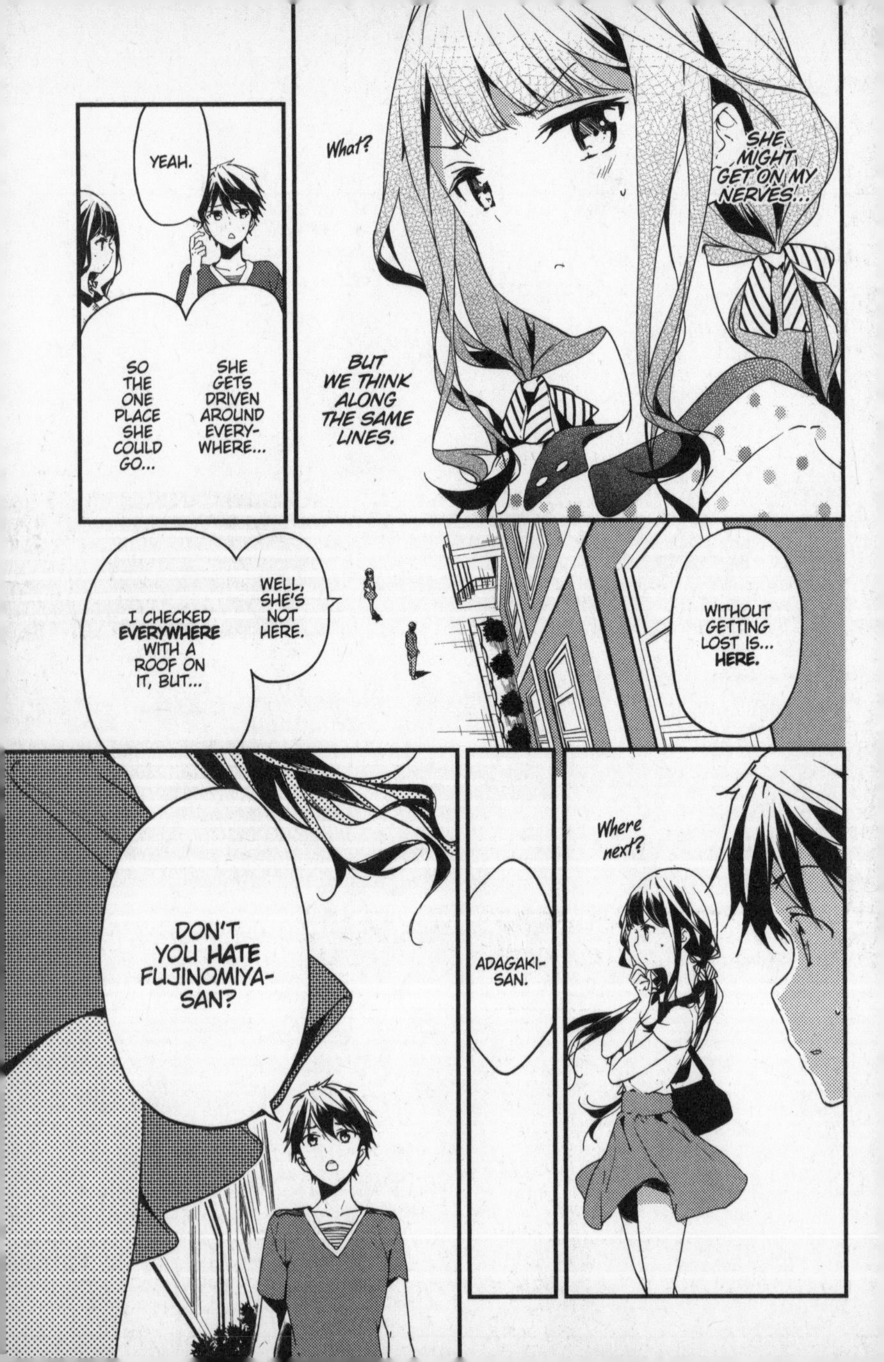
SHE MIGHT GET ON MY NERVES...
What?
BUT WE THINK ALONG THE SAME LINES.
YEAH.
SHE GETS DRIVEN AROUND EVERYWHERE...
SO THE ONE PLACE SHE COULD GO...
WITHOUT GETTING LOST IS... HERE.
WELL, SHE'S NOT HERE.
I CHECKED EVERYWHERE WITH A ROOF ON IT, BUT...
Where next?
ADAGAKI-SAN.
DON'T YOU HATE FUJINOMIYA-SAN?

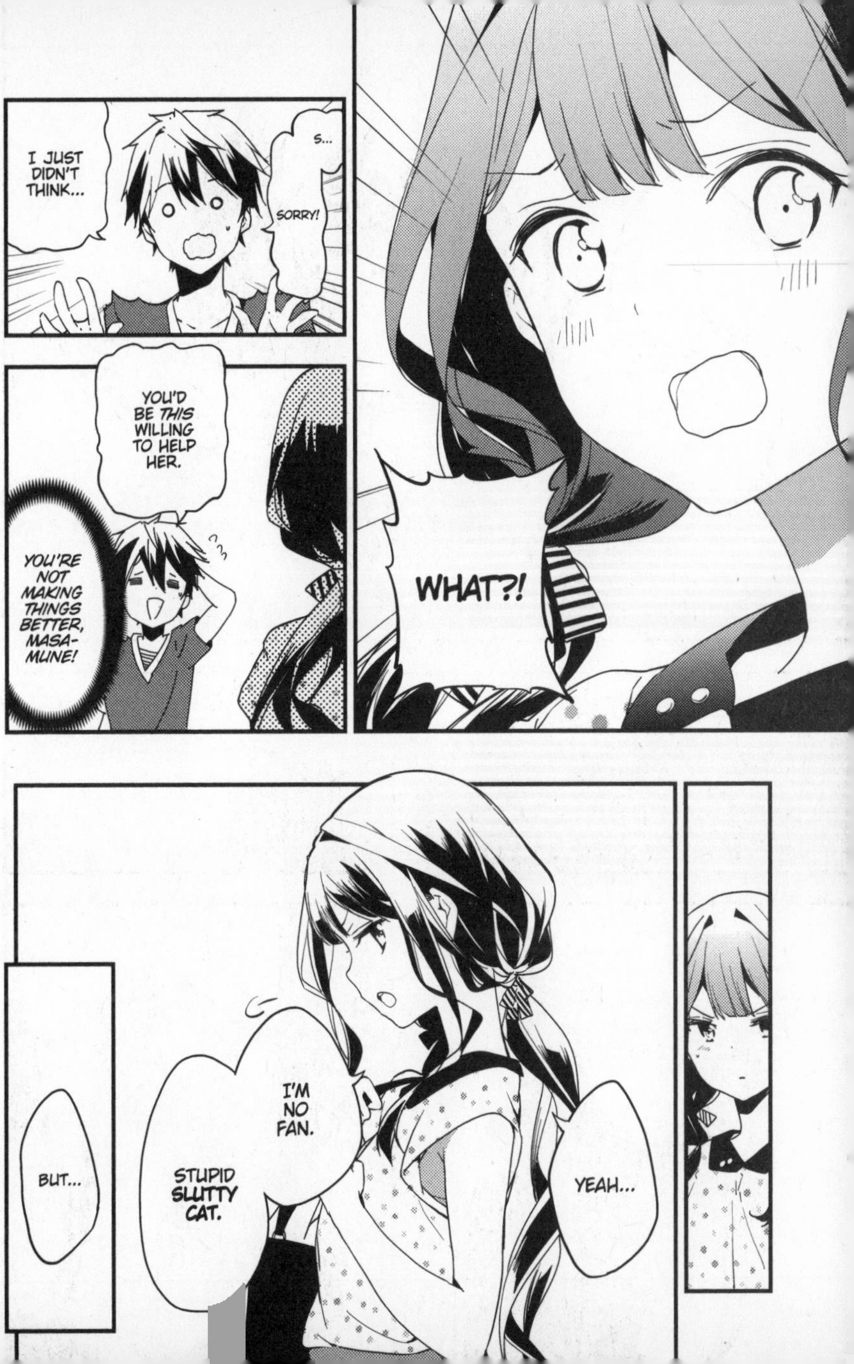
WHAT?!
S... SORRY!
I JUST DIDN'T THINK...
YOU'D BE *THIS* WILLING TO HELP HER.
YOU'RE NOT MAKING THINGS BETTER, MASAMUNE!
YEAH...
I'M NO FAN.
STUPID SLUTTY CAT.
BUT...

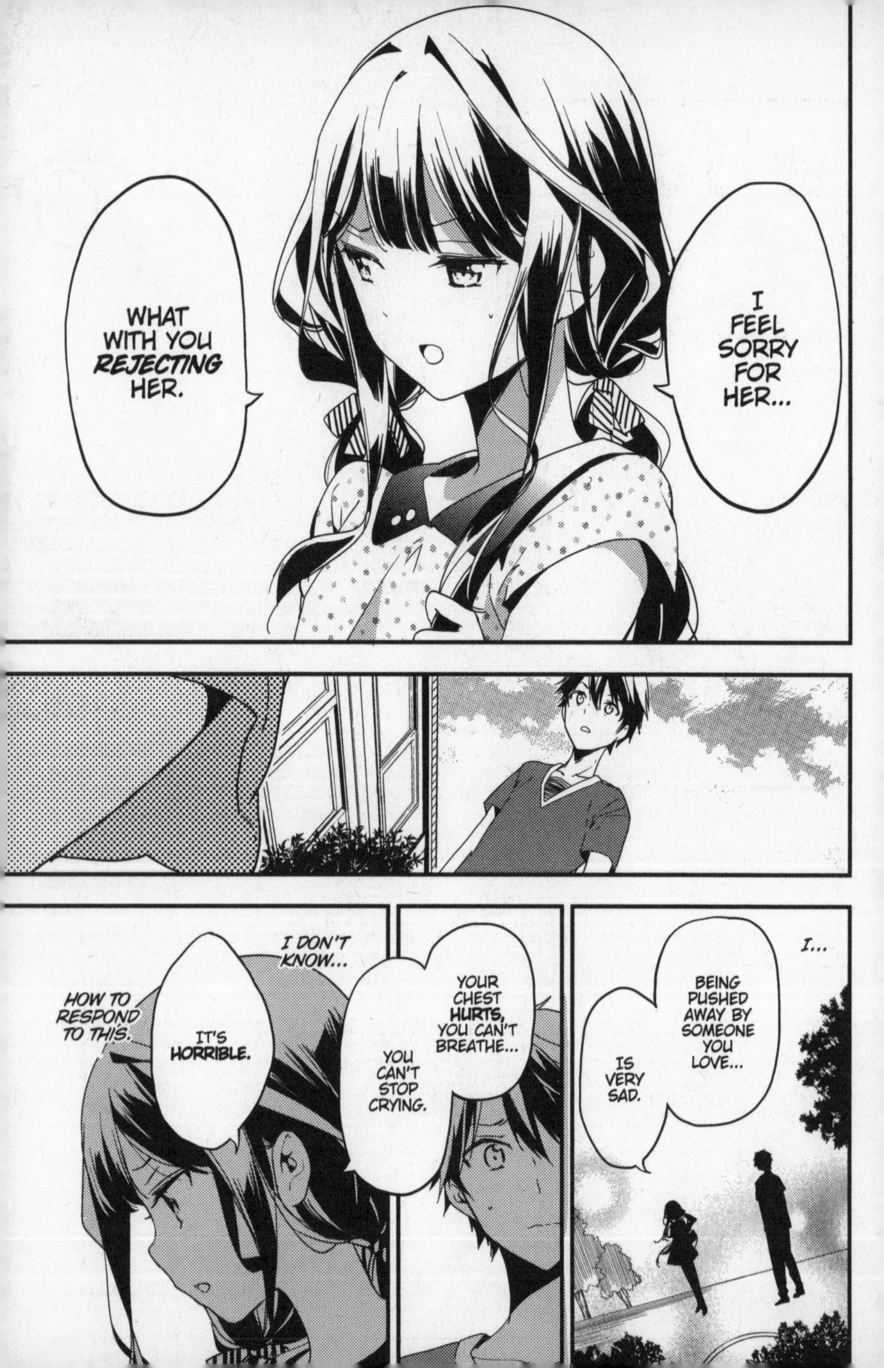
I FEEL SORRY FOR HER...
WHAT WITH YOU *REJECTING* HER.
I...
BEING PUSHED AWAY BY SOMEONE YOU LOVE...
IS VERY SAD.
YOUR CHEST **HURTS**, YOU CAN'T BREATHE...
YOU CAN'T STOP CRYING.
IT'S **HORRIBLE**.
I DON'T KNOW...
HOW TO RESPOND TO THIS.

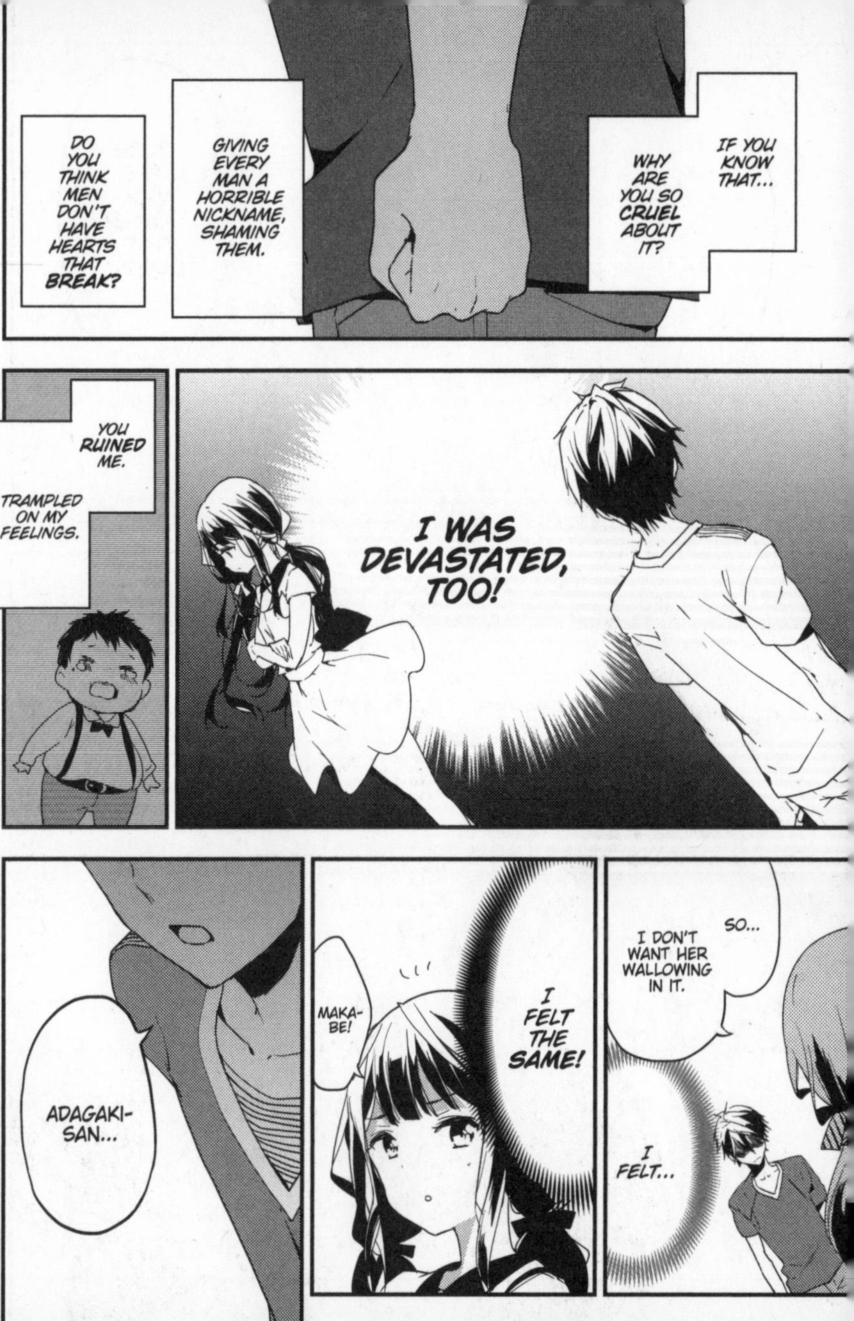
IF YOU KNOW THAT... WHY ARE YOU SO CRUEL ABOUT IT?
GIVING EVERY MAN A HORRIBLE NICKNAME, SHAMING THEM.
DO YOU THINK MEN DON'T HAVE HEARTS THAT BREAK?
I WAS DEVASTATED, TOO!
YOU RUINED ME.
TRAMPLED ON MY FEELINGS.
SO... I DON'T WANT HER WALLOWING IN IT.
I FELT...
I FELT THE SAME!
MAKA-BE!
ADAGAKI-SAN...

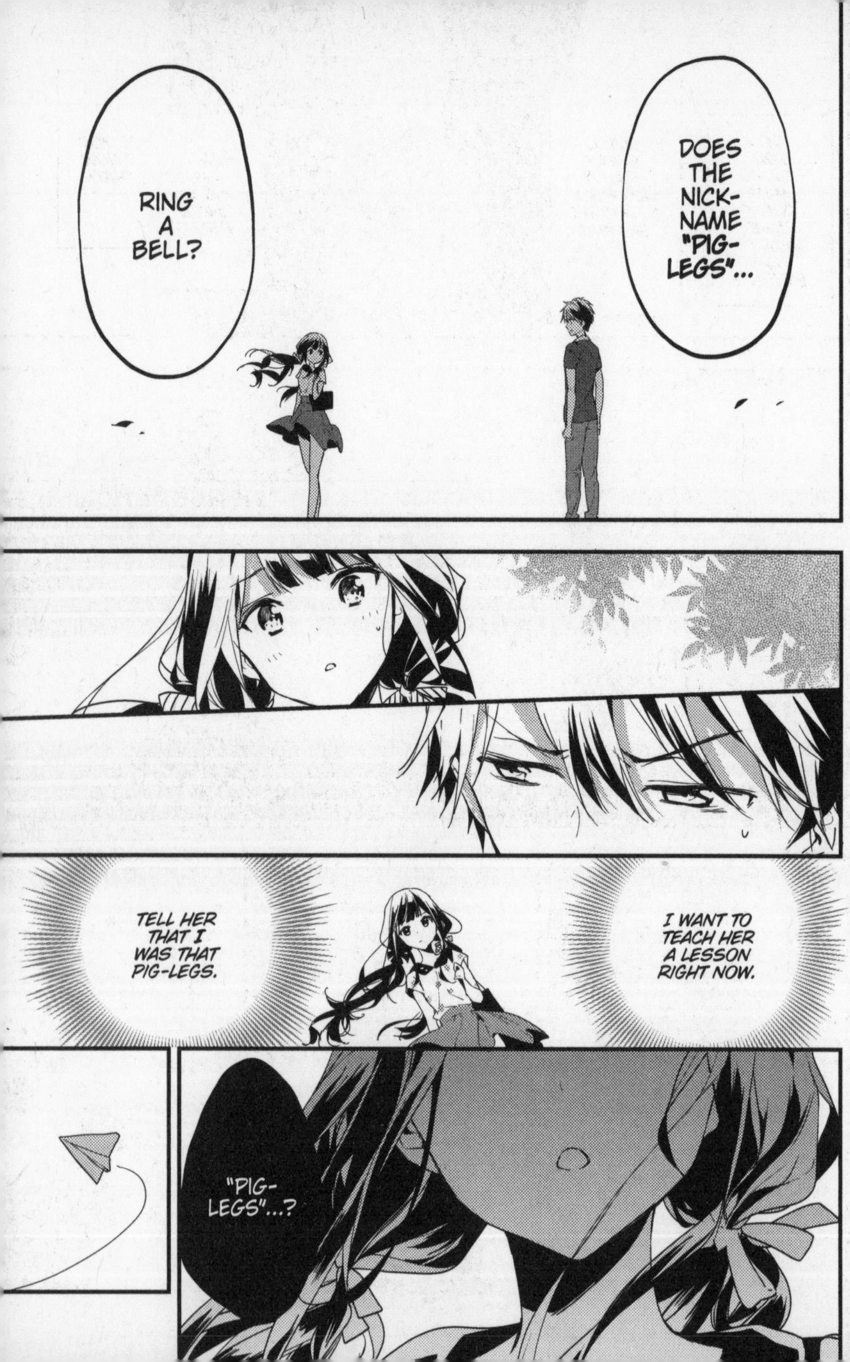
DOES THE NICK-NAME "PIG-LEGS"...
RING A BELL?
I WANT TO TEACH HER A LESSON RIGHT NOW.
TELL HER THAT I WAS THAT PIG-LEGS.
"PIG-LEGS"...?

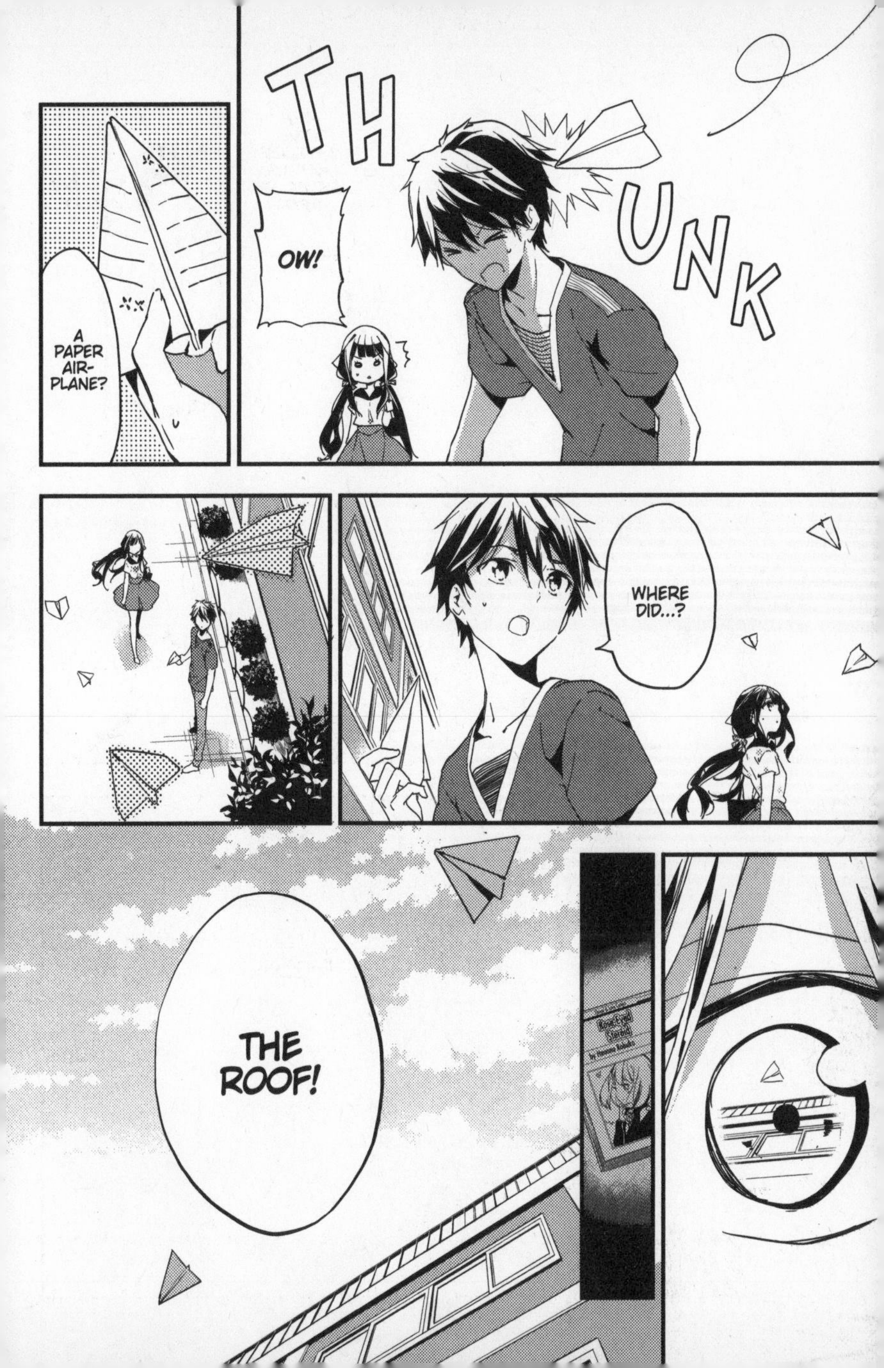
THUNK
OW!
A PAPER AIR-PLANE?
WHERE DID...?
THE ROOF!

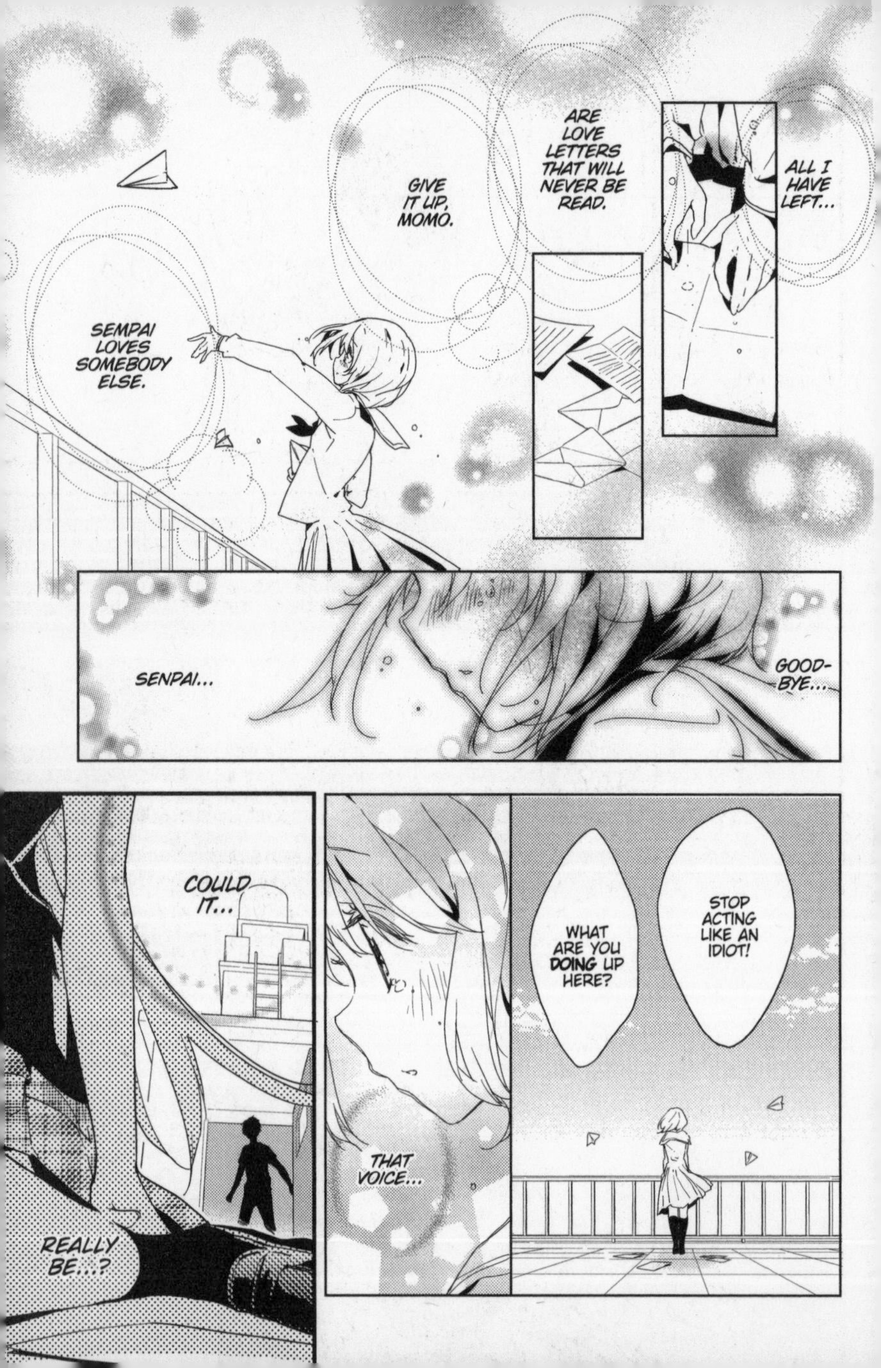
ALL I HAVE LEFT...
ARE LOVE LETTERS THAT WILL NEVER BE READ.
GIVE IT UP, MOMO.
SEMPAI LOVES SOMEBODY ELSE.
GOOD-BYE...
SENPAI...
STOP ACTING LIKE AN IDIOT!
WHAT ARE YOU DOING UP HERE?
THAT VOICE...
COULD IT...
REALLY BE...?

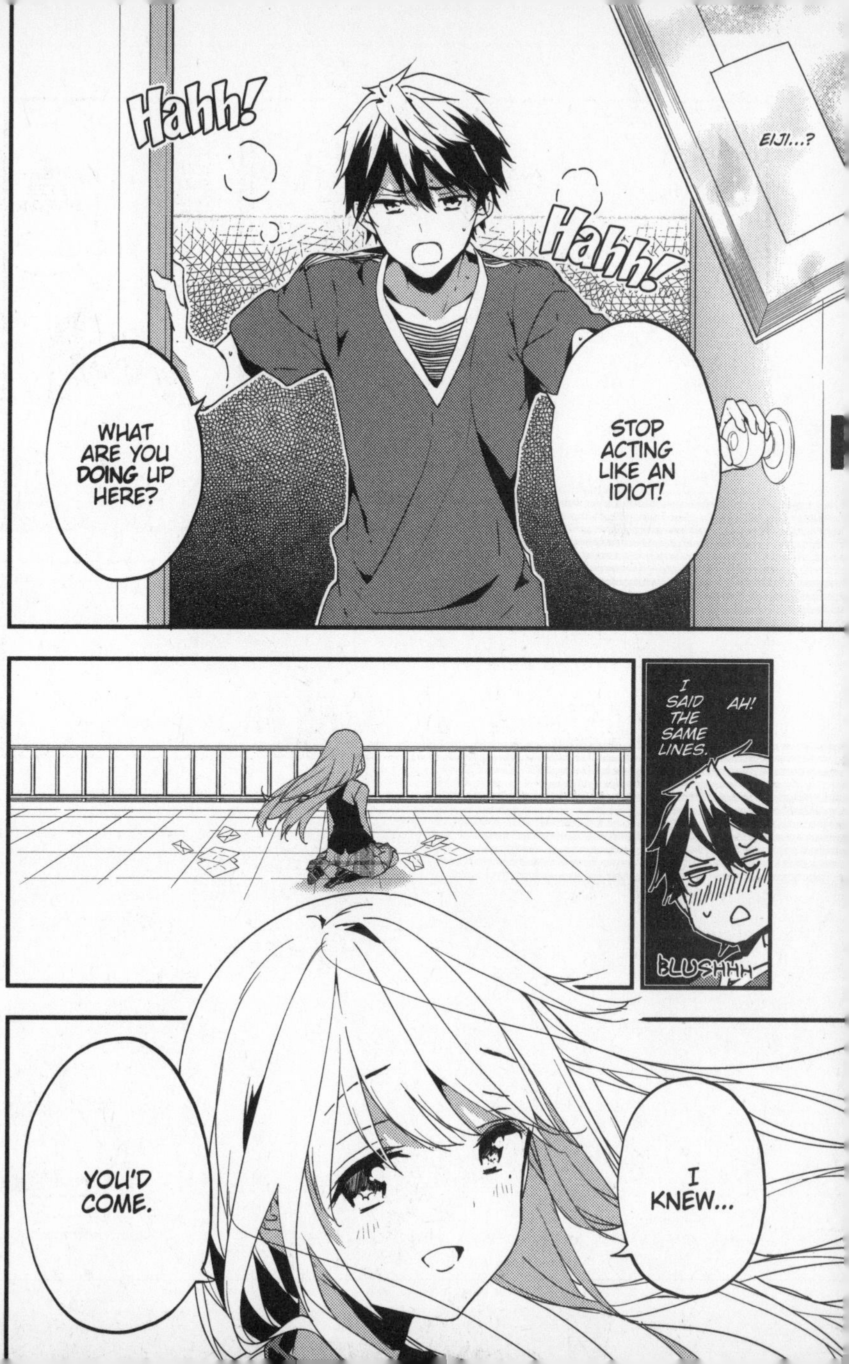
EIJI...?
Hahh!
Hahh!
STOP ACTING LIKE AN IDIOT!
WHAT ARE YOU DOING UP HERE?
AH!
I SAID THE SAME LINES.
BLUSHHH
I KNEW...
YOU'D COME.

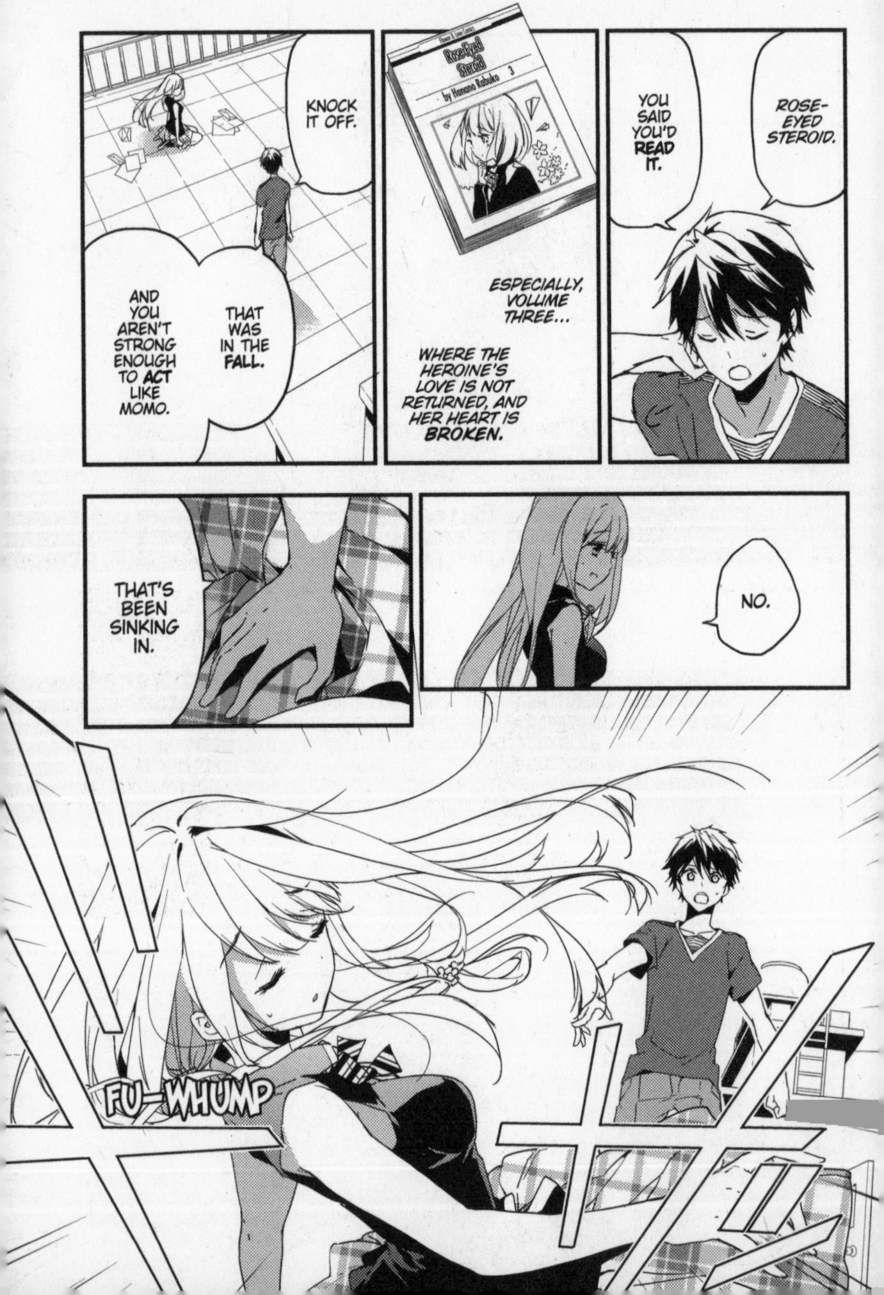
ROSE-EYED STEROID.
YOU SAID YOU'D READ IT.
Rose-Eyed Steroid 3
by Hanano Rabuko
ESPECIALLY, VOLUME THREE...
WHERE THE HEROINE'S LOVE IS NOT RETURNED, AND HER HEART IS BROKEN.
KNOCK IT OFF.
THAT WAS IN THE FALL.
AND YOU AREN'T STRONG ENOUGH TO ACT LIKE MOMO.
NO.
THAT'S BEEN SINKING IN.
FU-WHUMP

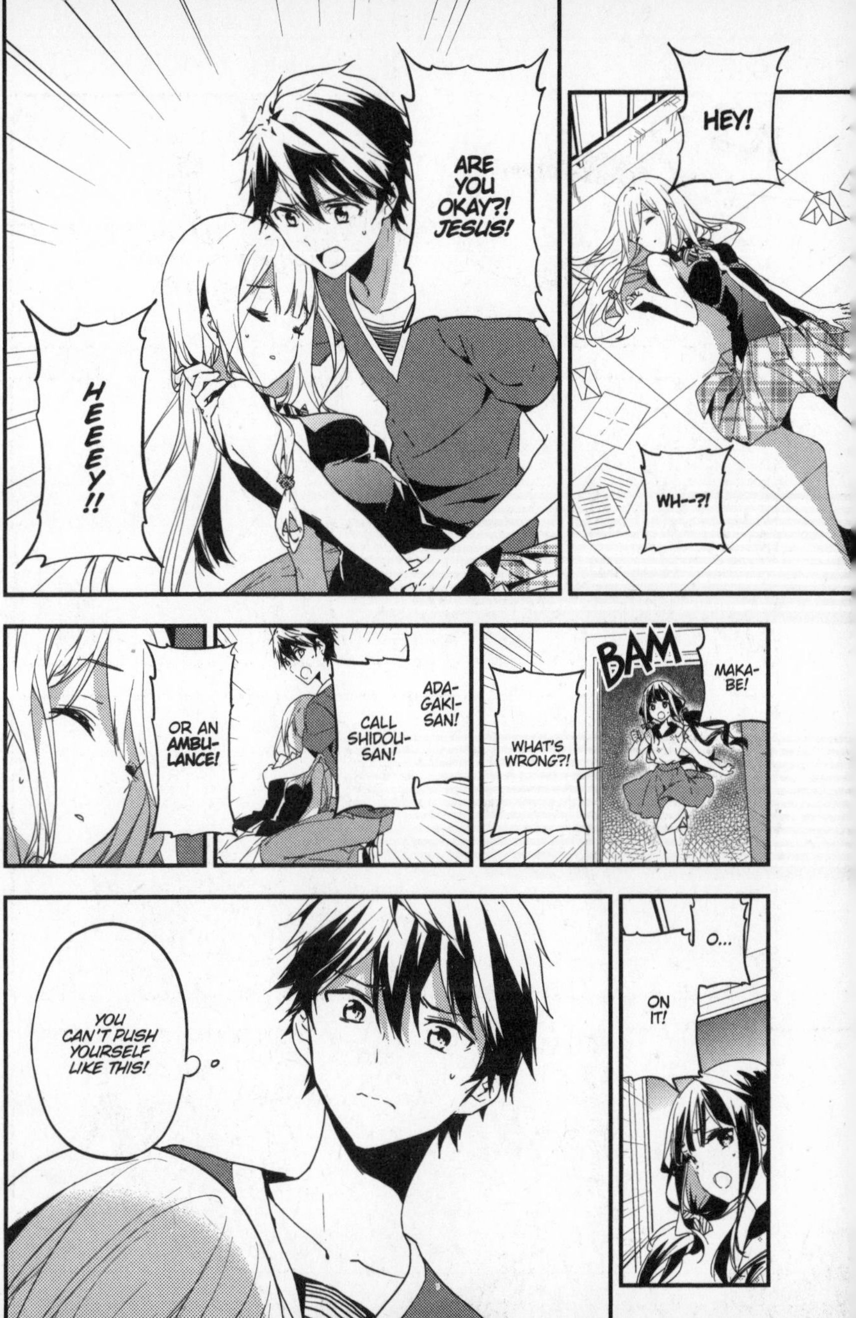
HEY!
WH--?!
ARE YOU OKAY?! JESUS!
HEEEEY!!
MAKA-BE!
WHAT'S WRONG?!
ADA-GAKI-SAN!
CALL SHIDOU-SAN!
OR AN AMBU-LANCE!
O...
ON IT!
YOU CAN'T PUSH YOURSELF LIKE THIS!

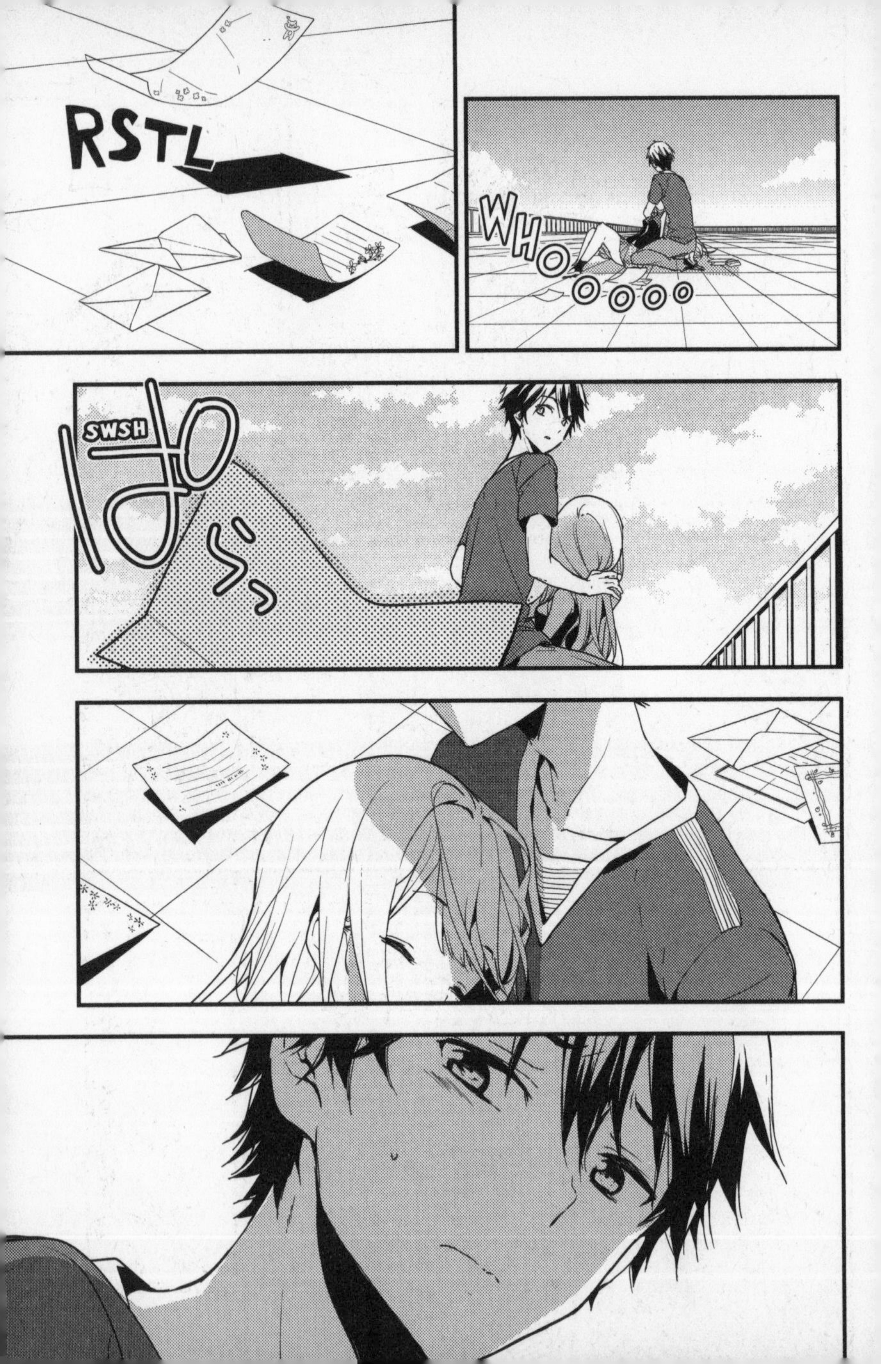
WHOOOOOO
RSTL
SWSH

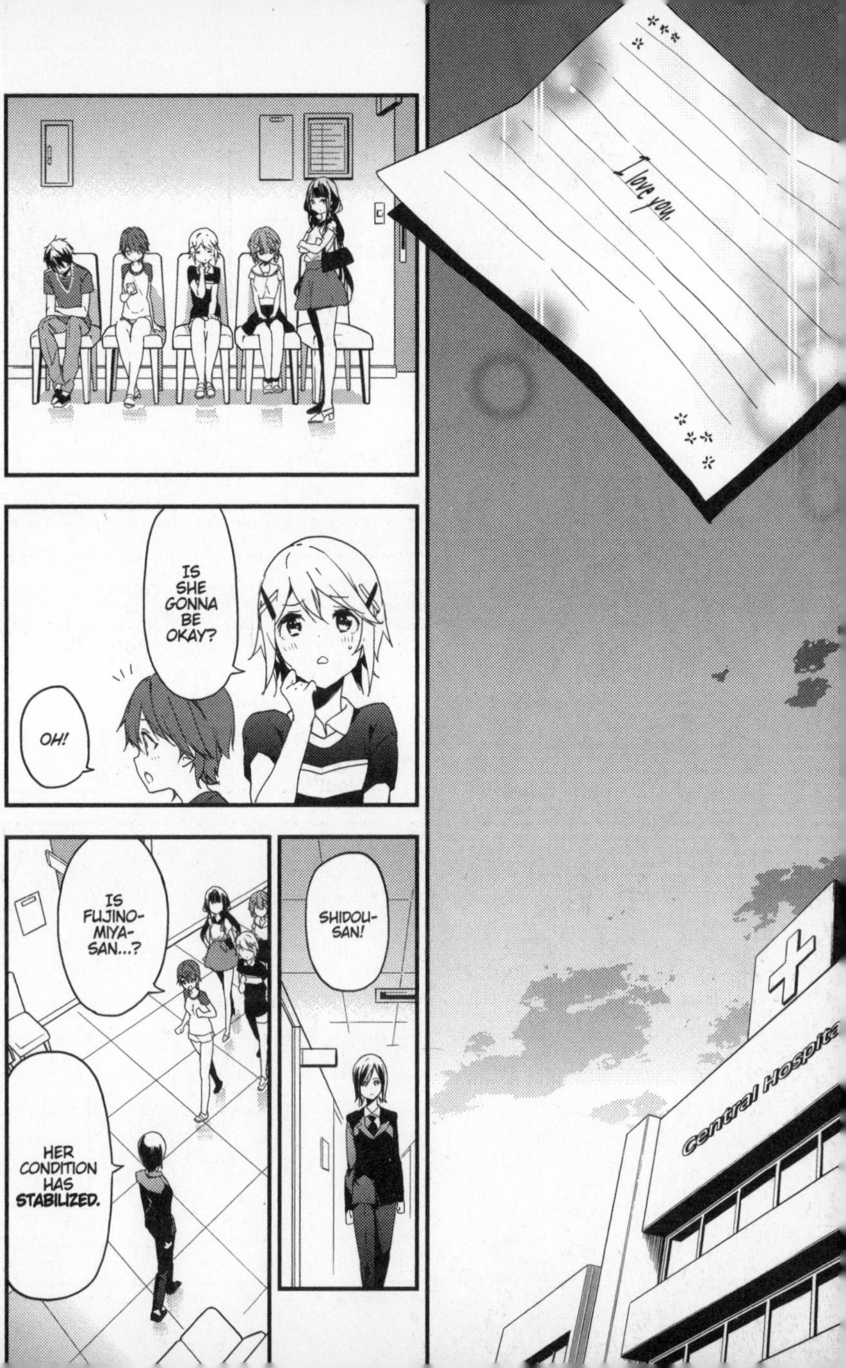
I love you.
Central Hospita
IS SHE GONNA BE OKAY?
OH!
SHIDOU-SAN!
IS FUJINO-MIYA-SAN...?
HER CONDITION HAS STABILIZED.

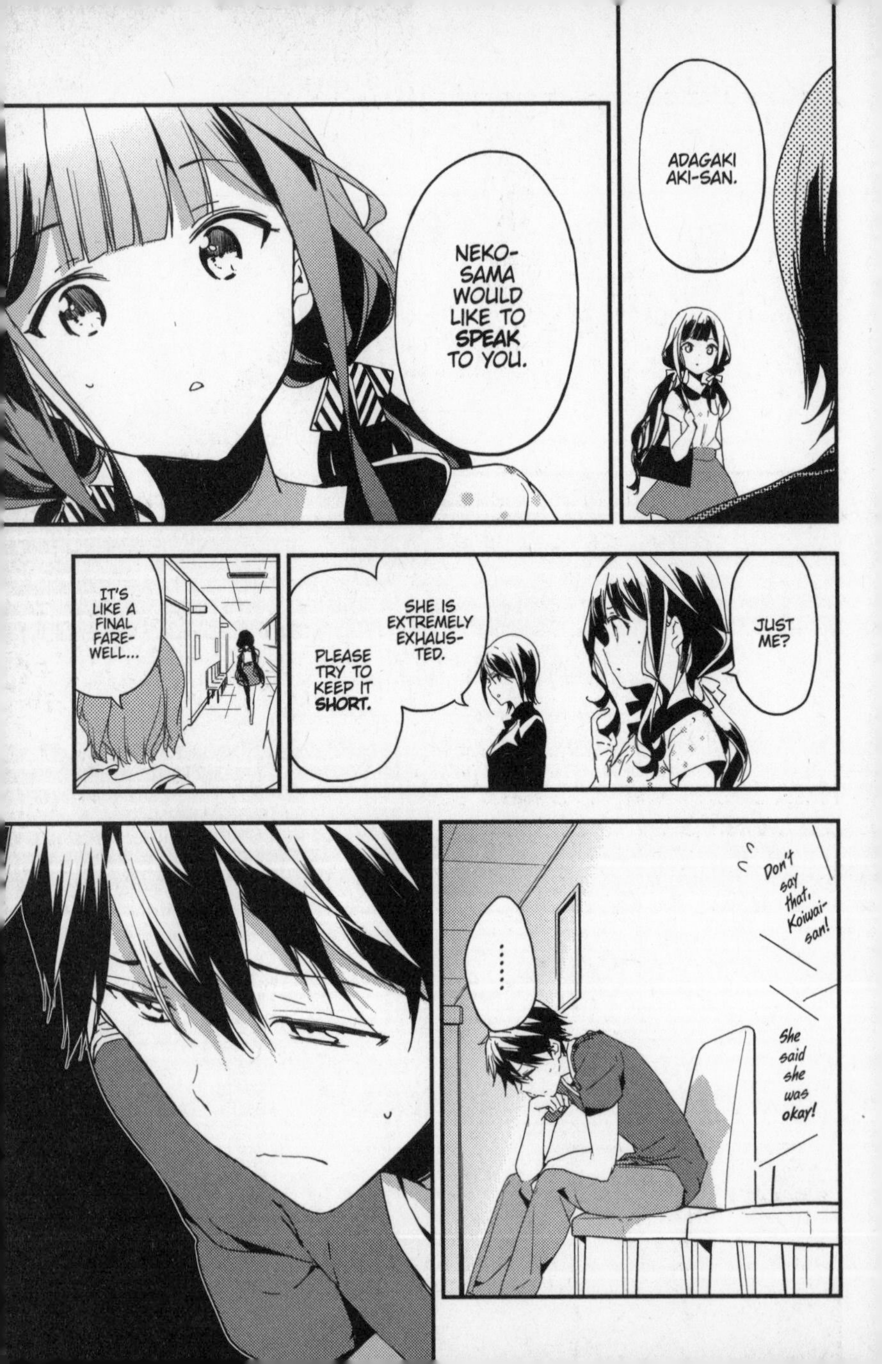
ADAGAKI AKI-SAN.
NEKO-SAMA WOULD LIKE TO SPEAK TO YOU.
JUST ME?
SHE IS EXTREMELY EXHAUSTED.
PLEASE TRY TO KEEP IT SHORT.
IT'S LIKE A FINAL FAREWELL...
Don't say that, Koiwai-san!
......
She said she was okay!

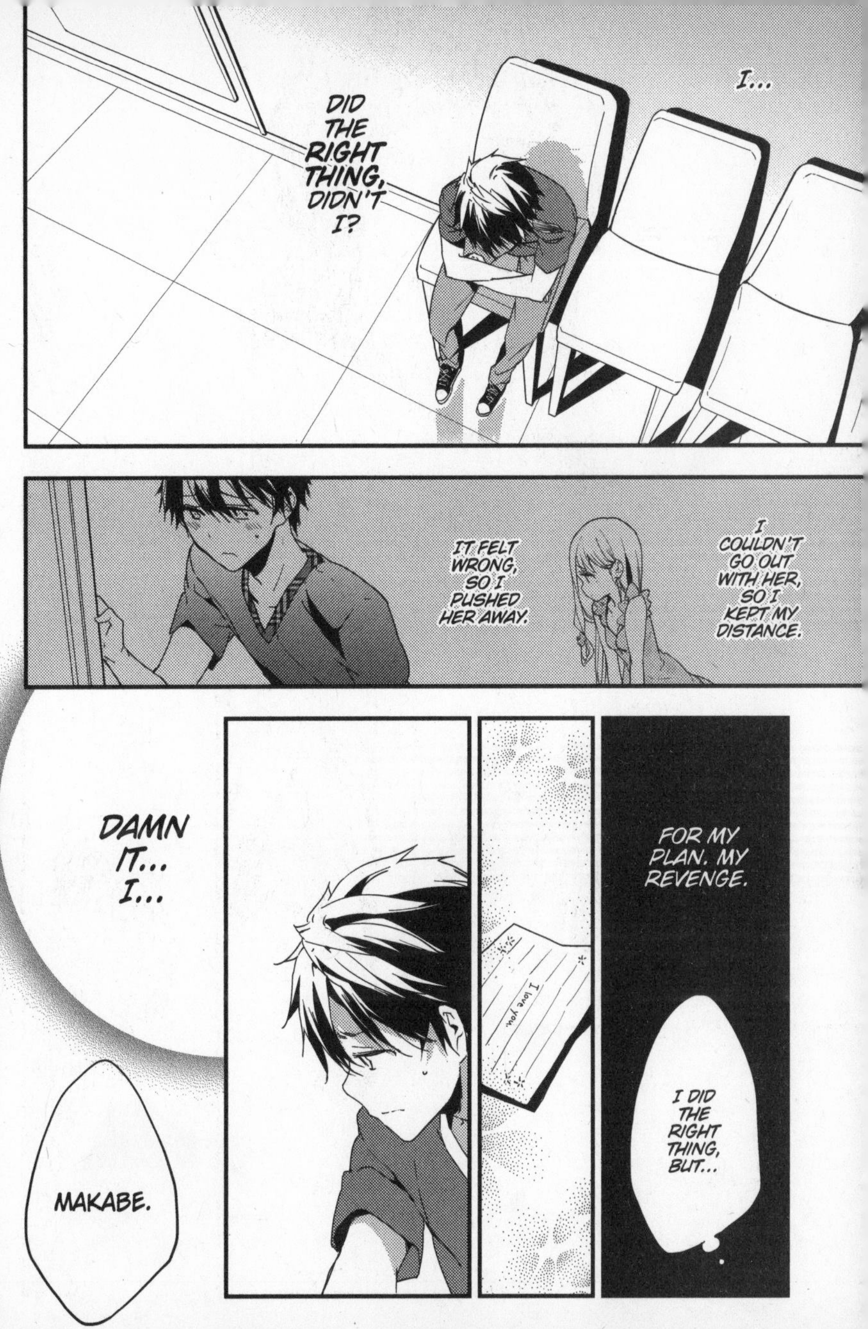
I...
DID THE RIGHT THING, DIDN'T I?
I COULDN'T GO OUT WITH HER, SO I KEPT MY DISTANCE.
IT FELT WRONG, SO I PUSHED HER AWAY.
FOR MY PLAN. MY REVENGE.
I DID THE RIGHT THING, BUT...
I love you.
DAMN IT... I...
MAKABE.

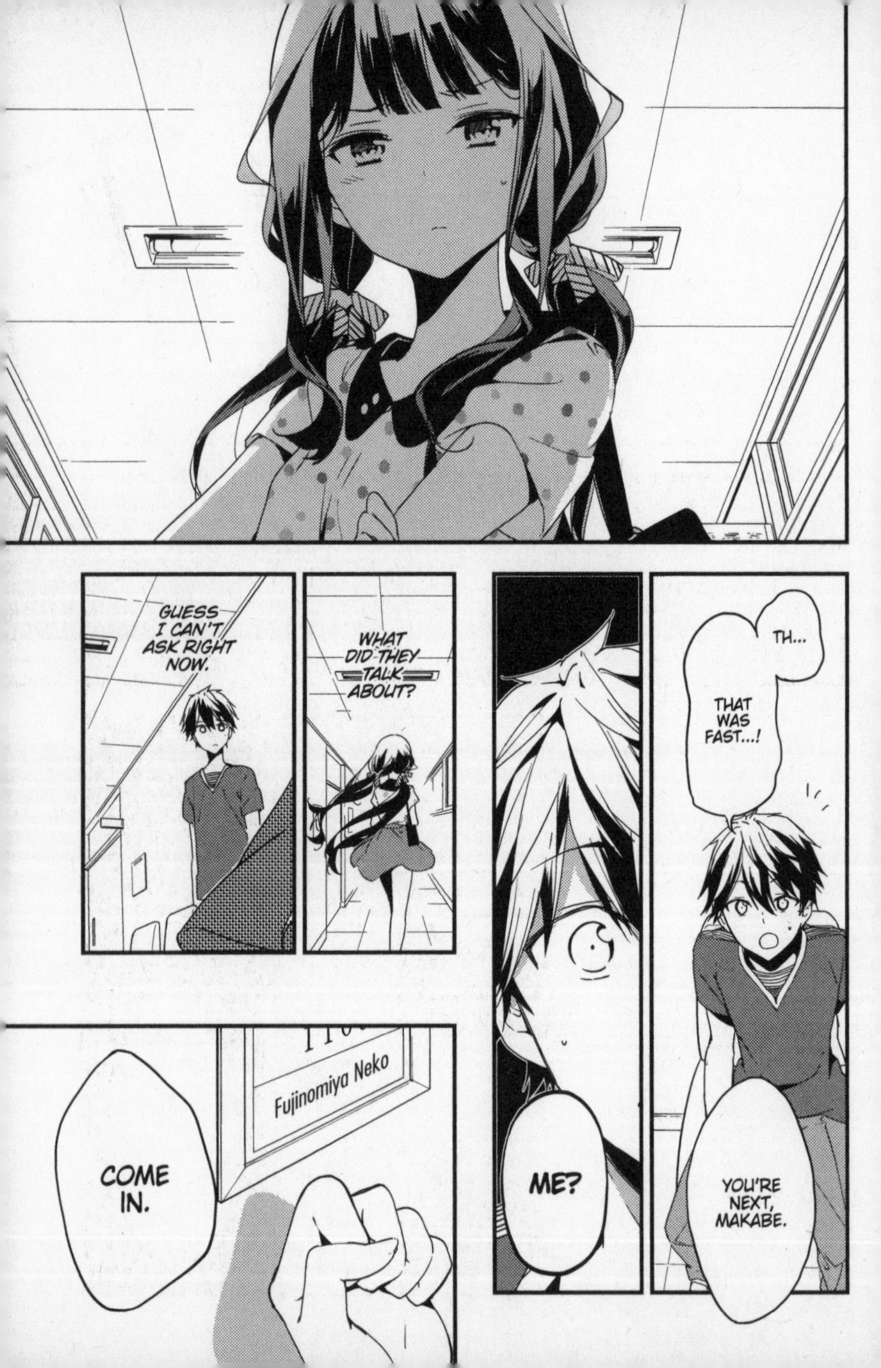
TH...
THAT WAS FAST...!
YOU'RE NEXT, MAKABE.
ME?
WHAT DID THEY TALK ABOUT?
GUESS I CAN'T ASK RIGHT NOW.
Fujinomiya Neko
COME IN.

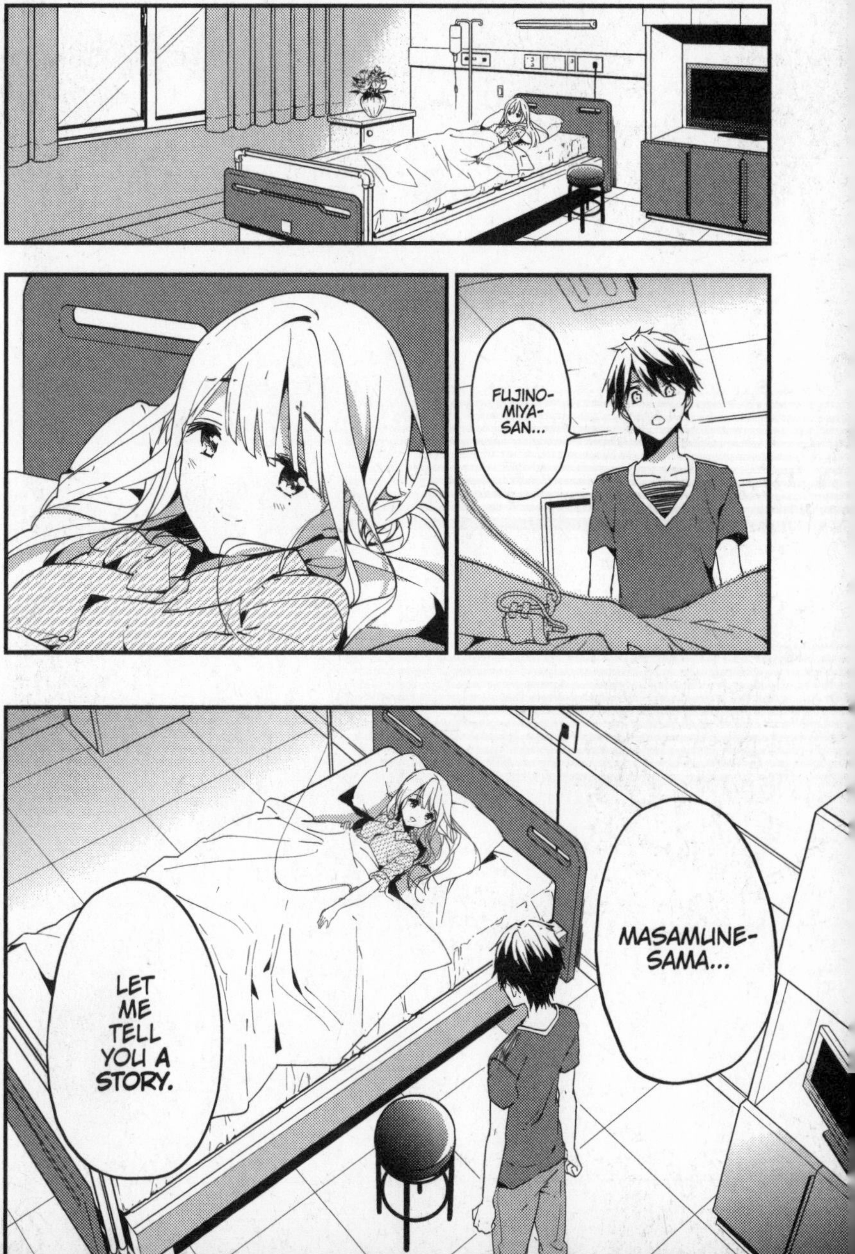
FUJINO-MIYA-SAN...
MASAMUNE-SAMA...
LET ME TELL YOU A STORY.

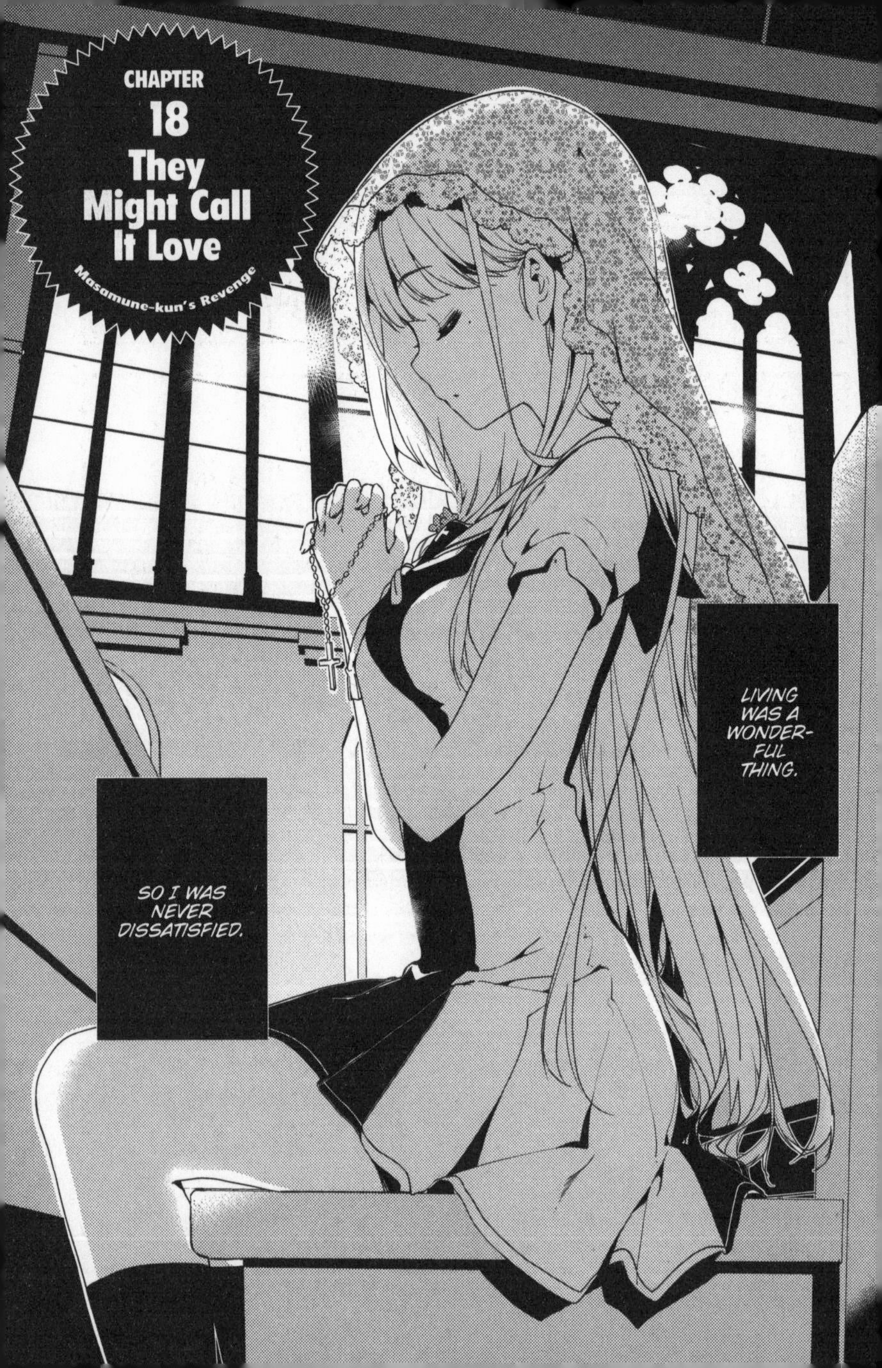
CHAPTER
18
They Might Call It Love
Masamune-kun's Revenge
LIVING WAS A WONDER-FUL THING.
SO I WAS NEVER DISSATISFIED.

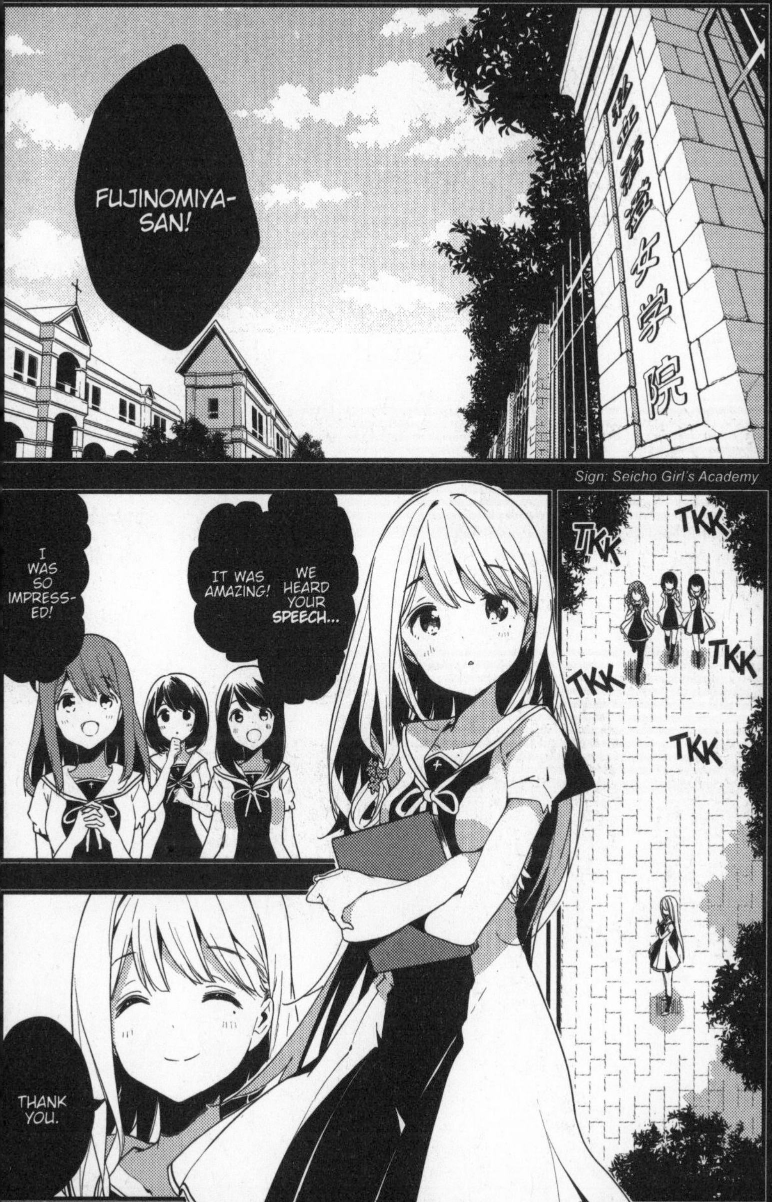
FUJINOMIYA-SAN!
Sign: Seicho Girl's Academy
TKK
TKK
TKK
TKK
TKK
WE HEARD YOUR SPEECH...
IT WAS AMAZING!
I WAS SO IMPRESSED!
THANK YOU.

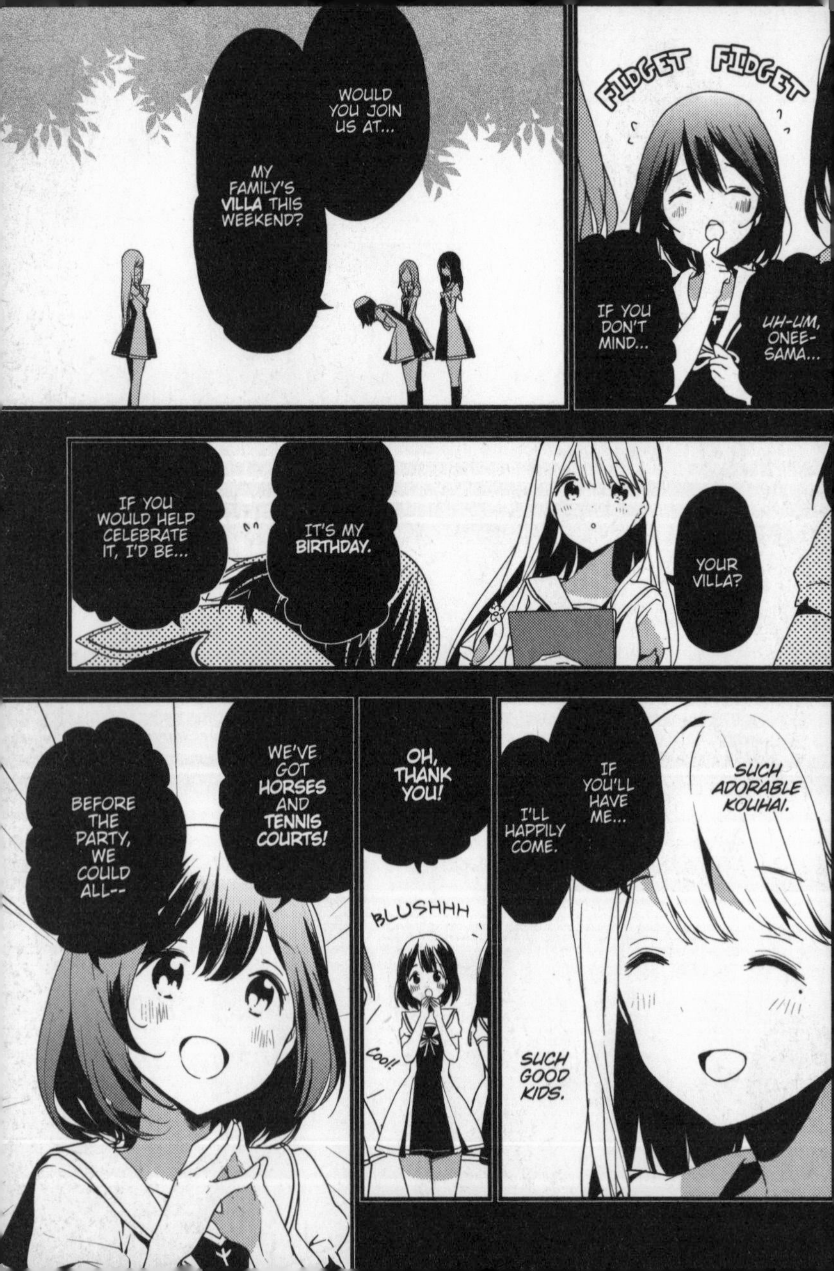
FIDGET FIDGET
UH-UM, ONEE-SAMA...
IF YOU DON'T MIND...
WOULD YOU JOIN US AT...
MY FAMILY'S VILLA THIS WEEKEND?
YOUR VILLA?
IT'S MY BIRTHDAY.
IF YOU WOULD HELP CELEBRATE IT, I'D BE...
SUCH ADORABLE KOUHAI.
IF YOU'LL HAVE ME...
I'LL HAPPILY COME.
SUCH GOOD KIDS.
OH, THANK YOU!
BLUSHHH
COO!!
WE'VE GOT HORSES AND TENNIS COURTS!
BEFORE THE PARTY, WE COULD ALL--

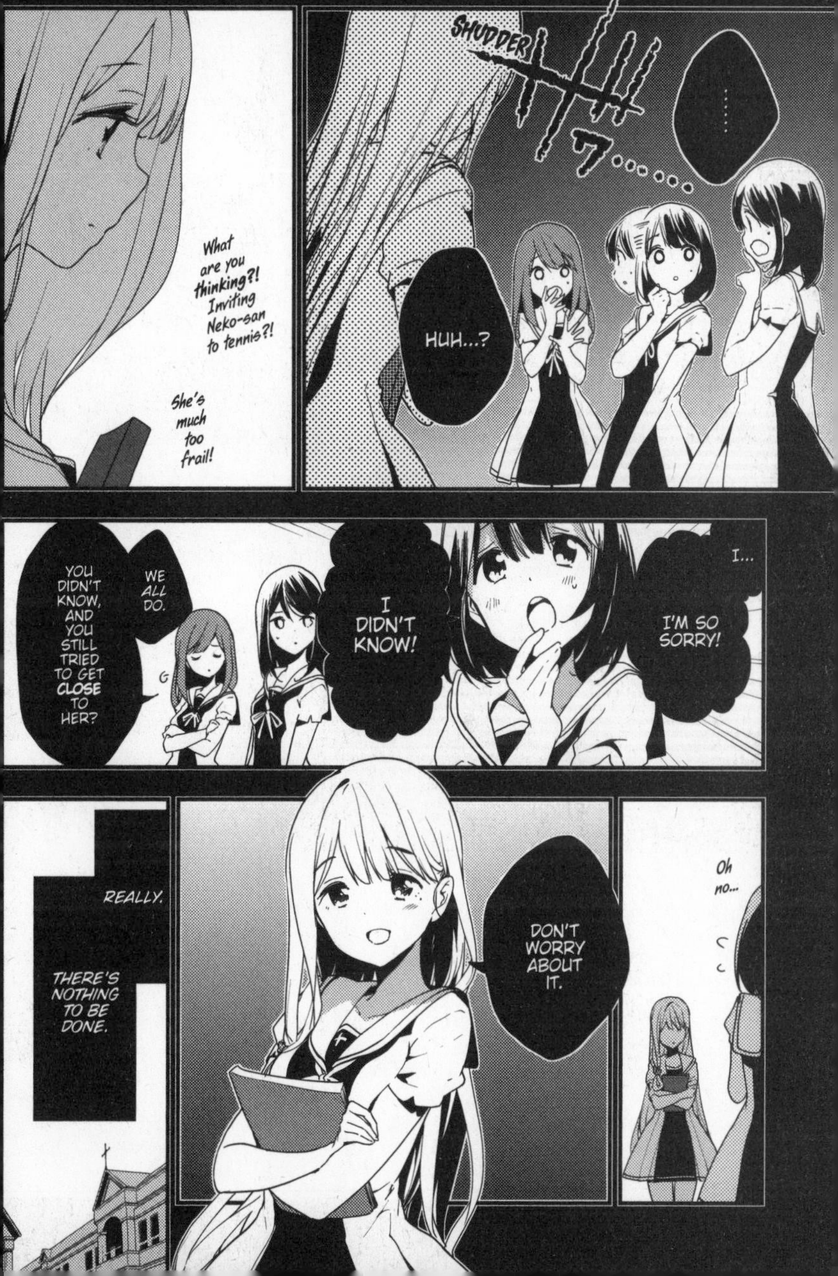
SHUDDER
ワ
......
HUH...?
What are you thinking?! Inviting Neko-san to tennis?!
She's much too frail!
I...
I'M SO SORRY!
I DIDN'T KNOW!
WE ALL DO.
YOU DIDN'T KNOW, AND YOU STILL TRIED TO GET CLOSE TO HER?
Oh no...
DON'T WORRY ABOUT IT.
REALLY.
THERE'S NOTHING TO BE DONE.

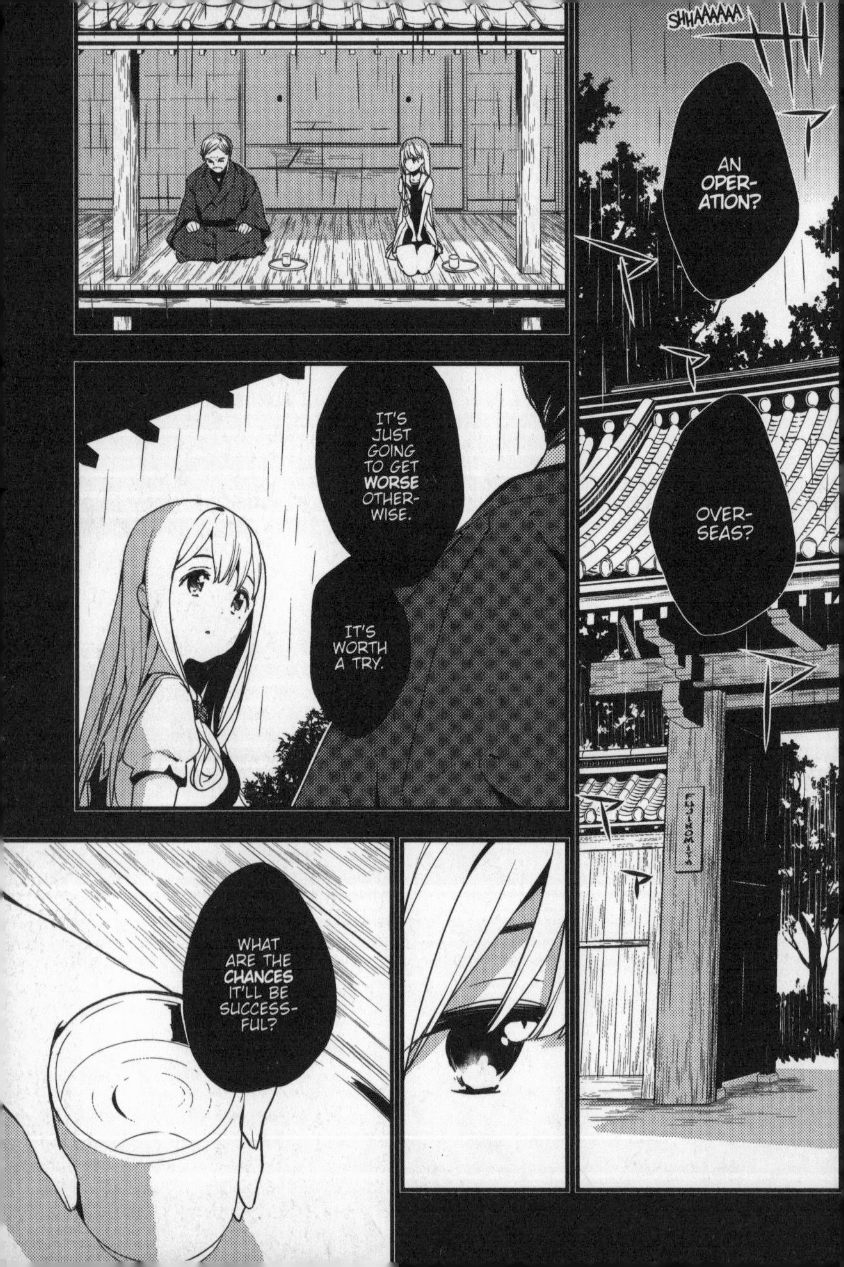
SHHAAAAA
AN OPERATION?
OVERSEAS?
FUJIKOMIYA
IT'S JUST GOING TO GET **WORSE** OTHERWISE.
IT'S WORTH A TRY.
WHAT ARE THE **CHANCES** IT'LL BE SUCCESSFUL?

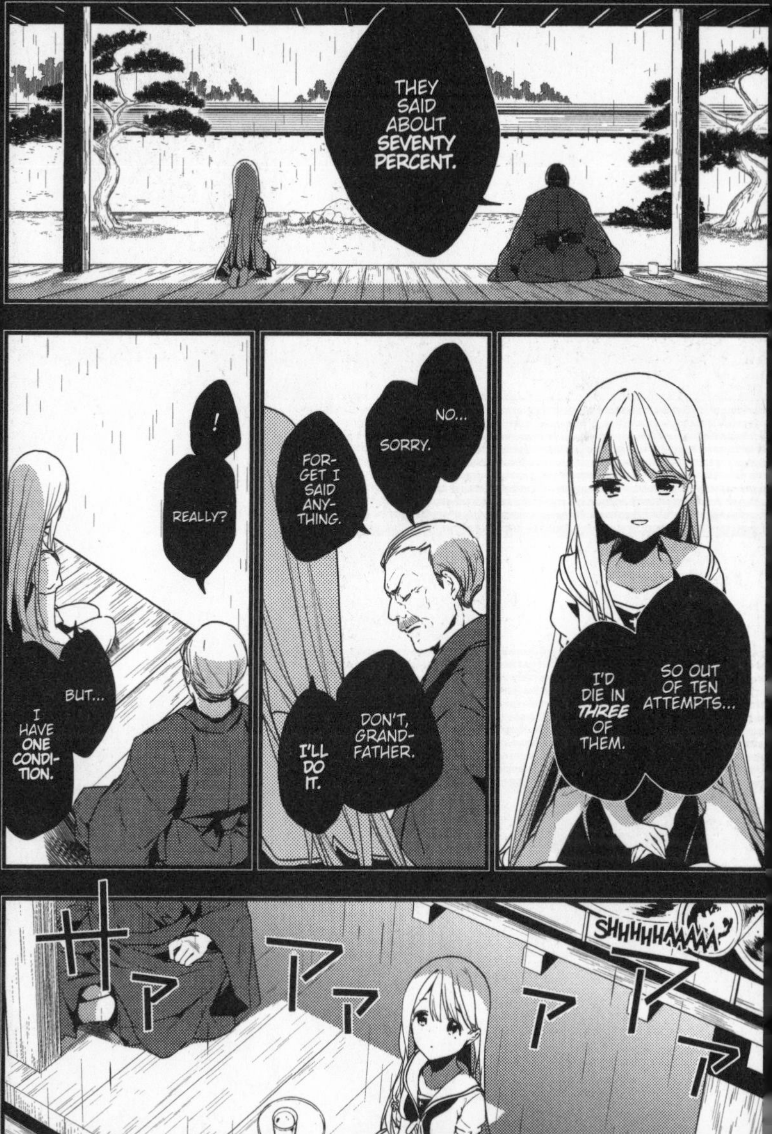
THEY SAID ABOUT SEVENTY PERCENT.
SO OUT OF TEN ATTEMPTS...
I'D DIE IN THREE OF THEM.
NO...
SORRY.
FORGET I SAID ANYTHING.
DON'T, GRANDFATHER.
I'LL DO IT.
!
REALLY?
BUT...
I HAVE ONE CONDITION.
SHHHHHAAAAA

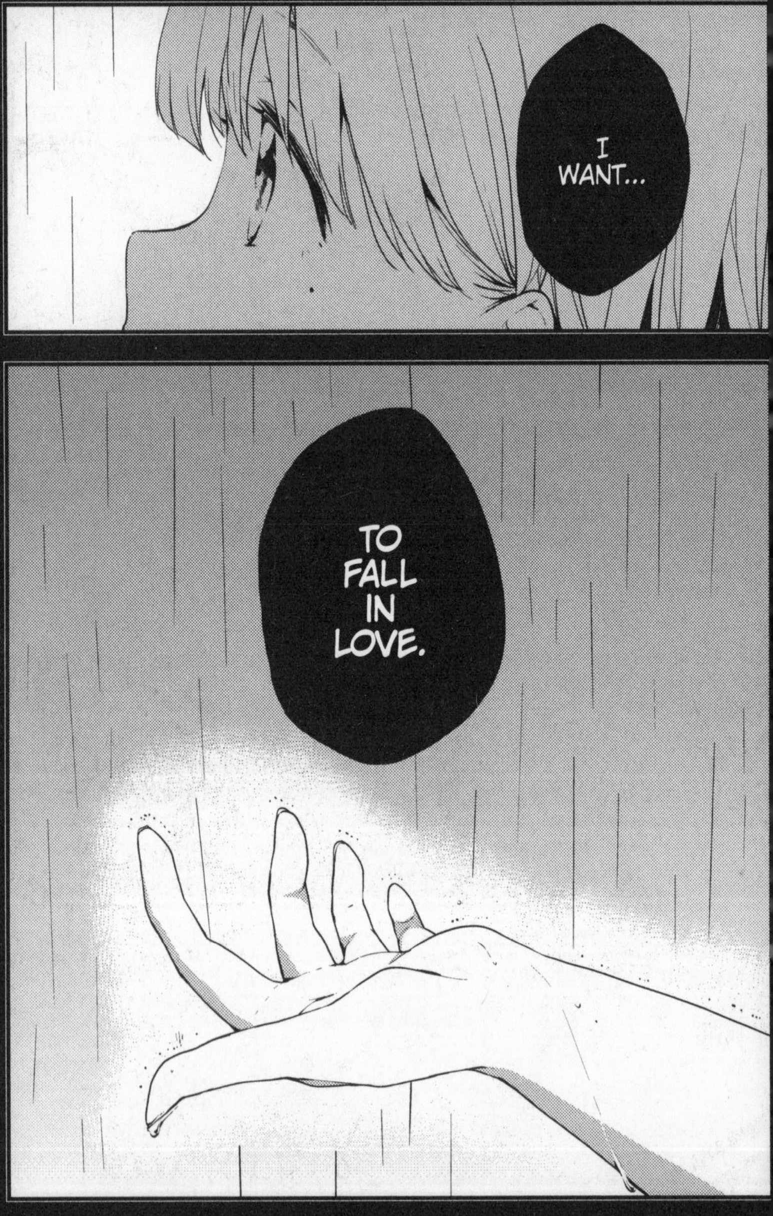
I WANT...
TO FALL IN LOVE.

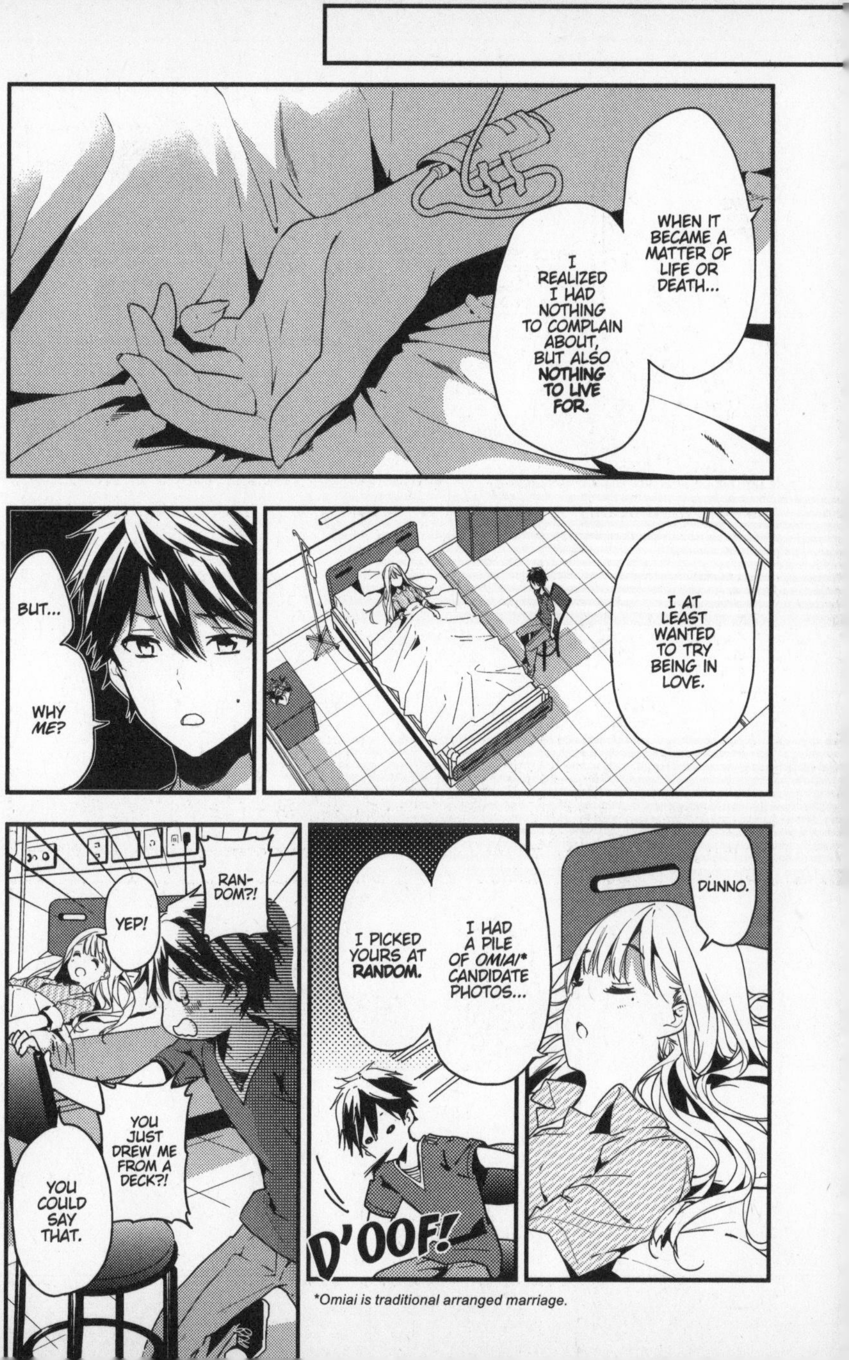
WHEN IT BECAME A MATTER OF LIFE OR DEATH...
I REALIZED I HAD NOTHING TO COMPLAIN ABOUT, BUT ALSO **NOTHING TO LIVE FOR.**
I AT LEAST WANTED TO TRY BEING IN LOVE.
BUT...
WHY *ME*?
DUNNO.
I HAD A PILE OF *OMIAI** CANDIDATE PHOTOS...
I PICKED YOURS AT **RANDOM.**
D'OOF!
RAN-DOM?!
YEP!
YOU JUST DREW ME FROM A DECK?!
YOU COULD SAY THAT.

*Omiai is traditional arranged marriage.

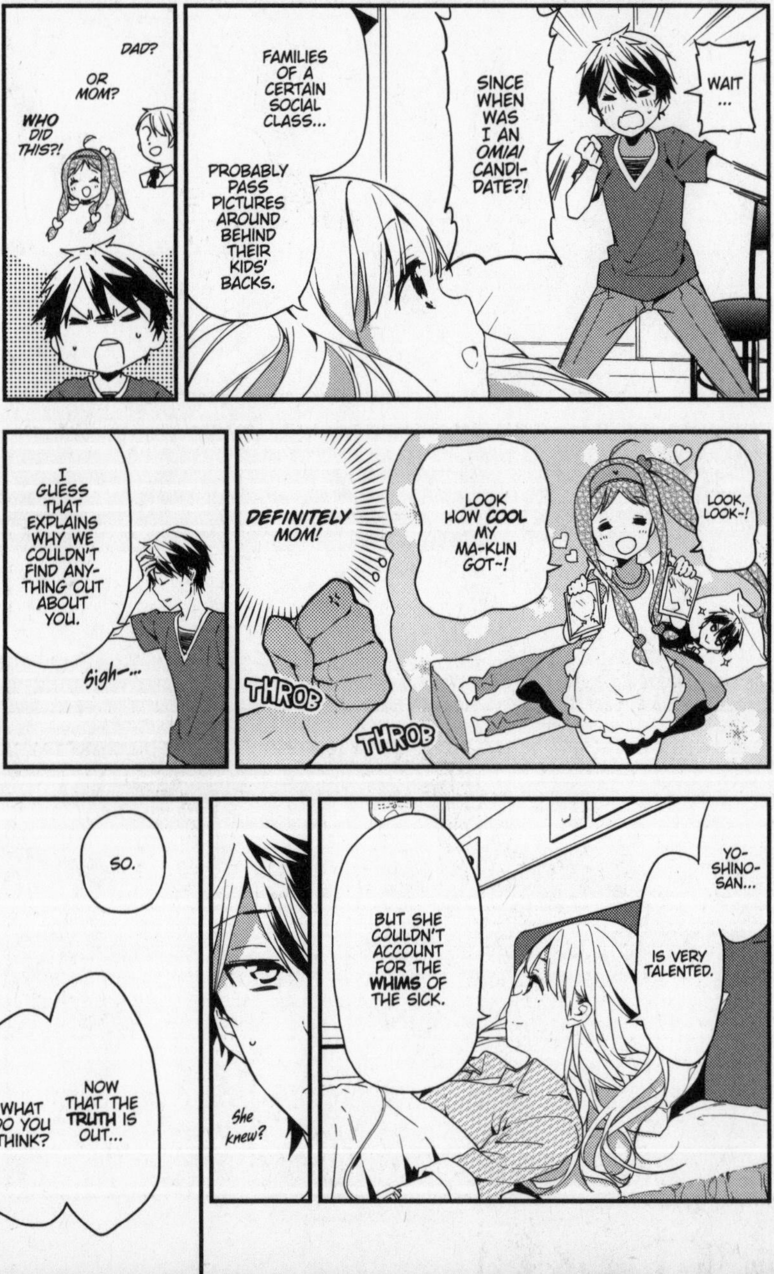
WAIT ...
SINCE WHEN WAS I AN OMIAI CANDIDATE?!
FAMILIES OF A CERTAIN SOCIAL CLASS...
PROBABLY PASS PICTURES AROUND BEHIND THEIR KIDS' BACKS.
DAD?
OR MOM?
WHO DID THIS?!
LOOK, LOOK~!
LOOK HOW COOL MY MA-KUN GOT~!
DEFINITELY MOM!
THROB
THROB
I GUESS THAT EXPLAINS WHY WE COULDN'T FIND ANY-THING OUT ABOUT YOU.
Sigh~...
YO-SHINO-SAN...
IS VERY TALENTED.
BUT SHE COULDN'T ACCOUNT FOR THE WHIMS OF THE SICK.
She knew?
SO.
NOW THAT THE TRUTH IS OUT...
WHAT DO YOU THINK?

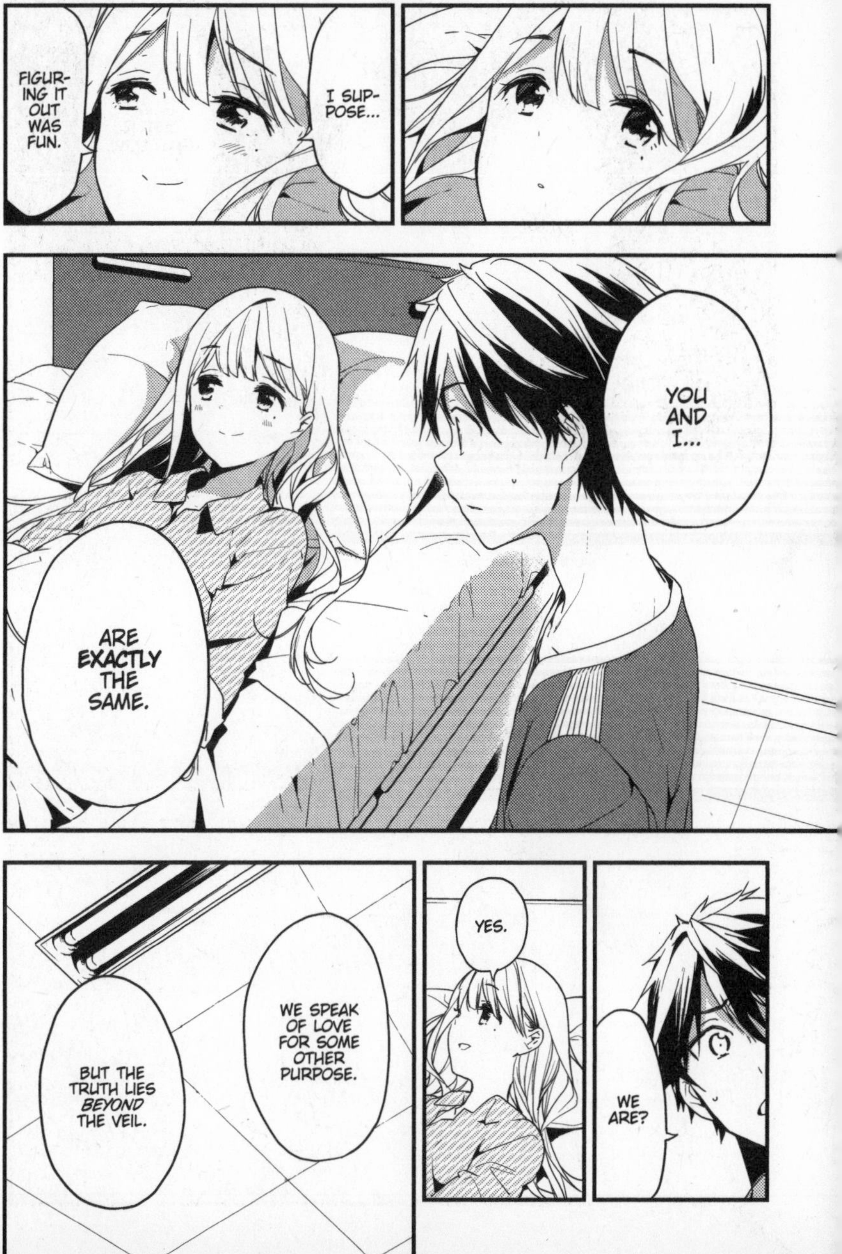
I SUP-POSE...
FIGUR-ING IT OUT WAS FUN.
YOU AND I...
ARE EXACTLY THE SAME.
WE ARE?
YES.
WE SPEAK OF LOVE FOR SOME OTHER PURPOSE.
BUT THE TRUTH LIES *BEYOND* THE VEIL.

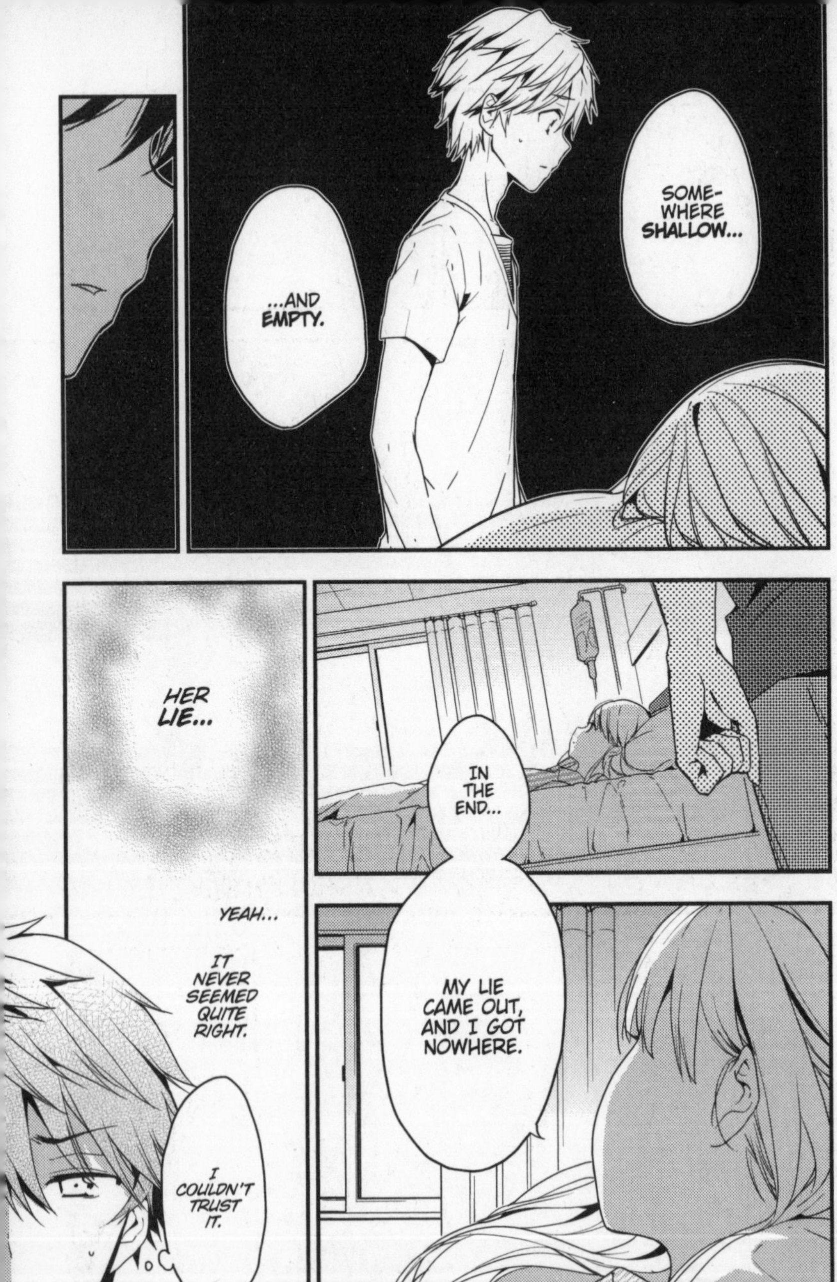
SOME-WHERE SHALLOW...
...AND EMPTY.
IN THE END...
HER LIE...
MY LIE CAME OUT, AND I GOT NOWHERE.
YEAH...
IT NEVER SEEMED QUITE RIGHT.
I COULDN'T TRUST IT.

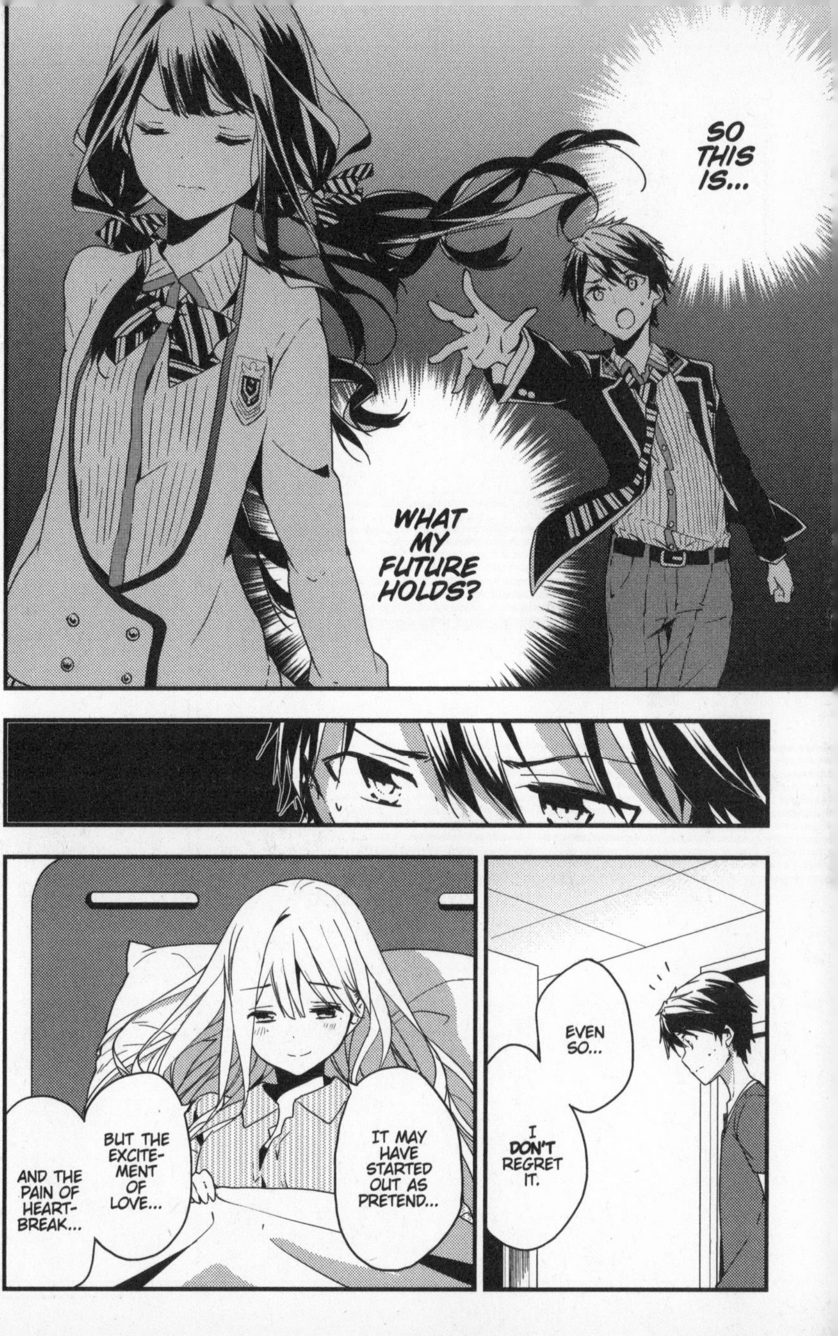
SO THIS IS...
WHAT MY FUTURE HOLDS?
EVEN SO...
I **DON'T** REGRET IT.
IT MAY HAVE STARTED OUT AS PRETEND...
BUT THE EXCITEMENT OF LOVE...
AND THE PAIN OF HEARTBREAK...

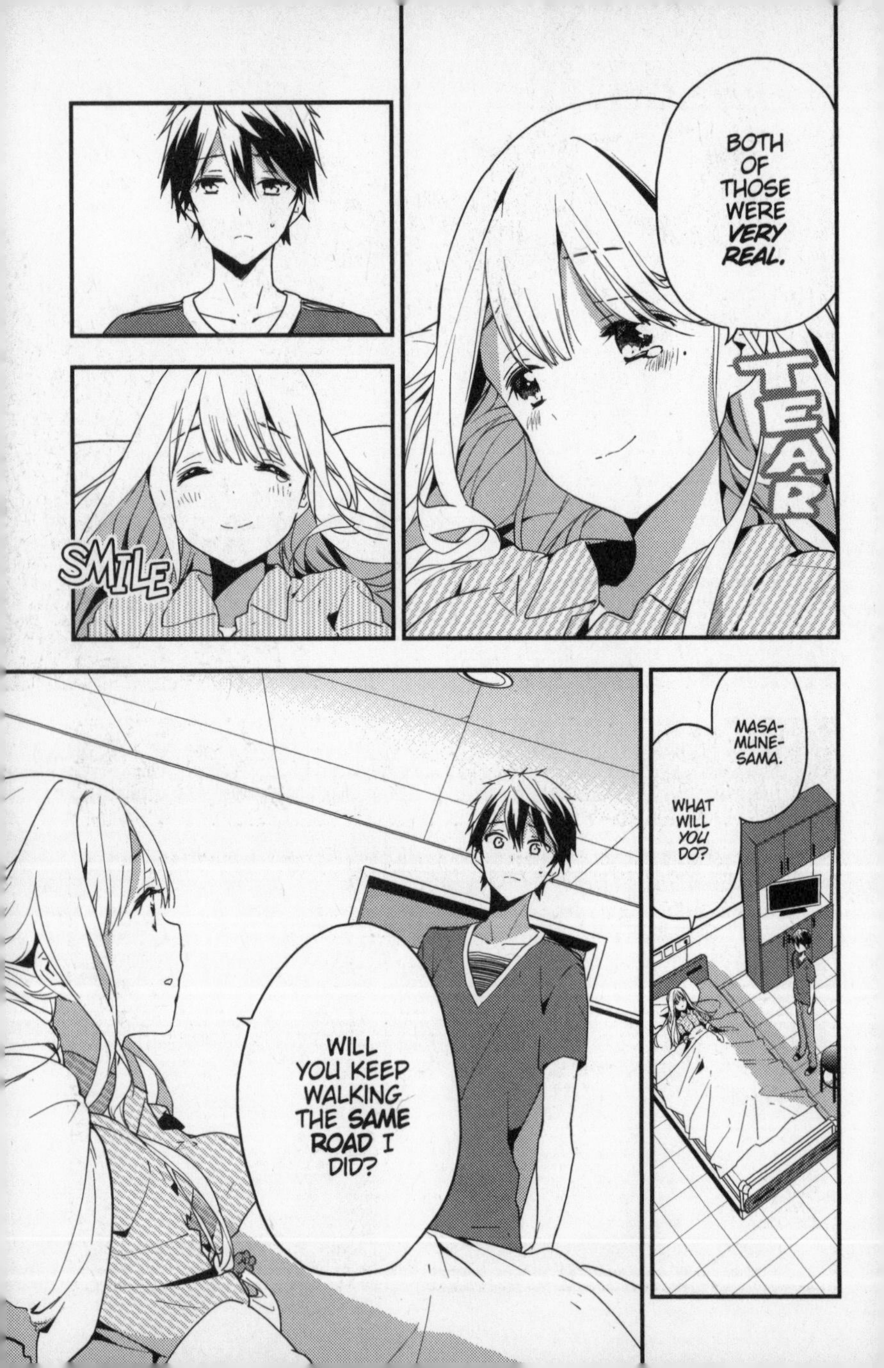
BOTH OF THOSE WERE VERY REAL.
TEAR
SMILE
MASAMUNE-SAMA.
WHAT WILL YOU DO?
WILL YOU KEEP WALKING THE SAME ROAD I DID?

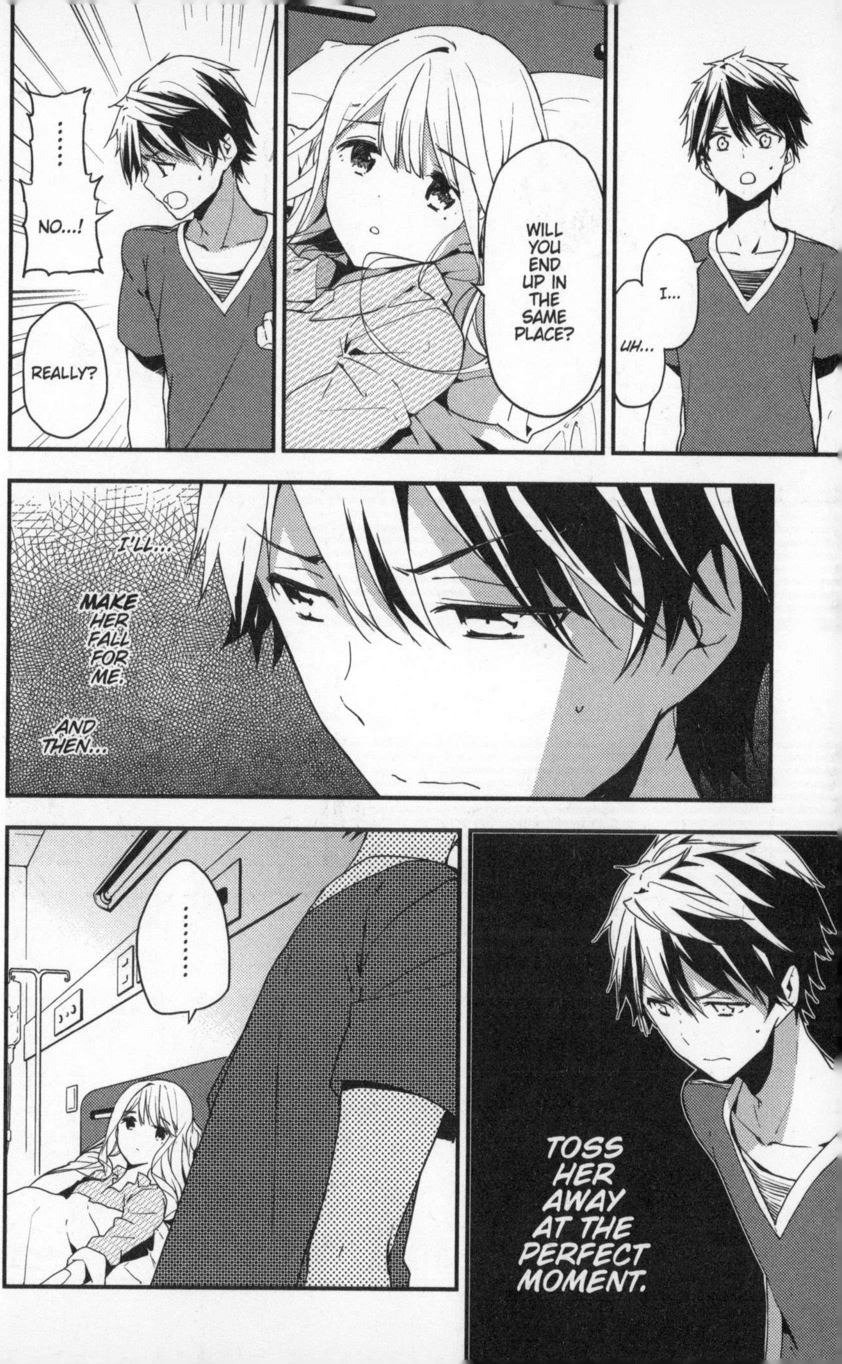
I...
UH...
WILL YOU END UP IN THE SAME PLACE?
......
NO...!
REALLY?
I'LL...
MAKE HER FALL FOR ME.
AND THEN...
TOSS HER AWAY AT THE PERFECT MOMENT.
......

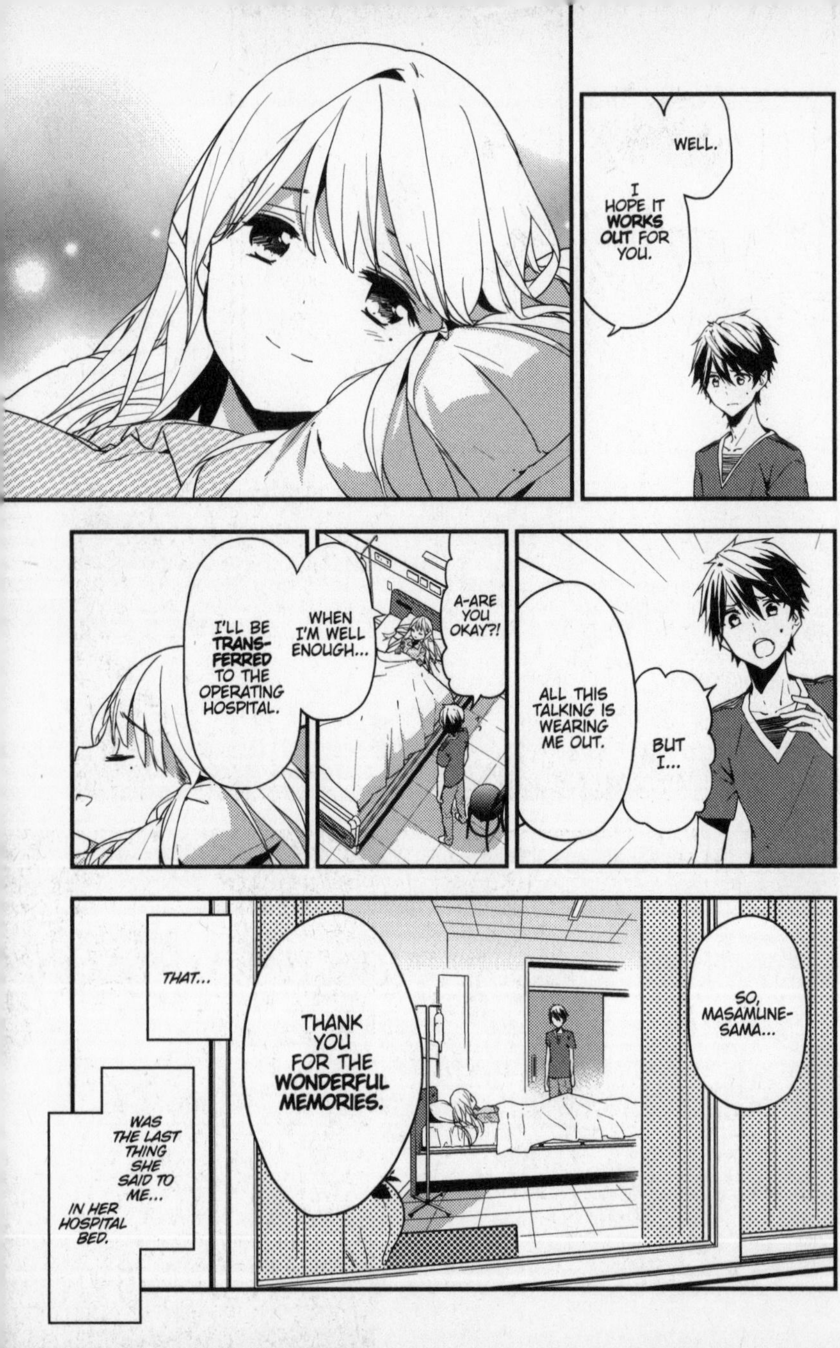
WELL.
I HOPE IT WORKS OUT FOR YOU.
BUT I...
ALL THIS TALKING IS WEARING ME OUT.
A-ARE YOU OKAY?!
WHEN I'M WELL ENOUGH...
I'LL BE TRANSFERRED TO THE OPERATING HOSPITAL.
SO, MASAMUNE-SAMA...
THANK YOU FOR THE WONDERFUL MEMORIES.
THAT...
WAS THE LAST THING SHE SAID TO ME...
IN HER HOSPITAL BED.

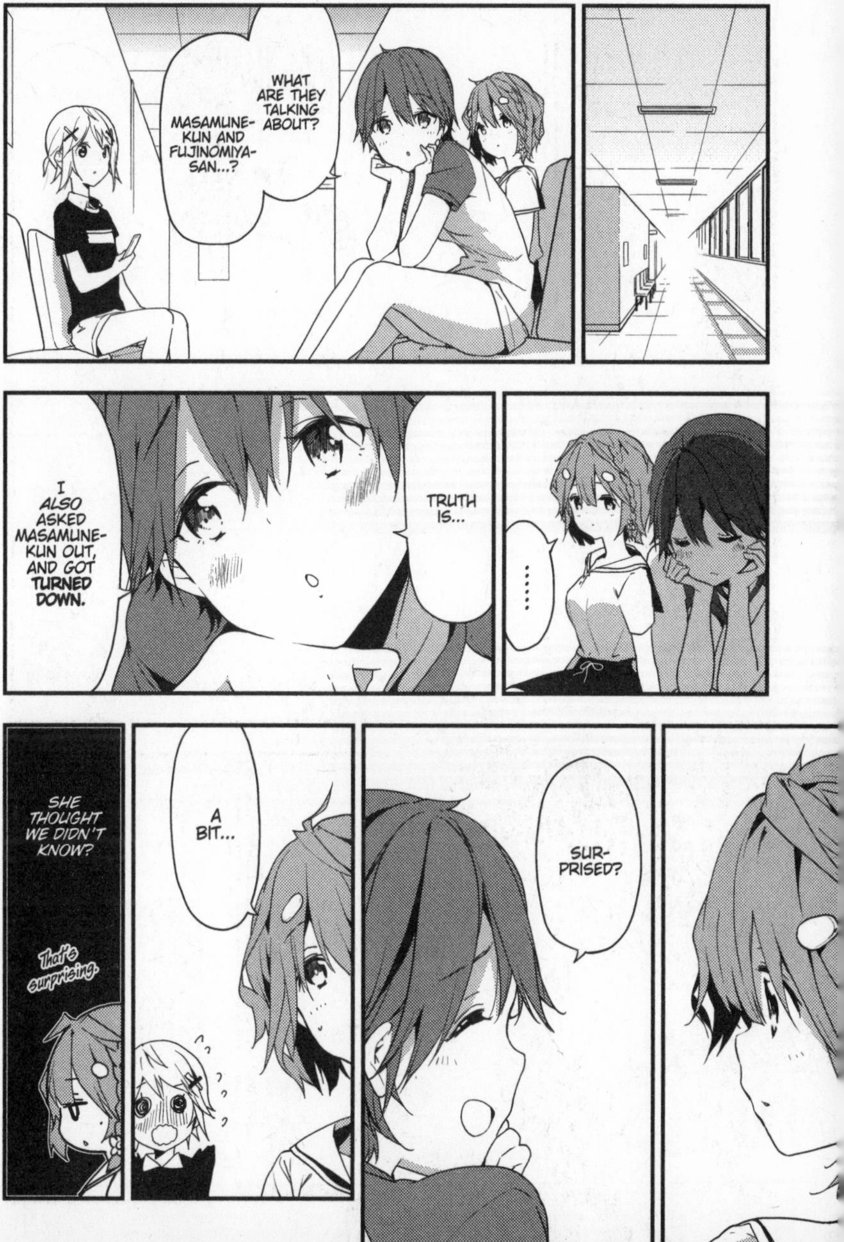
WHAT ARE THEY TALKING ABOUT?
MASAMUNE-KUN AND FUJINOMIYA-SAN...?
......
TRUTH IS...
I ALSO ASKED MASAMUNE-KUN OUT, AND GOT TURNED DOWN.
SUR-PRISED?
A BIT...
SHE THOUGHT WE DIDN'T KNOW?
That's surprising.

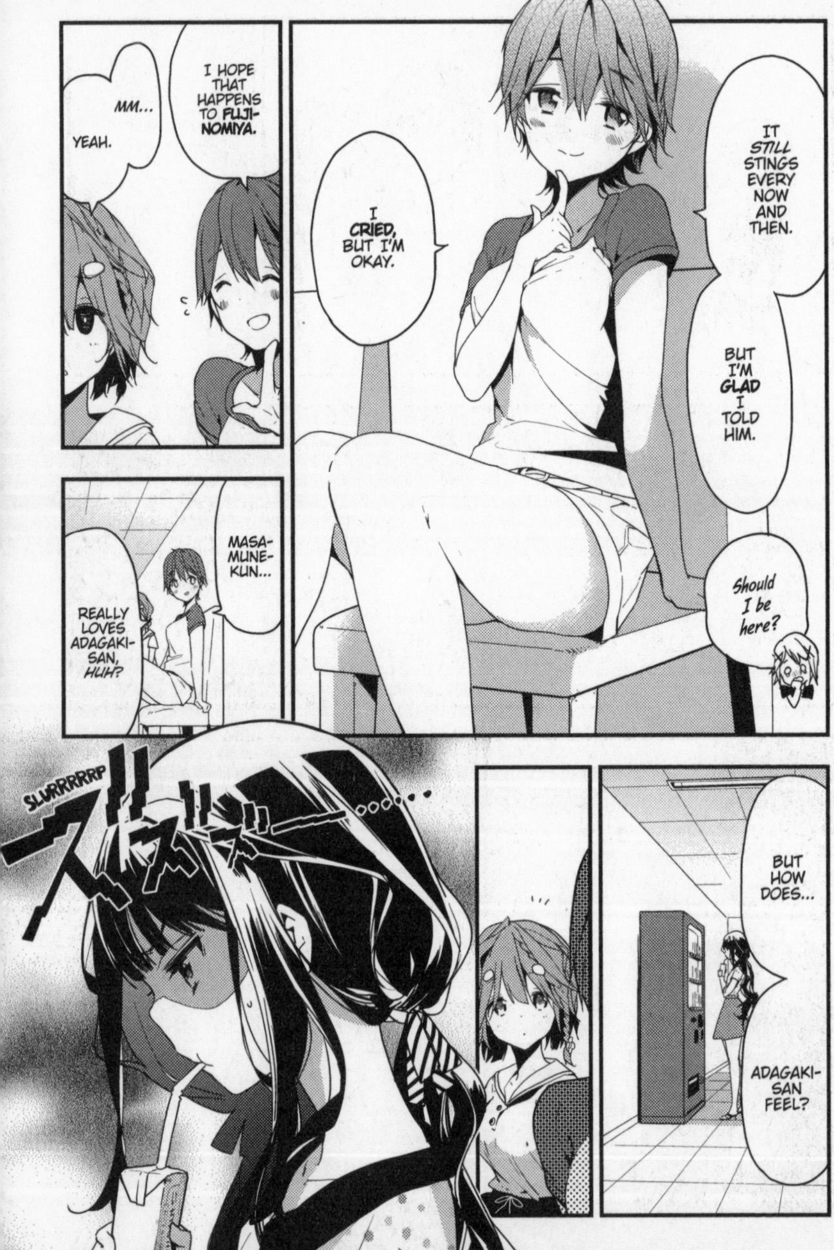
IT STILL STINGS EVERY NOW AND THEN.
I CRIED, BUT I'M OKAY.
BUT I'M GLAD I TOLD HIM.
Should I be here?
I HOPE THAT HAPPENS TO FUJI-NOMIYA.
MM... YEAH.
MASAMUNE-KUN...
REALLY LOVES ADAGAKI-SAN, HUH?
BUT HOW DOES...
ADAGAKI-SAN FEEL?
SLURRRRRP

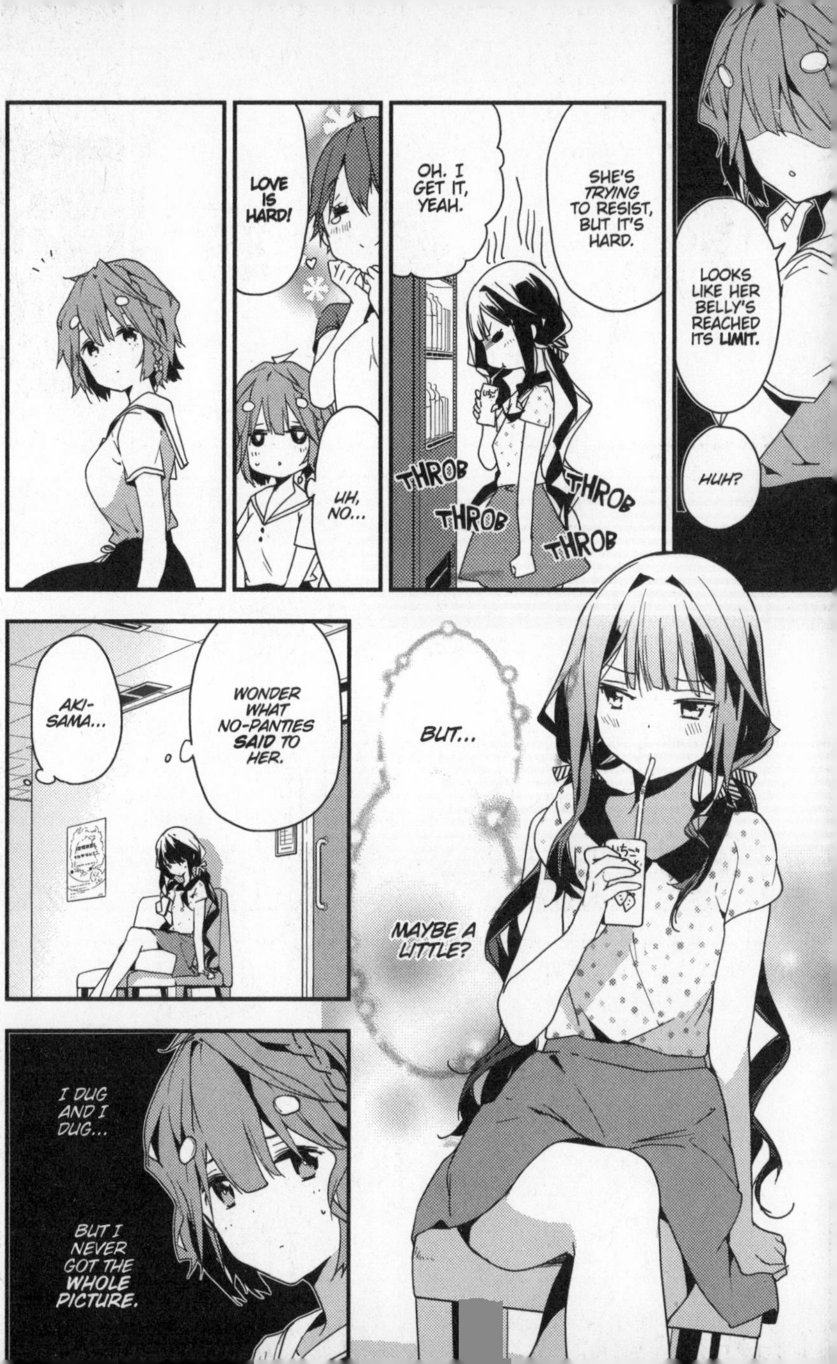
LOOKS LIKE HER BELLY'S REACHED ITS LIMIT.
HUH?
SHE'S TRYING TO RESIST, BUT IT'S HARD.
OH. I GET IT, YEAH.
THROB
THROB
THROB
THROB
LOVE IS HARD!
UH, NO...
BUT...
MAYBE A LITTLE?
WONDER WHAT NO-PANTIES SAID TO HER.
AKI-SAMA...
I DUG AND I DUG...
BUT I NEVER GOT THE WHOLE PICTURE.

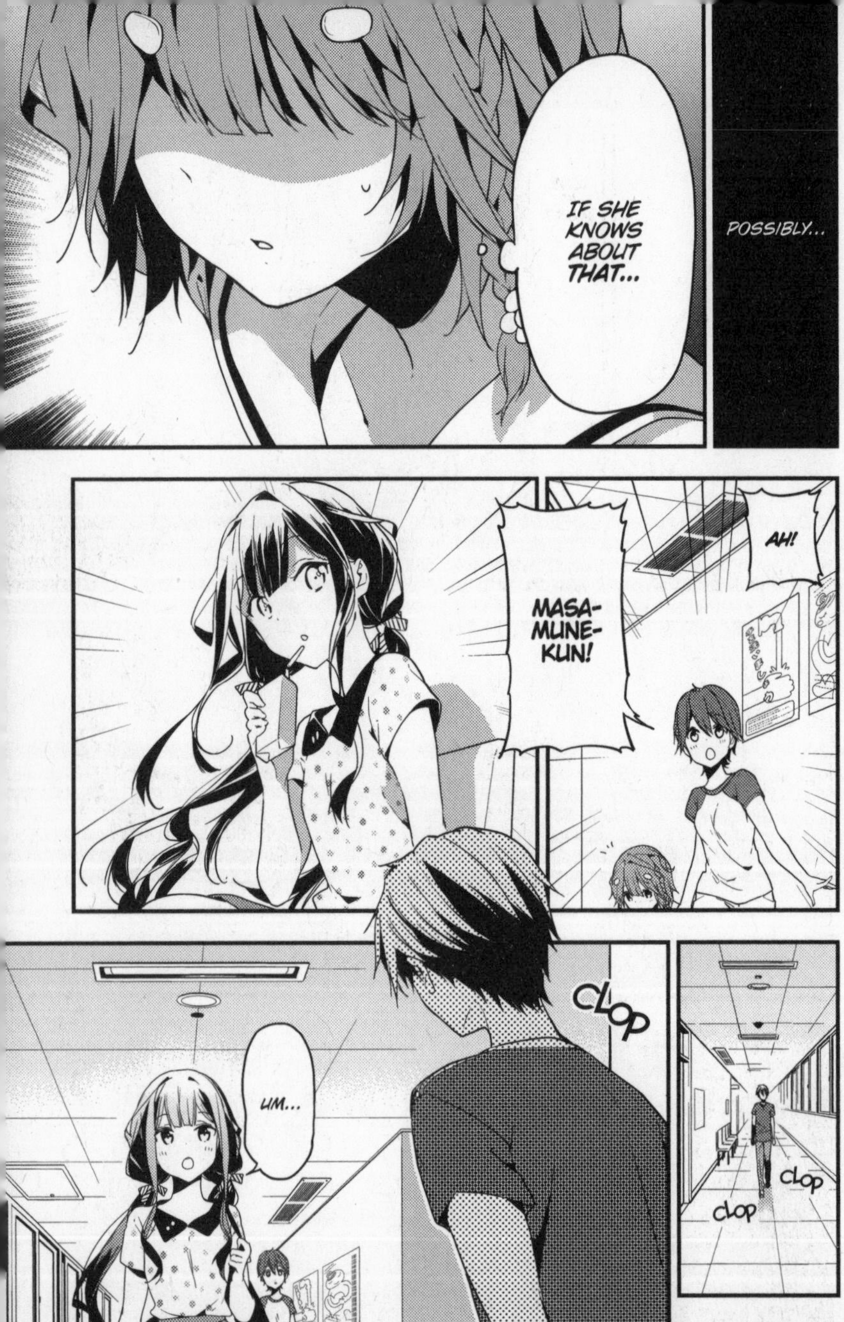
POSSIBLY...
IF SHE KNOWS ABOUT THAT...
AH!
MASA-MUNE-KUN!
CLOP
CLOP
CLOP
UM...

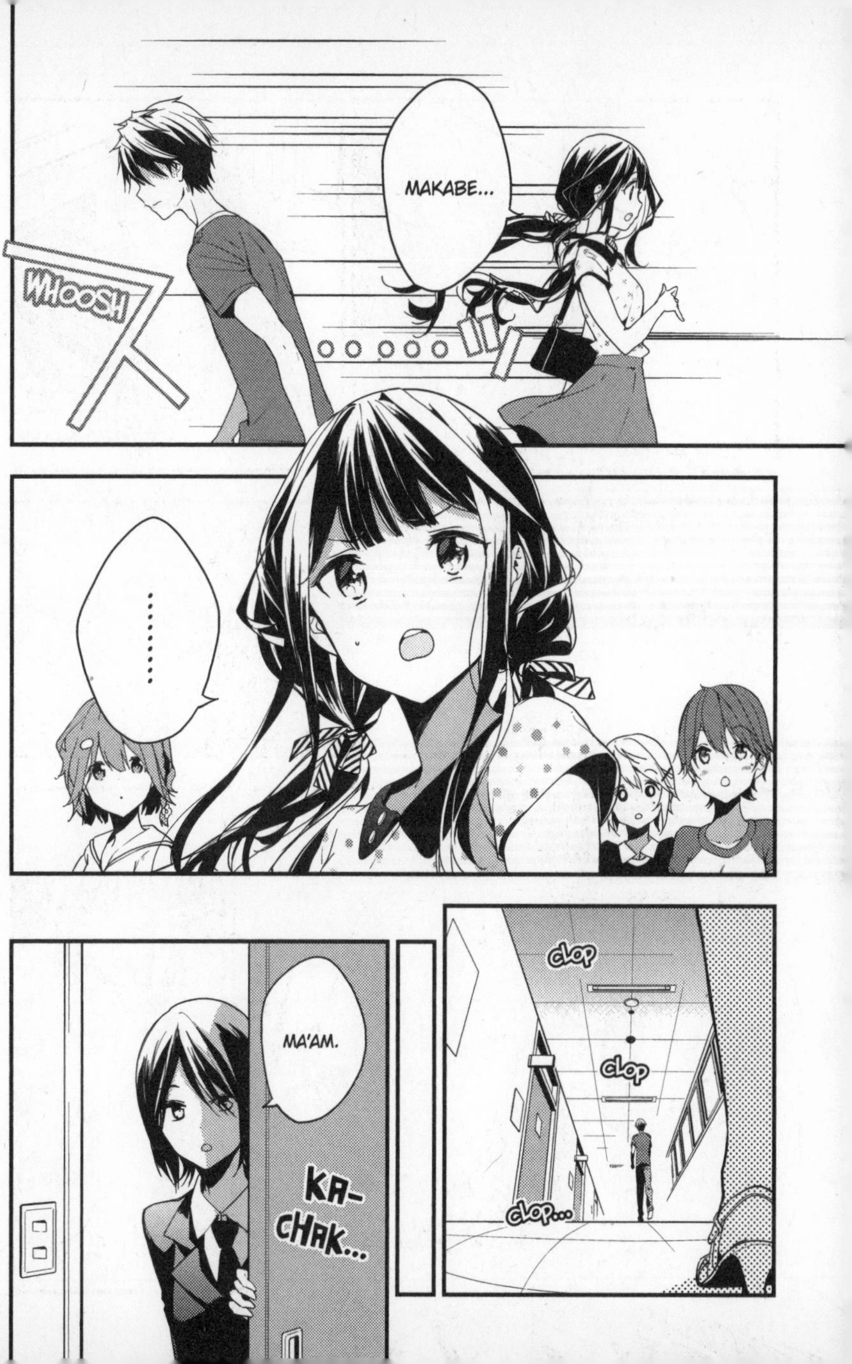
MAKABE...
WHOOSH
......
CLOP
CLOP
CLOP...
MA'AM.
KA-CHAK...

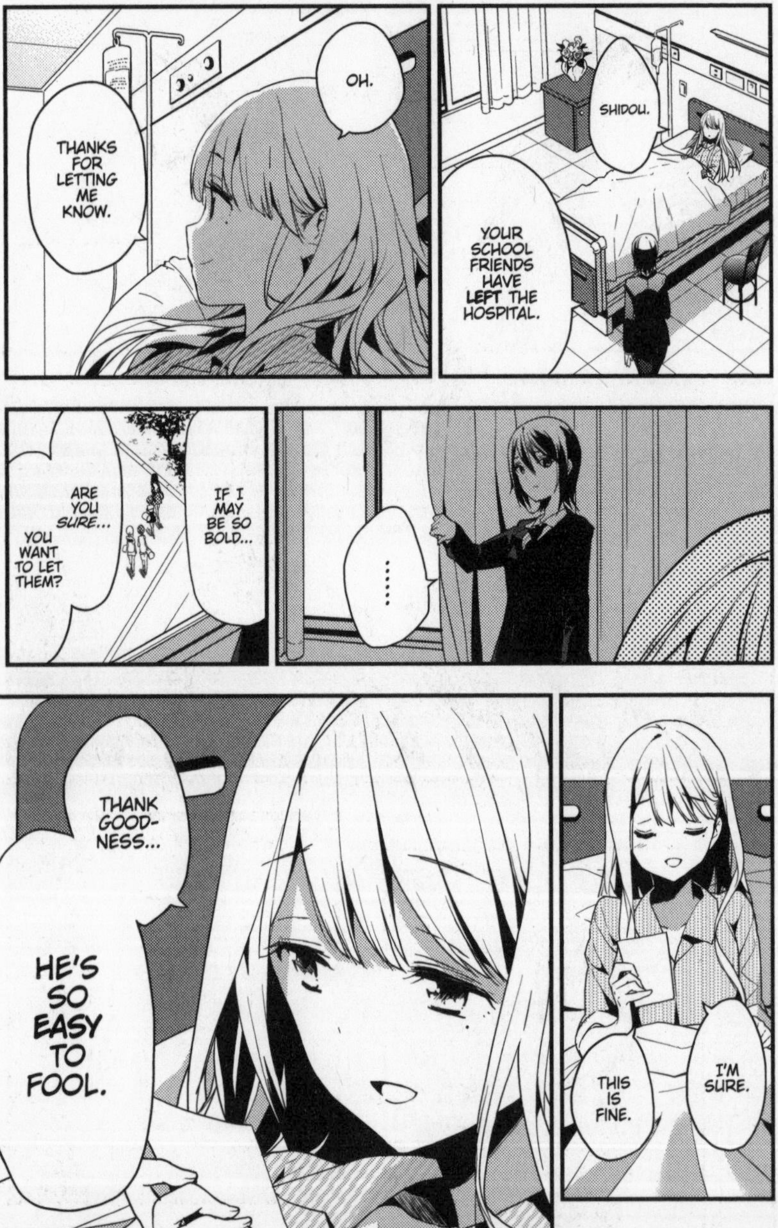
SHIDOU.
YOUR SCHOOL FRIENDS HAVE LEFT THE HOSPITAL.
OH.
THANKS FOR LETTING ME KNOW.
......
IF I MAY BE SO BOLD...
ARE YOU SURE... YOU WANT TO LET THEM?
I'M SURE.
THIS IS FINE.
THANK GOODNESS...
HE'S SO EASY TO FOOL.

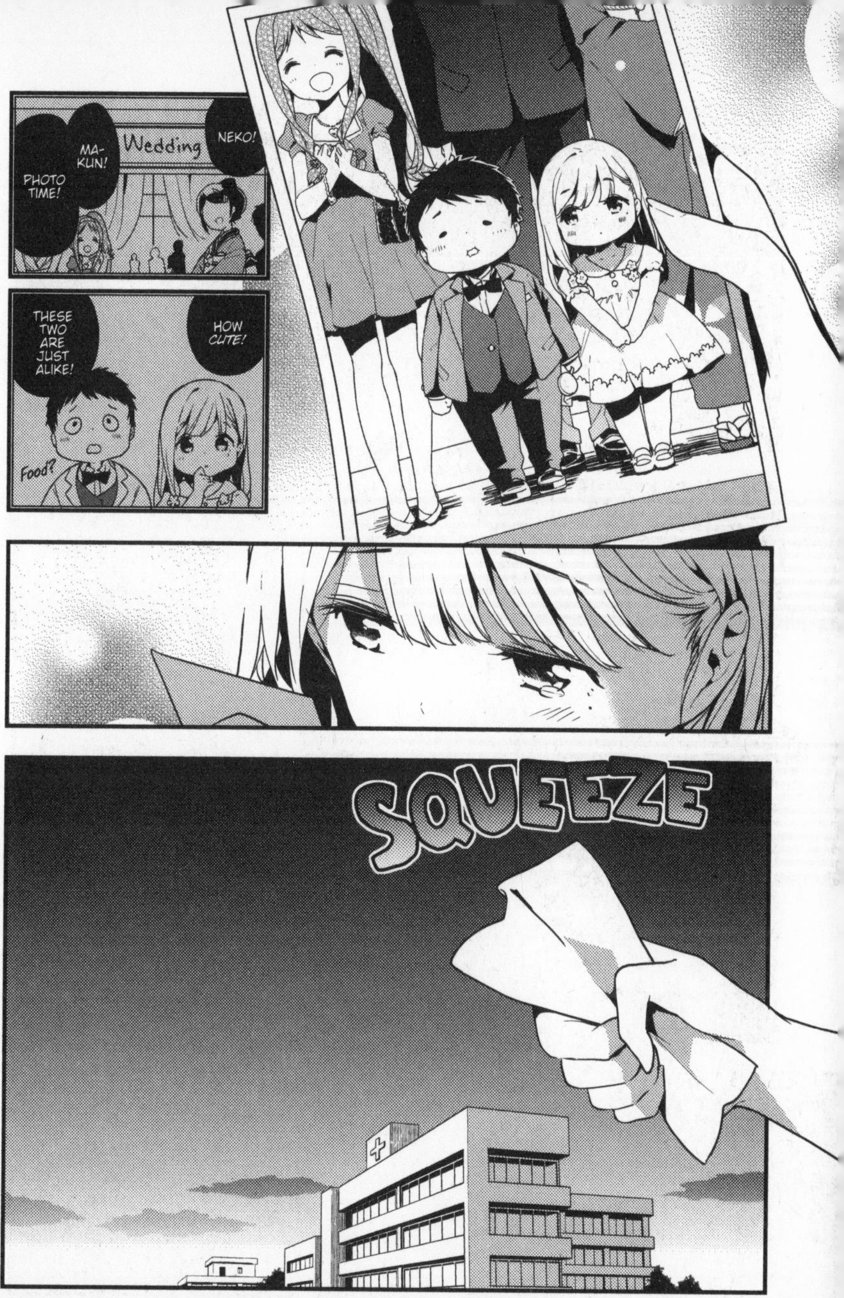
NEKO!
Wedding
MA-KUN!
PHOTO TIME!
HOW CUTE!
THESE TWO ARE JUST ALIKE!
Food?
SQUEEZE

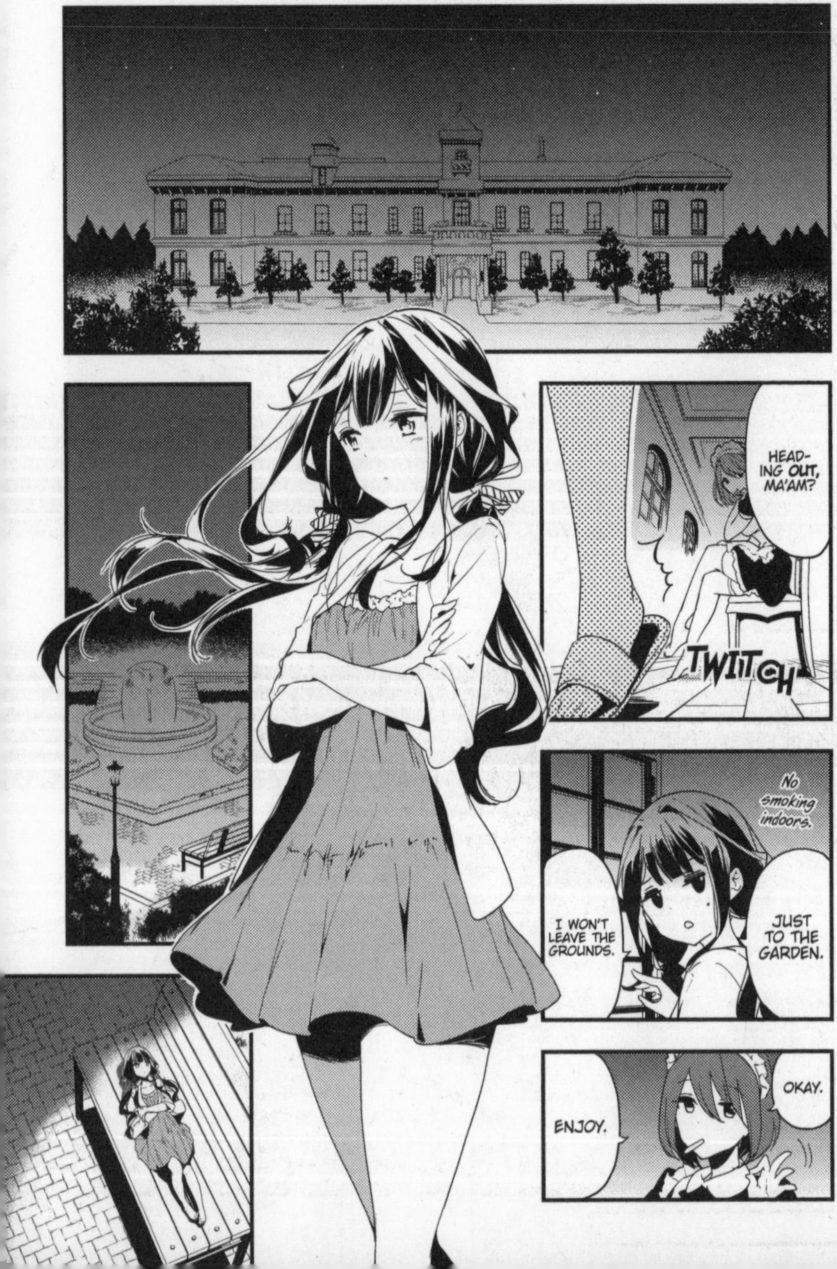
HEADING OUT, MA'AM?
TWITCH
No smoking indoors.
JUST TO THE GARDEN.
I WON'T LEAVE THE GROUNDS.
OKAY.
ENJOY.

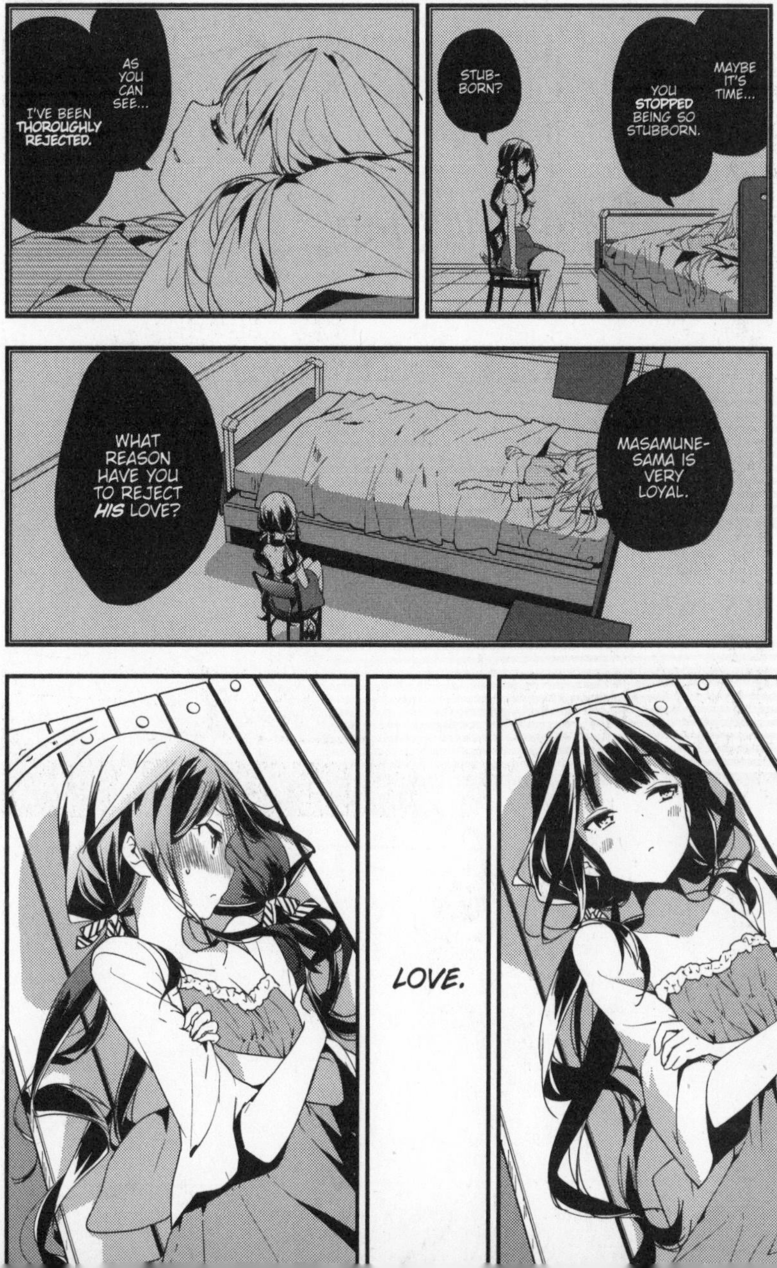
MAYBE IT'S TIME...
YOU STOPPED BEING SO STUBBORN.
STUB-BORN?
AS YOU CAN SEE...
I'VE BEEN THOROUGHLY REJECTED.
MASAMUNE-SAMA IS VERY LOYAL.
WHAT REASON HAVE YOU TO REJECT HIS LOVE?
LOVE.

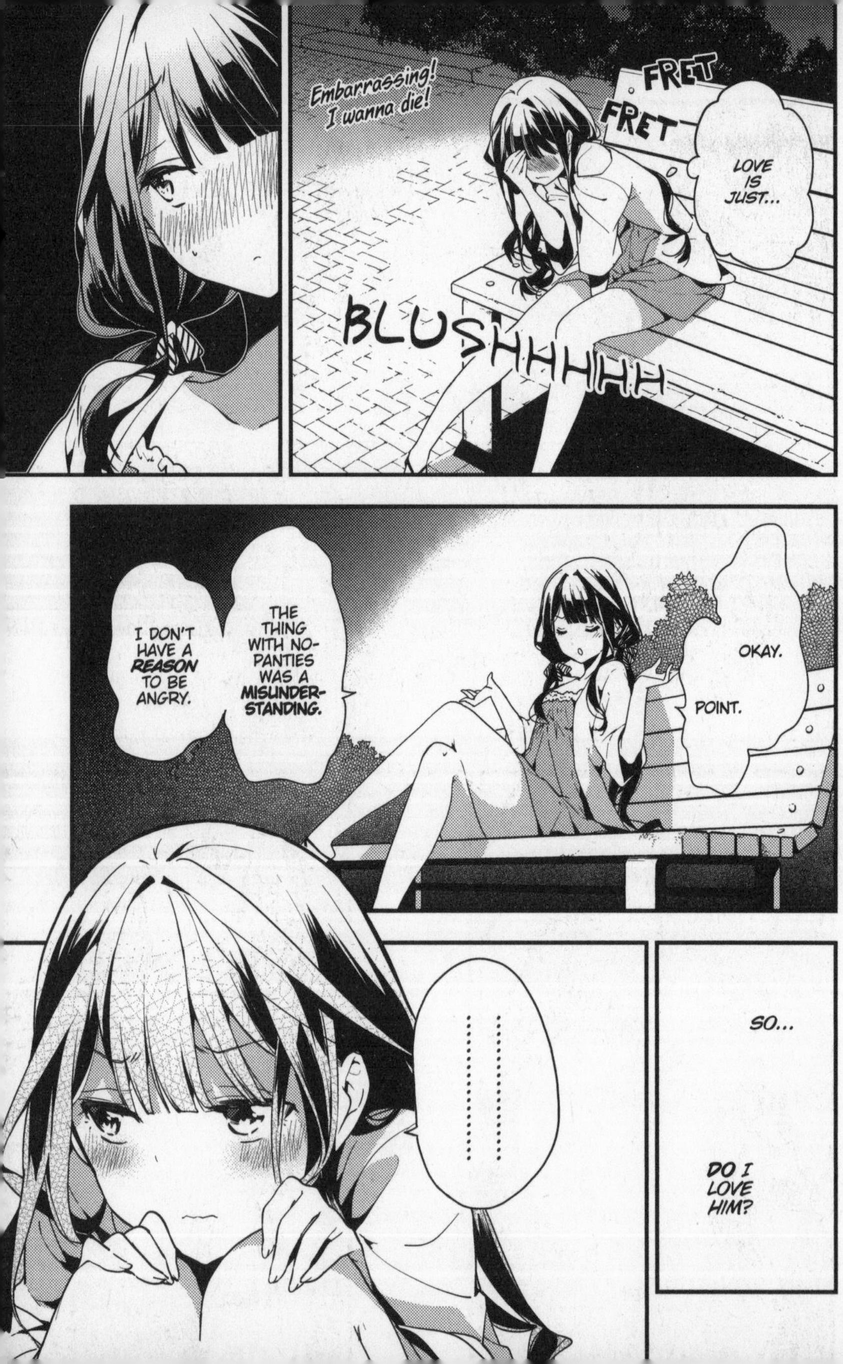
FRET
FRET
LOVE IS JUST...
Embarrassing! I wanna die!
BLUSHHHHH
OKAY.
POINT.
THE THING WITH NO-PANTIES WAS A MISUNDERSTANDING.
I DON'T HAVE A REASON TO BE ANGRY.
SO...
DO I LOVE HIM?
......

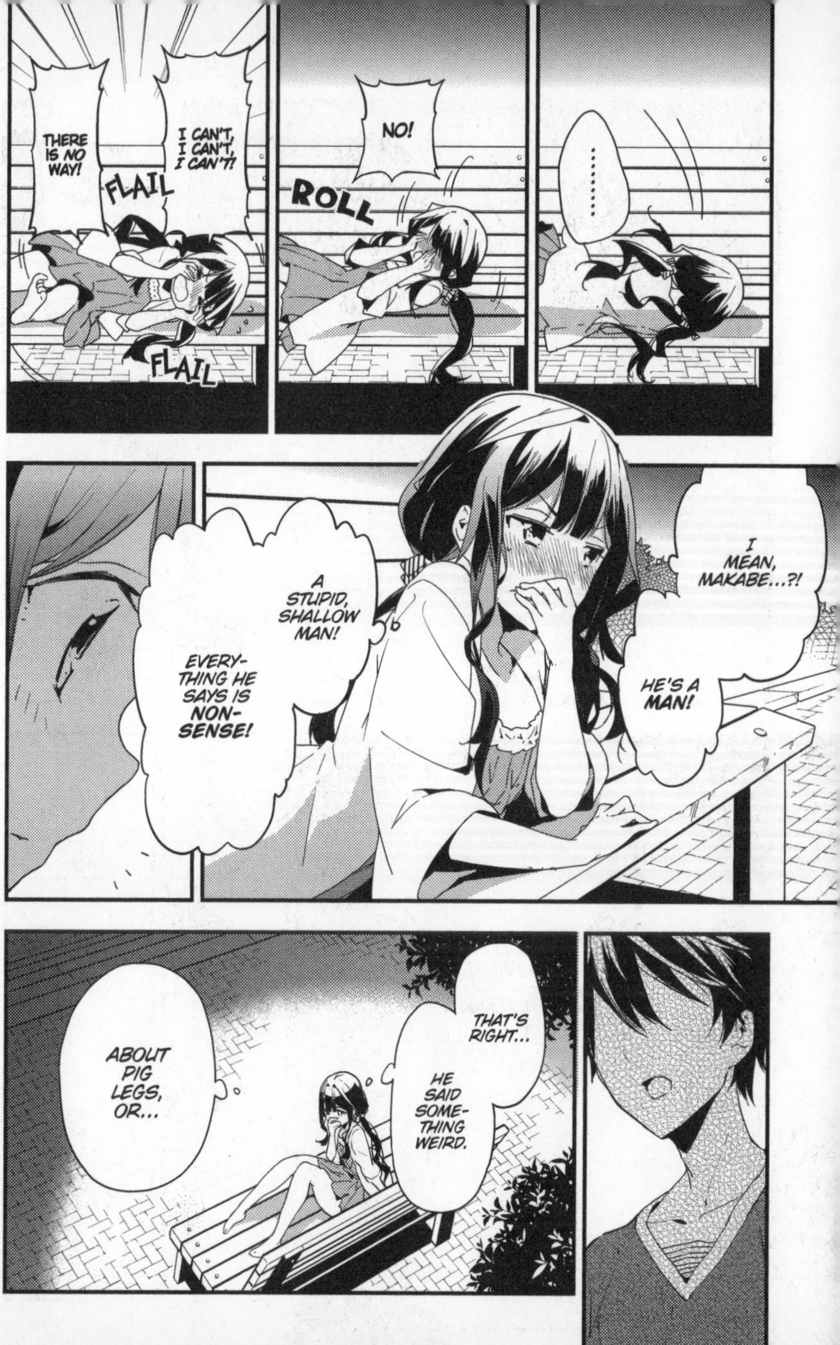
......
NO!
ROLL
I CAN'T, I CAN'T, I CAN'T!
THERE IS NO WAY!
FLAIL
FLAIL
I MEAN, MAKABE...?!
HE'S A MAN!
A STUPID, SHALLOW MAN!
EVERY-THING HE SAYS IS NON-SENSE!
THAT'S RIGHT...
HE SAID SOME-THING WEIRD.
ABOUT PIG LEGS, OR...

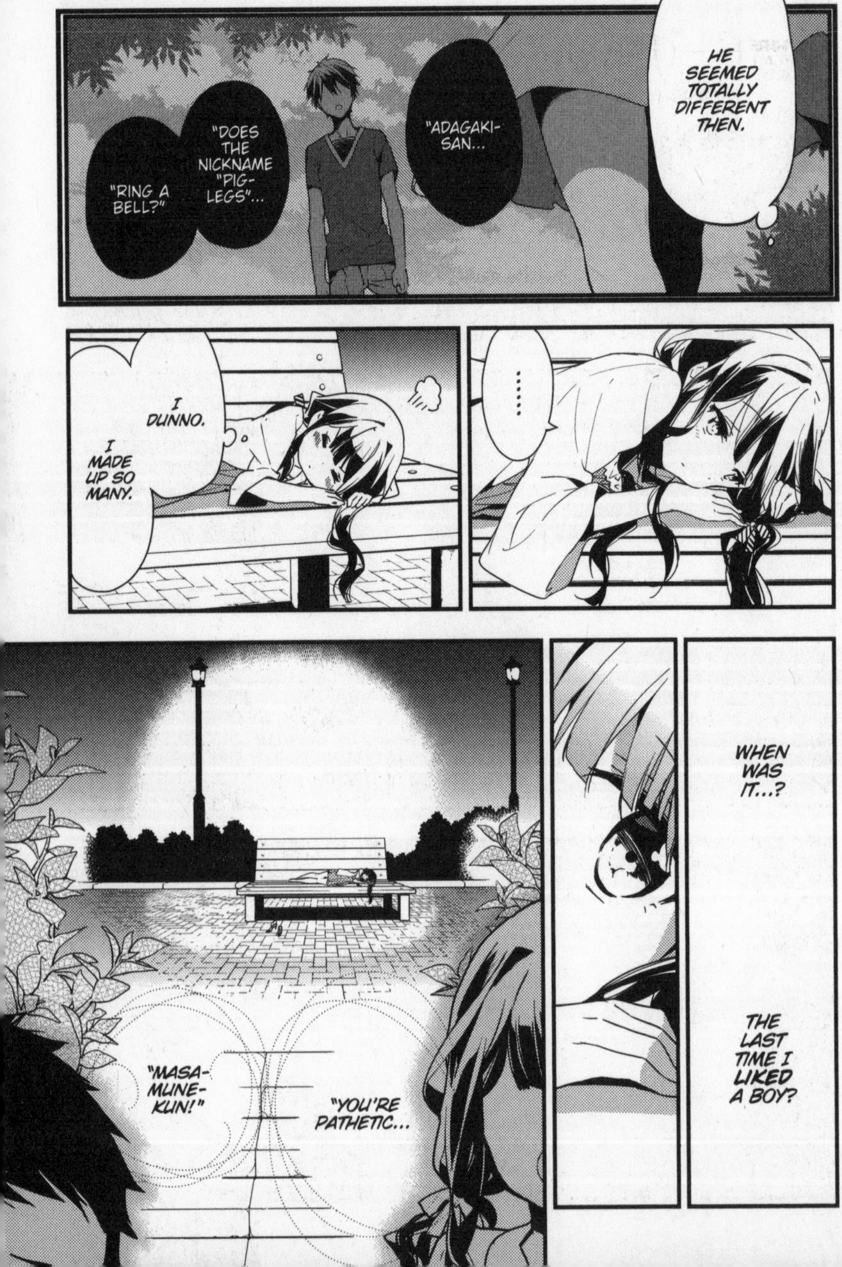
HE SEEMED TOTALLY DIFFERENT THEN.
"ADAGAKI-SAN...
"DOES THE NICKNAME "PIG-LEGS"...
"RING A BELL?"
......
I DUNNO.
I MADE UP SO MANY.
WHEN WAS IT...?
THE LAST TIME I LIKED A BOY?
"YOU'RE PATHETIC...
"MASA-MUNE-KUN!"

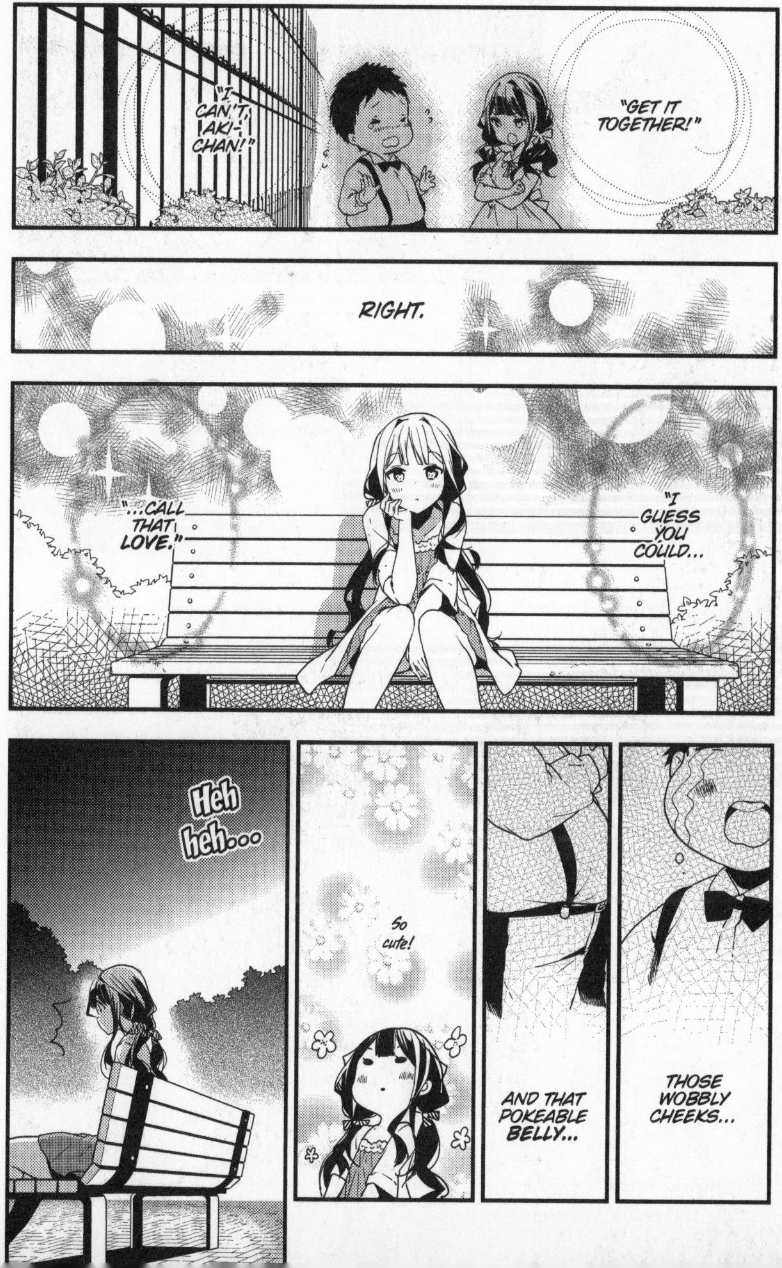
"GET IT TOGETHER!"
"I CAN'T, AKI-CHAN!"
RIGHT.
"I GUESS YOU COULD...
...CALL THAT LOVE."
THOSE WOBBLY CHEEKS...
AND THAT POKEABLE BELLY...
So cute!
Heh heh...

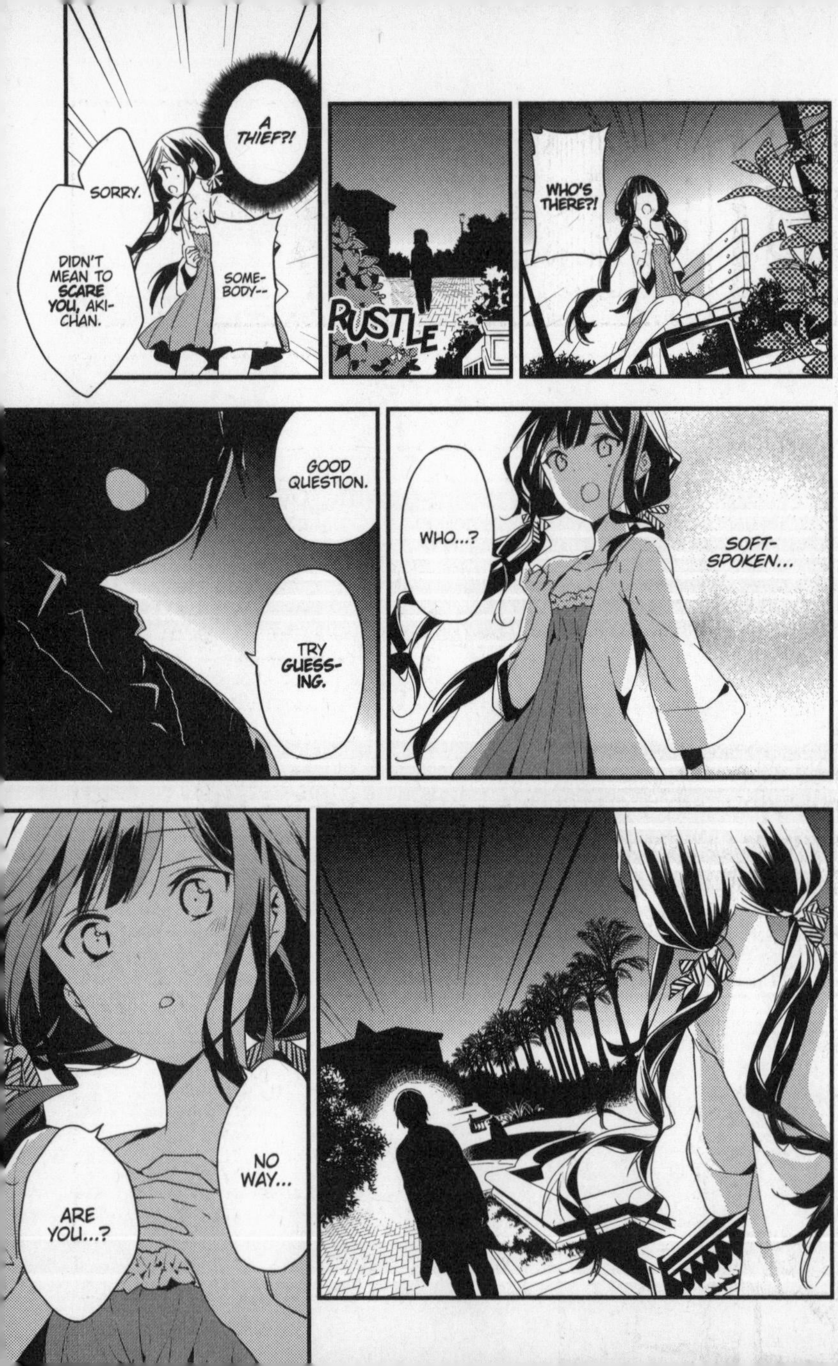
WHO'S THERE?!
RUSTLE
A THIEF?!
SOME-BODY--
SORRY.
DIDN'T MEAN TO SCARE YOU, AKI-CHAN.
SOFT-SPOKEN...
WHO...?
GOOD QUESTION.
TRY GUESS-ING.
NO WAY...
ARE YOU...?

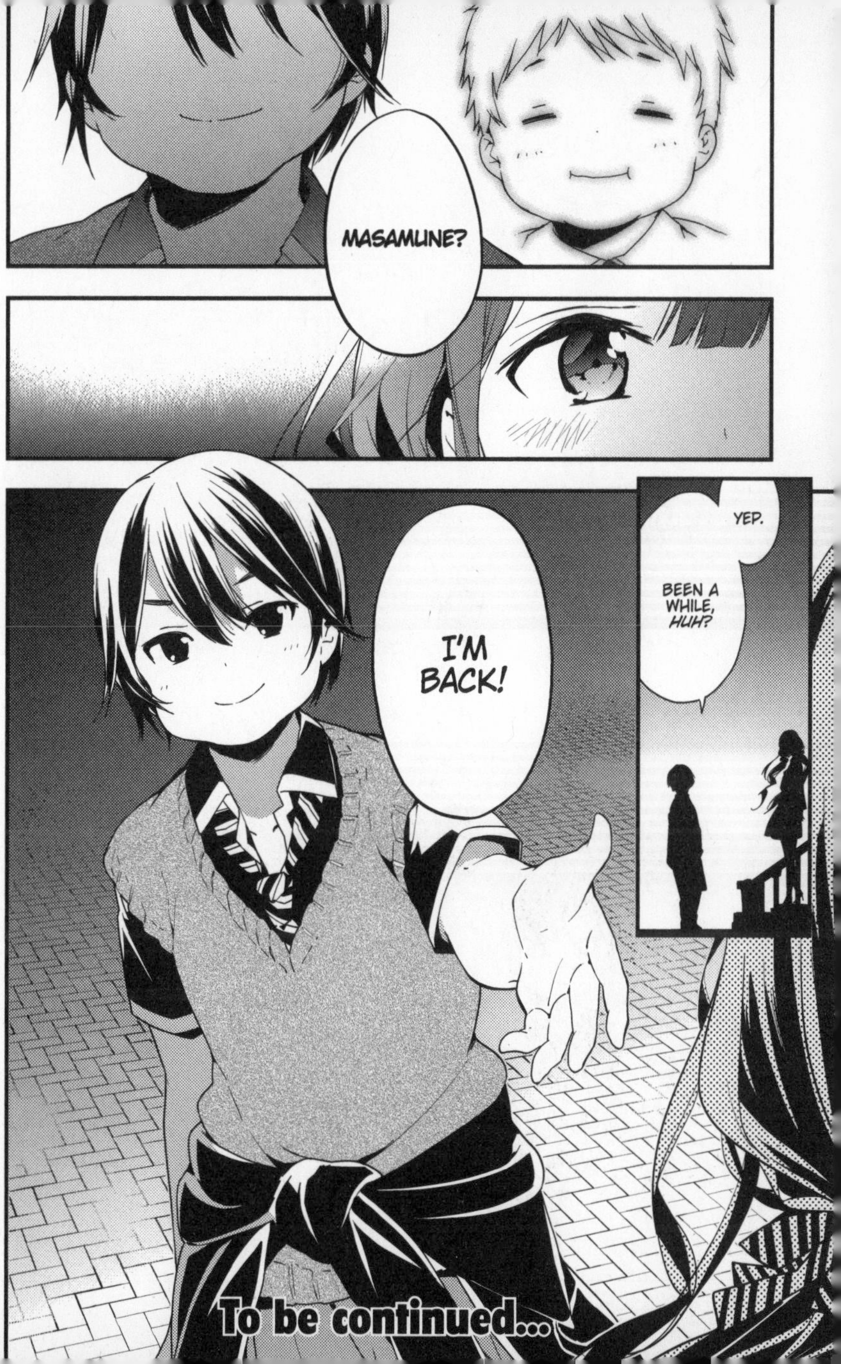
MASAMUNE?
YEP.
BEEN A WHILE, HUH?
I'M BACK!
To be continued...

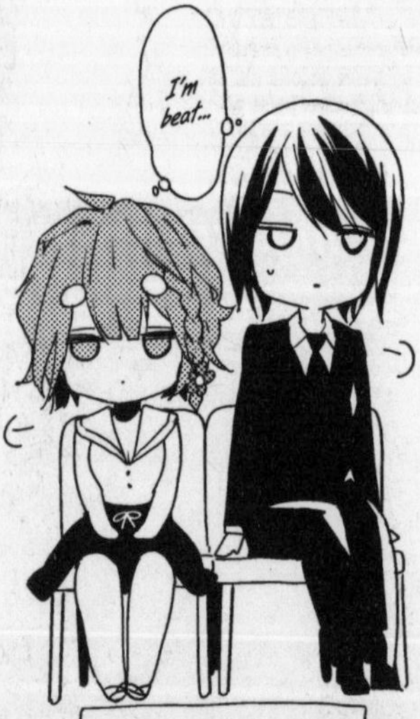
I'm beat...
Servants

SEVEN SEAS ENTERTAINMENT PRESENTS

Masamune-kun's REVENGE 4

story by HAZUKI TAKEOKA   art by TIV

TRANSLATION
Andrew Cunningham

ADAPTATION
Carol Fox

LETTERING AND LAYOUT
Jennifer Skarupa

LOGO DESIGN
Karis Page

COVER DESIGN
Nicky Lim

PROOFREADER
Holly Kolodziejczak

ASSISTANT EDITOR
Jenn Grunigen

PRODUCTION ASSISTANT
CK Russell

RODUCTION MANAGER
Lissa Pattillo

EDITOR-IN-CHIEF
Adam Arnold

PUBLISHER
Jason DeAngelis

MASAMUNE-KUN'S REVENGE VOL. 4
©HAZUKI TAKEOKA · TIV 2014
First published in Japan in 2014 by ICHIJINSHA Inc., Tokyo.
English translation rights arranged with ICHIJINSHA Inc., Tokyo.

Seven Seas books may be purchased in bulk for promotional, educational, or
business use. Please contact your local bookseller or the Macmillan Corporate
and Premium Sales Department at 1-800-221-7945, extension 5442, or by
e-mail at MacmillanSpecialMarkets@macmillan.com.

Seven Seas and the Seven Seas logo are trademarks of
Seven Seas Entertainment, LLC. All rights reserved.

ISBN: 978-1-626924-38-3

Printed in Canada

First Prin

10 9 8

D1308115

FOLLOW US ONLINE: w

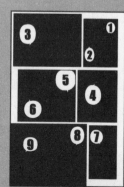

READING DIRECTIONS

This book reads from *right to left*, Japanese style.
If this is your first time reading manga, you start
reading from the top right panel on each page and
take it from there. If you get lost, just follow the
numbered diagram here. It may seem backwards at
first, but you'll get the hang of it! Have fun!!